Pelican Books
Israel and the Arabs

Maxime Rodinson was born in Paris in 1915; his father was one of the founders
of the Jewish Workers' Trade Unions in Paris. He received his primary
education in Paris, then worked as an errand boy before taking advanced
studies in the École des Langues Orientales Vivantes and at the Sorbonne,
where he studied Semitic languages, ethnography and sociology. After serving
in the army in Syria he stayed for seven years in the Lebanon working as a
teacher in a Muslim high school and as an official in the French Department of
Antiquities for Syria and the Lebanon; during this time he made frequent trips
across the Middle East. He had joined the Communist Party in 1937 and he
became acquainted with the Communists and the Left in these regions. He
returned to France in 1947 to take charge of oriental printed books in the
National Library, and from 1950 to 1951 he published *Moyen-Orient*, a
political monthly on the Middle East. Maxime Rodinson left the Communist
Party in 1958, but stayed in the Marxist Left as a .... writer and
theoretician. His publications in English .... *Ideology, Lenin in
His Own Words, Mohammed*. *M.........* and *Islam and
Capitalism*.

Maxime Rodinson

Israel and the Arabs

Translated by Michael Perl and Brian Pearce

Second edition

Penguin Books

Penguin Books, 625 Madison Avenue, New York, New York 10022, U.S.A.
Penguin Books Australia Ltd, Ringwood, Victoria, Australia
Penguin Books Canada Ltd, 2801 John Street, Markham, Ontario, Canada L3R 1B4
Penguin Books (N.Z.) Ltd, 182–190 Wairau Road, Auckland 10, New Zealand

First published as a Penguin Special 1968
Reissued in Pelican Books 1969
Reprinted 1970, 1973
Second edition 1982

Acknowledgement is made to Victor Gollancz Ltd for permission to quote
a passage from *Golda Meir: Woman with a Cause*

Made and printed in Great Britain by
Richard Clay (The Chaucer Press) Ltd, Bungay, Suffolk

Contents

Publisher's Note

The essential tenets of this book remain unaffected by events following the revision of the text for the second edition, including the outbreak of war between Iran and Iraq in the autumn of 1980; the election of Ronald Reagan to the Presidency of the United States of America at the end of 1980; and the assassination of President Anwar El-Sadat of Egypt on 6 October 1981.

I
Jewish Nationalism and Arab Nationalism

Once again in the course of human history, events in a tiny Middle Eastern province (in area about the size of Wales or of three French *départements*) have shaken the world and unleashed fierce passions from San Francisco to Karachi. The province is that little patch of Palestinian soil, barren and inhospitable, in which only the imaginations of half-starved nomads could see 'a land flowing with milk and honey'. But it is from here that a sizeable proportion of mankind have chosen to derive their God, their ideas, and everything that governs their life, customs, loves and hates.

A new epoch in the history of this land opened less than a century ago. This new phase, strange as it seems, was heralded by events and situations which arose in territories far removed from that land in distance, customs, social structure and ideas. Just as at the time of the Crusades almost a thousand years ago, Palestine's tribulations stemmed from the fact that far away men and women longed for her, and were ready to die for her, like lovers pining for an absent mistress.

In the eleventh century, Palestine's lovers were Western Christians moved by the memory of their God and the danger threatening his tomb. In the nineteenth century, they were Eastern European Jews. For almost two thousand years, Jews all over the world had dreamt of their old homeland as the land in which God would reign in their midst, a dream-world where the wolf would lie down with the lamb and a little child would lead them. But then God discreetly disappeared from the vision, and a very terrestrial kingdom emerged instead. Far from any Messianic prophecy, it was hoped that this would be an 'ordinary' kingdom where the rulers and the ruled, the rich and the poor, wise men and fools would live side by side, just as anywhere else. There would even be, like everywhere else, murderers, thieves and prostitutes – from which no anti-Jewish inference should be drawn.

The Jews, once inhabitants of Palestine, had emigrated and scattered over almost the whole of the earth's surface – like their Syrian neighbours and many other peoples. The independence of their national home, again like many others, was destroyed by the Romans. But the cult of their national god Yahweh had certain characteristics which rendered it peculiarly attractive to many people. Their prophets had proclaimed that he was not only their God but the God of all peoples, although he had conferred a special privilege on the people of Israel, as they called themselves. One of their heresies, Christianity, had conquered the Roman world and spread beyond it. Many Jews were converted to pagan cults, then to Christianity, and later still, in the East, to Islam, a new religion born in the heart of the Arabian peninsula, which also drew its authority from their God, their laws and their prophets.

But as predicted by its prophets, a 'remnant' of the Jewish people was left, scattered over a multitude of different communities, remaining faithful to the old law, to the old scriptures, to ancient, complicated, archaic and cumbersome rituals. These, Jews in the true sense of the word, practising a minority religion, had been tolerated by the Christian states, but came to be viewed with increasing mistrust and hostility. Their failure to recognize the divine nature of one of themselves, Jesus of Nazareth, appeared more and more scandalous. After centuries of more or less grudging tolerance came the era of violent persecutions, of torture and the stake. Again, many became Christians. But as before, a 'remnant' was left, and multiplied in Eastern Europe where the Jews were at first welcomed. In the territory of Islam they were, like their Christian rivals, tolerated and 'protected', at the price of certain special taxes and discriminatory measures, and at the price also, from time to time and under special circumstances, of outbreaks of intolerance on the part of the Muslim mob – the 'poor white' reaction of those who cling to the last vestige of their superiority, their membership of the dominant community.

Within this network of self-contained minority communities, interpolated like cysts in states professing a rival ideology, the hope of salvation survived. This salvation was to be prepared by God on behalf of his chosen people, whom in his mysterious but infinite love he had allowed to suffer, no doubt so that the happiness they were to inherit should be all the more splendid. The old homeland, Palestine, the land of Israel as they called it, together with its centre the Holy City of Jerusalem, were still worshipped as the place appointed for the final victory, the kingdom of peace and plenty at the end of time. The Jews visited it whenever possible; they hoped to die there; they had themselves buried there. But the task of preparing their return to the promised land was left to God.

After the fall of the Jewish State of Palestine and the last struggles for Jewish independence from the Romans in the years 70 and 135, up to the fateful day of 1948, only two Jewish states were ever formed. The first appeared in the Yemen in the course of the fifth century, and took the form of a core of original Jews ruled by natives of southern Arabia converted to Judaism. The other was likewise an empire of the converted: the Khazars, a people of Turco-Mongoloid stock dwelling on the lower Volga. It lasted from about the eighth to the tenth century. For nineteen centuries these were the only instances when Judaism was anything other than a group of minority communities, and became itself a state religion.

The new spirit running through Western Europe in the eighteenth century was to change all this. Terrestrial communities were no longer built up around a god, but only within the framework of a state. The world of religious communities began to disappear, to be replaced by the world of nations. And for many men and women, God himself gradually receded from the earthly scene, to the point of disappearing altogether. The French Revolution drew the logical conclusions from these new conditions and new ideas. It proclaimed aloud and carried through to the end the abolition of every act of discrimination – a change already accepted by the enlightened despot Joseph II and by the young American Republic. Faith in a system of dogmas, the practice of certain rites, adherence to one or other religious community were no longer relevant criteria by which citizens of the same nation could be isolated from one another. Jews became Frenchmen like any other. They worshipped their own God after their own fashion, within the framework, if they so desired, of their own religious association, just as did the Catholics.

The logic of the French solution conformed so well with the social and ideological conditions of the time that Western Europe and America gradually came to accept it. The consequences for the Jewish situation were enormous. In this new world, religious communities no longer formed nations or quasi-nations to which the individual was bound, whether by choice or by force, but had become hardly more than free associations much like political parties or chess clubs. In this situation, a Jew who lost faith in the religion of his ancestors was no longer obliged either to be converted to another religion or somehow to sidestep the innumerable practical and moral problems with which he was faced as the subject of a community whose creed he did not accept. He became a Frenchman, an Englishman or a Belgian, of Jewish origin, and even this fact would probably fade from men's memories. No one could hold him to account for his religious opinions. No bond tied him to Judaism. And in conformity with the general tendencies at work in European society, such cases occurred with increasing frequency.

Of course not all Jews went as far as this. But cultural assimilation, which had always existed, became much greater. The notion of a 'Jewish people' had now become outdated. It had some justification when Jewish communities were universally regarded as foreign bodies encapsulated in the different nations, or as minority groups with no right of participation in the government of their states, when a multiple network of common interests united them wherever they might happen to be. Under the new order, all were full citizens of the various states; some of them happened to practise a certain religion, while others were descendants of practitioners of that religion. Even if their common religion created a bond between the Jews of different countries, the example of the Catholics and others showed that this common membership was easily reconciled with total commitment to each separate fatherland, a commitment which extended as far as mutual bloodletting without a trace of remorse or bad conscience.

Thus assimilation triumphed, to a greater or lesser degree. This is not to say that it was accepted and recognized by all non-Jews. For too long the Jews had been denounced as God's murderers and the servants of Satan. The Catholic Church and reactionary elements in every Christian confession smelt the hand of the Jew in every enterprise which undermined, to a degree increasingly dangerous to them, their ideological monopoly and the many advantages they drew from it. It is a commonplace of conservative ideological conventions to refuse to recognize that a progressive movement which attacks acquired privilege is the normal reaction of those classes in society who are discriminated against and oppressed. To denounce the motives of such a movement as a dark conspiracy of the forces of evil is much more convenient for the conscience of the privileged and much better propaganda material to direct at the ignorant masses. And who better to represent these forces than the Jews, to whom liberalization opened the doors of Christian society?

Moreover, it was true that the Jews detached themselves more easily than others from traditions in flagrant discord with the spirit of modern civilization; they were anxious to escape from the stigma of their underprivileged minority position to become a part of a larger society, and found themselves still the object of ancestral enmities. Hence in proportion to their numbers they always provided a very large contingent of liberals, reformers, even revolutionaries.

From time to time – and this is especially evident in the history of

British Jewry – almost total assimilation would be freshly imperilled by the arrival of immigrants from parts of the world where the old order still persisted. These immigrants came from communities closed in upon themselves, cysts in the body politic of states in whose life they played no part, and hence having developed, in differing degrees, their own peculiar cultural characteristics. This was true of the Russia of the Tsars and of the whole of Eastern Europe, where the Jews (who had mostly come from the western parts of Germany in the Middle Ages) even spoke their own special language, Yiddish, a Germanic dialect with its own literature, existing in the midst of Slav populations. And then the Jews from Eastern Europe would appear in the West, re-populate the deserted synagogues, and once again build up their own community life until they, in their turn, were assimilated.

In 1879 a fateful event took place. Bismarck, personally devoid of any prejudice against the Jews, found it expedient for his internal policy to launch a campaign of 'anti-Semitism', to use the term which had recently become popular in Germany, where certain writers of small influence had been developing this theme as a stick with which to beat liberalism. The weapon proved effective, and it was taken up to meet similar political circumstances in Austria, France and Russia in the years which followed. As James Parkes very rightly says,

Political antisemitism had extremely little to do with the Jews as such. . . . The enemy was 'liberalism', 'industrialism', 'secularism' – anything the reactionaries disliked; and they found by experience that there was no better way of persuading their electors to dislike these things also than to label them 'Jewish'.*

Extremely violent verbally, political anti-Semitism provoked relatively little physical violence in Western Europe until the victory of Nazism. But in Russia, where Jewish communities of the medieval type still survived in large numbers, the reactionary Tsar Alexander III decided to avenge the death of his father on the Jews (Alexander II was killed by revolutionaries in 1881). The Tsarist administration likewise deliberately developed anti-Semitism as a political weapon against liberal ideas, and used it with great success among the more backward classes of the population, who were unleashed on the defenceless Jewish communities. The Russian pogroms filled the civilized world with horror.

The Jews reacted in various ways. Many of them gritted their teeth and waited for the storm to pass, remembering that similar persecutions

* James Parkes, *An Enemy of the People: Anti-Semitism*, Penguin Books, Harmondsworth, 1945, pp. 10–11.

had in the past struck at the French Protestants and the English Catholics. Some emphasized their assimilation, changed their name, and broadcast their attachment to the religion and cultural values of their adoptive homeland, in an effort to obliterate their origins. Others fought with intensified fury, side by side with liberals or revolutionaries of Christian origin, for a society from which anti-Semitism would be extirpated root and branch. In Eastern Europe, where the Jews still formed almost a nation of their own with its own Yiddish language and culture, a local cultural nationalism grew up, broadly socialist in spirit. This was the ideology of the Bund, the Jewish Socialist Party of the Russian Empire, founded in 1898.

Another reaction was openly nationalistic in spirit: this was political Zionism, created by a thoroughly assimilated Jew, the Viennese journalist Theodor Herzl. Appalled by the demonstrations of the French mob against Dreyfus, Herzl feverishly wrote his *A Jewish State* in 1896. In it, he showed himself converted to nationalism and in agreement with the anti-Semites on the diagnosis that the European Jews were an alien element, unassimilated for the most part, and in the long run unassimilable. They constituted a people, a nation. The remedy to the situation lay in departure, in the possession of a homeland, such as other nations had. Somewhere a Jewish State, purely Jewish, autonomous and independent, had to be created. But where? A number of possible solutions were canvassed, including the Argentine. But the clear preference was for the ancient homeland, Palestine, abandoned by most Jews for almost two millennia. The messianic fervour of religious Jews, the emotions aroused by Biblical texts, and traditions which retained their power even over Jews who had ceased to identify with Judaism, all contributed to an effective mobilization of Jewish opinion towards this end.

Palestine was at that time an Arab province of the Ottoman Empire. This did not appear a great obstacle. Around 1900 colonization projects did not have the unfavourable aura that surrounds them today. More or less backward populations were being introduced to progress and civilization, even at the cost of being displaced or somewhat subordinated. It is hardly surprising, therefore, that this project, originating in Europe, showed little concern for the fate of the inhabitants of the one-time promised land. Likewise, as was normal in the atmosphere of the times, the only strategy considered was a pact with some power or group of powers in exchange for favours which the would-be settlers might be in a position to bestow. The terms 'colonization' and 'colony' were used quite without inhibitions by the pioneers of political Zionism. Herzl wrote of Palestine: 'We should there form a portion of the rampart of Europe against Asia, an outpost of civilization as opposed to barbarism.' *

Small Jewish colonies did exist within Palestine. Jews of many different origins had come to settle in the Holy Land, side by side with an already motley population. In 1880 they numbered some 24,000 of a total of perhaps 500,000 inhabitants. After the new wave of anti-Semitism had begun in Russia in 1881, great numbers of Russian Jews fled to Western Europe or the United States, but some directed their steps towards Palestine. A movement had sprung up among the Russian Jews advocating the establishment of Jewish agricultural settlements in Palestine or Syria. Agricultural labour was supposed to regenerate the Jewish people, degraded or at least denatured by centuries in the ghetto. A variety of Tolstoyan socialism became manifest in the movement of the 'Lovers of Zion'. It was possible that a true Jewish socialist society might grow up in Palestine. But the Jewish settlements in Palestine were not numerous, and before the advent of Herzl the prospect of a Jewish State was ignored or considered to be extremely far off. Then came Herzl, and the first Congress of the Zionist Movement held in Basle in 1897 marked a new departure.

Throughout all this, the actual inhabitants of Palestine were ignored by practically everybody. The philosophy prevailing in the European world at the time was without any doubt responsible for this. Every territory situated outside that world was considered empty – not of inhabitants of course, but constituting a kind of cultural vacuum, and therefore suitable for colonization. And in fact the European nations were able to impose their will in most parts of the world without too much difficulty.

It was unfortunate for the form of Jewish nationalism represented by Zionism that just at the moment when it decided to direct its efforts towards achieving a Jewish State in Palestine, the natives of that country began to be affected by a similar ideological movement, namely Arab nationalism.

The Arabs were an ancient people from the Near East, whose language, like that of the ancient Hebrews, was a branch of the family known as 'Semitic'. Ancient Hebrew mythology recognized them as close relatives of the Hebrews, together with all the other neighbouring peoples, and it is certainly true that the same ethnic or racial characteristics appeared, perhaps in slightly varying degrees, in all these peoples

* Theodor Herzl, *A Jewish State*, London, 1896, p. 29.

of the ancient Middle East. Of course this by no means prevented bitter rivalries, sometimes going as far as outright hostility. The Arabs, inhabitants of the Arabian peninsula, began at a very early date to make frequent incursions into neighbouring territories. At the beginning of the seventh century they were politically and ideologically united by their prophet Muhammad (or Mahomet), who preached a new religion, Islam, which drew heavily for its inspiration on Judaism and Christianity. The Arabs subsequently conquered an enormous area of the earth's surface, extending from India and the fringes of China to Spain and Southern France. They did not force their religion on the conquered Jews and Christians, since they granted that these religions were in possession of a certain element of the truth. Religious minorities were 'protected', though obliged to pay special taxes. However, the political and social conditions of the state ruled by the Muslim Arabs (soon to become fragmented) gradually induced the majority of its subjects to embrace the Islamic faith. Some of these subjects, between Mesopotamia and Morocco, were gradually 'Arabized' and became indistinguishable from their Arab conquerors.

Arab domination was brief among those peoples – principally the Persians and the Turks – who, although they had become Muslims, had not been Arabized. Native Persian and Turkish dynasties very soon came to power and before long dominated the Arabs and their Arabized subjects. National feeling certainly existed at that time, in that part of the world as elsewhere, but had not as yet acquired an ideology. To be ruled by sovereigns of foreign origin was a perfectly normal phenomenon, in many cases accepted for thousands of years. Co-religionism between rulers and ruled (except for some minority groups) seemed a far more important characteristic.

From the fourteenth century a Muslim state, that of the Ottoman Turks, began to show its strength in Anatolia. By the sixteenth and seventeenth centuries it had subjugated most of the territories with Arab populations, in particular Egypt, Palestine and Syria, which had for two or three centuries been under the suzerainty of the Mamelukes, rulers who were themselves of Turkish origin. The Ottoman Empire was an immense structure, governed from Istanbul (previously Constantinople). The Sultan who resided there ruled over a tremendously varied population, extending from Belgrade and Bucharest to Algeria and the Yemen. His power was, of course, sanctified by Islam. The minority religions, Christianity and Judaism in particular, were allowed considerable autonomy; but the governors of the various provinces of the Empire made their authority felt by all their subjects through their highly arbitrary rule, and above all by extracting the maximum tribute in taxes, dues and rents.

Towards the end of the eighteenth century the preponderance of Europe began to make itself felt. The economic, technological and military superiority of this part of the world, which had for some time been foreshadowed by increasingly spectacular scientific advances, became more and more overwhelming. European merchants who had long had a foothold in the Muslim countries enjoyed an increasingly privileged position. European ambassadors who had earlier had little status were now admitted to the Sultan's counsels and even began to dictate policy. They were frequently aided and abetted by the local Christian community, their common ideology providing a means of mutual understanding, and also by the local Jews, many of whom came from Europe, and who in any case maintained close relations with their European co-religionists. The Ottomans, who as recently as 1683 had stood before the gates of Vienna, now retreated through the Balkans before the Christian powers. The Balkan subject peoples revolted one by one, with European encouragement, eroding the frontiers of the Empire. The French took Algiers in 1830, the British Aden in 1839, thus beginning the movement of direct colonization. After a pause during which the European powers consolidated their indirect but terribly effective hold over the whole of the Ottoman Empire, Anglo-French colonial expansion moved inexorably forwards: Tunisia in 1881, Egypt in 1882, the Sudan in 1899, Libya and Morocco in 1912. At the same time, the cultural influence of Europe grew everywhere stronger. Its values, its forms of organization, even its fashions had increasing impact, penetrating first the rich and cultured elite, then gradually the poverty-stricken masses. Europe brought domination and humiliation; but at the same time she introduced a new style of political and cultural life. She showed that a political structure was possible in which the state's subjects could also have their say in its government, and that a culture was conceivable in which the masses could be educated to a degree enabling them in principle to understand and participate in decisions taken at the topmost level. Moreover it was these organizational forms which appeared to express European superiority, enabling an advance along the path of infinite progress towards greater liberty and greater welfare. Slowly new aspirations, new loyalties, new ideas began to appear and to spread.

This new mentality, the new horizons which Europe had revealed, only served to make European domination, whether direct or indirect, even harder to bear. The most universal sentiment was an immense humiliation, shared by an entire people, from sultan to the humblest peasant. Moreover those who were most determined to learn European ways and share the secret of her power usually did so as a first step on the road towards an implacable revenge.

The Muslim rulers, who had to make decisions from one day to the next, reacted as best they could, according to the pressures acting on them and their different temperaments. Some clung to the old forms and structures on which their power was based, and resisted all change except under duress. Others attempted to introduce reforms, in a more or less consistent manner. In a society in which the old order of things largely persisted, under the watchful eye of the European powers who made sure that such reforms would in no way threaten their dominant position, these measures usually came to nought, or resulted in deadlock or crisis.

The future was being forged elsewhere. Intellectuals of a new type were gradually beginning to appear, who although educated in the traditional disciplines of the old culture were sensitive to the new situation, open to new ideas, and convinced of the need to lead their peoples out of the dark tunnel of backwardness and humiliation. Their level of culture was uneven and frequently superficial, they varied greatly in intellectual power and moral standards; it would be easy to highlight the unscrupulousness of some of them, the deficiencies of others, the defects of all. Nevertheless, it was their function as intellectuals to create dynamic and appealing ideologies; and they fulfilled this function. This was not done as an abstract exercise but with direct reference to the objective situation as they saw it. Their ideas, inasmuch as they reflected the situation accurately and held out some hope of a solution to universal problems, evoked an increasingly powerful response.

The men who won influence over increasingly wide sections of society and ultimately left their mark upon history were the prophets of immediate or eventual liberation. They expected a more or less Utopian breakthrough towards a new set of values: the suppression of privilege; liberty; welfare; in short, happiness. Naturally enough, this liberating upsurge was at first conceived within the old framework of society. The existing frameworks were the Muslim religious community, the *umma*; and the political structures – the Ottoman Empire, Iran and the state of Egypt. The first great mobilizer of opinion was Jemal ad-din al-Afghani (1839–1897). He belonged to the select line of great nineteenth-century nationalist and liberal revolutionaries. Like them, he was a conspirator, and a secularist freemason. By plots, ex-

pedients and lies, he dedicated his life to the cause which he hoped to
lead to victory. Actually a Persian Shiite, he posed as an Afghan Sunnite
in order to gain greater influence over the orthodox Mohammedan
world (hence his pseudonymous surname, al-Afghani, the Afghan). At
some time in his career he had decided that religion was still a powerful
force and not to be despised. He hoped, indeed, to exploit it in arousing
the masses to revolt against reactionary despotism, allied in his view
with foreign domination. He thus assumed the character of a Muslim
Holy Man, not without revealing quite different features to his European friends. He attempted to play off one European power against
others, frequently changing his tactics and running the risk of being
himself more exploited than able to exploit these powers. But he sowed
ideas; simple and sometimes wrong but always dynamic ideas. They
were to fall on fertile ground.

He won many disciples, in Iran, in the Ottoman Empire and
throughout the Muslim world. Their attitudes towards Islam, towards
the modernization of their society and social progress, and towards the
use of violence differed considerably. But they were united by one
fundamental aspiration, the most common characteristic of that mass
of society which they represented: the recapture of national independence from the European colonial powers.

This central theme was argued on different grounds and with different emphasis by the various ideologies. But it was always present. And
around these ideologies there grew up very gradually small and at first
insignificant groups of men dedicated to putting the programme of
liberation into effect.

Who was to be liberated? The Muslim community, the Ottoman
Empire, the Egyptian nation, the Arab people? It mattered little at
first, since the enemy was in every case the same – the European
imperialist powers, and especially the most dynamic of them at that
time and the most actively interested in the area, Great Britain.

Nevertheless, European nationalist ideas infected all the political
ideologues of the Muslim world; and they based themselves on a European model – the nation-state built up around a people defined by a
common language. This alien model, which ultimately captured the
imagination first of the elite and then of the masses, must have struck a
chord in pre-national feelings of identification – inhibited no doubt by
community of religion, but nonetheless always present in more or less
repressed form.

The Turks were the first to be affected by this type of nationalism.
The 'Ottomanists' had originally wanted merely to create an Ottoman

nation of the modern, liberal type in an atmosphere of romanticism. But because most of the members of this group were Turks, it was soon guided by feelings of specifically Turkish national pride. This found expression in increased interest in Turkish national origins, and a love for historic monuments to the ancient grandeur of the Turks. The Young Turk movement overthrew the despot Abdul Hamid in 1908, and replaced him by a regime which appealed to all the different national elements in the Ottoman Empire, but increasingly tended to maintain and reinforce the supremacy of the Turks in that Empire. This was bound to provoke a reaction among the other nationalities and favour the crystallization of Arab and other nationalist ideologies.

The broad outlines of such an ideology had already been drawn. Not surprisingly, a considerable number of the new ideologues were Christian Arabs from the Lebanon, who were not bound by any ties of religion to the Turks. After 1908, resistance to Turkish supremacy reinforced the movement in this direction. The minimum demand was for the decentralization of the Ottoman Empire; the maximum was Arab independence. But support for these demands was still hesitant. Most Arabs had not forgotten that 'the principal contradiction' (as Mao Tse-Tung was to say half a century later) was the struggle against European imperialism, even if some did not hesitate to court the aid of, say, France against Great Britain. Moreover the Muslim Arabs shrank from conducting a ruthless struggle against the Turks.

In Palestine, which had an Arab majority, the situation was complicated by the gradual growth of the Jewish settlements. These had now generally accepted Herzl's doctrine of political Zionism. Herzl (who died in 1904) had attempted to win the support of various European powers and of the Sultan Abdul Hamid for the establishment of his Jewish State in Palestine. At first this was to take the relatively innocuous form of an autonomous territory under Ottoman suzerainty, on the pattern of the Lebanon. This scheme was unsuccessful. Herzl's successors then put off the achievement of the final objective for a more auspicious time, but never lost sight of it. Meanwhile they continued to found Jewish settlements in Palestine to help reinforce their claims. By 1914 the Jews comprised 85,000 out of a total population of 739,000.

The Palestinian Arabs, in direct contact with the Jewish settlers, had realized the danger of having grafted on to them a foreign community isolated from the life of the local inhabitants. It did not require great perspicacity to understand the aspirations of this alien community to form a new national entity, and hence to subjugate or displace the native peoples. They had protested vigorously in the Ottoman Parliament. However, the virile nationalism of the Young Turks made any early cession of territory seem extremely unlikely. Jewish immigration was restricted by the Ottoman state, although bureaucratic corruption made the restrictions easy to circumvent. Some Arab nationalist leaders, especially non-Palestinians, contemplated an alliance with the Zionist movement against Turkish supremacy. Contributions from the Diaspora put considerable funds at the disposal of the Jews, who were far more advanced both technologically and economically, and were culturally on a level with Europe. They would therefore have been a formidable ally to the young Arab movement, which was poor and inexperienced, with a thoroughly underdeveloped social basis, to express it in fashionable terminology. And some negotiations towards an Arab-Zionist alliance did in fact take place.

But on 2 November 1914, the Ottoman Empire under the rule of the Young Turks entered the world war on the side of Germany and Austria-Hungary against Great Britain, France and Russia. A new era had opened.

2

From Nationalism to Nations

War is said to be the midwife of revolution. It is also the midwife of nations. The world war of 1914–18 was a turning point in the destinies of both the Arab and Jewish nationalisms.

No one can say what would have happened if the Ottoman Empire had not been the ally of the Central Powers. But it was, and any weapon could be used against it. In April and May 1916, Great Britain, France and Tsarist Russia drew up a plan of partition for the greater part of the Empire in the secret Sykes-Picot Agreement. At the same time Great Britain incited Hussein, Sherif of Mecca, to revolt and proclaim a Holy War against the Turks. The Arab nationalist secret societies of Syria-Palestine and Iraq vacillated, torn between hostility to Turkish supremacy and their awareness of the European threat. Many Maronite Christians in the Lebanon, followed by Muslim Arab nationalists, looked towards France. The Turks got wind of these secret dealings, and were aware of a certain diffuse hostility. They thought that the Arabs' tentative plans were on the point of fruition. The Young Turk proconsul Jemal fired the powder-keg by hanging for treason some Muslim and Christian Arab nationalists at Beirut and Damascus. This precipitated Hussein's decision, and he began the revolt on 5 June 1916, proclaiming himself King of the Arabs on 29 October. Britain, France and Italy, however, only recognized him as King of the Hejaz. The exploits of the Bedouin forces led by his son Feisal and T.E. Lawrence, fighting side by side with British troops commanded by Allenby, have passed into legend.

The imminent collapse of the Ottoman Empire was now obvious even to the most short-sighted. It seemed a huge, inexhaustible cake, and every claimant promised portions to those whom they wished to attract to their cause. Great Britain wooed the Jews, many of whom sympathized with Germany out of hatred of anti-Semitic Tsarist Russia. The pacifist tendencies of the American Jews, who played such a major role in American industry, had somehow to be overcome; Russian Jews, said to be influential in the revolutionary movement, and Jews from all over the world had to be won over to the Allied cause. The British Zionists, led by Chaim Weizmann, persuaded the

British Cabinet, in the face of opposition from anti-Zionist Jewry, that favours bestowed on the Zionist movement would win Jewish approval and gain powerful support for the Allies. The strong Biblical leanings characteristic of Protestants, the desire to counterbalance French claims on Syria and the Lebanon, the need to establish a base closely connected with Britain by ties of gratitude and interest (and, moreover, flanking the Suez Canal and the route to India) all helped to sway the British mind. On 2 November 1917 the Balfour Declaration promised the establishment of a Jewish national home in Palestine.

The Ottoman Empire crumbled, as predicted. As might also have been predicted, the ordering of its succession proved an extremely difficult task, in view of the multiplicity of contradictory promises made as to the distribution of its former lands. The Syrian National Congress meeting at Damascus in July 1919 claimed political independence for a united Syrian state (covering what is now Syria, the Lebanon, Jordan and Israel). The new state was to be a constitutional monarchy, with Feisal as king. French and Zionist pretensions were to be rejected and no mandate system could be accepted unless restricted to technical aid. On 8 March 1920 the Congress did in fact proclaim the independence of Syria-Palestine with Feisal as king, and a programme of decentralization, the Lebanon being guaranteed a certain degree of autonomy. At the same moment, a meeting of Iraqi Arab nationalists was choosing Feisal's brother Abdullah as first King of Iraq under similar conditions.

On 5 May the conference of the Allied powers at San Remo announced very different decisions. Without waiting for the meeting of the League of Nations, which was in theory supposed to 'bestow' the mandates (a new and hypocritical formula for colonization disguised as benevolent aid), the powers shared the mandates out amongst themselves. Two separate states of Syria and Lebanon were to be formed and placed under French tutelage. Iraq and Palestine (whose frontiers were not strictly defined) were to come under British mandate, with a clause inserted providing for the application of the Balfour Declaration.

This announcement was a betrayal of all the promises made to the Arabs, and that betrayal was to condition subsequent events. At once it aroused a chorus of protests. In the Middle East as elsewhere, great faith had been placed in President Wilson's Fourteen Points containing the principle of the self-determination of peoples. Great Britain had made specific promises to the Arabs in order to gain and retain their support. They might have been couched in somewhat vague and equivocal terms; but they had been understood to guarantee the Arabs of the old Ottoman Empire freedom to decide their own destinies and also, to some extent, the right to form a unified state. They had indeed been so formulated as to be understood in this way. An American commission sent by Wilson to Asia Minor to sound out the wishes and complaints of the inhabitants had returned with recommendations based on their findings. All was in vain – given the intransigent claims of France, based on the secret Sykes-Picot agreement, the will of Britain to keep sure control of the region, and the strength of the Zionist pressure group. Instead of independence and unity came division and the subjection of the native peoples to the control of the great powers under the hypocritical form of the mandate. The disappointment, frustration and indignation were immense, and their effects were felt long afterwards. They have indeed lasted to the present day. The political situation in this area cannot be understood without reference to this background of profound and general resentment.

The year 1920 was called by the Arabs *âm an-nakba* – the year of the catastrophe. On 14 July General Gouraud, stationed in Beirut, sent an ultimatum to King Feisal of Syria in Damascus. The ultimatum was accepted; in spite of this, French troops marched on Damascus and occupied it. Feisal fled. Anti-Zionist riots had broken out in Palestine; Iraq was in the throes of insurrection. This did not prevent the San Remo decisions from being gradually brought into effect. Great Britain alone did make some attempt to limit Arab resentment against her, and made especially strenuous efforts to turn the fury away from herself on to others. She made some 'prestige' concessions by giving Feisal the throne of Iraq and recognizing his brother Abdullah as Emir of Transjordan. Transjordan was thus clearly cut off from Palestine and therefore placed beyond the scope of Jewish colonization. The French accentuated the division of the territories placed under their mandate. Gouraud created a State of the Lebanon, where France had many sympathizers among the Maronite Christians, by enlarging it to the north, south and east with additions of predominantly Muslim territory. This was Greater Lebanon, founded on 1 September 1920, which was to become later (May 1926) the Republic of Lebanon. The rest of French Syria was divided into three states: Damascus, Aleppo and the Alawi territory. In addition, two separate administrative areas were created: the autonomous territory of the Jebel Druse and, to the northeast, the Sanjak of Alexandretta (Iskenderun), with its partly Turkish population. In 1925 Damascus and Aleppo were joined to form the state of Syria.

The fate of the other Arab countries was rather different. In Arabia Sherif Hussein, ruler of the Hejaz, whose sons now reigned over Iraq and Transjordan, was supplanted in 1924 by a chieftain from the interior named Ibn Saud. This Ibn Saud had had dealings during the war with the British Viceroy of India, as a result of which he was favourably regarded by the British. The old Sherif, on the other hand, had to pay the price for his obstinacy towards Great Britain. He had repeatedly refused to sign an agreement which would have secured his throne, although he would have been prepared to endorse the innovations introduced by the British and French in the Arab world, in particular their acceptance of Zionist settlement in Palestine. In 1930, at Mecca, Ibn Saud had himself crowned King of Hejaz and Nejd, later to be called Saudi Arabia, a region still largely populated by nomads untouched by the ideological storms of the outside world. The Yemen continued its remote, archaic existence under the rule of the Zaydi Imamate, freed in 1918 of Turkish tutelage, which had in any case been somewhat hypothetical. The Emirates of the Persian Gulf, peopled by scattered tribes of nomads and fishermen, remained under British influence.

The ideology of Arab nationalism had at this time hardly touched the Arab countries to the west of the Suez Canal. Egypt, a British protectorate, rebelled in 1919 under the leadership of the Wafd party and claimed independence. On 28 February 1922 Britain declared Egypt a sovereign nation, and on 15 March the Khedive Fuad took the title of King of Egypt. Italian Libya, the French Maghreb and the Sudan, to all intents and purposes British, remained under colonial administration; only a few squalls foreshadowed the coming storm.

At the heart of the Arab countries of Asia lay Palestine, where the British vainly tried to reconcile their contradictory promises. During the war the Jewish population had fallen to some 60,000 souls. In the autumn of 1919 it began once again to increase. Between 1919 and 1923, 35,000 Jews entered Palestine. Jewish settlers flocked in from all parts of the world, encouraged by the hope that Zionist dreams might now be near realization; after all, they were now embodied in documents of international law. The Jewish community set up a sort of Parliament and an Executive Council. The British military administration had given way to a civil government. But the first British High Commissioner to occupy the seat made famous in earlier times by Pontius Pilate was an English Jew, Sir Herbert Samuel, who had distinctly Zionist leanings and who remained in office until 1925.

Arab hostility was not slow to show itself in Palestine, and in the most violent fashion. In the spring of 1920 the first explosion of rioting against the Jewish immigrants broke out. Arabs in other countries gave increasingly clear indications of their hostility to the Zionist project of making Palestine Jewish. British governors gradually became aware of the enormous difficulties that Jewish colonization would cause. But the British had gone too far along the road of support for Zionist ambitions to retreat. The Zionist lobby was still extremely powerful; the British tried therefore to moderate Jewish ambitions so as to make them acceptable to the Arabs, whom they were in danger of alienating once and for all.

These considerations resulted in the British statement of policy known as the Churchill Memorandum, published on 3 June 1922. The Balfour Declaration, upheld in principle, was fairly subtly but unmistakably reinterpreted. What was to be the nature of the promised Jewish national home? Not, as some had been led to believe, a Palestine as Jewish as England was English. The intention had been simply 'the further development of the existing Jewish community with the assistance of Jews in other parts of the world in order that it may become a centre in which the Jewish people as a whole may take, on grounds of religion and race, an interest and pride'. Immigration would be limited according to the 'economic capacity of the country at the time to absorb new arrivals'. There was no intention to bring about the 'disappearance or the subordination of the Arabic population, language or culture in Palestine'.*

The British government gave the Zionist organization to understand that it would have to declare its official approval of this interpretation of the Balfour undertaking if it wished the British mandate over Palestine to become official. The organization's executive acceded, thus officially repudiating the project for a Jewish State, and hoping, as Weizmann put it, for 'a framework for building up a Jewish majority in Palestine'.† When such a majority had been established, the Jewish State would come about through force of circumstances. Hence it was with official Zionist endorsement of the reinterpretation of the Balfour Declaration excluding a Jewish State that the draft resolution according the Palestine Mandate to Great Britain was presented to the League of Nations, and ratified by it on 24 July 1922.

*

* Correspondence of Colonial Office with Palestine Arab Delegation and the Zionist Organization. Cmnd. Paper 1700, H.M.S.O., 1922.

† Chaim Weizmann, *Trial and Error* (illustrated edition), London, East and West Library, 1950, p. 361.

The basis for future developments had now been created. The new situation had received the official seal, and now dictated the areas of political choice open to the various protagonists. Great Britain and France were now concerned to preserve and consolidate the dominant position in the Middle East given to them by the war. The frustrated Arabs fought for independence and unity. The Jewish Zionist colony in Palestine (the *Yishuv* in Hebrew) sought to consolidate its gains and to swell its numbers by immigration. The majority of the settlers remained faithful to their final goal – the Jewish State. Their preparatory measures, moreover, could not fail to bring this objective about.

In every Arab country resistance to direct or indirect foreign domination manifested itself in strikes, demonstrations and innumerable riots. Repression only reinforced the feeling of frustration and revolt. In some instances the population went as far as full-scale insurrection –witness Syria in 1925 to 1927 and Palestine in 1936. Even the revolt led by Abd-el-Krim (1921–1926), in distant Morocco, which arose out of local conditions, might possibly be included in this category. In any case it appeared to the Eastern Arabs as another manifestation of the Arab revolt. In the East especially, the struggle against Zionism was on every programme. No matter which ideology happened to be leading the revolt, this projected foreign colonization of an Arab country, with the ultimate aim of amputating that country from the rest of the Arab world, was an affront to Arab nationalism, to Islam and to anti-colonialism alike.

The two colonizing powers, faced with this ever-present smouldering revolt, vacillated between two contrasting attitudes – as would any power in such a situation. Sometimes the policy would be to bestow power on well-trained puppet regimes, suppressing nationalist conspiracies by force. At other times, moderate nationalists with an impeccable record of loyalty to the Arab nation would be chosen as spokesmen for the Arab case. The colonial power would then enter into negotiations with these men in order to find a way of giving some satisfaction to the aspirations of the people without abandoning their foothold in the country concerned. Leaders contacted under these conditions shortly found themselves faced with an agonizing choice. Either they would have to agree to make concessions, and then proceed to suppress more intransigent elements, thus condemning themselves in the eyes of the masses as foreign agents; or they would have to go back into opposition.

A common tactic on the part of the colonizing powers was to apply the policy of 'divide and rule'. They would give support to minority interests and ethnic groups to counterbalance the unifying and assimilatory tendency of the Arab nationalist movement. The French, for instance, attempted to exploit in this way the Druses and the Alawi in Syria, and the Berbers in the Maghreb. The British did the same in Iraq with the Assyrians, Nestorian Christians speaking an Aramaic dialect.

Similarly minority religious communities such as the Jews and, above all, the various denominations of Christians were supported against Islam, the majority religion, itself historically linked with Arab nationalism. This was the key to French policy in the Lebanon, in particular. The unsurprising result of this policy was to compromise in the eyes of the masses – who tended to be profoundly nationalist – all who agreed to play the colonialists' game. *Some* members of minority groups were of course quite eager to do this. At times when concessions to Arab nationalism were being made, these found themselves suddenly abandoned by their protectors, and suffered retaliation for their earlier apparent complicity. Retribution was sometimes terrible. In 1933 for example, the Assyrians paid by wholesale massacre for their earlier enrolment as 'levies' in the British armies of repression. It often happened that members of minority groups became hyper-nationalist so as to avoid this kind of consequence of the suspicions to which they were vulnerable.

The intensity of national feeling, manifested in a thousand everyday incidents, finally drove the colonial powers to grant independence to all the Eastern Arab countries under mandate or protectorate – except Palestine. This formal independence was supposed to satisfy national feeling, but care was taken not to make it full and comprehensive. The European patron states often retained very extensive powers, particularly in military matters and foreign policy. 'Treaties of alliance' signed after independence were sometimes used to restrict or camouflage these limitations to independence, in an attempt to appease general discontent. Thus Great Britain recognized Egypt's independence in 1922, while the mandates were in theory independent anyway. Treaties were signed with Iraq in 1922 and 1932, with Transjordan in 1928, with Egypt in 1936. France made the Lebanon an 'independent' republic in 1926, and in 1936 signed a treaty with Syria which the French Senate refused to ratify.

The Republican leaders of the French mandated territories and the kings of the countries under British influence had to steer a difficult course between their own peoples and the colonial powers. They frequently shared the aspirations of their own peoples, and they could not afford to become too alienated from them; yet at the same time they mistrusted them. On the other hand, they were dependent on the colonists for their own authority. The Hashemites (sons and descendants of Sherif Hussein) had been deceived by the British, but nonetheless continued to throw in their lot with them, hoping to extract increasingly important concessions which would justify them in the eyes of their peoples. Above all, they would exploit British support against third parties, notably France and the Zionists. The British Secret Service and a host of officials in British pay, varying in number according to the vagaries of British policy, viewed France as an enemy power, and attempted to direct all the hostility of the Arab nationalists on to her. These same circles represented British support for the Zionists as an unfortunate side-effect of the war, destined gradually to disappear; and, indeed, a powerful pro-Arab lobby in London was working in this direction. This did not prevent the contempt and hatred felt for 'collaborator' governments from steadily increasing and spreading to ever-wider sections of the population. The fine past record of some Arab leaders in the struggle for independence and unity did not save them from their countrymen's resentment. The only ones to escape contumely were Feisal (who died in 1933), who charmed the populace by his romantic personality and was always felt to be the victim of the English rather than their accomplice; and his son Ghâzi, himself fiercely nationalistic, who was killed in a motor accident in April 1939 – public rumour seeing in his death the hand of the British Intelligence Service.

The mass of the population remained oppressed by feelings of disillusion, humiliation, frustration and anger. The Arab people itself had been cheated, used as a pawn; promises had been made and immediately broken, once the desired end had been achieved. The Arab world as a whole burned with the desire for revenge, to throw off the yoke of foreign occupation and achieve independence. Vague feelings of identity among the Arabic-speaking peoples, based on their common tongue, cultural heritage and history, were now reinforced by their struggle to free themselves from their common plight, a struggle directed against a common enemy. Upheavals in one country had major repercussions in all the others, whatever their outcome. The ideology of Arab nationalism, born in the Asian part of the Arab world, gradually spread.

Social conditions assisted this development. The growth of a modern economy, the creation of bureaucracies to sustain the new states, the wants of the occupying powers, all accompanied or followed by a widening of education, combined to expand and develop the tertiary sector, producing a new and numerous middle class. The new intelligentsia in particular were closer to the people and hence more militant and uncompromising than the older leaders of the nationalist movement, who tended to be large landowners and merchants with their own intellectual coterie, with international connections and a cosmopolitan culture. Leadership of the nationalist movement gradually passed into the hands of these new elements, who had no strong ties with traditional intellectual culture and subscribed to a new ideology.

The influence of international ideologies was also felt. Marxism had only limited influence, although some of its ideas were taken up subsequently in a very general form. Only the Syrian-Lebanese Communist Party, after 1936, achieved anything significant. Fascism, on the other hand, especially in the form of Nazism, won considerable success after 1933 in the Eastern Arab world. Seen from a distance, it represented the ideal of a strong and unified state from which all internal dissensions had been eradicated, founded on the nation's will to autonomy and strength. This corresponded exactly with the current phase of the Arab national struggle. Added to this identity of aim was the coincidence of a common enemy. The principal enemies of Germany, and subsequently of the Axis, were the well-endowed colonial powers, Britain and France; and, artificially, the Jews. These were the very enemies of the Arabs. Sympathy between the two movements was therefore inevitable. However, the Arabs were not blind to the darker side of the Fascist regimes and were mistrustful of their promises. After all, they too were European states, and if they had no colonies at the moment, this was only because the others had taken them away, a fact of which the Axis powers never ceased to complain. It was wiser not to trust interested allies too far; in any case, they gave little assistance. But a common enemy has always tended to move political groupings closer together, and the Arabs had at any rate nothing to lose from an upheaval bringing about the collapse and humiliation of the colonial powers.

Centrifugal forces also existed. However artificial the new frontiers may have been, they had created regional networks of economic and political interests. Local patriotisms had grown up – Iraqi, Lebanese etc. Some of the more realistic leaders had appreciated the need for flexibility and manoeuvre.

By and large however, the most striking feature of the situation was the Arabs' hatred for the occupying powers, especially Great Britain. This was stirred up by very skilful German and Italian propaganda.

The idea of Arab unity was an additional factor; Egypt espoused the cause in about 1936, and it spread westward. The role of the press, radio and books gained in importance as the level of education rose, exerting a markedly unifying influence. It was at this stage that the war of 1939 broke out.

In Palestine, the *Yishuv* had increased in strength and level of organization, while Arab opposition to it became increasingly violent. The British were forced to take serious account of this Arab opposition.

British protection had enabled the *Yishuv* to increase its numerical strength through Jewish immigration. At the end of the Great War, there were some 60,000 Jews in Palestine, out of a total population of 700,000. A further 117,000 Jews entered the country between 1919 and 1931. But political crisis and unemployment forced many to leave again. From 1924 to 1931, 29 out of every 100 immigrants left the country after a brief stay. In 1927 there were more departures than arrivals – 5,000 as against 3,000. Nevertheless, in 1931 the Jews constituted 175,000 of the 1,036,000 inhabitants, or 17.7 per cent. Hitler's persecutions unleashed a new flood of immigrants, which saved the *Yishuv*. Numbers more than doubled. Between 1932 and 1938, 217,000 Jews entered Palestine, mainly from Poland and Central Europe. Many of them had some capital. 1,250 'capitalists', each possessing more than £500 sterling, arrived between 1926 and 1930; from 1931 to 1939 inclusive, immigrants owning more than £1,000 numbered 24,247. In 1939 the Jews numbered 429,605 out of an estimated population of 1,500,000, i.e. 28 per cent.

The Jewish *Yishuv* was a thoroughly well organized force, practically autonomous, progressive and dynamic. Jewish agriculture was partly organized in settlements with a collectivized internal structure, and was geared to the production of high-quality, profitable and readily marketable produce. Every effort was made to use the most up-to-date techniques. Products were marketed through a network of cooperatives. A large-scale industry, by the standards of the country, had grown up. Practically all the electricity in the region was supplied by a Jewish company, the Palestine Electric Corporation. As mentioned earlier, the *Yishuv* was self-governing, through an elected Representative Assembly which controlled various social activities such as the organization of education. The Assembly could levy taxes on its own authority. Purely Jewish trade unions were united in the powerful *Histadruth* (trades union confederation), which as well as its trade union activities fulfilled the functions of capitalist entrepreneur, banker, insurance company, landowner and social security service. The *Yishuv* was divided into several political parties, and at its fringes some extremist religious Jews declared themselves anti-Zionist and refused to recognize the authority of its institutions. Nonetheless it formed a coherent bloc, a quasi-state, ready to take over full power in part or the whole of Palestine if occasion should offer. The majority, it is true, did not at this time place great hope in the objective of a purely Jewish State, and tended rather to explore the possibility of some kind of bi-national state. This meant negotiation with the Arabs, but these negotiations always came up against the question of immigration. Unrestricted immigration must necessarily one day lead to Jewish preponderance in a bi-national Palestine, and this the Arabs were not prepared to accept. An extremist wing within the *Yishuv*, the Revisionists, reproached the majority for its indecision, its dealings with the English, its consideration for the existence of the Arabs. It demanded a revision of the mandate, the extension of Jewish colonization to Transjordan, and the formation of a Jewish army which would establish the Jewish State by force.

The Arabs were divided into clans and factions, and found it difficult to achieve unity, despite the fact that the religious differences between Muslims and Christians counted for little, and that all agreed on the main issue: the need to prevent the *Yishuv* from creating, by whatever means, a Palestinian State dominated by the Jews in which the Arabs would be forced to choose between a position of inferiority and exile. One by one, they used every means of opposition open to them: political action, strikes, demonstrations which degenerated into brawls, and sometimes terrorism. Some were in favour of moderate tactics, leaving open the channels of communication with the British authorities, and even attempting to reach a basis for agreement with the Zionists. Others pressed for violent action, some turning hopeful eyes towards the Fascist powers. These, however, had more taste for inflammatory propaganda than for specific promises or concrete assistance. Hitler Germany even favoured the emigration of German Jews to Palestine. By 1936 tension in Palestine had risen to such a degree that the increasing spate of minor incidents finally erupted into a state of war. Armed bands of Palestinian Arabs supplemented by Syrian, Iraqi and other volunteers took to the hills, defying a British force of several tens of thousands of men (including Jewish auxiliaries) armed with tanks and aeroplanes. Strikes, street-fights and assassinations followed thick and fast upon one another's heels. The Arab rebels were divided into all kinds of different factions. In the countryside, full-scale peasant revolts took place, just as dangerous to the big Arab landowners as to the Zionists. Thanks to the Haganah, the illegal but tolerated Jewish secret army, the Jews were able to defend themselves. Some even undertook reprisals. They collaborated closely with the British Army, which gave them arms. Development of the Jewish economic sector benefited from Arab strikes and disturbances. On the other side, the Mufti of Jerusalem, an extreme nationalist leader, had Arab moderates executed. Just as a large number of wealthy Jews from Germany and Austria were entering the country, the Palestinian economy was in a state of paralysis, social life was disrupted, and the British army was fully occupied in obscure and dangerous missions.

The British themselves were divided into several different factions, in varying degrees sympathetic or hostile to one or other of the warring parties, and interested to a greater or lesser degree in the protection of the Suez Canal and the route to India. The Labour Party tended to support the Zionist cause, presented by the Zionist lobby as being in keeping with socialist ideals. Another major factor was hostility to Nazi anti-Semitism. In Palestine itself, British officials and the military were frequently hostile to the Jews; but in any case, all attempts on their part to give objective consideration to the claims of one race was immediately interpreted by the other as shameful collusion with its enemy. By and large, however, the English were beginning to appreciate the substance of the Arab grievances and the dangers inherent in ignoring Arab public opinion in the current state of world crisis, when the conviction was growing that war was now inevitable. Various commissions were sent to the area to inquire into the causes of the difficulties and strife, and to suggest possible solutions. In 1937 the report of the Peel Commission first proposed the partition of Palestine into an Arab State and a Jewish State, with a third small state containing Jerusalem and a corridor to the sea to remain under British mandate. To the great astonishment of the British and the Arabs, it was the Jewish population and the Zionists, conditioned by Messianic propaganda proclaiming an all-Jewish Palestine, who forced their leaders to an ambiguous answer, amounting practically to rejection of the plan. In 1938, when the civil war in Palestine broke out with renewed violence and the British had practically to reconquer the country and forcibly put down the Palestinian rebellion, the Woodhead Technical Commission concluded that the Peel plan could never be put into effect. A round-table meeting held in February 1939 broke down in deadlock.

War was approaching. London was deeply preoccupied with the

Anglophobia and pro-German sympathies of the Eastern Arab world. In May 1939, the question was brusquely settled by the British White Paper, which dictated the following terms: Palestine was to continue to be ruled by Britain. Negotiations for a constitution were to take place after five years, and for independence after ten years. 75,000 more Jews would be allowed to immigrate within the next five years, but after that the level of immigration would be conditional on the consent of the Arab majority. Sales of land to Jews were restricted in certain areas, and prohibited in others. Palestine was to be neither an Arab state nor a Jewish state. In fact, in the bi-national state envisaged, the Jews would be kept down to a level of one third of the population. Zionist indignation reached its highest pitch.

War broke out three months later. The White Paper did much to convert most Arab leaders from their policy of declared hostility to Great Britain. The Arabs' favourite policy was 'wait-and-see'. At first they hoped for an Allied defeat, which promised to liberate them from Anglo-French tutelage. The anti-British insurrection in Iraq in April and May 1941, led by Rashîd Alî Kaylânî, was motivated more by anger at Britain's Arab and Palestinian policies than by any great love for the Axis powers. The revolt failed. The Grand Mufti of Jerusalem, who had played a part in it, fled to Germany, there to assist the Nazi propaganda machine. The British made strenuous efforts to win back Arab friendship. In May 1941, Anthony Eden announced that Britain's attitude towards Arab unity was 'sympathetic'. England played a decisive role in putting an end to the French mandate over the Lebanon (1943) and Syria (1945), thus contributing to the achievement of full independence by these countries. On 22 March 1945 the founding charter of the Arab League was signed in Cairo under the aegis of the British.

In Palestine, the Jews were in general committed to assist the struggle against Hitler in every way possible. Many held important positions in the British Near-Eastern armies. They nevertheless continued to protest vigorously against the White Paper. Militant minorities among them, right-wing extremist groups, soon decided to begin terrorist activities against Britain, which they regarded as a colonial oppressor. Those most attracted to this form of action were, naturally enough, the young, who had not known the period when the English were primarily the protectors of the Jews – ill-disposed and harsh at times, no doubt, but protectors nonetheless. These youthful elements soon carried with them increasing numbers of adults, embittered especially by the restrictions on immigration imposed at a time when European Jews were being massacred wholesale. The organization which gave the first signal for terrorist action was the *Irgun Zvai Leumi* (National Military Organization), a splinter-group of the Revisionist party, from which in turn emerged the Stern Gang (or *Lehi*, for *Lohamei heruth Yisrael*, 'Fighters for the Freedom of Israel'). The latter rejected the truce the former had accorded the British at the outbreak of war. But the Stern Gang broke up on the death (probably by assassination) of its leader. The struggle started again in earnest at the beginning of 1944. It was condemned by the Jewish Agency and the Haganah, but supported by an uncompromising Jewish public opinion, outraged by the British refusal to allow free entry into Palestine to European Jews fleeing Nazi persecution. At the end of 1945, with the world war over, the Haganah also entered the war against the British, who continued to maintain restrictions on immigration. A deadly round-dance of terrorist raids, assassinations and blind reprisals followed. The situation soon became untenable for the British. The Arabs desired the victory of neither of the two antagonists and therefore remained passive spectators. Besides, any force they might have raised to dispute the issue had been broken by the suppression of the Palestinian rebellion of 1936–39 and the political differences that arose out of that event.

On 14 February 1947 Bevin capitulated. He announced that Great Britain would withdraw from Palestine, and handed over responsibility for deciding the country's future to the United Nations. Discussions then began at international level. The strength shown by the *Yishuv*, the solidarity of its local base, its single-mindedness and will to independence, and the efficiency with which it had conducted the 'war' against the English had convinced the great powers that peaceful coexistence with the Arabs was a pipe-dream. On 29 November 1947, the United Nations passed a resolution prescribing the partition of Palestine into an Arab State and a Jewish State, the internationalization of Jerusalem, and economic union of all three parts.

But the U.N. proved incapable of putting the plan into practice. The British refused to supervise its implementation, stating only that their troops, the only force capable of maintaining peace, would evacuate the country on 15 May 1948. From that moment, a bloody head-on collision between the two races became inevitable. The day after the U.N. decision was announced the Arabs repudiated the international resolution and firing broke out in Jerusalem. The Jews, who had become wiser since their rejection of the Peel plan, accepted a Jewish State far below their expectations; one which, nonetheless, might provide them with a firm base and, perhaps, a nucleus for further gains.

The Arabs indignantly rejected what they regarded as an amputation of their territory and a confirmation that they were to be sacrificed to a project of colonization.

Guerrilla warfare raged throughout the months preceding the fateful day of 15 May 1948. Each side attempted to seize as much territory as possible in preparation for the departure of the English. The British troops, who were gradually being concentrated in the major centres ready for evacuation, observed an ambiguous neutrality tending, if anything, to favour the Arabs. The only truly military engagements in which they were involved were in an unsuccessful move to prevent the Jews from conquering points attributed by the U.N. to the Arab zone, notably Jaffa. The Palestinian Arabs embarked on a few isolated, sporadic and thoroughly ill-organized attacks. Then the volunteers of the Arab Liberation Army, numbering several thousands under the leadership of Fawzi al Kawakji (who had earlier commanded a similar force from 1936 to 1939), entered Palestine in January 1948 and launched several abortive attacks against the Jewish settlements. The daring raids, skirmishes and street-fights in which this Army engaged provoked Jewish reprisals on an even greater scale. These were at first led by the Right-wing extremist groups, the *Irgun* and the *Lehi*. The official Zionist leaders who controlled the Haganah, the semi-clandestine official army of the Jewish Agency, took a more sober view of the recourse to arms, and still entertained some hope of effective international intercession. But the response which nationalist extremism evoked among the Jewish populace forced them also into the attack. The flames of this nationalist fervour were fanned by the *Irgun* and the *Lehi*, and ample fuel provided by the havoc wrought by the Arab irregulars, who began more systematic attacks, notably the blockade of the Jewish quarter of Jerusalem. Reprisals became increasingly indiscriminate, spectacular 'warnings' to discourage further Arab attacks and to win as much territory as possible before the British left. Some also hoped that the Arabs too would be driven to leave, thus ensuring a homogeneous Jewish population of the future Jewish State. Terror against the Arabs was carried to its logical conclusion by the *Irgun*. On the night of 9 to 10 April, a commando detachment systematically massacred all 254 inhabitants, men, women and children, of the Arab village of Deir Yassin. A full-scale military campaign was conducted to take Jaffa, an Arab island in the middle of Jewish territory according to the U.N. plan; in fact it constituted a major military threat to Tel Aviv. Similar campaigns were mounted to relieve the Jewish quarter of Jerusalem (international territory according to the

same plan) and to clear the road connecting the H
Jewish areas.

On 14 May 1948 the British High Commissioner I
the evacuation of British troops was begun. On the s
Ben Gurion proclaimed the foundation of the Jewish St
The next day the regular armies of the neighbouring *A*
moved into Palestine. They may have prepared far-reac   ...ns of
campaign, but in the end they were only able, with one or two exceptions, to occupy part of the areas granted to the Arabs by the U.N.
plan. They were defeated by the Jews on every front. The Jewish
troops were well-trained, their morale was extremely high, and they
were totally dedicated to their cause. Their numbers were at first about
equal to those of the Arab forces, but their lines of communication
were much less extended. In the final phase of the war, there were
60,000 Jewish soldiers facing 40,000 Arabs. The Haganah networks in
Europe and America had excellent connections, and organized the
purchase of arms, the recruitment of volunteers and mercenaries and
their shipment to Palestine with tremendous efficiency and panache.
The Arabs were handicapped by military inexperience, the uneven
morale of their soldiers, the slackness of many of their officers, the
corruption and incompetence of their bureaucracies, and above all
perhaps by the rivalry between states supposedly acting in concert who
never communicated to one another their respective plans of campaign.
The two cease-fires imposed by the U.N. seem to have served chiefly
to allow the Jews to rearm and gather reinforcements. In order to
maximize his advantages, Ben Gurion broke the truce and the various
partial cease-fires on several occasions. The last time this was done,
the operation code-word was, significantly, '*Fait accompli*'. Only an
Anglo-American ultimatum prevented him from pressing on into the
Sinai Desert, beyond the Egyptian frontier.

The U.N. finally secured a prolonged cessation of hostilities on 7
January 1949. The last cease-fire dates from 11 March. Between February and April, a series of armistices were concluded between Israel
and the various Arab states. The war was over, but peace had not been
made.

The Zionists had achieved their aims. A Jewish State now existed.
While its territory did not cover the whole of the Mandate of Palestine,
still less the lands of ancient Israel (which extended eastwards beyond
the River Jordan), most Jews were content with the substantial plat-
form they had won. As for the Arabs, they felt that a foreign colony
had succeeded in seizing a part of their territory and driving out a

ber of its Arab inhabitants – and this with the support of the ntire Western world, regardless of ideology, from the capitalist United States to the socialist U.S.S.R. The British Mandate, imposed by force, had prevented them from taking any political or police action to halt the immigration of this new population. Once this population had achieved a firm base and sufficient strength in numbers it demanded its independence, first from its erstwhile patron, then from the native population which it hoped to dispossess or dominate. It had achieved this autonomy by force of arms, with the blessing of the whole of Europe and America, represented by the United Nations. Virtually all its violations of the decisions and 'orders' of the U.N. had been crowned with success. Even the murder of the U.N. mediator, Count Bernadotte (who had proposed a revision of the U.N. partition plan, and demanded the return of the refugees), by Jewish terrorists was not allowed to count against it. The policy of the *fait accompli* never failed. The Arabs, full of bitterness and rancour, refused to recognize this European *Diktat*, this colonial amputation which had been imposed on them. Hostilities were only broken off because of their own impotence, which they hoped would be temporary. One way or another, for them the war would go on.

3
Israel's First Decade

Israel was founded by a group symbolized by one man: David Ben Gurion. The secret of Ben Gurion's success was that his militant attitude was in perfect harmony with the logic of the Zionist movement. He had made his choice as a young man, and he was always able to see which actions accorded with the general direction of Zionist policy and which drew their inspiration from some other source. Like all great leaders of ideological movements, he held firmly to his central idea and was able at any point in history to understand its implications in terms of action. Again like many such leaders, there were times when he may have suspected that the chosen course itself might one day prove a dead end. But men of action cannot retrace their steps or allow themselves any doubts. They will pursue their ends through fire and water; it is left to history to make the final decision.

David Ben Gurion, like others in his group, was a non-Marxist socialist. But socialism was for them a means, not an end. Their dream was not to create a more just and freer society for all men, but to regenerate the Jewish people within its own state. Those among the Jews most deserving of sympathy and most capable of realizing such a project were the workers. Jewish society of the future was to be a hard, pure society of workers not ruled by any leisure class, a society which they alone were capable of sustaining just as they alone had been capable of creating it.

Ben Gurion's impatience, even hatred, for middle-class Zionists who were usually careful not to soil their hands in Palestine is thus understandable. In all their decisions he saw a dangerous leaning towards solutions which endangered the realization of Zionist aims. This was his opinion of Chaim Weizmann himself. In recognition of his historic services, Weizmann was offered the Presidency of the new state. But he was not allowed the right to append his signature to the declaration of independence of 14 May 1948 (he was in New York at the time) and it was made clear that his functions would be purely honorary.

There were at the outset 21 parties in Israel, but the state centred on Ben Gurion and his party, the Mapai. The first elections, held in January 1949, gave the Mapai 35 per cent of the votes, 20 per cent more than its nearest rival. But the majority was not absolute, and has never become so. Attacks on the Mapai from both the Right and the Left were numerous, violent and venomous. Since only a coalition government was possible every party haggled long and skilfully before granting its support. None failed to take advantage of the opportunities for political blackmail. Nevertheless, the Mapai always came out on top.

Despite the violence and aggressiveness of the internal jealousies and struggle for power, the instinct for unity always prevailed. Israel was a besieged fortress, and no one could afford to forget it. The frontiers, defined merely by the front lines on the last day of hostilities, were tortuous. At its narrowest point the country was less than ten miles across.

The state began to take shape. Essential institutions were set up. Israel became a parliamentary democracy. Instead of a written constitution, it had a series of fundamental laws voted by the Assembly, or *Knesset*.

Administrative questions were, however, less important than the fulfilment of the Zionist dream. To make this dream a reality was the State of Israel's first priority. It was made plain from the beginning that Israel did not wish to be a Levantine state among others, but the setting in which the destiny of the Jews was to be accomplished, the place where the exiles were to be reunited, the true home of all the Jews of the world. All restrictions on immigration were lifted, and a solemn appeal was sent out to all members of the 'Jewish people' to come and settle in Israel. A law, regarded as fundamental, and without parallel in any other legislation, was promulgated in July 1950. This is the famous Law of the Return: 'Every Jew has the right to come to this country as an *'oleh.'* *'Oleh* is a Hebrew expression, not strictly translatable, literally 'One who ascends', a Jew who comes to settle in the land of Palestine. It was found impossible (or dangerous) to define the term 'Jew'. A law of nationality, adopted after years of discussion in April 1952, emphasized the special nature of the state. Israeli nationality belonged to every *'oleh* by right, whether or not he renounced his original nationality. The same applied to every person residing in Israeli territory on the day on which the state was proclaimed, or who had legally entered that territory before the date on which the law was promulgated. It applied to Arabs who had remained in their homes or who had legally been accepted into the country since. By contrast, every Palestinian Arab who left his home at the time of the war and had not since been able to return had to apply for naturalization, and swear an oath of loyalty to the State of Israel like any other foreigner.

Acceptance of the application would then depend on the result of inquiries and on the good will of the Minister of the Interior. His only privilege by comparison with other foreigners was that he was not obliged (in principle) to know Hebrew. A similar fundamental law accorded official status to the World Zionist Organization.

Under these conditions, Jewish immigration began again in earnest. Just before the war there were 650,000 Jews on Israeli territory compared with 740,000 Arabs. Only 160,000 Arabs remained. Between 1948 and 1951, 687,000 new Jewish immigrants arrived, more than the original number. Among the first to arrive were 70,000 survivors of Nazi concentration camps and 300,000 from the Peoples' Democracies (especially Rumania and Poland, whose governments at that time left the door open to Jewish emigration). But above all, between 1948 and 1951, 330,000 Asian and African Jews 'ascended' to Israel. On the one hand, the conditions under which the State of Israel had been created rendered the Jewish minority in Arab countries (from which came 247,000 of the 330,000 immigrants) suspect of being sympathetic to the Arabs' enemy. This led to hostility, and in some cases (witness Morocco and Libya) full-scale pogroms. On the other hand, these events appeared to the pious Jews of the Third World, usually grouped into orthodox communities, to presage the coming of the Messiah and to demand their return to Zion. Between 1952 and 1954 the flow thinned considerably, and in 1953 Jewish departures from Israel even surpassed the arrivals. But the wave was swollen once again at the end of 1954 by the influx of some 100,000 Jews, mainly from North Africa; these came mainly out of fear of the rabid nationalism which seemed to have been revealed in the course of the Algerian War. By 1956, there were 1,667,500 Jews in Israel, as against 200,000 Arabs. The composition of the Jewish population changed markedly in favour of Orientals. In 1948, 54.8 per cent of Israeli Jews were of European birth, 35.4 per cent had been born in Palestine and 8.8 per cent in the rest of the Middle East. In 1956, 37.7 per cent were born in Europe, 29.4 per cent in the Middle East and 32.9 per cent in the country itself. The European Jews were from then on in the minority.

This enormous flood of immigrants more than doubled the population, and naturally caused considerable economic difficulties. Even in the period of the Mandate the *Yishuv* had subsisted largely on foreign aid. The trade deficit of Palestine under the Mandate was very large. In the period from 1933 to 1937, exports paid on average for only 29 per cent of imports. The young State of Israel was in an even worse position. The rupture with the Arab countries forced it to trade mostly with distant countries: England, Canada, the United States, Germany. Furthermore, it was an uphill struggle for Israeli products to compete in these markets with the local products of a better equipped and better organized local agriculture and industry. In 1952 exports were only 11 per cent of the value of imports. Integration of the immigrants was very costly. From the proclamation of independence to the end of 1952, the cost of bringing them to Israel, receiving them and housing them was 2,250 dollars per head.

The usual sources of funds proved inadequate to cope with this situation. At the time of the Mandate they had been composed chiefly of a flood of voluntary contributions from the Jews of the Diaspora, especially American Jews. Between 1917 and 1942, 86.8 per cent of the £22,535,000 sterling total receipts of Jewish institutions and national funds came from such contributions. The means of conducting the war of 1948 were secured largely thanks to the eloquence of Golda Myerson, who managed to extract 50 million dollars from the American Jews. Eighteen months later she returned to the United States to appeal for funds for construction. On 27 April 1949, Ben Gurion said in announcing his austerity programme to the Knesset:

It would be a cruel illusion to imagine that the absorption and housing of the immigrants is an undertaking which can be quickly and easily accomplished. We believe that despite the enormous financial, technical and administrative problems, the State will be able to absorb this immense flood of immigrants if it succeeds in obtaining every possible assistance from Jews abroad.*

Thus was the Zionist programme to be carried out, in spite of the enormous economic problems to which it gave rise, and at the cost of a heavy dependence on the outside world.

Massive immigration, however, was not the only burden which the young state's situation and programme obliged it to bear. Surrounded by a hostile world, it had to have arms. The Haganah had proved its strength in the war against the Arabs. In its new role of the National Army, it now needed to be strengthened, provided with superior equipment, and kept in a constant state of readiness for immediate mobilization. Military expenditure and special budgets in 1950 and 1951 amounted to 44 per cent and 42 per cent respectively of the whole of government expenditure. This proportion then fell to 30 per cent in 1953, then rose once more to 37 per cent in 1955. The state was threatened with financial collapse when, in January 1952, Ben Gurion proposed the acceptance of reparations payments from Germany. This

* Quoted in *Cahiers de l'Orient contemporain*, nos. 18–19, Paris, 1949, p. 148.

proposal had to overcome opposition from a wide spectrum of public opinion, from Right to Left, outraged that the debt to millions of victims of Nazism should be considered atoned for by this means. Ben Gurion won the assent of Parliament by only 61 votes to 50, after having had to suppress a popular uprising in Jerusalem.

Militarization did not exclude democracy, and in a sense was one aspect of it. Hence the contrast between Israel as seen by the Arabs and the vision of her cherished by Europeans. To the former, Israel was a colonial offshoot of the Western world, imposed on the Oriental world by force and therefore the very epitome of injustice and oppression. The word 'Zionism' has acquired in Arabic a meaning sinister in itself, evocative of evil, like the words 'imperialism', 'colonialism' and, for many people nowadays, 'capitalism'. For them, seen on the world scale, Israel is an armed camp peopled by aggressive conquerors. Indeed, Israel is an armed camp set in the midst of hostile territory, like the makeshift forts surrounded by palisades which European pioneers erected feverishly, Western-style, in every alien territory to which they penetrated, posting lookouts to scan the prairie anxiously for the movements of unfriendly tribes. But the West had solemnly endorsed the legitimacy of this island transplanted from the Western world, and no longer questioned it; what interested Westerners was the internal structure of the state. To admit and even exalt its virtues helped to eradicate, retrospectively, all the wrongs which had been done to the European Jews. It helped Westerners to forget the religious persecutions of old, the hatred and contempt still contained in many religious books, the massacres carried out by some while others looked on and did nothing, the repugnance felt for an alien people. This repugnance had become almost instinctive over a thousand years of history and was aggravated by intellectual, cultural and social cleavages which assimilation had not yet succeeded in effacing. The Jews of Europe and America had not on the whole been very eager to emigrate to this barren land, a country foreign to them and speaking a strange tongue. But they could not help feeling a thrill of pride at the success of those, their own cousins and brothers, who had shared their humiliation, and at seeing in them the resurgence of the Maccabean virtues. While before the war Zionism had been only a minority cult among the Jewish masses, now, after the holocaust which had devoured so many of their people, they felt uneasy about refusing their support to an independent community where so many had found refuge. Sometimes discreetly, sometimes with militant ostentation, they therefore became highly effective propaganda agents. For them, any attack or criticism of Israel smacked of the furies of Nazism, and they would at the least brush it aside, with secret unease, or else passionately denounce it. Films showing the action of the war of 1948 from the Israeli point of view were vigorously applauded all over the world. The showing of a film shot from the Arab point of view was inconceivable. The only Jews who (apparently) did not share such sentiments were either the fervent adherents of militant anti-Zionist ideologies such as Communism, or the admittedly very large number who had opted for assimilation and had taken to it with such enthusiasm that they were well on the way to breaking all links with Judaism. The latter group tended to take refuge in silence, however, and therefore passed unnoticed – especially since they had merged with widely differing peoples and nationalities.

Europe was also led to idealize Israel and to see in her the image of its own aspirations. Paradoxically, some saw a parliamentary, pluralistic democracy, with a capitalist free-enterprise economy; while others saw at least the beginnings of an egalitarian socialist society, free of the privilege conferred by wealth, allowing to all the free development of their potentialities in their own chosen direction. Both of these opposite schools were able to adduce facts to support their conflicting analyses.

The Palestinian *Yishuv* was largely founded by settlers from Tsarist Russia strongly influenced by socialist or progressive ideologies of the Marxist or Tolstoyan variety. Indeed it was this class of settlers which furnished a large number of the leaders and chief administrators of the new state. Some set up agricultural colonies on the collectivist principle, the famous *kibbutzim*. Other settlements quickly sprang up representing a transitional form of small peasant ownership. For the distribution of their products these production units were then interconnected by networks of cooperatives. This sector is undeniably socialist in character. As far as the collectivist settlements are concerned, there is a great deal of truth in G. Friedmann's assertion that 'the *kibbutzim* seem to us . . . the most successful attempt so far to replace the individual's own private interest by community principles as the basis for social existence'.* It is hardly surprising, therefore, that a major section of European intellectuals should have viewed this socialistic sector with admiration and hope, particularly since it is free of the unpleasant associations which the Stalinist system has given to other existing forms of socialism.

On the other hand, both under the British mandate and to an even

* G. Friedmann, *The End of the Jewish People?*, London, Hutchinson, 1967.

greater extent in the young State of Israel, this socialist sector within the Palestinian *Yishuv* formed part of a social structure dominated by economic considerations which had nothing specifically socialist about them; the market economy was paramount. The *kibbutzim* float in a mixed-economy capitalist environment, to which they have to adapt. The apologists of private enterprise need therefore have nothing to fear from this kind of micro-socialism. As a certain Israeli banker has stated:

To the outside world, the *kibbutz* behaves exactly like a capitalist enterprise, and keeps to its contracts better than an individual. If the *kibbutz* is internally composed of people who renounce private property, who bring up their children collectively or who ... crawl about on all fours, that is none of our concern.*

As for the workings of Israel's parliamentary democracy, it may well live up to all the (theoretical) principles of liberalism. Elections to the Knesset are surrounded by a network of precautions guaranteeing maximum electoral freedom. Seats are distributed by a system of proportional representation. In 1959 as many as 24 lists of candidates were submitted to the electorate. 75 to 83 per cent of electors actually go to the polls. The seats are distributed among about 10 parties, all with a fairly stable representation. Coalitions form and re-form. As mentioned before, the Mapai (Labour) party generally polled 40 to 47 per cent of the votes. It was therefore never able to govern alone. Government coalitions have usually been between the Mapai and the religious parties, which obtain about 12 to 15 per cent of the votes and of the seats. The result is that these religious parties have a permanent lever for blackmail, and only give their support at the price of further concessions to clericalism. The alternatives – support from the Left or the Right – also present problems. Ben Gurion campaigned for a long time for the adoption of the simple mjority system, on the pattern of the Anglo-Saxon countries, but without success. Simple-majority voting would lead to a simpler and more stable two-party system which would ensure greater security of office for the government.

Clerical influence is an embarrassment to the pro-Israeli Left in the outside world. It is more difficult to idealize than the micro-socialism of the *kibbutzim* or political democracy. It does not only stem from the unique position of the religious parties, but also from the expectations of American Jewish organizations who would be unwilling to finance bodies exhibiting anti-clerical tendencies. Thus the salvation of the

* B. Goriely, *Cette année à Jerusalem*, Paris-Lausanne-Bâle, ed. Vineta, 1951, p. 69.

American Jews is conveniently assured by the strict religious observance imposed on Israeli Jews, while their consciences are assuaged and their supposed duty as Zionists fulfilled at the price of certain financial sacrifices. Also, Israel inherited from before the time of the British Mandate the community structure of the Ottoman Empire. Every religious community is self-governing and is empowered to regulate legally the personal status of its members. Hence the impossibility of mixed marriages in Israel, as in the Lebanon, which has a comparable structure in this respect. The fear of a purely secular constitution has driven the religious parties to oppose the introduction of any constitution whatsoever. Thanks to the support of the Mapai and against opposition from all the other parties, they have succeeded in their aim, because the Mapai was not prepared to go against the express wishes of its political allies. As a result of this political situation the Israeli people is obliged to conform to strict religious observance which it finds repugnant, or at least irritating: cessation of all transport on the Sabbath, the imposition of Kosher food, etc. In several cases, clerical tyranny has actually harmed the national interest.

A deeper consequence, and one no doubt more serious in its long-term implications, has been the growth of a common ideology, which was deeply rooted in many minds though not always made explicit. This ideology is a rather incoherent mixture of nationalism with racialist overtones, and religion. Ancient Israel has the great distinction that it developed, at the time of the prophets, one of the very first universalist ideologies in the world. This transcended the old ethnic religion of the national god Yahweh fighting against the gods of other peoples. At a certain stage in social evolution, this ideology corresponded so closely to a real human need that it conquered, in the shape of the Christian and Islamic 'heresies', a large part of mankind. This universalist tendency has now been practically abandoned. God is with His people Israel in work and in battle. Those who do not believe see in their religion primarily a national value, and are externally all the more faithful to it. For many, nationalism has been one step on the road to faith. To believe in dogmas about the universe and man in general merely because they are the ones which your race or nation has adopted many years since is an affront to reason and morality. It is, indeed, a common phenomenon; but in Israel it has been developed into a State theology to an extent which is fairly uncommon in the modern world. The reading, veneration, meditation and teaching of the Old Testament has had the most deplorable effects, as it has in some Puritan Christian communities devoted to the imitation of Israel. In

Israel's present situation, what most minds, and especially children's minds, retain most easily are the battles fought by the ancient nation against its neighbours, Moabites, Amalekites, Philistines and others, the exaltation of carnage, the wrath called down by God on the heads of Israel's enemies, the supreme value accorded to the nation. Next to these tendencies, the universalist values emerging from the tradition of the great prophets do have some influence, but it is (not surprisingly) small by comparison.

The State of Israel is only a purely Jewish State in its leadership and in its official ideology. Several hundred thousand Arabs fled their homes in the territory later to become Israel at the time of the war of 1948. The official line is that they were incited to leave by the Arab leaders themselves. This theory is accepted by most foreign commentators, but except in a few limited cases without any historical evidence. There were many causes for the Arab exodus, the main one being simply that which operated in Spain during the Civil War or in France in 1940: to get away from the theatre of military operations. The fear of Jewish terrorism also played a major part, even though the terror was sporadic and restricted. The massacre of Deir Yassin, despite the condemnation of it by the ruling Jewish bodies, was fearfully effective as an act of terror. Many leading Jews were glad to see the departure of a population which by its very presence presented an obstacle to the realization of the Jewish State projected by the Zionists. At all events, most of the refugees hoped to return to their towns and villages when hostilities had ended, but could no longer cross the front lines, now congealed into the new frontiers.

There were about 580,000 refugees. 160,000 Arabs remained in Israel, their number eventually increasing to 380,000 around 1967. About one third of these are Christians. Israel was greatly embarrassed by this minority, which never wanted to become integrated into a Jewish State, and which prevented that state from being purely Jewish. Should it be treated as a Trojan horse, a danger to the security of the state? Or as a bridge to the hostile Arab states, providing a model example of coexistence between the two races? It was doubtless impossible to take up an unequivocal position between the two policies. Clearly nothing would entirely disarm the hostility of the Arabs inside the country, while those outside would remain irreconcilable. The Israeli Arabs were excused military service – any other course would have been unthinkable. Many of them lived in frontier areas – or rather, in view of the small size of the country, one should perhaps say areas closer to the frontier than others. 80 per cent were under military administration.

Army passes were required in order to travel short distances. Since it is not always possible to tell an Arab from a Jew at first sight, special identity cards carrying the letter 'B' were issued to Arabs. All this was done for reasons of security, and followed logically from the way in which the state had been constituted. Moreover, thanks to the Arab exodus, 80 per cent of Israeli territory after the war consisted of abandoned land, one quarter of which was cultivable. Israeli land laws settled the question by massive confiscations with offers of monetary compensation, which many people thought inadequate. But in any case, the vast majority of Israeli Arabs refused to give their consent to the confiscation. It has been estimated that they lost 40 to 50 per cent of their land.

Seen from another angle, however, it is certainly true that the Israeli Arabs benefited from the general rise in the standard of living compared with that of neighbouring Arab countries. They enjoyed political rights, and entered to some extent into the internal political game. They joined various parties, usually of the opposition, the Communist Party in particular. Arab deputies sat in the Knesset (and still do). This did not help them to forget their status as second-class citizens, the discrimination from which they suffered in the allocation of administrative posts and all positions of responsibility, and the natural mistrust with which Jewish society regarded them. Consequently they could hardly be expected to accept completely the new state which had been imposed on them. This led to many incidents, which the Arab states outside seized upon to denounce the oppression to which their Arab brothers in Israel were subjected.

Naturally enough, the Palestinian refugees left outside the country gave even greater cause for denouncing the Israelis. They had a high birth rate, and their numbers increased. In June 1956 there were estimated to be 922,000 refugees in all, of which 512,000 were in Jordan, 216,000 in the Gaza Strip, 102,000 in the Lebanon and 90,000 in Syria. At the end of 1949 the United Nations created U.N.R.W.A. – the United Nations Relief and Works Agency for Palestine Refugees in the Near East, with headquarters in Beirut. The aim of this body was to provide minimum rations (which always proved insufficient), shelter, medical services, education and professional training to all those who had not been integrated in the economies of the various countries. Because financial resources were limited, the aid was wholly inadequate. In 1964–5 U.N.R.W.A. aid came to 37 dollars per refugee per annum. Many Palestine refugees did, however, find employment in the country to which they had emigrated. In the Lebanon, for instance, they actually acquired a reputation as an active and industrious minority, with considerable achievements to its credit. But the great mass of unskilled labourers and landless, destitute peasants stayed in the U.N.R.W.A. camps with their wives and children. There they lived in conditions of extreme privation, frustrated, bitter and vengeful, clinging to the hope that they would one day be able to return to their villages and win back their land. They represent for the Arabs the living evidence, the symbol of the great injustice which has been collectively perpetrated on them.

The consequences of the Israeli victory in the Arab countries were enormous, but it was some time before they were fully felt.

Their defeat was a rude shock to the Arabs, an unprecedented humiliation. At the very moment when they had a real hope of liberation from the Western yoke, a Western colony gave the Arabs a brutal reminder of how weak they were, and how easily vanquished. They were then preached at by the whole world and told that their defeat was just.

They were attacked both ways [writes Michael Ionides]. It was morally wicked of them to fight to prevent the Zionists enjoying what was theirs; they were weak and incompetent to fight and fail. As aggressors they had no right to win; for their military incompetence they deserved to lose. They should have been loyal to the United Nations' decision to partition, for the rule of law must be honoured; they must accept the consequences of defeat, for victory goes to those who are strong. The Jews were there as of right; anyway, they had beaten the Arabs in war. It was right for the Jews to fight to acquire; wrong for the Arabs to fight to hold.*

The old political groupings in power in the Arab countries found defeat as mortifying as any of their subjects. But they were incapable of conducting policy in any other way than the familiar, traditional fashion. Out of the universal indignation new forces arose which attacked their policies, remorselessly unmasking the internal vices of these regimes. Furthermore, these very policies and vices were seen as the real reasons for failure. The sociologically minded probed the endemic vices of Arab society and the mentality which they engendered, seeking the 'Meaning of the Disaster', to quote the title of a book on the subject by the Lebanese historian Constantine Zurayq. But these new forces, especially young people belonging to social classes so far excluded from power, were impatient and had no time for

* M. Ionides, *Divide and Lose: The Arab Revolt 1955 to 1958*, London, Geoffrey Bles, 1960, p. 79.

distant reforms laboriously prepared for by a long-term educational programme. In any case, how was it possible for such reforms to be carried out within the framework of a decayed political structure? The time was ripe for an attack on that structure to be launched.

The old ruling classes had fought for independence and against Zionist encroachment. But their internal weaknesses were only too apparent. This band of kings, aristocrats, large landed proprietors and wealthy merchants were concerned above all with sectional and personal interests. They had been unable to make the sacrifices necessary to achieve unity. They had no conception of technology, which is the key to power in the modern age. Absorbed in their court intrigues, they failed to consider wider social alternatives, they were incapable of effective mobilization of the masses. They were corrupt and incompetent. They had put their trust in the support of the European world, especially Great Britain. Great Britain did indeed help them to get rid of the French, but only in order to take their place. Under the provision of treaties signed by the dynasties, British troops were stationed everywhere except Syria and the Lebanon, ready to intervene if necessary in any part of the Eastern Arab world. But Great Britain had not even succeeded in preventing the Israeli victory – if one can assume that that was her object. And the entire Western world had actively assisted this victory. The first priority was to get rid of these ill-starred regimes, identified with policies which had failed so spectacularly.

Only one of the Arab rulers, a survivor from the period of the revolt against the Turks, was so preoccupied with the realization of his personal ambitions that he failed, despite his adroitness, to appreciate the profound social transformation that was taking place. This was Feisal's brother Abdullah, Emir of Transjordan, who had himself proclaimed king in April 1946. He had made several attempts to reach an understanding with the Zionists over the partition of Palestine, and even looked beyond this. While the talks which he had with Golda Myerson on the eve of the outbreak of war may not have resulted in a signed pact, the strategy followed by his troops could easily be interpreted as dictated by a tacit agreement with Ben Gurion. At all events, in December 1948 he seized the available portion of the cake by annexing all the Arab territory remaining to the west of the River Jordan, ignoring the protests of many Palestinians and the other Arab states. It became customary to call the kingdom Jordan, in accordance with the name chosen in 1946, and the name Transjordan, confining the state to the East Bank of the river, fell into disuse. In 1949 and 1950 he entered into top-secret discussions with Ben Gurion's special envoy, Moshe

Dayan. He agreed to sign a peace with Israel, in return for a corridor to Haifa. His cabinet opposed the project, however, unless a proper Jordanian corridor several miles wide were accorded. Ben Gurion only wanted to allow a free road, with a few hundred feet on each side. Abdullah beat a retreat, but continued to seek agreement despite his cabinet. Rumours of these secret discussions leaked out, and Abdullah, who had for some time been regarded as a puppet of the British, became increasingly unpopular. On 20 July 1951 he was assassinated by a Palestinian Arab in the mosque of al-Aksa in Jerusalem.

Agitation against the regimes responsible for the conduct of the Palestine war combined with the violent anti-Western movements which had grown up in response to British domination and the Western support for Zionism. Everyone not already corrupted by the existing regime by sumptuous gifts and favours spoke out against domination by Europe, joining either Right-wing or Left-wing organizations according to their predilections. The U.N. vote in November 1947 in favour of partition of Palestine inflamed the anger of the Arabs. In December 1947 the Egyptian prime minister Nokrashi Pasha, who had outlawed the Muslim Brotherhood, a Right-wing extremist organization, and suppressed the Communist Party, was assassinated by a student, a member of the Muslim Brotherhood. The prime minister of Iraq, Saleh Jabr, signed a treaty with Bevin at Portsmouth on 16 January 1948 which provided for the evacuation of British troops, but allowed Great Britain the right to bring them back in case of the threat of war, to use military airfields, and to train the Iraqi army. The riots which greeted the announcement of the treaty were so violent that the Crown Prince, who was intensely pro-British, was forced to declare that the treaty would not be ratified. The prime minister resigned and fled to Jordan, fearing assassination.

Once the defeat had occurred, of course, matters only became worse. Discontent showed itself most openly in Syria. This was the first centre of Arab nationalism, deeply wounded by the defeat because of its geographical proximity. Until 1918 no frontier had divided Syria from Palestine. Syria was a republic with a more open political structure than the Arab kingdoms, with no foreign troops on its territory, and without the Lebanese preoccupation with holding the balance between Muslims and Christians. Syrian intellectuals had added the influence of the French Left to the ideology of Arab nationalism. Popular anger could be more easily expressed there than elsewhere, and after December 1948 violent demonstrations broke out against the old ruling clique of Shukry Kuwatly. The situation became so troubled that the army was called in to restore order, and became immediately aware of its own strong position. On 30 March 1949 Colonel Husni Zaim seized power. This was the first Arab military coup to take place since the war. It was not to be the last.

Radicalism made great strides in every part of the Arab world in the years which followed. Syria was beset with intractable problems. Torn between the Saudi-Egyptian alliance and the possibility of union with Iraq, and between American, English and French factions, the country was subjected to two successive military dictatorships: Hinnawi (August – December 1949) and Shishakli (December 1949 – February 1954). The latter had fought in Palestine. But the military rulers had to take account of their public opinion, of clandestine and legal parties, of pressure-groups of every description. By 1950 it was clear that in foreign policy the neutralist school had overwhelming popular support. The Communist Party's following was stronger than in any other part of the Arab world. There was also a new force emerging: the Ba'ath party (Socialist Party of Arab Resurgence). This party set out to re-formulate the ideology of pan-Arab nationalism on a strictly secular basis, with a seasoning of socialism. In September 1954, in the first elections after Shishakli's downfall, 22 Ba'athists were elected to the Parliament, together with the Communist leader Khaled Begdash. This was the Left's first great success in the Arab world.

In Iraq, the old pro-British politician Nuri es-Said, a survivor from the times of King Feisal, seemed to have the situation well under control, despite popular unrest. But his authority was only apparent. The opposition parties attracted more and more attention. Neutralism and socialism increased in strength, and so, despite brutal repression, did Communism. The elections of June 1954 saw the appearance of a block of 26 opponents of Nuri's policy, while his party lost seats. He dissolved Parliament, suppressed 18 newspapers, took repressive measures against the Communist Party, and searched and closed down the offices of the main opposition party. After this, the September elections naturally produced more satisfactory results. It was however a Pyrrhic victory.

In Egypt the king had been forced, in July 1949, to admit into his coalition cabinet the Wafd, the old bourgeois anti-British party. The Wafd had fallen into disrepute to some extent, because the British had imposed it on the king during the Second World War, needing a popular government capable of maintaining peace. Its social policy (or rather its absence of a social policy) had been a disappointment. But there had been no other party available capable of expressing the popular will. In the elections of January 1950 the Wafd won 228 seats out of a total of 319. This victory unseated the team held directly responsible for the defeat in Palestine. Driven forward by public opinion and the Left wing of his party, Nahas Pasha, leader of the Wafd, demanded from Britain the revision of the Anglo-Egyptian Treaty of 1936. This move was designed to eliminate British influence in the Sudan and expel British troops from the Suez Canal Zone. The British refused. The Wafd became all the more intransigent. The government began to move towards a neutralist position. In October 1951 Nahas unilaterally renounced the treaty, anti-British riots broke out, and detachments of volunteers and auxiliary police attacked British troops guarding the Canal. British reprisals further antagonized public opinion. On 26 January 1952 groups of terrorist incendiaries began burning and looting in the streets of Cairo. 277 fires were started. The police and the public fraternized with the rioters. The army restored order, and the king dismissed Nahas. But a clandestine group of young officers, most of whom had fought in the Palestine war, had formed within the army. United by their common resentment against those responsible for and profiting from the defeat, they seized power and drove out King Farouk, symbol of a corrupt and unrepresentative hierarchy. This was on 23 July 1952.

It is true that the Egyptian revolution only represented a danger to Israel in the long term. The nationalist officers undoubtedly desired a free and strong Egypt, able in case of need to settle all accounts with its rivals. But up until March 1954 they were primarily occupied with their internal struggle against the forces of the old society – including the Communists and the Muslim Brotherhood – who had combined behind the figure of General Neguib to demand a return to pluralist Parliamentary rule, in which they might stand a chance of gaining power. The Palestine problem, while it served to illuminate the depths of corruption of the old regime, was far from being first on the list of priorities. The younger officers were at the time particularly attracted by the prestige and wealth of the United States, which meant that they would have to put off to a later date any project of revenge against Israel. On the other hand, they wanted to liberate their country once and for all from the remains of British tutelage. They effected a compromise with Great Britain over the Sudan in February 1953, and signed a treaty on the Suez Canal on 27 July 1954. Though this treaty did promise the evacuation of the Canal Zone, it also committed Egypt fairly deeply to a pro-Western policy: the British were to be allowed to return in the event of an attack on Egypt, the members of the Arab

League, or Turkey. This last provision was no doubt directed against the Soviet Union. These pro-Western measures certainly helped to secure British good will. At the same time, the barrier of British troops between Egypt and Israel was now removed.

The Western powers were at this time completely blind to the strength of Arab aspirations. The Eastern specialists and others who advised Western politicians only pushed them further towards monumental errors of judgement, which the experts proceeded to justify. The burning desire for complete independence and the irreconcilable hostility towards Israel were seen as minor infantile complaints which greater political maturity, coupled with the wise counsels of the great powers and backed by their wealth and military strength, would quickly cure. The rise of new forces attacking the old structures was seen as the product of the machinations of Moscow, which also explained the demonstrations against the Western presence. Broadly speaking, the Atlantic powers were incapable of viewing Middle Eastern problems in any other light than that of the Cold War. Their only interest in the area was as a barrier against possible Soviet attack. They totally failed to appreciate that the world struggle on this level was not of the slightest interest either to the peoples or the politicians of the Arab world. Nobody in the Middle East felt remotely threatened by any Soviet danger. What they feared, rightly or wrongly, was Israeli expansionism, and what they wanted was to get rid of the last vestiges of Western occupation. Arab politicians who wished to retain their connections with the West were acutely aware of the danger of an internal upheaval, even if they did not consider the danger immediate. Thus Nuri es-Said, the most important pro-Western politician, begged the British to provide him with some moral capital to help disarm his own public opinion, either by forcing Israel to make major concessions, or at least by coming down firmly on the Arab side. His efforts were in vain. Similarly fruitless were Nasser's public declarations in August and September 1955, to the effect that Arab public opinion would be prepared to align with the West as long as the Arab states were not bound by any treaties making provisions for a military presence, even conditional. This would be unacceptable to peoples who had already suffered too long from the West and had become profoundly suspicious of Western intentions.

These problems, which to the Arabs were crucial, were seen by the Western powers as rather small flies in the ointment. They were only interested in them to the extent that they interfered with the great cause of the 'Defence of the Free World'. They were irritated by requests for arms from the Middle Eastern countries, arms which the Western powers needed for the struggle against the 'Communist menace'. On 25 May 1950 the United States, Great Britain and France published a joint declaration expressing opposition to the use of force in this area. Arms would only be sold to those who promised not to embark on any act of aggression. If any danger of this arose, 'The three Governments . . . would . . . immediately take action, both within and outside the United Nations, to prevent such violation.' The states concerned finally agreed to declare that the arms would be used purely for defensive purposes. But the Tripartite Declaration was widely interpreted as a guarantee of the status quo favouring Israel and as a threat of direct intervention. Shortly after this, the Korean War broke out. The United Nations claimed to be giving military support to the victim of aggression – South Korea – and thus punishing a violation of the international organization's decisions. The Arab states, whose attitudes to the war varied, did not fail to notice that not so long before the three powers had expressed their 'unshakable opposition' to the use of force, and that Israel's violations of United Nations decisions had not provoked any similar action.

The Western powers were profoundly disturbed by the Korean War, and they redoubled their efforts to gain the support of the Arab countries in the Cold War. The Soviet threat was gradually transformed in Western minds into a danger of internal subversion, against which the Middle East had to be supported by economic aid and the supply of arms, and bound to the West by military treaties. But the Arab reaction to this viewpoint was the same as ever, to the great astonishment of the Americans, who found it difficult to understand that such a conservative, religious people should have so little enthusiasm for defending themselves against the insidious menace of Communism. The missions of the British General Brian Robertson and the American Secretary of State McGhee in 1951 met with little success so far as the Arab governments were concerned, and excited violent popular reaction. J. Foster Dulles' trip in 1953 had the same effect. Dulles took note of the setback, and resorted to a different plan: to create a shield (or a launching-base) against the Soviet Union by means of a 'Northern Tier' of sincerely anti-Communist, Muslim nations: Turkey, Iran and Pakistan. Turkey had been a member of N.A.T.O. since February 1952, and had sent troops to Korea. In Iran, a coup d'état organized by the C.I.A. had overthrown Mossadeq in August 1953. A pact was signed between Turkey and Pakistan on 2 April 1954, followed by a military aid agreement between the United States and Pakistan on 19 May. In April the United States announced a military aid programme to Iraq.

Britain was shocked by this American intrusion into the Middle East, which it regarded as its own sphere of influence. The Arab governments were still divided. Egypt pleaded for a policy of non-alignment sympathetic to the West, but with no pacts entailing any automatic obligations. It would have been absurd for them to place themselves once again in a position of inferiority in an alliance with powers whose only concern was the defence of their interests against the U.S.S.R., and who paid not the slightest attention to Arab grievances over Israel and the needs of Arab defence against Israel. The Western powers had shown nothing but indulgence towards Israel; Turkey had good relations with her. Most Arabs were sympathetic to the Egyptian standpoint. At the very least, any agreement with the West should be conditional upon some kind of bargain. Benefits would have to be mutual. If the Arabs were to throw in their lot with the West, it would have to be in return for Western pressure on Israel to negotiate her frontiers on the basis of the U.N. partition plan of November 1947. There seemed, moreover, to be signs of a more conciliatory attitude in Israel itself in this respect. But Nuri es-Said and Abdulilah Crown Prince of Iraq were not primarily concerned with Israel. A settlement could in any case not be imposed on the West by Arab weakness, and would depend on the friendship of the Western powers. These rulers were much more afraid of Communist and nationalist subversion. They were attached to the alliance with Britain and sought Turkish and Iranian support against the claims of the Kurds. Iraqi rivalry with Egypt for supremacy over the Arab world made them suspicious of the plans of the young and inexperienced officers in Cairo. Attempts to reconcile the two opposing viewpoints failed. On 24 February 1955 Nuri signed a pact with Turkey in Baghdad, and on 4 April an agreement with Great Britain endorsing the Iraqi-Turkish pact. Shortly afterwards Pakistan and Iran also joined the pact. In November the Baghdad Pact, as it was called, was consolidated by the establishment of a joint secretariat.

The first pact had been signed on 24 February. On 21 February Ben Gurion returned from retirement on the *kibbutz* to become Israel's Minister of Defence. On the 28th he launched a massive reprisal raid on Gaza and destroyed the Egyptian headquarters there, killing 38 Egyptian soldiers and wounding 31. These events were connected in Arab eyes. The Arab revolution against the Western alliance, which had proved incapable of dealing with the Israeli threat, was about to erupt.

In 1948, the primal choice in international politics was that between the Western power bloc and the Soviet Union, flanked by its socialist satellites. The policy of cooperation between the Big Three, an extension of the wartime alliance, was dying. The Cold War began in earnest in the autumn of 1947. In October, Zhdanov laid down the principle that 'All those who are not with us are against us'.

One of the few points on which the leaders of the two blocs, the United States and the Soviet Union, were in agreement was the decision to partition Palestine, taken in November 1947, and to recognize the new State of Israel in May 1948. The newborn state had had to face British hostility, but was greatly aided by the United States, both as a state ('Truman is incontestably one of the principal architects of the State of Israel',* writes M. Bar-Zohar, the Zionist historiographer) and through the numerous and influential American Jewish community. Truman did have a passing moment of indecision, in March 1948, when the gravity of the situation in Europe and the outcry raised by the American ambassadors in the Arab countries moved him to renounce the partition plan and propose international control over Palestine. This was also due in part to the fears for the safety of the new state entertained by friends of the Jews, foreseeing the imminent Arab attack. Israel also possessed highly influential supporters in the West, especially in France. On the other side, she very opportunely acquired a consignment of Czech arms, a deal in which the Yugoslavs were also involved. This combination of both blocs in Israel's favour made the subsequent choice between them doubly difficult.

A policy of non-alignment was theoretically possible, and naturally enough this was the policy officially announced by the Israeli government. Moshe Sharett (previously Shertok), first Minister for Foreign Affairs of the new state, was a sincere advocate of this policy, while the Left clamoured for a policy of active friendship with the Soviet Union.

But irresistible forces pushed Israel towards the Western bloc, a development clearly foreseen by David Ben Gurion from the outset. Neutrality between the blocs was still possible as long as it only needed to be expressed by diplomatic gestures with no great influence on events, but not beyond this. Israel's strength depended in very large measure on money provided by American Jews and by the pressure they were able to exert on the American government. In February 1948

* Michel Bar-Zohar, *Ben-Gourion, le prophète armé*, Paris, Fayard, 1966, p. 117.

an alert American observer was able to write: 'Without a continuous flow of money and political support from the American Jews, the new Judaea would head for almost certain destruction.'* In January 1949 the Export–Import Bank of Washington, a government agency, granted Israel a loan of 100 million dollars, 35 million of which could be drawn upon at once. The Labour government which ruled the state may in part have considered non-alignment a necessary expedient on the diplomatic plane. But its whole sympathy was with the Western camp. In Palestine as in the Second International, to which the Mapai was affiliated, it had always had to fight against the Communists. The brand of socialism represented by the Mapai entailed the defence of working-class interests without excluding the use of capitalist investment. In 1950 an Investment Centre was set up to assist foreign capitalists. Approved companies would benefit from special privileges in taxation, writing-off invested capital, etc. This appeal to foreign capitalists was given wider scope, and the facilities made available to their shareholders were extended.

The U.S.S.R. for its part quickly cooled in its attitude to the new state. The Communist International had always been opposed to Zionism in principle, since it distracted Jewish workers from the struggle to overthrow capitalism in every country. Within the Soviet Union itself, Zionism offered the Jews a second loyalty to a foreign state. While this may be acceptable in a pluralistic society – although difficult for any state to accept openly – it was intolerable for a totalitarian state. Nonetheless, the *Yishuv*'s hostility to Great Britain gave Stalin the idea of exploiting the situation of the Jews in the Middle East. At that time, the Arab states were reactionary and for the most part pro-British, and seemed hardly likely to be sympathetic to the Soviet cause. Marxism evidently gave the Soviet leaders no better inkling of the revolutionary rumblings within the masses than the capitalist politicians had. Hence the U.S.S.R.'s support for partition (which was to strike a terrible blow at the Communist parties in the Arab countries) and the fleeting support given to the new state.

Disillusionment was not slow to follow. The first steps taken by Israel, seen from close quarters, might have suggested to Stalin the very thoughts expressed above. The demonstration of the Moscow Jews in September 1948 had a profound effect on him. It took place on the day of the Jewish New Year, when the new Israeli ambassador, Golda Myerson, attended the Moscow synagogue. From 30 to 50,000

* T. W. Van Alstyne, *Current History*, February 1948, p. 80.

people invaded the streets to welcome her. Here was clear evidence that many Soviet Jews were attracted to the new state. The Zionist programme continued to call for their emigration to Israel. The elections to the Knesset in January 1949 gave 34·7 per cent of the votes to the Mapai, 14·54 per cent to the neutralist Mapam and 3·44 per cent to the Communists. Israel's orientation now seemed obvious, and Stalin quickly drew his own conclusions. At the beginning of 1949, the Soviet bloc put into effect severe anti-Zionist measures. In the U.S.S.R. itself these soon assumed a more ominous character, leading to decisions which deprived the Yiddish culture of its means of expression, to malignant discrimination against the Jews, to executions and deportations. In short, anti-Zionism had turned into anti-Semitism. The other countries of the Soviet bloc followed Russia's example, and emigration to Israel was made extremely difficult.

This process rapidly accelerated. In 1950 Israel aligned herself with the Western camp over Korea. In 1951 Ben Gurion paid a triumphal visit to the United States. He made advances to Great Britain, then to the United States. In order to give them an interest in Israel's existence, he offered a military alliance, the right to use Israeli ports and aerodromes, service depots, a whole military infrastructure. The Old Man was very farsighted; he knew very well that these were the only means of support on which he could rely to ensure Israel's survival in the long term, permanently threatened as she was by the Arab desire for revenge. In 1955 he offered the United States bases, point-blank, in exchange for a firm guarantee of Israel's frontiers. But after some hesitation the British and the Americans, aware of the importance of the Arab world, refused these offers, which would automatically commit them to support Israel.

What of the Arabs? Surely it was possible to mollify their hostility? Again, there were two schools of thought. Some wished to make concessions to the Arabs to secure peace – Sharett because of his essentially conciliatory temperament, and the Left wing for ideological reasons. Ben Gurion detested the Arabs, but being himself a nationalist, he understood them. He did not believe that it would be possible to neutralize their desire for revenge by any other means than force, although it occurred to him at times that the force would perhaps not always be on the same side. Such a contingency was distant, however, and he left it to his successors to worry about it. Meanwhile, he considered that the territory so far conquered was a minimum. He would not hear of yielding an inch of it. And the Jewish state already had too many Arabs, on the whole more prolific than the Jews. He was not prepared to take one single extra refugee.

This question was bound up with the Israeli attitude to the U.N. Ben Gurion the realist despised the international organization. He knew very well that united action to impose a solution on Israel was inconceivable. He rightly reckoned with disagreement among the great powers and the weight of public opinion in Europe and America working in Israel's favour.

In theory, the United Nations' plan of partition of November 1947 was still valid. The Arabs had rejected it in principle, but in practice they had, willy-nilly, occupied only areas accorded to them by the plan. The Israelis had added considerably to their portion of Palestine by their military successes, and the frontiers won by force of arms were frozen into immobility by the armistice agreements of 1949. On 11 December 1948, during a break in the fighting (which was to prove more or less permanent), the General Assembly of the United Nations adopted a resolution creating a Conciliation Commission for Palestine, comprising representatives of the United States, France and Turkey. The Assembly declined to deal with the question of frontiers, but nonetheless 'resolved' that Jerusalem and its immediate environs would be internationalized, as provided for in the partition plan. It was also decided that 'refugees wishing to return home and live in peace with their neighbours would be allowed to do so as soon as practicable, and that compensation would be paid for the property of those choosing not to return'. * Israel was admitted to the U.N. on 11 May 1949; the Assembly specified its views on the internationalization of the zone around Jerusalem on 7 December, in a resolution sponsored by France, the U.S.S.R. and the Arab countries. Jerusalem was to be governed by the U.N. Trusteeship Council. Ben Gurion, against the advice of Sharett, decided to brave the U.N. and on 13 December he transferred the capital to Jerusalem. Protests by the powers were of no avail.

Defying the proposals of the U.N. mediator Bernadotte and American pressure for the return of the refugees, Ben Gurion had declared in July 1948: 'We must do everything in our power to ensure that they never return.'† In 1949 Israel announced to the Conciliation Commission that she was ready to accept as Israeli citizens the 200,000 refugees in the Gaza Strip, plus the 70,000 native inhabitants of the Strip, provided the zone passed under Israeli sovereignty. Naturally the Arabs rejected this offer, emphasizing that priority should be given to

---

* U.N.G.A. Resolution 194 (III/1), para. 11, 11 December 1948.

† See Michel Bar-Zohar, *Ben-Gourion*, op. cit., p. 207.

the unconditional return of the refugees in accordance with the U.N. resolution, without being subject to the territorial settlement and peace treaty desired by Israel. Sharett then made a major concession. He would allow 100,000 refugees to return. The Arabs did not reject this offer, but demanded first the unconditional return of the refugees originating from the areas conquered by Israel and lying outside the territory accorded her by the U.N. partition plan. This entailed recognition, in some measure, of that plan and hence of the existence of Israel within these limits – already recognized in practice by the armistice agreements of 1949 and by the promise not to resort to force. Israel refused, despite American pressure. Israeli public opinion was practically unanimous against Sharett, who gave way. In 1953 the Arab states signed agreements with U.N.R.W.A. for the reintegration of a fairly large number of refugees in their respective countries. Mounting tension led to the abandonment of the agreements. Contacts between Nasser and Sharett, set up in 1954 through the intermediary of the Labour Members of Parliament Richard Crossman and Maurice Orbach, seem to have been cut short. But at the same time, Arab reactions to the Charles T. Main plan were encouraging. This was a plan for the utilization of the waters of the River Jordan by all the countries through which it flows, presented under the auspices of the American government to the various states by Eisenhower's personal representative Eric Johnston.

The Arabs were constantly forced to operate on two different levels. They were accustomed to haggling, in which the speaker's intention is only understood via hints and allusions. This is not merely an Oriental idiosyncrasy, but the common practice of international diplomacy. But Zionist activists and their innumerable sympathizers throughout the world caught them in the trap of their own words, pointing to actions which were or might be represented as confirmation of those words. Ideologically, the Arabs could not openly accept the *fait accompli* of colonial encroachment of their territory. Moreover it was in their interest, diplomatically, not to throw away their trump card: non-recognition of Israel, rejection of diplomatic relations and therefore of any possibility of negotiations with Israel. Ideologically again, they could not disavow, in the face of public opinion in their own countries, the raids and incursions of the Palestinian Arabs; on the practical plane, they were unable entirely to prevent them. Neither could they accept Israel's constant encroachments on the status of the demilitarized zones, and had to do something to prevent limitations of their rights.

Something more needs to be said in regard to these latter problems since European opinion is commonly familiar only with the Israeli point of view. The 1948 frontiers, arbitrarily delimited by the front lines reached on the cessation of hostilities, were the cause of much trouble. Villages were cut in two, pastures were separated from the source of drinking water for the animals, farmers were cut off from their fields. Traditional bonds between villages were broken. Large numbers of Palestinians tried to return clandestinely, and many succeeded. The Bedouin always moved about freely in the border areas, ignoring the frontiers. Looters, bandits and smugglers also crossed the frontier. In a population in which the blood-feud was a customary feature of social life, some crossed the border to seek vengeance for wrongs they had suffered.

In addition, the 1949 armistice agreements had made provision for demilitarized zones, which presented serious problems and were variously interpreted. These zones caused a number of incidents, despite the presence of joint armistice commissions presided over by officials of the U.N. truce supervisory body.

Generally speaking, Israel's attitude in the innumerable cases of friction resulting from these fragile frontiers was for the most part roundly condemned by the various military commanders of the U.N. truce supervisory force. With monotonous regularity, the Israelis denounced them as anti-Semites. The repeated accusation led to the recall of some of the commanders, and induced others to take up a conciliatory attitude towards Israel. It seems unlikely that the U.N. should have placed a series of anti-Semites at the head of its mission. In reality, Israel's intransigent and aggressive attitude emerges clearly from all these incidents, and it is an attitude which is readily explicable. The Israelis considered that the Arabs had refused to negotiate a final peace on the basis of the 1948 frontiers, and had therefore, according to them, violated Article 1 of the armistice agreements referring to a gradual transition towards the re-establishment of peace. They in turn, therefore, were not bound to any scrupulous respect for the other provisions of these agreements, they could refuse to cooperate with U.N. representatives, etc.

In Israeli eyes, the neighbouring Arab states were responsible for all infiltrations, lootings, rapes and murders committed within her frontiers, even when police investigation was not able to place the responsibility for the crime outside the country's borders. Israel had no confidence in inquiries carried out by the U.N. officials, even less in those conducted by the Arab police forces, and refused to cooperate in them. In any case, the Arabs were responsible for everything by refusing to negotiate a peace, i.e. to recognize Israel within the frontiers of 1948, and by conducting an unremitting campaign of verbal propaganda against her. Force was the only means of winning respect. Force was all the Arabs understood. The policy of collective reprisals had its roots in this attitude.

The policy was applied with rigorous severity. On 13 October 1953 a grenade attack in a Jewish village killed a woman and two children. The tracks left by the assassins indicated that they had taken refuge in Jordan, and the Jordanian police took up the case, under the direction of Glubb Pasha, the British commander of the Arab Legion. On the night of 14 to 15 October a contingent of the Israeli Army bombarded and attacked the Jordanian village of Kibya, blowing up 40 houses, killing 53 villagers, men, women and children, and injuring 15.

Two months later Ben Gurion, who had ordered the attack, resigned and withdrew to the *kibbutz* of Sde Boker. Leadership of the government now fell to Sharett.

Moshe Sharett governed from December 1953 to February 1955. He favoured a more flexible policy, and the contacts established with Egyptian officers date from this period. Nasser was well-disposed towards him. The Arabs could not officially give way over non-recognition nor cease their propaganda activities, but they had shown de facto recognition of Israel while still contesting the frontiers, and they waited for feelers to be extended aiming at an agreement based on the U.N. resolutions. It is not impossible that an Israeli declaration of principle in this direction would have resulted in some intimate bargaining. Territorial adjustments and the return of refugees might have been discussed. The outcome of the discussions might well have approximated to an acceptance of the status quo. Israel would have been recognized, and perhaps saved.

It might have been the salvation of Israel. But it would have been the end of Zionism. What neither the Left nor Sharett saw was clearly perceived by the old chief, tucked away in his *kibbutz* in the Negev. An Israel recognized, an Israel become a Levantine state like any other, admitting a certain number of Arab refugees to her breast, abandoning some of her conquests, conforming to the decisions of the U.N., was necessarily subject to a certain limitation, a definite restriction of Jewish immigration. This would have meant the extinction of the proud dream of reviving the kingdom of David and Solomon, bridgehead of the Jewish Diaspora, able to call on the aid of the whole of the world Jewry for its defence and ultimate victory. The 'normal' progress of events was fatal for Zionist Israel. Internally, the increasing number of

Levantine Jews would become a majority and gain the upper hand. Once the external danger had disappeared, Messianic fervour would decline. The pioneer spirit was in jeopardy. Ben Gurion's call for the colonization of the Negev had aroused little response. If Israel was just a country like any other, why go there, why become attached to it? By 1953 more Jews were leaving the country than arriving. In external affairs the big powers would be inclined to ignore this rather awkward little state. By contrast, Zionist Israel throve on a bellicose atmosphere and the threat of danger. The world could not allow her to be destroyed, Jews the world over would rally to the aid of those whom in times of peril they could not help regarding as their brothers. Zion's salvation lay in permanent danger.

The shady Lavon affair – based on a programme of provocation planned by the Israeli Secret Service to force the British to stay in Egypt by simulating Egyptian outrages against British institutions – brought Ben Gurion back to power on 21 February 1955. He immediately gave notice to the Arabs that Israeli policy was now reverting to the hard line, that Israel would react violently to infiltration, to the non-recognition which justified it and the propaganda which accompanied it. The powers which had just formed the Baghdad Pact were shown that Israel was an important factor, which they ignored at their peril. The immediate pretexts for this policy were no more urgent than at any other time. The previous year Egypt had prevented an Israeli ship from passing through the Suez Canal. On 2 February, three agents of the Israeli intelligence network in Egypt were found guilty of acts of terrorism and hanged. Sharett had appealed to Nasser for clemency. But members of the Muslim Brotherhood had earlier been executed on similar charges, and Nasser could not therefore show favour to Israeli agents. On 28 February Ben Gurion unleashed the massive reprisal raid on Gaza mentioned earlier.

The Gaza raid marked a turning point. The Arabs had been given a severe shock. They realized that Zionist Israel had resumed its traditional policy. They were afraid of its expansionist tendencies. The 1955 elections, in which the Mapai lost five seats, were interpreted as a repudiation of Sharett's policy of appeasement. The Egyptians, together with all politically aware elements in the Arab world, feared that the Baghdad Pact would deprive them of all possibility of independent action, and tie them to the chariot of the West; and Israel was the West's favourite son.

In their eyes, the threat of Israeli expansionism was again taking shape. With Ben Gurion the partisan of unlimited immigration back at the wheel, Ben Gurion the friend of the activist military clique dominated by Dayan and Peres, Ben Gurion who always wanted more, who always imposed his own policy regardless of U.N. decisions, all hope of concessions which might lead to peace faded into the distance. The Arabs therefore had to get arms. The Arab world was aware of its own weakness. According to a military spokesman, Egypt had at this time six serviceable aeroplanes and enough tank ammunition to last through one hour of battle.

Nasser and the ruling officer group in Egypt continued to press the United States for arms. But Foster Dulles kept the carrot too far in front of them, and used the stick too hard: no arms without entry into a regional 'defence pact', i.e. into commitment to the Western military system against the U.S.S.R. Great Britain's attitude was the same. France, who supplied arms to Syria, had become shy of arming the Arabs since the outbreak of the Algerian War. Faced with these pressures and with the threat of a pro-Western military bloc actually protecting Israel, and covering the whole of the Middle East under the leadership of Turkey and Iraq, the Egyptian tendency towards neutralism was accentuated. Nasser drew closer to Nehru, and established links with Tito. In April 1955, at the conference of the 'Third World' held at Bandung, he opened a line of communication with Chou En-Lai. The Third World hesitated, appreciating that the Arabs were in the same boat as the rest of them, while Israel properly belonged in the Western camp. Israel was excluded from the conference. Nasser's requests for arms were transmitted to the Soviet Union by the Chinese. Nasser had got the Americans and the British in a corner. They thought he was bluffing. On 27 September 1955 Nasser announced the conclusion of an agreement with Czechoslovakia for the supply of arms to Egypt. In response to Baghdad, in October he concluded pacts with Syria and Saudi Arabia. A wave of neutralist fervour swept over the Arab world. The pro-British regimes were threatened. In Jordan, a popular revolt prevented the government from signing the Baghdad Pact. King Hussein gave way to popular pressure in dismissing Glubb, the British commander of his army, on 1 March 1956. The elections held on 21 October brought a Popular Front government including Ba'athists and Communists to power. On the 25th, Egypt signed a military pact with Jordan and Syria. In Syria likewise a neutralist coalition hostile to the Baghdad Pact was in power. Saudi Arabia supported the movement through fear that her old enemy, Hashemite Iraq, would win hegemony over the Arab world.

After the Gaza raid, Egypt was preoccupied with her potential loss of face in the confrontation with Israel; somehow public dissatisfaction had to be quelled, and Arab claims upheld. So-called death commandos, the *fedayeen*, were organized in Egypt to conduct guerrilla raids inside Israel. The Strait of Tiran was closed to ships carrying strategic materials to Israel. Ben Gurion responded to the challenge. In October a raid was conducted on the Syrian frontier; on 2 November the demilitarized zone of al-Auja on the Egyptian frontier was occupied; in December an attack in force was carried out against Syrian positions – to the anger of Sharett, who was at that moment attempting to obtain arms from Dulles. But Ben Gurion wanted to demonstrate to the Arabs the emptiness of the Egypto-Syrian pact. The Burns plan, providing for local agreements to prevent frontier incidents, with joint Israeli-Egyptian patrols, was accepted by Egypt and rejected by Israel.

At the same time, final attempts at conciliation were made. An American politican of high standing was sent to act as a secret intermediary between Nasser and Ben Gurion. The plan foundered on the question of the return of refugees, which Ben Gurion would not have at any price. An official plan proposed by Dulles, which he rather clumsily tied to the Main-Johnston water allocation plan (which if accepted on a purely technical basis might have had a chance of unfreezing the situation in the long run), suffered the same fate. On 9 November 1955 Sir Anthony Eden, rather more realistically, spoke of a compromise between the Arab demand for a return to the 1947 plan and Israeli insistence on the frontiers of 1949. On the 12th the Israeli government refused any territorial concessions. At the end of November Nasser again mentioned, to Jean Lacouture, the possibility of recognizing Israel on condition that negotiations were held on the basis of the Eden proposals. On the same date, Ben Gurion submitted to the Israeli cabinet Dayan's plan for attacking Egypt and opening the Strait of Tiran to all Israeli shipping by force. The majority of Ministers, including Sharett, rejected the plan. Ben Gurion submitted – for the moment.

Sharett made superhuman efforts to achieve a peaceful solution. Ben Gurion meanwhile prepared for war. Failing to obtain arms from Great Britain and the United States, he approached France. Guy Mollet's Socialist Party, which had come to power in January 1956, was well disposed to Israel's request. The Socialists had capitulated to the Algerian settler lobby, and abandoned all thoughts of bringing peace to Algeria by carrying out far-reaching reforms. Reduced to desperate expedients, they resolved to put an end to the war by bringing about the overthrow of Nasser, who was supposed to be supporting and even directing it. Sentiments of socialist solidarity with the Mapai, the primitive identification of aid to Israel with an anti-racist, and hence anti-Fascist, socialist and 'Left-wing' position, all played a part. The British, for their part, attributed to Egypt the upsurge of Arab nationalist feeling, and hoped also to avenge the rejection of the Baghdad Pact. Eden, who enjoyed good social relations with Nuri es-Said and the youthful King Feisal of Iraq, was scandalized by Nasser's coarse and indelicate competition against them. The British and French governments and the press in both countries launched the myth that Nasser = Hitler, which was to be carried so far and do so much damage.

Alone among the Western countries, the United States tried to maintain contact with the Arabs and to woo Nasser away from neutralist, let alone Communist, influence. The financing of the Aswan High Dam, a supposedly essential project if Egypt was to escape from her disastrous economic situation, was projected by Washington on relatively favourable terms. Funds for this purpose were released in December 1955, and a loan from the World Bank was envisaged, but with controls and conditions irksome to the Egyptians, who were suspicious from bitter experience. Great Britain had a finger in the pie. The British, French and Israelis all tried to dissuade Dulles from granting the loan. The American Congress jibbed at voting it. Nasser conducted parallel negotiations with the Soviet Union for the money, but announced to the Americans that he would prefer the aid to come from them.

At the same time Ben Gurion, prevented for the time being from embarking on a full-scale war, continued his campaign of harassment. He refused to make any concessions to the U.N. on the al-Auja demilitarized zone, launched a military expedition on the southern frontier, and shelled Gaza. On 18 June he drove Sharett, who opposed his policy, to resign from his post of Foreign Secretary. Ben Gurion's way was now clear.

On 18 July Dulles, learning that the U.S.S.R. was unable to finance the Aswan Dam, announced that the United States was cancelling the offer of aid, adding some disparaging remarks by way of explanation. Great Britain followed suit. Nasser had been taught a good lesson. Egypt and the Arab peoples were humiliated, their backs to the wall. To the Western powers, capitulation seemed certain.

But the Egyptian officers' group refused to take the snub. They bridled, and on 26 July, at Alexandria, Nasser found his answer. He announced the nationalization of the Suez Canal.

There then took place the event which was to engrave the image of Israel in the mind of the Third World (at that time still unsure of its attitude), an event which was to give the final impetus to the radicalization of the Arab world: the Suez expedition, undertaken jointly by Britain, France and Israel after a secret treaty signed at Sèvres on 23 October. Of course the motives of the three partners were very different. For Ben Gurion, who took the lead on the Israeli side, the object was to strike a crippling blow at the Arabs, forcing them to recognize Israel in its present boundaries, to call off the state of virtual war and the now quite serious attacks of the *fedayeen*, together with the blockade of the Strait of Tiran. No doubt the possibility of territorial gains also entered his head. Any upheaval might bring about potentially advantageous changes. But Ben Gurion had in any case long been haunted by the spectre of a united Arab revival. He wondered whether Nasser might not prove the Arab Mustafa Kemal, who would lead his people out of chaos; he watched the development of the Arab alliance with the East, and the influx of arms and munitions. He decided that the time had come to strike, to crush the power that was now arising, or at least gain recognition while Israel held the upper hand, before it was too late. Also, it seemed foolish not to profit from the happy circumstance of finding two major, well-armed Western powers on Israel's side. Such an opportunity might not occur again for a long time.

The French Socialist government, strangely upset by the nationalization of a large capitalist enterprise, were hoping to win in Egypt the war they were incapable of winning in Algeria, both to make peace and to win the war. For the British Conservative government, the main aim was to overthrow Nasser, the symbol of anti-imperialist radicalism in the Arab world, and the number-one adversary of the faithful Nuri es-Said, whose policy was based on alliance with Britain. The latter had again attempted, on 8 October, with British support, to achieve a peace on the basis of a return in principle to the U.N. partition plan. Israel's response to this was naturally a scornful and vigorous 'no'. The English and French were certain that the slightest setback would set the Egyptian people against Nasser and bring a rival group to power. They were confirmed in their opinion by their own expert advisers, themselves prisoners of the same prejudices.

The situation was eminently favourable to the conspirators. The U.S.S.R. was busy suppressing the Hungarian revolt. Eisenhower was kept in ignorance by the C.I.A., who knew what was afoot. On 29 October the Israeli army invaded Sinai. French aeroplanes kept the Israeli columns supplied, and machine-gunned Egyptian convoys, at the same time protecting Israeli air space. French warships patrolled the coast, by secret agreement behind the backs of the British. On 30 October, as agreed by the three allies, an Anglo-French ultimatum was delivered, masquerading as a peace-keeping manoeuvre; it demanded that Israeli and Egyptian troops should withdraw to a distance of 16 km from each bank of the canal. The Israelis would thus keep the territory they had occupied, except for a strip of 16 km, while the Egyptians would retire from a part of their own country which had not even been conquered. It was calculated that this obvious and deliberate partiality would force Nasser to reject the ultimatum.

On 1 November the General Assembly of the U.N. ordered a cease-fire. On the 3rd, once their troops had overrun Sinai, the Israelis agreed to comply, but then withdrew their acceptance to give their allies, who were a little slow in moving, a pretext for military intervention. On the 5th, British and French paratroops were dropped on the Canal Zone. But the Soviet Union threatened atomic reprisals. The U.N. Assembly decided to send an international peace-keeping force. On the 6th Eden capitulated, carrying with him Guy Mollet, who was eager to continue. At midnight on the 6th, a cease-fire was announced in Egypt. Nasser had not fallen, as the British and French had hoped. But Israel was victorious. On 7 November Ben Gurion, intoxicated by success, declared to the Knesset: 'We have created the third Kingdom of Israel!'

4
The Rise of Arab Socialism

Like most of the manoeuvres of the Western powers, at least during this period and in this area, the Suez campaign achieved precisely the opposite result to that intended. Nasser was supposed to fall. Instead, he achieved the status of an Arab national hero and the stature of a near-legendary figure at the summit of his popularity.

Independence of the West was the consuming passion of the Arab world; no voice dared raise itself, no party dared take its stand against this aspiration. Israel, a Western enclave in Arab territory, appeared in Arab eyes as the living symbol and busy agent of Western imperialism. The Suez campaign was hardly calculated to make the Arabs change this opinion. Nasser had been the first to dare defy the West, and had been the West's first victim. He had emerged victorious – diplomatically if not militarily. His people had put up a spirited resistance to the Anglo-French paratroops in Port Said, chalking up the Arabs' first glorious feat of arms for many years.

In 1952 Nasser had been a nobody; he remained in the background till 1954, while the myth of the Egyptian revolution was symbolized by Neguib. Subsequently his halo was successively brightened by the moves taken in the direction of neutralism, his attack in 1955 on the Baghdad Pact, his presence at Bandung, and his decision to purchase arms from the Eastern bloc. To the West, neutralism meant Communism. To the masses of the East, it meant anti-imperialism. This implied intervention in Arab affairs. The possibility no doubt existed of Egypt standing alone, in isolated neutrality; the politically conscious element in the Egyptian masses had only been aware of the affairs of the Arabs of Asia for perhaps a score of years, while the Egyptian army officers had been very reluctant to commit themselves to the imbroglio of pan-Arab politics. But how was Egypt, the most heavily populated Arab country, and the pole of the cultural, intellectual and social life of the Arab world, to hold aloof from the Arab masses, who all looked up to her in admiration and hope? Had not the enemy powers and Israel themselves nominated Egypt head of the Arab world by making her their principal adversary and directing all their fury on to her? 'Nasserite' movements sprang up in every Arab country. This does not mean that Egypt's internal policy was everywhere approved (in so far as anybody knew what it was). But everywhere there was tremendous enthusiasm for the challenge to Western domination thrown down by Nasser.

The social struggle was a secondary consideration. All Arabs wanted to modernize their countries and raise their desperately low standard of living. Most were undecided on how to set about achieving these ends. Experience had already shown, and was to continue to prove, that every effort in this direction tied to a liberal-style economy and alliance with the West only produced a degree of economic growth wholly dependent on exterior forces and having nothing in common with a healthy and self-sufficient internal development. More important still, this economic dependence carried with it a political dependence. An unmistakable indication of this was the passivity which the more dependent regimes displayed towards Israel, their tendency towards capitulation and the abandonment of Arab claims.

Nasser was the incarnation of the Arab drive towards independence and modernization. From the point of view of the Arab middle class, the most active politically, he had the further merit of standing for independence from Communist ideology too, which had its own recipes for attaining the same ends (a point completely overlooked by Western analysts, blinded by myth and prejudice). The popularity of the U.S.S.R. among the Arab masses did not in the main stem from an enthusiasm for Communism as such. The Soviet Union had merely assumed the popular role played by pre-war Germany. In both instances, the Arab masses saw simply a European power not involved in the colonial dismemberment of the world, and hostile to the two great colonial powers whose domination the Arab countries had had to endure: Great Britain and France. As for the United States, also apparently a non-colonial power, initial good will towards her had been dissipated by her friendship for Britain and France, her eagerness to enrol the Eastern countries in the anti-Communist crusade (which seemed to be nothing but a thin disguise for Western domination), her support for Israel and for the more reactionary Arab regimes. Finally, Lenin's idea of imperialism was gaining increasing credence among all sections of the population, and seemed confirmed by the outpourings of American wealth, invariably tied to Foster Dulles' obsessional pact-making schemes.

Immediately after Suez the United States almost managed to win back popularity in the Arab world. Eisenhower was anxious to avoid losing the area entirely, and furious with the French and British for

their duplicity towards him. He was eager to cooperate with the U.S.S.R. to prevent a conflict which might snowball beyond the control of the two super-powers, and had played an important part in forcing the British and French to retreat. Again in conjunction with the U.S.S.R., which threatened Israel with atomic retribution, he succeeded in obtaining an Israeli withdrawal from the occupied areas. Ben Gurion struggled furiously in his efforts to avoid this result, only retreating step by step, trying to keep at least some of the fruits of his victory. But Israel's dependence on the United States had a telling effect. American economic pressure proved far more persuasive than Soviet threats, which would have been very difficult to carry out. Ben Gurion knew this from the start. He is said to have declared to the Israeli cabinet on 28 October, on the eve of the attack: 'The Americans will force us to leave. America need send no troops to achieve this result; she need only state that she will break off diplomatic relations, prohibit collections for the Jewish fund, and block Israeli loans. She will ask herself: what is more important to her: Israel or the Arabs?' *
Calculations of this kind duly played their part. The result was unfavourable to Israel. The U.N. unanimously condemned the Israeli conquest. An American loan was blocked. Israel feared that the Americans might press West Germany to stop the payment of reparations, they feared international economic sanctions, and what might follow from them. France, Israel's last ally, was in favour of a compromise.

Ben Gurion gave in. He would evacuate the conquered territory. All he would get was the presence of U.N. troops in the Strait of Tiran, guaranteeing free passage to Israeli shipping in the Gulf of Aqaba. These troops would also be stationed in the Gaza Strip, providing a barrier between Egypt and Israel to prevent frontier incidents. They would thus be stationed on Egyptian or Arab territory. Because Israel was the victor, she was spared encroachment on her own territory.

The fund of Arab goodwill which the United States had won by forcing Israel to evacuate was shortly to be dissipated. This was once again due to the Americans' anti-Communist phobia, to their profound lack of comprehension for Middle Eastern problems, and to their backing of Israel in the 1949 frontiers. Suez led to the exclusion of the British and French from the region and weakened the position of Nuri es-Said, Great Britain's staunch friend. The Soviets and the Americans were the only powers left to compete for influence in the Middle East. The Americans were afraid of the force of the neutralist wave, behind which they of course saw the hand of Moscow. They were apprehensive

* Michel Bar-Zohar, *Ben Gourion*, op, cit., p. 313.

of the 'vacuum' created by the disappearance of British and French influence. On 5 January 1957 Eisenhower put forward a doctrine annotated by Dulles and accepted by Congress. The President was authorized 'to include the employment of the armed forces of the United States to secure and protect the territorial integrity and political independence of such nations requesting such aid against overt armed aggression from any nation controlled by international Communism'. *
In March, the Eisenhower Doctrine was approved by Congress, James P. Richards, the Special Assistant for Middle Eastern affairs, left on a tour of the Middle East to exhort the countries of the area to join the Pact, and the United States became a member of the Baghdad Pact's Military Committee.

As usual, the immediate reaction on the part of some Middle Eastern governments was extremely favourable to the United States, while the effect on the masses was disastrous and was to have long-term repercussions. Iraq, of course, immediately supported the Eisenhower Doctrine, as did the Lebanon, ruled by its pro-Western president Camille Chamoun. In Jordan Hussein officially rejected the Doctrine, but at the same time dismissed his neutralist ministers. Encouraged by the Americans, Saudi Arabia decided to attempt a reconciliation with her old Hashemite enemies, Iraq and Jordan.

But violent riots broke out in Iraq, accompanied by a full-scale peasant revolt. Martial law was proclaimed. In Jordan a wave of strikes and riots also forced the government to resort to martial law, backed up by a general curfew, the suspension of Parliament and the suppression of political parties. Dulles was obliged to put up a show of force by sending the Sixth Fleet into the Eastern Mediterranean, and take charge of the financial affairs of the little kingdom.

The Egyptian and Syrian governments alone remained faithful to the neutralist line. But they had the support of all the Arab peoples. The hostility of the West only pressed them further. Nasser did not intend to burn all his bridges to the United States, far from it. But he no longer needed to pay any attention at all to the British and French, and in January 1957 all British and French companies in Egypt were 'Egyptianized' (and the Jewish ones too). The State had to intervene in the financing and management of the new Egyptian companies, but the Egyptian bourgeoisie also participated, to its own great profit. A certain degree of political liberalization followed the proclamation of a

* Text from the *New York Times*, 6 January 1957, quoted by G. Lenczowski, *The Middle East in World Affairs* (3rd ed.), Ithaca, N.Y., Cornell University Press, 1962, pp. 676–7.

Constitution in January 1956 and the elections to the Legislative
Assembly, held in July. Left-wing detainees were set free. Nasser succeeded in mobilizing the natural Left-wing sympathy for his new
foreign policy. He allowed the Left its own press outlet, and made use
of its services, especially to reinforce the internal ideological front. But
the military clique still kept firm hold of the reins of power.

In Syria, where a neutralist coalition was in control, policy also took
a new direction. The government included the Ba'ath party, a socialist
and nationalist party committed above all to Arab unity, which at that
time was symbolized in the person of Nasser. The Ba'ath saw in him
their natural leader, in control of the powerful resources of Egypt,
without whom no unity was possible. Sharing power with the Ba'athists
was the Communist Party of Syria, the best organized in the whole of
the Middle East. It possessed in its leader, Khaled Begdash, an eloquent public speaker, able to move the masses, gifted, intelligent and
ambitious, overshadowing bourgeois politicians with his formidable
political expertise, yet bound with every fibre of his being to the Communist International in which he was trained, and to the Soviet Union
in which he continued to see the torch-bearer of world progress. His
strength rested less on the Syrian proletariat, which was small and
divided in its loyalties, than on the support of middle-class groupings
attracted by an alliance with the Soviet Union. These were primarily
represented on the political scene by the millionaire Khaled el-'Azm,
scion of an old Damascan aristocratic family. The coalition was led and
held together by a skilled politician, Sabri al-'Asali.

The policy of reliance on the Soviet bloc took shape in June 1955. A
series of arms contracts, long-term credits, and the construction of an
oil refinery bound Syria to the Soviet Union and the other countries of
its orbit. Suez reinforced this trend. Washington was horrified to witness, as it thought, the creation in the Middle East of a people's democracy subject to the authority of Moscow. The Americans were the
victims of their own ideological mythology. They were quite unable to
understand that Syrian policy was primarily conditioned by local factors, and in the final analysis by the popular desire for independence
and modernization, not in the very least by the daemonic machinations
of international Communism. Nor did they appreciate that the
U.S.S.R. had not the slightest desire to burden itself with a Middle
Eastern Soviet state, unruly, dangerous to Soviet international policy,
and requiring the investment of enormous sums to drag itself out of its
material backwardness. The Soviet Union, and Begdash also, only
wanted a Parliamentary regime sympathetic to Soviet foreign policy,

and guaranteeing this orientation by permitting the existence of a Communist Party able freely to make its own propaganda and exert its influence. In contrast to the Americans, the middle-class Syrians led by Khaled al-'Azm understood this attitude very well.

The Americans behaved in the clumsiest fashion possible in their attempts to exorcize the imaginary menace. Clandestine moves by the American Embassy to achieve the overthrow of the Syrian government resulted in the expulsion, in August 1957, of three American diplomats. This was the first rebuff of its kind to American power in the region, and it was bitterly resented. The Syrian government appointed as Chief of Staff in Damascus 'Afif al-Bizri, denounced in Washington as pro-Communist. From that time on the Syrian government was outlawed by the West. If it was not possible to achieve its overthrow from within, external measures would be tried. At the end of August the American Under-Secretary of State Loy Henderson was sent to Ankara, where he met President Menderes, of the Democratic Party, loyal to the American alliance, together with the kings of Jordan and Iraq and the Iraqi Chief of Staff. He then went to Beirut for talks with President Shamoun. All were promised arms. Turkey, which had had long-standing territorial disputes with Syria, became an increasing menace. Ben Gurion seized the opportunity to play on American anti-Communist susceptibilities, and wrote to Dulles offering him the benefit of his advice and services, sent Golda Meir [formerly Myerson] on a special mission to Washington, and contacted the friendly French and German governments to try to obtain a N.A.T.O. guarantee of Israel's frontiers in exchange for Israeli cooperation.

Neutralist Syria justifiably felt threatened. Her only recourse was to Soviet aid. American policy, in its habitual fashion, had resulted in creating the very situation which it sought to avoid. The Soviet Union dispatched two warships to the Syrian port of Lattakieh. The pro-American Arab states were embarrassed by America's antics, which only resulted in condemning them in the eyes of their peoples as accomplices in the suppression of Syrian and Arab aspirations to independence, unity and modernization. King Saud of Saudi Arabia intervened; he visited Damascus in September, preached moderation to Washington, and brought Jordan and Iraq round to his point of view. All declared their opposition to any threat to Syrian independence.

Egypt could not stand aside. In October Egyptian troops disembarked at Lattakieh to take their stand at the side of the Syrians on the Turkish frontier. The successful launching of the first Soviet sputnik was received with enthusiasm by the Arabs. In the face of the

American threat, exerted from its bases in Turkey and Israel, the great protector from the North had shown that it, too, was powerful. Patrick Seale writes: 'In short the net effect of America's brusque intervention in Arab affairs in 1957 was to confirm the Soviet Union and Egypt as Syria's twin protectors in the face of Western hostility.' * One might add the two champions not only of Syria but of Arab aspirations in general.

This was not the end of the matter. Soviet influence, up till then a myth, established itself. The Syrian Communist Party was stimulated by these developments, and many Syrians, feeling the way the wind was blowing, joined the party. Others began to share some of the American apprehensions. Begdash's voice was heard increasingly loudly, though he still made no reference to a socialist economy or to political power on the Soviet pattern. In fact, neither he nor the Soviet Union envisaged any such measures. But many could not avoid the fear that they might.

The Ba'ath party was especially nervous of Communist influence, reinforced as it now was by the Soviet alliance. This party had won a considerable following by virtue of the seductive appeal of its immediate programme and rousing slogans, which corresponded closely to the trends and aspirations of the masses. But it lacked a numerous party membership and a stable core of supporters. It was an elite, dominated at the time by a thorough-going intellectual, the French-educated Michel Aflaq. Aflaq's ideas of socialist nationalism were developed in Paris before the war. They were largely a reaction against Stalinist Communism, whose world strategy was contemptuous of national claims and accorded them no place in it. He was greatly influenced by André Gide's *Back from the U.S.S.R.*, and feared the Communist Party's organizational ability, however potential.

The Ba'ath saw one hope of salvation, and one only: the Arab nationalist, anti-imperialist state of Egypt, which even exhibited some socialistic tendencies. Above all, Nasser the national hero was seen as the only man able to marshal all the Arab masses behind himself. His immense popularity alone could woo them away from the seductions of Communism. The Ba'ath's preoccupations were shared by that section of the Syrian middle class which really feared Communism, while remaining ardently nationalist, and by the Syrian army, disillusioned with civilian politicians and envious of the privileged position enjoyed by the Egyptian military caste. There emerged throughout Syria an increasing enthusiasm for the plan of federal union with

* Patrick Seale, *The Struggle for Syria*, Oxford University Press, 1965, p. 306.

Egypt, as a first step towards the realization of the dream of Arab unity.

The greatest obstacle was Nasser himself. He certainly favoured strong Egyptian influence over Syrian policy, which would remove the danger of this key country's falling under the domination of a hostile Arab power such as Iraq. But he was loath to become too closely embroiled in Syria's turbulent politics and in the complex rivalries of the Eastern Arabs' multifarious pressure-groups. The problems created by Egypt alone were already quite difficult and complex enough.

The Ba'athists and the Syrian army were insistent. As for the Syrian Communists, they had always been in favour of Arab unity, like everybody else. But like many others, they were afraid of its realization in practice. Egypt, where Communists were persecuted, did not attract them, and their excellent prospects in Syria itself were liable to suffer from the union. Knowing Nasser's reservations, they outbid him in their efforts to abort the scheme. The only effect of this was to encourage the Ba'ath to demand, not federation, but total union with Egypt. Perhaps in the new united Arab state, the Ba'ath would provide the source of the nation's ideology and so come to control its policy while Nasser would be content with the role of symbolic leader.

In the end, Nasser agreed. It was a dangerous gamble, but one from which he intended to extract the maximum advantage. He laid down his conditions. The Syrian army was to withdraw from politics, and the political parties were to be disbanded. The Ba'ath hesitated for the last time. Would they be committing political suicide? The party's leaders considered that although dissolved, the Ba'ath would re-emerge strengthened in the form of the National Union (the sole party according to the Egyptian prescription). Military leaders were sceptical of the practical applicability of the measure directed against them. Khaled Begdash and Khaled el-'Azm tried in vain to avert the danger threatening them by falling back on the old proposal of federal union. The ideological power of the idea of Arab unity swept away all resistance. The Syrians accepted Nasser's conditions. The United Arab Republic was proclaimed on 1 February 1958. The Communist menace had been removed. On the 4th, Khaled Begdash left Damascus, and the Communist Party went underground.

Unity had carried the day. The old-style Arab nationalists were jubilant. In their eyes, the sovereign ideal of Arab unity, which had previously floated somewhere between heaven and earth like some

Platonic Idea or Hegelian concept, was finally incarnate upon earth. An initial kernel had been formed. It could only grow – as Germany had grown from Prussia, as Italy had grown from Piedmont. The Arabs were bound to turn to this centre of the Arab nation. Their hour of triumph was at hand.

Actual developments were very different from these dreams. For a few months of 1958, however, circumstances lent them some measure of verisimilitude.

In the Lebanon, the tensions between the faiths usually resulted in driving the Christians – especially the Maronite community – into the arms of the West. For some time, however, this tendency had been balanced by the ideological force of Arab nationalism, especially powerful among the Muslims, but rapidly gaining ground among the Christians as well. It was from them, after all, that the idea had originated. Loyalty to the little homeland of Lebanon was extremely strong in the Christians, but in the case of the Muslims it was less ideological than utilitarian; they accepted it, after 1943, on condition that it remained compatible with allegiance to the larger Arab nation. The Lebanon's endorsement of the Eisenhower Doctrine roused Muslim indignation; but it also offended all pan-Arab sympathizers, not to mention those with special or sectarian interests. Even the Patriarch of the Maronite Church found himself in the ranks of the so-called 'Nasserites'. This term is rather misleading, since outside of Egypt itself Nasser was primarily a symbol. These people were anti-imperialist Arab nationalists with pan-Arabist leanings, vaguely socialist in inclination, but not partisans of any specific doctrine.

The formation of the United Arab Republic awakened extraordinary enthusiasm in this shade of opinion and filled the opposite faction with dismay. The situation became explosive when the pro-Western President, Camille Chamoun, gave indications of his intention of standing for re-election. This would have entailed amendment of the Constitution, which forbade the re-election of a President of the Republic for a second term; Chamoun himself had earlier opposed a similar attempt by his predecessor. The murder on 8 May 1958 of a 'Nasserite' Maronite journalist provoked a general strike against Chamoun, which then exploded into civil war. The war was a very curious one, conducted by scattered armed bands with no central direction, under the command of local leaders. The Lebanese army took no part in the affair. The Army chief, General Chehab, regarded the whole business as a violent quarrel between politicians, and his troops only intervened to restore equilibrium between the warring factions when it seemed in danger of being upset. The pro-American rulers of the country, Camille Chamoun and Charles Malik, his Foreign Minister, represented the conflict as foreign aggression, a planned piece of subversion directed by Nasser. They took the matter before the United Nations, hoping for Western intervention to come to their support.

In Iraq, too, the gulf separating neutralist public opinion, sympathetic to the Egyptian and Syrian position, from the country's pro-Western rulers, bitter enemies of Nasser and the Syrians, only widened. Social tensions aggravated the situation. Nuri es-Said and the Regent Abdulilah (who coveted the throne of Syria) had undertaken a programme of public works (mostly large dam projects) financed by the royalties on Iraq's oil revenue. But the masses derived no benefit from these projects, which could only have very long-term effects upon the economy. No money and no technical resources were left over for small improvements whose effects might have been more rapidly felt.

Nuri had taken decisive control of the anti-Nasser party. He saw the formation of the United Arab Republic as a challenge, and as a counterblast he arranged a Federation with Jordan. He had close ties with Great Britain, the United States and Turkey, and by the summer of 1958 dominated the bloc in which Chamoun of the Lebanon and Hussein of Jordan were associated with him in opposition to the Syrian and Egyptian neutralists. This was not all. At the time of the Jordan crisis in April 1957, when Hussein had dismissed his neutralist ministers and stifled a popular revolt, Eisenhower had declared the integrity of Jordan a vital interest, and Israel had reserved freedom of action in the event of any threat to Jordan's status. This could only mean that Israel would occupy the West Bank if Jordan were swallowed up in any Arab union. Objectively, therefore, Israel appeared as the ally of Western imperialism and of the coalition of pro-Western Arab governments.

In May 1958 Moshe Dayan revealed to Field-Marshal Montgomery a plan, supported by Ben Gurion, for an alliance to contain Arab turbulence between all the states on the periphery of the Arab world: Iran, Turkey, Ethiopia and Israel. Dulles continued to emphasize the threat of armed Soviet aggression, which he considered imminent. In June 1958 Nuri arrived in London. On the 27th, in an interview with *The Times*, he made a thinly veiled plea for Anglo-American intervention. On his way home he stopped off for conversations with the Turks, and a meeting of the Baghdad Pact members was announced for 14 July. It was common knowledge in the Arab world that he planned a joint military assault by the United States, Great Britain and Iraq to detach Syria from the U.A.R. and place the Fertile Crescent under the rule of a Hashemite king, who would be a client of the British. He sent troops into Jordan, no doubt as part of this plan, perhaps to start the war with Syria in the hope that the Western powers would follow. But the commanders of these troops, Brigadiers Kassem and Aref, marched instead on Nuri's villa and the Royal Palace. The King and the Crown Prince were killed, and Nuri fled, only to be found the next day disguised as an old woman and lynched. The Baghdad mob ran riot in the streets. On 14 July 1958, to the strains of the *Marseillaise*, the last powerful pro-imperialist regime in the central zone of the Arab world was overthrown. The Arab Revolution was victorious.

Naturally, the Iraqi Revolution was interpreted in the West as the outcome of a cunning Muscovite plot. It is quite certain that the Soviet Union was overjoyed to witness the abrupt collapse of the military edifice erected against her in the South. But the primary responsibility for the revolution must rest with the West, and especially the Americans. Their obstinate insistence on press-ganging the Arab countries into an anti-Soviet crusade in which they had not the slightest interest, and the British preoccupation with bolstering up unpopular monarchs in an attempt to win back their lost sphere of influence, sapped the foundations of their policy. The Western attitude towards Israel, which was looked upon as a firm base in a troubled world, and not as a problem confronting the Arabs and a threat to them, only made matters worse. It resulted in the strengthening of the militant clique in Israel, instead of encouraging conciliation. Behind these attitudes lay total lack of comprehension of the sociological factors. The political games played with chieftains and governments took no account whatsoever of Arab public opinion. Arab nationalism was regarded as the artificial creation of Nasser and the Russians, whereas in fact it was an entirely spontaneous, deeply rooted passion, which forced governments to obey its will, or else swept them away, dragged them down and cut them to ribbons, as happened to Nuri es-Said and Regent Abdulilah.

The Iraqi Revolution naturally filled the Arab nationalists – that is to say the vast majority of the Arab peoples – with exultation and terrified those who stood opposed to the wave: Hussein and Chamoun. They appealed for aid, which was hardly necessary. On 15 July American marines landed at Beirut, and on the 17th British paratroops from Cyprus were flown to Amman, permission having been obtained from Israel to overfly her territory. The Saudi rulers, fearing too much unpopularity, refused to allow American fuel intended for Jordan to pass their borders. It was therefore transported by plane from the Lebanon over Israeli air space, with Israel's consent. 'Where an Arab nation refused,' Hussein writes bitterly in his memoirs, 'an enemy agreed.' *

A new pattern was emerging. And it was by no means characterized by the unconditional victory of Nasserism, as the Arab masses hoped and the Western powers feared. The idea of Arab unity was not to carry all before it, as the Arab ideologues had believed. One phase of development had come to an end. New problems were about to arise.

Up until this point, anti-imperialist Arab nationalism had been represented by Nasser. The Ba'ath, his only competitor, was comparatively weak, and the formation of the U.A.R., as will be seen, had apparently subordinated it to Egyptian power. A new alternative to Nasserism now arose, a new competitor appeared on the scene: Kassem's Iraq.

Although it was unleashed by a purely military action, the revolution of July 1958 was the first real revolution in the Arab world. In 1952 the Egyptian officers had waited in vain for a positive massive popular reaction to their coup – although as lovers of order, they also did all in their power to prevent such a reaction. In Iraq, from the very first hours of the insurrection the masses came out into the streets, acted on their own initiative, and gave passionate, violent, even cruel vent to their aspirations and hatreds. Scenes which vividly conjured up the France of 1793 were accompanied by singing of the *Marseillaise* and the *Carmagnole*. Kassem, the new Leader (*Za'im*), gave popular spontaneity a free rein, and the attitudes and decisions taken by him manifested a still unaccustomed radicalism. From the start, the nationalist narrow-mindedness typical of so many Arab movements was overruled by a spirit of generosity, exhibited in the recognition of a Kurdish nationality, which was granted equal rights with the Arab race. Diplomatic relations were established with the U.S.S.R. and the Soviet bloc. Political refugees, including Communists, returned. A military tribunal was set up, very revolutionary in tone, which sat in public; sessions were broadcast and televised, and presided over by a Communistic colonel of ferocious truculence, Mahdawi, Kassem's cousin. Peoples' Militias were organized.

The Iraqi Communists, ruthlessly persecuted under the old regime, and apparently eliminated from the political scene, re-emerged surrounded by all the glamour of the underground, the prestige of a persecuted but tough and resilient group with a firm, apparently unequivocal political line. Party membership grew, despite the theoretical

* Hussein of Jordan, *Uneasy Lies the Head*, London, Heinemann, 1962, p. 168.

ban on political parties imposed by the regime. The party's first objective was to canalize, under Soviet influence seemingly communicated via Khaled Begdash, popular enthusiasm and especially the reactions of the peasantry, which pressed for an extension of the revolution. Without more ado the peasants seized the lands of the big proprietors. Once again the U.S.S.R. stated her preference for a parliamentary regime sympathetic to her own foreign policy. Party pressure was exerted on Kassem with the principal object of obtaining major concessions to relieve the plight and calm the revolutionary fervour of the most poverty-stricken layers of the population. Agrarian reforms were rapidly decreed, but their actual execution was delayed or sabotaged by the civil service and the bourgeoisie, and it was therefore a long time before they took any effect.

On the national level, the regime's protestations of Arab solidarity and the solemn declaration contained in the Provisional Constitution of 27 July 1958, according to which 'The Iraqi State is an integral part of the Arab nation' (Article 2), did not solve all its problems. Kassem was not eager to relinquish the privileges of independence, and supported no doubt by a large section of the army he resisted the pressures towards organic union with the U.A.R. He was also supported by part of the nationalist middle class, which disliked Nasser's military authoritarianism, and by the very numerous racial and religious minorities (together constituting a majority of the population), which were apprehensive of Sunnite Muslim domination in a Greater Arab State. The Communists assumed the role of protector of the minorities, and did not hesitate to enlist the aid of the bourgeoisie. 'The idea of union with the U.A.R.,' declared the Political Bureau of the party on 3 September 1958, 'is unwelcome to the people, because such a union would limit the opportunities for growth and development of the national economy and the nation's capital.' * The party and Khaled Begdash proposed simple federal union, which they knew Nasser would refuse. Kassem upheld this point of view, in opposition to the Ba'athists and the Nasserite section of the middle class represented by his team-mate Brigadier Abdul Salem Aref. Aref was excluded from power in September 1958. His conspiracy to stage a come-back resulted in his being condemned to death in January 1959. He was subsequently pardoned by Kassem.

The existence of Kassem as an alternative to Nasserism, the competition between the two movements, and the endemic geopolitical

---

* Quoted in *France Nouvelle* (weekly of the French Communist Party), 22–28 January 1959, pp. 16–17.

rivalry between Egypt and Iraq led to a number of realignments. As recently as the beginning of 1956, the U.S.S.R. had decided finally to abandon the Zhdanov–Stalin theory of the two blocs, and to recognize the progressive character of the non-Communist regimes in the Third World. She supported Nasser, hero of the anti-imperialist struggle. The general stiffening of the party line after the Hungarian and Polish rebellions in 1956, renewed hostility towards Nasser's friend Tito, the suppression of political parties in Syria, including the Syrian Communist Party, while the Iraqi Communist Party enjoyed a privileged position, all helped to increase Soviet suspicions of Nasser and favour Kassem.

Events in Syria tended towards a similar conclusion. In this 'Northern Province' of the United Arab Republic, Egyptian army officers often behaved as though they were in a conquered country. In every field of activity, Syrians were subordinated to Egyptians. As has already been mentioned, the political parties had been disbanded and replaced by a National Bloc on the Egyptian pattern. The Ba'ath, which had pressed for Union and had hoped to dominate the National Bloc, was undermined by Nasser, who simply dispensed with its services. Meanwhile both Communists and conservatives became increasingly enraged at Egyptian depredations of their economic and other interests, and held the Ba'ath responsible as instigator of the Union. Instead of the Ba'athists, the only Syrian given power and support by Nasser was the sinister Colonel Sarraj, Minister of the Interior for the 'region', who stocked the prisons with his opponents and practised torture on a grand scale. The fall of Nuri es-Said removed any danger of annexation by a British-dominated Iraq – one of the hazards which had pushed Syria into the arms of Egypt.

The Communists and a growing proportion of the Syrian middle class, including even some of those who had been appalled at the excesses of the Iraqi Revolution, turned against Nasser. At successive Congresses of Eastern European Communist Parties (and for a time in Syria itself), Khaled Begdash denounced his authoritarianism, which had previously been overlooked, and condemned his 'Titoist' foreign policy as insufficiently attuned to that of the U.S.S.R. This irritated Nasser, and at the beginning of January 1959 he had a large batch of Egyptian Communists arrested. This action further aggravated Egyptian-Soviet relations. On 16 March Khrushchev pronounced his verdict: the Iraqi regime was the more progressive. At the same time, the cold war between Egypt and Iraq was intensified. The radio stations of the two countries rained insults on one another. In March 1959 a

Nasserite revolt at Mosul was nipped in the bud with the aid of local Communists and Kurds. In July 1959 Kurdish Communists instigated a massacre of 'reactionary' Turkmens in Kirkuk. Kassem shifted his ground and condemned these excesses. The Iraqi Communist Party was penitent, and Kassem retained the support of the Left and of a section of the middle class. The Nasserites continued to denounce the Red Terror reigning in Iraq, while condemning Iraq's refusal to join the Union. Nasser then outdid himself with public protestations of Muslim piety and inveighed against the atheistic Communism to which Kassem had delivered Iraq. This led him towards a reconciliation with the so-called reactionary Arab states, Jordan and Saudi Arabia. In defiance of the U.S.S.R., which had become hostile, he improved relations with the United States and the Western powers. From October 1958 the U.A.R. once again began to accept American aid.

Despite his slanging match with the U.S.S.R., Nasser did not break with the Soviet Union altogether, and attempted to maintain reasonable relations with both blocs. The economic ties which he had established with the socialist countries were difficult to undo and replace. But the West was by now also contributing to Egypt's economic effort. Internally, Egyptian businessmen found the Syrian market open to economic penetration, and were able to realize large returns on their capital by cooperating in state-controlled enterprises or by taking advantage of other openings left free to them. However, the nationalization of English, French and Jewish companies after Suez had caused a considerable loss of confidence in Egyptian business circles, many of whose members had close financial connections with these companies. Most of the holders of the nation's capital had shown little inclination to invest it where the government considered it most necessary. Despite all the soothing assurances made to them, capitalists felt a vague unease, and many looked back with longing to the old days of the free economy and parliamentary government, which had guaranteed them their power. The more these reservations made themselves felt, the more the government was forced to nationalize, in order to ensure that vital functions which private capital refused to perform were fulfilled. It was then obliged to justify these actions in speeches which became, perforce, increasingly socialistic in tone, thus arousing yet further alarm among the capitalist classes. All in all, the State's role thus expanded considerably, at the expense of the private sector. In February 1960 Egypt's two largest banks were nationalized. The centralization of power made rapid strides. The old middle class fell increasingly under the domination of the military machine. Nasserite rule remained true to its two great aims: independence and modernization. But it now took the view that the Western powers were resigned to abandoning any claims on Egypt's independence and that good relations with these powers could therefore be resumed without fear, and even to Egypt's advantage. Private capital had proved incapable of achieving modernization or the building up of an autonomous industry. The participation of the Communist Left had proved dangerous, in that it provided a possible nucleus for an alternative policy. The development of industry was therefore controlled by the State, in which the military caste enjoyed a near-monopoly of power and very considerable privileges. A further step was taken in June and July 1961. The entire cotton trade, all banks and insurance companies, and 44 companies in the primary industries were nationalized. State control over foreign trade and over a large number of firms in commerce and light industry became paramount. However, it was made clear that the object of all these measures was merely to ensure economic growth and to raise the standard of living. Capitalism was only condemned for its excesses. No appeal was made to class consciousness or the class struggle. Compensation for expropriated possessions, the inviolable right to private property, the regime's protection of the civil rights of its subjects, its fidelity to Islam, respect for the value and dignity of the human person were strenuously insisted upon. Naturally, opponents of this programme were tortured. When Heykal, Nasser's confidant, published a newspaper article entitled 'A Workers' and Peasants' Revolution', it transpired that he meant a revolution *on behalf of* the workers and peasants.

Egypt's new external policies, especially the *rapprochement* with the United States and the reactionary Arab regimes, caused her sympathizers abroad considerable disquiet. The Ba'athists became increasingly cool in their attitude. Worse followed. At the end of June 1961 Kassem laid claim to the Arab sheikhdom of Kuwait, which had only six days previously been granted full independence by a treaty with Great Britain. Claims to a share in Arabia's oil wealth, monopolized by a handful of despotic rulers while so many heavily populated Arab countries were tragically lacking in resources, was one of the theme songs of Arab nationalism. However, hostility to Kassem drove the U.A.R. to defend the integrity of the sheikhdom, in conjunction with Jordan and Saudi Arabia and even with Great Britain, who dispatched troops to protect the feudal oil magnate's interests, closely bound up with her own. The replacement of British troops by a mixed contingent of Jordanian, Saudi Arabian and Egyptian soldiers did not help much to improve matters.

Egypt's authoritarian rule in Syria, the eclipse of the Ba'ath, the exploitation of Syria to bolster up the Egyptian economy finally became too much for the Syrians. Sarraj himself was dismissed and transferred to Egypt, with some honorary titles but stripped of all power. General discontent finally exploded in a military coup at Damascus. Syrian officers arrested the Egyptian proconsul, Marshal Abdul Hakim Amer, on 28 September 1961 and deported him to Egypt. They proclaimed Syria's secession from the U.A.R. The formation which was to have been the nucleus of Arab unity had blown apart.

Nasser wisely decided against any military campaign to reconquer Syria. But he was profoundly disturbed, and undertook a painful re-appraisal of his policy at every level. This was expressed in a series of self-critical speeches covering the last quarter of 1961, and in one in particular which he made on 16 October. The tenor of these texts throws light on the whole process of the Arab Revolution.

Nasser, with whom the great majority of the Arab masses identified, saw this movement as above all else a national movement. In his *The Philosophy of the Revolution*, written at the beginning of the Egyptian Revolution, he explains that it (the Revolution) was 'the realization of the hope held by the people of Egypt since they began in modern times to think of self-government and complete sovereignty'.* The principal object of modernization was to guarantee the nation freedom of decision in its own affairs. The democratization of economic and social life were merely the corollary to these two things. As in every other ideology, the end was seen as possessed of every virtue. An independent and powerful nation ought automatically to abolish privilege and injustice. In his view, in fact, Egypt's ills were the result either of foreign influence or of the moral turpitude of individuals.

This nationalist outlook, extrapolated from Egypt to apply to all the Arab peoples, resonated with the feelings of the masses. Under conditions of foreign oppression, everything is attributable to that oppression. Likewise, every aim is subordinated to the primary aim of national liberation. Under the influence of Marxist thinking, Nasser had admitted the necessity for a second revolution. This would be a social revolution, bringing into play the class struggle with the object of ensuring 'equity to all the children of the same fatherland'. This, however, was a disagreeable necessity. Significantly, Nasser depicted the national revolution as fostering a host of noble qualities: unity, mutual love, the spirit of sacrifice. By contrast, the social revolution would

* Gamal Abdul Nasser, *Egypt's Liberation: The Philosophy of the Revolution*, Washington, Public Affairs Press, 1955, p. 18.

induce ('despite ourselves' he writes) division, hatred, selfishness. This is the precise opposite of the classical Marxist view, according to which it is the internal struggle which is healthy, which develops the most noble qualities. External struggles on the other hand – however necessary to achieve liberation – are to be deplored, divide the workers who ought to unite ('Proletarians of all lands, unite!'), bring out prehistoric instincts of group interest, and are generally symptoms of retrogression.

Nasser must have admitted to himself that some blame attached to the Egyptians for the way in which they had governed Syria. But he thought it his duty to take a more profound view of the matter. In his eyes, the Syrian secession was a betrayal by the Syrians of the ideal of the Arab nation, united and free. How was he to account for this unnatural phenomenon? Basically he saw in it a reaction on the part of the Syrian privileged classes against the socialist character of the regime, which had been accentuated by the wave of nationalizations in July. The subsequent policy of the secessionist Syrian government was to appear to justify this opinion. These privileged classes had succeeded in misleading the people by taking advantage of Egyptian errors and of grievances against the Egyptians, whether legitimate or not. Therefore the conclusion drawn from this was that not enough had been done to combat privilege, either in Egypt or Syria, and the masses had not been sufficiently enlightened. Nasser thought he detected a universal conspiracy directed against Egyptian socialism – a conspiracy both external and internal.

I have given the matter much thought [he declared on 16 October], and I have made my choice. I have chosen to pursue the revolution begun nine years ago on both the political and the economic plane, whatever the cost. . . .We over-estimated our strength and our opportunities by under-estimating those of the reactionaries. We have, as a result, had to make terms with the reactionaries, and we have been thrown off our stroke. . . . We have suffered a serious setback in organizing the people by opening the gates of the National Union to reactionary forces. Our efforts to educate the masses have been inadequate . . .*

The Egyptian reaction to Syrian secession therefore expressed itself in the form of a more radical social policy. The revolutionary movement exemplified by Nasser had not at first possessed any specifically socialist ideology. However, the logic of unyielding anti-imperialist nationalism, in continual conflict with the blind reactions of the imperialist powers in order to maintain itself, led Nasser's group through the

* Quoted in *Cahiers de l'Orient contemporain*, no. 47, Paris, 1961, p. 401.

elimination of the large landed proprietors first into a centralized statist economy controlled by the military caste, and then to an appeal to the revolutionary fervour of the underprivileged classes. This appeal was unquestionably sincere in Nasser's own case, and in that of some of his colleagues. They were also fully aware of the immense difficulties facing Egyptian economic development. The country possessed an extremely limited acreage of usable soil, which the Aswan High Dam had not as yet been able to increase significantly; the mineral resources necessary to build up a prosperous industry were totally lacking; and the population was multiplying at a dizzy rate. A superhuman effort, a Great Leap Forward according to the Chinese prescription, was needed – not to progress, but simply to avoid catastrophe. Who was capable of mobilizing the masses? It would perhaps be possible with the aid of a network of some hundreds of thousands of small, completely dedicated revolutionary cells, capable of enormous sacrifices, to set an example to the millions of peasants who had viewed their rulers with mistrust and scepticism ever since the time of the Pharaohs. It was becoming apparent that the military bureaucracy, whose principal concern was to extract the maximum profit from positions of responsibility, bore not the slightest resemblance to the completely dedicated cells which had carried with them the Chinese and the Vietnamese masses, or those which had earlier ensured the relative success of Soviet economic development. It was now essential to establish militant cells drawn directly from the ranks of the suffering masses. And in order to win their enthusiasm for such a project, it was essential to offer them other prizes than external independence, which had now been assured. They would have to be promised a relentless struggle against privilege and the privileged – and not only those of the old society, but also those with whom the masses were in daily conflict. It had become necessary to promise the people liberty and equality – in brief, to have recourse to a socialist ideology.

In the immediate aftermath of the schism, nationalization measures were extended and stepped up. A wave of arrests and confiscations struck the members of the old property-owning classes. Above all, Nasser arranged for a National Congress of People's Forces to be elected, in which farmers, workers and peasants almost formed the majority. The Congress gave rise to a lively debate on the draft of a 'National Charter'.* This spoke of the 'will to revolutionary change, which rejects every tie and every limitation other than the rights and the claims of the masses', of the dangers of bureaucracy, and of liberty,

* *Mashroû' al-Mithâq*, Cairo, Department of Information, 1961, p. 10, 62.

which alone could overcome the passivity of the masses. 'A powerful public sector will direct progress in every field, and will bear the main responsibility for planning development.' The draft was accepted as it stood, with a reference to Islam inserted as the sole concession to the Right. The National Union, Egypt's only party, formed in 1957, was replaced by an Arab Socialist Union, half of whose party officials at every level had to be workers or peasants, except in the very highest ruling body of the party. A Constitutional Proclamation on 27 September 1962 laid down – in theory – that power at the top must be shared.

In his relations with the other Arab states Nasser returned to ideological intransigence. He broke off diplomatic relations with Jordan, denounced the regime in Saudi Arabia and refused to recognize the new Syrian government. He ended the vague confederation he had entered with the ultra-reactionary Yemen. Egypt's effective withdrawal from Arab affairs was accompanied by ringing proclamations of revolutionary Arab unity, and of unyielding hostility to the combined forces of imperialism, among which Zionism figured prominently.

Nasser's diagnosis of the causes of the Syrian secession did have some justification. The Syrians' irritation at Egyptian hegemony in their country was aggravated by the Syrian bourgeoisie's hostility to nationalization. Hardly had secession become an accomplished fact than the nationalization measures were reversed, to loud applause from the Communists, who laid emphasis on the services performed by Syrian industrialists in the national struggle. Agrarian reforms were largely abolished, and many proprietors regained, sometimes by force, possession of the lands which they had lost.

Nasser's socialist, Arabist and anti-imperialist stand gave a new dynamism to these three guiding principles throughout the Arab world. In Syria the leaders of the Ba'ath had through their hatred of Nasser publicly approved the secession. But faced with the defection of all their supporters, they had to eat their words and go into opposition. Young Ba'athist officers, more Left-wing than their elders and supporters of a truly socialist policy, were appalled by the shiftiness and incompetence of the traditional leaders of the party, and formed their own clandestine breakaway party.

In September 1962 the wave of revolutionary feeling sweeping the Arab world led to the most unexpected developments. A Republic was proclaimed in the medieval Imamate of the Yemen, and recognized by the U.A.R. and the U.S.S.R. But a hard core of royalists regrouped under the leadership of the Imam Badr, with the support of Saudi Arabia; the United States refused to recognize the Republic. In October

Nasser sent Egyptian troops to the aid of the threatened Republic. More than ever, he was acclaimed as the hero of revolutionary pan-Arabism.

Kassem's Iraq had also recognized Republican Yemen, but could do no more than this, being entangled in inextricable difficulties of its own. Kassem, a wild and fantastic personality, attempted to steer an even course between the various Iraqi pressure-groups and the international powers, but succeeded only in sowing the greatest mistrust on every side. He had given free rein to a wave of popular demands and claims at the beginning of his rule. The result had been neither a proletarian dictatorship (for which neither Moscow nor the local Communists had the slightest enthusiasm), nor a stable state with a smoothly running institutional machinery for the peaceful and permanent settlement of clashes between different interests, different aims and different ideologies. Demonstrations, expropriations, the excesses perpetrated by unruly mobs (rendered more severe by the rivalries between religious and ethnic communities), the televized sessions of the revolutionary tribunal, all these only succeeded in terrifying the bourgeoisie and the privileged classes of every sort. In self-defence they mobilized the forces of religion and of pan-Arab nationalism, helped from outside by Nasser. He for his part was only too eager to make use of the tactical weapon placed in his hands by indignation at Iraqi impiety and Kassem's separatism (Nasser's propaganda fortuitously gained from the fact that Kassem's name, in Arabic, can mean 'the Divider'). Kassem busied himself with appeasing the Right while endeavouring to retain the support of the Left, to whom he therefore also had to make concessions. But his attitude towards his competitor Nasser remained intransigent. His international policy was also one of maintaining a shifting balance between the Western powers and the Soviet bloc. Kassem attempted to harness the nation to his own ends by adopting a policy of repression towards the Kurdish minority's claims to autonomy, and continually putting off the promised implementation of administrative and cultural autonomy. The Kurdish revolt broke out in April 1961, and Kassem had the Kurdish villages shelled. The claiming of Kuwait in June 1961 was also intended to stimulate national unity, but the ridiculous aspects of the claim did not contribute to gaining mass support for it, especially since the issues dividing the masses were of much greater consequence.

The army was united on a programme of pan-Arab nationalism. Weary of the crazy oscillations of Kassem's policy, the leading Army officers made a pact with the Ba'ath with the object of achieving an organized party with mass support. A military coup on 8 February 1963 (known as the Revolution of the 14th Ramadan, after the corresponding date of the Hegiran calendar) dethroned Kassem, who was killed. Power was taken over by a coalition of Nasserites and Ba'athists, with the latter at first in the dominant position. Conservative forces rejoiced at the abrupt disappearance of the danger of a gradual slide into Communism. A neo-Ba'athist militia was formed to hunt down suspected Communists and fellow-travellers; some 5,000 were slaughtered. This bloody settlement of accounts lanced the boil of five years' accumulated hatred and resentment. From their position of dominance, the Ba'athists then turned to the elimination of their Nasserite allies. Their pan-Arab nationalism caused them to step up the war against the Kurds, which became bitter and frequently horrific. One month after the Iraqi putsch, on 8 March 1963, Syrian army officers brought off a similar military coup at Damascus, overthrowing the weak parliamentary regime which had governed since the secession in 1961 and bringing the Ba'ath to power, in Damascus as in Baghdad.

Thus in the spring of 1963 the Eastern Arab world was dominated by two regimes, both avowedly socialist in spirit and both pan-Arab nationalist: the Ba'ath in Iraq and Syria, and Nasserism in Egypt. The two blocs entered into negotiations at Cairo in March and April 1963 to find a basis for unity. But the two parties, made wary by the Egypto-Syrian experiment in unity of 1958–61, rivalled one another in mistrust and suspicion. Each accused the other of authoritarianism – not without reason in both cases – and each blamed the other for the failure of the earlier experiment. The Ba'ath would have liked to have been able to take advantage of Nasser's prestige without giving up any of its own power. Nasser was not prepared to accept unity unless Egyptian ideas were given precedence. The negotiations ended in an 'agreement' which put off a final solution to a later date.

Relations between the Ba'ath and the Nasserites became extremely strained as a result of the Ba'athists' manoeuvrings to preserve their hegemony on the Syrian political scene, in violation of the Cairo agreements. A purge of Nasserite officers was followed by the bloody repression, on 18 July 1963, of an attempted Nasserite coup in Damascus. Nasser began to denounce Ba'ath 'fascism', pointing to the paucity of the latter's social reforms in respect of the Egyptian Charter. It had, moreover, become common to refer to the Ba'ath in this way since the massacres of Communists in Iraq. The Ba'ath's reign in Iraq was brief, however. The National Guard which it had set up and which had all the characteristics of a military organization had begun to make itself intolerable, especially to the army. The party governed under the cover of a non-Ba'athist President, General Abdul Salem Aref. This individual was a religious traditionalist and a fervent admirer of Nasser, with little taste for socialism and even less for the secularism of the Ba'athist ideology. In a coup carried out on 18 November 1963, he rid himself of the Ba'ath and established closer links with Cairo.

By the end of 1963 the Arab world had never been more divided. Syria was engaged in a cold war with Egypt and Iraq; her relations with the capitalist Lebanon were far from cordial, and she was hostile to Jordan and Morocco. Egypt and Saudi Arabia were in military conflict in the Yemen, each giving more or less open aid to the opposing sides in the civil war. Outside the Near East itself, Algeria was embroiled in frontier disputes with Morocco (with whom there had been actual military clashes) and Tunisia; these two were themselves at loggerheads over Mauritania. But Israel stirred, and all quarrels were forgotten.

5
Israel Softens

In the course of the general outline just given of Arab political developments from the Suez expedition to the end of 1963, the name of Israel has hardly been mentioned. Certainly no Arab forgot the presence of this outpost of the Western World implanted in the Near East, none forgot the common aim of all Arabs to avenge the humiliating defeats suffered in 1948 and 1956, none was resigned to the loss of forcibly stolen Arab territory nor to the running sore of the refugee problem. Action, however, was always put off until later, to some unspecified time in the future. Some hoped that this time would not be far off, while others wished it as far in the future as possible, even hoping that some unforeseen development might some day solve the problem painlessly. The Arab rulers' principal preoccupations for the moment were in some quarters the creation of a more modern, more independent and more just society, in others to make the maximum profit with the minimum effort out of a society deliberately left archaic, unjust and very largely dependent – albeit profitably dependent – on the outside world. All were also intent on protecting a chosen system, maintaining or acquiring power for a given group, or extracting the benefits of power for the class supporting that group. In practice, Israel was a long way down the list of priorities. But no ruler would or could allow Arab rights to go by default – rights which had been violated through sheer brute force. The Arab claims were kept up in verbal proclamations delivered in a more or less impassioned style, coloured by every metaphor in the repertoire of Arab rhetoric and animated by all the fire of total ideological commitment. Various propaganda outlets were made available to the Palestinians, the most violent and most interested group in the Arab world. But a barrier of 'Blue Berets' conveniently prevented any incidents with Egypt, while a garrison of these same U.N. forces enabled shipping to and from Israel to pass the Egyptian Strait of Tiran without difficulty, thus symbolically absolving the U.A.R. from the responsibility of authorizing such traffic. Incidents remained possible and frequently occurred on Israel's frontiers with Jordan, Syria (where the question of demilitarized zones was a continual source of conflict) and even the

Lebanon, whose military weakness and mercantile pacifism naturally inclined her towards appeasement. But the incidents were limited and less serious than in the preceding period.

At the same time, Israel felt more secure. Her rulers were able to consider their long-term foreign policy. As in any country benefiting from a relatively peaceful situation, the masses were able to pay more attention to internal problems. A specific pattern in Israeli politics began to emerge.

Ben Gurion was still in power. As ever, his policy was conceived on the global scale. His object was to consolidate Israel's position despite Arab hostility, and force was the only means in which he had any faith. He therefore had to seek the support of the strong. As ever, his main hope lay in the United States; but he also made advances to Great Britain and Federal Germany, and kept up the alliance with France. In the course of a triumphal tour in March 1960, he visited Eisenhower in Washington to extract a vague promise of rockets. He shook Adenauer by the hand in front of press photographers. At the same time he won some substantial advantages, including a loan of 500 million dollars, and a free and secret supply of arms. Also secretly, Israeli troops and officers were trained in the use of the new arms on German territory. These arrangements were best kept secret in view of the sensitivity of Jewish public opinion to reports of dealings with Germans; the deals were nonetheless extremely useful. Also secretly, France helped Israel to build a nuclear reactor, allegedly for 'peaceful purposes'.

Ben Gurion was full of concern for his allies' welfare, and generous with his advice. This advice was obviously as much to Israel's advantage as to her allies'. In 1957, as we have seen, taking advantage of American anti-Communist hysteria, he had offered his services against the supposed threat of a Soviet take-over of Syria. Nonetheless, his efforts to win a N.A.T.O. guarantee of Israel's frontiers had failed. In 1960 he instructed de Gaulle as to how he, Ben Gurion, would solve the Algerian problem: partition Algeria and keep the most useful areas (the coast and the oil-rich Sahara), leaving the rest to the Arabs; then settle one million Frenchmen from the metropolis in the French zone. De Gaulle replied, appropriately enough but rather obviously, 'What, you want to create a new Israel in Algeria!' [*]

The support of the great powers remained of paramount importance, but it was always conditional and not entirely reliable. Following the age-old precepts of international diplomacy, it was necessary to have other allies outside the hostile Arab belt. Successful moves followed to

[*] Michel Bar-Zohar, *Ben Gourion*, op. cit., p. 357.

achieve an unsigned but firm agreement with Turkey – pro-American, anti-Soviet and estranged from Syria and Iraq by continual disputes; with Iran, likewise in constant difficulties with Iraq; and with Ethiopia, concerned about the possible effects of Nasserite propaganda on the Muslims of Eritrea and Somalia. Further off, Asia and above all Africa offered diplomatic opportunities for making friends and influencing people. It was not advisable for Israel to have all the Third World's votes at the U.N. against her. Israel was able to provide very useful technical advice, notably with regard to agricultural community development. Ben Gurion tried to get the Americans to finance these projects by extolling their usefulness in warding off Communism.

Ben Gurion was getting old. In 1960 he would be seventy-four. There were things that he failed to grasp with his old clarity of vision. For instance, he railed against overseas Zionists. He was particularly exasperated by the predilection exhibited by some of their representatives – notably Nahum Goldmann, president of the World Jewish Congress – to meddle in Israel's internal affairs. He failed, for once, to appreciate that this was the other side of a coin otherwise very valuable to Israel. The support of foreign Zionists was of the most crucial importance. For one thing, it enabled Israel to win the support of the Western powers without having to submit to all their demands. In December 1960 American reconnaissance aircraft discovered the secret nuclear reactor built with the aid of France. The Americans were furious at this breach of their own policy of non-dissemination of nuclear secrets. They demanded proof that the device was really only for peaceful purposes. They stormed and threatened, but Ben Gurion would not give way and refused to allow any inspection. The American super-state finally had to give in to the tiny state of Israel, and content itself with the reports from its intelligence agents. Once again, the more responsible Arab statesmen had to face the fact that Israel was strong, very strong indeed. In July 1961 the first Israeli rocket was launched.

From time to time the Americans were also forced to face the fact that Israeli-Arab tension had its disadvantages; it was impossible for them not to support Israel, and this support could not but discredit them in Arab eyes. They decided to work out a plan for the final solution of the problem, and exerted pressure to get it accepted. In 1961–2 Kennedy put forward two successive proposals for a settlement. Both began with a demand for the readmission to Israel of some of the refugees which the U.N. resolution had ordered Israel to take back. But the two parties were too mistrustful of one another, and both plans fell through. Significantly, Kennedy attempted to exert pressure on Ben Gurion through the Hawk missiles he had promised. The missiles would only be delivered if Israel accepted a plan for a settlement. Ben Gurion rejected the plans, and got the missiles all the same.

It should not be thought that he did not want peace. But he wanted it on Israel's terms, and his only strategy was to win it from a position of strength. From the end of the pre-war period, he had been convinced that demonstrations of force were the only way to wring recognition from the Arabs for the state which had been imposed on them. The failure of the 1948 war, the 1956 war and a large number of small frontier engagements to achieve this end could not persuade him of the ineffectiveness of the method. On each occasion, he felt that external circumstances had intervened to spoil the effect. A day would come when the international situation was favourable, and the major powers, behind Israel, would force this stubborn people, so unwilling to accept defeat, to bend the knee. He was not one of those dreamers who spoke of a Jewish Empire extending from the Nile to the Euphrates according to the promise made to Abraham by Yahweh (although Abraham was also supposed to be the father of the Arabs), a dream which had earlier inspired Herzl; nor had he any sympathy with Right-wing extremists like Menachem Begin and his Heruth party, successor to the old Irgun, who wanted all of Israel's ancient territory on both banks of the Jordan. He was ready to concede what he did not hold and content himself with the territory won in 1948. This was at any rate Ben Gurion's policy for the moment; he would leave to future generations of Israelis the task of constructing their policy on the basis of what he had given them. But he would not give up a single square yard of the land already won, nor allow a single man of those expelled to return. The Arabs, for their part, could not accept less than the announcement of some concession, even in principle, in the direction of the U.N. resolutions, which provided the only legal basis to which reference could be made, even though the Arabs themselves had at first rejected them. In the circumstances it is hardly surprising that Ben Gurion's proposals for a meeting with Nasser should have failed. These attempts were made through various intermediaries, including Tito, in 1962 and the beginning of 1963. Nasser had been wooed with fair words; but the difficulties facing him in the Arab world itself were too great. He could not hope to overcome them if he was handicapped by any gesture made to Israel, which would immediately have been denounced as a surrender. He knew that Ben Gurion was little inclined to make major concessions, and nothing less would enable him to emerge from the negotiations with his reputation more or less intact. In any case, he did not consider the matter urgent.

It all seemed rather a distant problem to the Israelis, too. They were growing used to the makeshift *modus vivendi* with the Arabs. Most Israelis were primarily concerned with their day-to-day difficulties, the economic situation, and with internal policy. Internal tensions were now free to emerge. Ben Gurion's authoritarian rule became increasingly irksome to many Israelis. The Old Man looked to the army, and to his younger colleagues who shared his militant approach: Moshe Dayan, one-time Commander-in-Chief of the Army, turned politician and subsequently Minister of Agriculture; and Shimon Peres, Director General of the Defence Ministry and then, in 1959, Deputy Minister of Defence. The opposition parties, naturally, became increasingly censorious of procedures which seemed to them undemocratic. But more seriously, increasingly bitter criticisms began to be heard in the heart of his own party, the Mapai. Sharett had never forgiven Ben Gurion for having forced him out of the government, and no doubt also saw quite clearly where the activists' policy would lead. The faithful Golda Meir, Minister of Foreign Affairs, was deeply offended at the major foreign policy initiatives taken behind her back by Ben Gurion and Peres. In March 1963, following the arrest of two Israeli secret agents in Zurich for threatening a German girl whose father, an engineer, worked in Egypt, a loud barrage of propaganda orchestrated by the Israeli secret service was let loose, condemning the collusion of German scientists with Egypt. A tremendously exaggerated picture was painted of the advances being made by Egyptian military technology with the aid of these Germans, all described as former Nazis. Some no doubt were, as no doubt were some of the Germans who made up the body of technicians in military establishments in the German Democratic Republic, and for that matter so were some of those West Germans currently giving aid to Israel and training her soldiers. Before long, every Israeli believed in his country's imminent annihilation under a hail of Arab-Nazi missiles. The Israelis' very understandable anti-German feeling was exacerbated, and Ben Gurion's friendly policy towards Germany was violently attacked. Ben Gurion was greatly embarrassed by the effects of his Intelligence Service's excess of zeal. He found himself opposed by Golda Meir, who was emotionally irreconcilable to a policy of friendship with the Germans. The head of the secret services was obliged to resign.

Ben Gurion then made the fatal mistake of providing the critics of his autocratic tendencies with a focal point of attack. This focal point was the sombre Lavon affair. Lavon, a former Minister of Defence and the sworn enemy of Dayan and Peres, and an influential member of the Mapai, had been convicted by his peers in 1954 of being responsible for an adventurist operation conducted by Israeli secret agents in Egypt, the objects and result of which have been described in an earlier chapter. He felt himself to be the victim of army machinations to place on his shoulders a responsibility which ought properly to have been assigned to certain highly placed officers in the Intelligence Service, perhaps to Peres himself. He felt that the oath of secrecy with regard to military operations had been used to prevent him from vindicating himself. He had since become General Secretary of the Histadruth, but still chafed at the bit, impatient for the day of his revenge. In October 1960 he demanded to be rehabilitated, and made allegations concerning the Army Intelligence services before several parliamentary commissions. Despite Ben Gurion's opposition, the government appointed a special commission of seven members to look into the secret dossiers of the affair. The commission exculpated Lavon. Ben Gurion was furious. He declared war on Lavon, and applied blackmail by threatening to resign. In February 1961 the Central Committee of the Mapai, rather than lose its leader, dismissed Lavon from the General Secretaryship of the Histadruth. But Lavon had attracted great popularity as the victim of the Prime Minister's authoritarianism; Ben Gurion was abandoned by his closest friends; the secret machinations of military cliques, the close extra-parliamentary connections between the Prime Minister and his favourites, who were quite beyond democratic control, were publicly denounced.

Ben Gurion's stiff-necked behaviour over the Lavon affair did him a profound disservice. It was everywhere seen as a sign of senility, superimposed on the old man's well recognized authoritarianism. In the spring of 1963 his panic at the still-born pact between Egypt, Syria and Iraq and his appeal for help to the big powers, who were justifiably sceptical of the imminence of any newfound Arab unity, caused his international stock to fall as well.

He was aware of the general hostility surrounding him, knew that he was considered 'past it', that many thought him incapable. On 16 June 1963 he resigned and retired to the *kibbutz* of Sde Boker. He probably hoped that his revenge would soon come. Israel would realize he was indispensable and recall him.

He was succeeded by Levi Eshkol. Eshkol was a man of much less brilliance, hesitant, a poor talker, but a good organizer, realistic, affable and easy-going. Of course he was a convinced Zionist, a member of the Mapai party machine. However, he was by temperament little inclined to military adventure, and he sensed the nation's weariness with the military burden and its small enthusiasm for periodic mobilization. It was in all conscience a strange nation which he represented. Hardly yet formed into a coherent whole, it was profoundly divided, chauvinistic and racialist from the Zionist ideology drummed into it in schools, in the army, in the party organizations, encouraged by reading the bellicose texts of the Old Testament and greatly heightened by the constant hostility of Israel's neighbours. But as soon as a relative relaxation of tension permitted, it was immediately ready to plunge into its internal quarrels, to clamour for reforms, to demobilize. It was largely composed of great numbers of Jews from the Arab countries, who had come to Israel not in the pursuit of any ideological dream, but quite simply because there did not seem to be anywhere else for them to go. How many even of the European Jews had made a practical rather than a spiritual choice, and had simply taken the path mapped out for them by the Zionists? A story told about Golda Meir by one of her friends, an American Zionist, is revealing. The story concerns an incident which occurred during a tour of inspection when she was Minister of Labour.

Once on an inspection trip to a recently completed housing development, Golda was surrounded by disgruntled immigrants from Eastern Europe, who, disdaining preliminary courtesies, besieged her with angry complaints about the houses, the climate, the scarcity of work for professionals and the neighbours. They had expected an easier life. The small four-room cottages assigned each family were unfurnished except for essentials; the plot of land around each house was bare; a hot sun beat down on the treeless, sandy road; and appropriate employment was hard to find. Golda, proud of the well-designed houses with running water, electricity and good plumbing given to destitute immigrants for a few dollars a month, and aware of what it had cost to transport and settle these newcomers, reminded one of the impatient women that flowers and vegetables had to be planted. Why had she come to Israel? 'Because I was afraid to stay in Poland. I don't care about Zionism,' the woman answered unblinkingly. The husband nodded in agreement.

'Not one word of gratitude,' said Golda bitterly to a companion as she left.*

Thus the nation's Zionist consciousness tended to abate the moment there was a let-up in tension. This filled the militant clique with fury, as they saw in it a slide towards the abyss. But Eshkol, without abandoning the fundamental principles of the movement, responded to the pacific urge to demobilize and explored the possibility of an alternative

* Marie Syrkin, *Golda Meir: Woman with a Cause*, London, Gollancz, 1964, p. 264.

to the activist sabre-rattling foreign policy of his predecessor. He thus inclined towards Sharett's old policy, and going further back still, to the policy of those who had hoped for a conciliatory attitude towards the Arabs. He was led therefore to seek ways of avoiding an arms race, to have recourse to the U.N. instead of despising it, to move towards non-alignment by disengaging himself from exclusive American support and making tentative advances to the Soviet bloc. At all events, he announced his intention of subordinating the military to the civil power and of placing restrictions on military reprisal actions against Israel's neighbours. He caused a stir by the changes he made in his cabinet, refusing to take Dayan or Peres into the Ministry of Defence.

The awkward problem which threatened to become a major cause of conflict was the question of the diversion of the waters of the River Jordan. As is well known, a large area of Palestine is near-desert. For a long time, a number of schemes had existed to use the water from the River Jordan for irrigation. A large part of this water originated from tributaries of the Jordan flowing through Syria and Lebanon. The main benefits of the proposed irrigation would accrue to Israel and Jordan. Ideally, an agreement between all four countries would have been necessary to arrive at an effective and equitable scheme. The political situation excluded such an agreement. As we have seen, the American Main-Johnston plan failed in 1955 because of Dulles. Fresh approaches in 1957 to get the plan put back on to the agenda proved futile. Jordan then obtained United States aid for a limited irrigation scheme using mainly water from the Yarmuk, a tributary of the Jordan. Israel then also decided to carry out a national irrigation plan, which would divert water from the Upper Jordan to the Negev Desert, which, said the Israelis, could then accommodate a further four million immigrants. This aroused great consternation among the Arabs. Jordan immediately feared a diminution in the river's volume and a proportionate rise in the saline content, which could have catastrophic effects on Jordan's arable land. Syria had similar fears for Lake Tiberias. The plan was announced at the end of 1959. The Arab countries then began a series of conferences to find a way of hindering its application or decide on effective retaliation. There was talk of diverting the headwaters of the Jordan flowing through Syrian and Lebanese territory. This proved difficult to implement and might not even be very effective. Israel replied with counter-threats in the time-honoured aggressive militant style. Officiously one paper stated: 'An attempt to divert the sources of the Jordan in Syria and the Lebanon will not be playing merely with water, but also with fire.'*

The first phase of the Israeli project was due for completion in 1964. For many years the Arab countries had made violent threats in their habitual style against the Israeli project, each outbidding the other in an attempt to put their neighbours in a difficult position. The impossibility of doing anything positive at once often led to conditional threats: 'Just wait and see what will happen when Israel acts.' The day of reckoning was now near.

In December 1959 Kassem had hit upon the idea of setting up a Palestine government, on the pattern of the Algerian G.P.R.A. His intention was to embarrass Egypt and Jordan, both of whom occupied portions of Mandate Palestine, rather than to attack Israel. The two Arab states were very well aware of this, and had reacted violently, accusing Kassem, naturally, of providing grist for Israel's mill. Nasser called him a criminal and a madman, alleging that this 'base manoeuvre' had been carried out 'on the orders of his Zionist, imperialist and Communist masters'. But the idea nevertheless gained ground, because it met a real need felt by the Palestinians, both those who had fled from the territory now occupied by the State of Israel and those remaining on the West Bank of the Jordan, since annexed by the Hashemite Kingdom of Jordan. The Palestinians were very mixed in their social structure, level of culture and political attitudes. Those who had remained on the West Bank or emigrated into Transjordan formed the most dynamic and progressive element in the Hashemite Kingdom of Jordan. The majority of them were opposed to Hussein's pro-Western policy, and could easily have enforced their own point of view – since they outnumbered the indigenous Jordanian population – were it not for the Bedouin tribes supporting the king. The refugees concentrated in the U.N.R.W.A. camps continued to chew over their nation's wrongs in bitterness and vengefulness. The most enterprising of them, or those most favoured by fortune, had succeeded in integrating in the various Arab countries, or at least in finding work. In many places they had settled in groups which behaved like a minority elite. Some had made fantastic fortunes. The intellectuals and militant trade unionists, full of ardour for the political and social struggle, were drawn from among them. But the old semi-tribal structure persisted – especially in the camps – dominated by village notables. All these groups felt themselves united by a common destiny which distinguished them from the Arabs of other countries. Together with their Arab brothers and

* *Israel Digest*, 6 January 1960, quoted by the *New York Times*, 16 January 1960, p. 7.

cousins inside Israel, they formed a torn and scattered national community. Their songs and poems made constant reference to 'the return' in tones which strikingly recalled the nostalgic songs of the Promised Land sung by the exiled Jews of old.

Kassem gradually developed the idea of the so-called Palestinian entity. He launched a Palestinian army, formed of a few volunteers who paraded in Baghdad, and created Palestinian passports. The other Arab countries were not to be outdone. Hussein, who was directly threatened by this manoeuvre, hastily convened a Congress, in May 1960, at which the Palestinians of Jordan reaffirmed their loyalty to his kingdom. Nasser created a radio station, the Voice of Palestine, in Cairo (October 1960). He then consolidated Egyptian rule in the Gaza Strip, giving it a constitution and a governor-general nominated by Egypt (March 1962). Hussein announced a chimerical plan for a solution. Syria called for an Arab military conference (December 1962) and Iraq demanded separate Palestinian representation at the Arab League (September 1963). All these moves were primarily directed towards the final elimination of the ghostly Palestinian Government in Exile, formed in 1948 by the Council of the League and consisting largely of followers of the former Mufti of Jerusalem, Haj Amin al Husseini, since widely discredited. Ahmed Shukairy, a Palestinian who had supporters among the Palestinian notables and had won friends in several Arab countries (especially Saudi Arabia), now came to the fore. He had previously been Deputy General Secretary of the Arab League. He had also been the Saudi Arabian Minister of State for Palestinian Affairs. In September 1963 he was appointed to sit on the Political Committee of the Arab League as official Palestinian delegate, despite Hussein's protests. At the same time the League, pressed to 'do something', called for a conference of Arab Chiefs of Staff to study what riposte to make to Israel's diversion of the waters of the River Jordan.

One man felt especially endangered by all this activity, which arose from the necessity to appear to respond to Arab expectations with regard to Palestine, thus threatening to detonate the whole explosive situation. This man was Nasser. He had for a long time advocated patience, bringing forward a convincing historical argument, the example of the Crusades. The Crusader Kingdoms had also, in their time, been a bridgehead of the Western World on Oriental territory. They had finally been eliminated after two hundred years. Israel would finish up the same way. There was no call for haste. Nasser was well aware of the weakness of the Arab armies, and their lack of coordination. His own army was fully occupied in the Yemen, bogged down in difficult terrain. He had his work cut out to keep the Egyptian economy from complete collapse, let alone achieve progress.

He was continually accused by his Arab rivals of being perfectly content with the cordon of U.N. troops which insulated him from Israel, while they were in daily confrontation with the Jewish state through numerous border incidents. He was afraid of the stigma of passivity, which would greatly harm Egyptian prestige and influence, but even more afraid of being dragged by irresponsible elements into an unequal contest with the powerful Israeli army under extremely unfavourable conditions. In June 1962 Akram Hourani, the dissident Ba'athist leader, let loose a broadside aimed at the Egyptian ruler, among others: all the Arab governments, with the exception of Syria, had accepted the Johnston plan for the irrigation of the Jordan valley in concert with Israel in 1955, and in 1959 Nasser had rejected a Syrian proposal for military intervention to prevent diversion of the Jordan waters.

Faced with this threat to his position, Nasser put out a clear warning. On 17 December 1963 an Egyptian journalist with official connections accused the Jordanians, Syrians and Saudi Arabians of trying to push Egypt into a hornets' nest, and of wanting to stab her in the back by making her attack Israel at an inopportune moment while standing aside themselves. 'The U.A.R.,' he declared, 'is not going to embark on any adventures. The U.A.R. will not let itself be pushed into a battle with Israel before the attainment of unity among all the Arab countries.'* This article provoked violent reactions in the countries concerned. Meanwhile Nasser brought off a great political stroke. In the course of a speech made at Port Said on 23 December he proposed that all the Arab states, so disunited and suspicious of one another, should come together in a summit conference to discuss what measures they should take on the question of the diversion of the waters of the Jordan. From 13 to 17 January 1964 all the Arab sovereigns and heads of state met in Cairo. General reconciliation was the order of the day. Differences were ironed out, or more frequently shelved. A united military command was created, under a high-ranking Egyptian officer. The 'Palestinian entity was to express the wishes of the Palestinians but would not take the form of a government and would have no constitutional authority over the Palestinians'.

The euphoria was great. Everyone went away contented. The danger felt by each of being driven too far by the game of chicken forced on

* Malcolm Kerr, *The Arab Cold War 1958–64*, Oxford University Press 1965, p. 131.

him by his neighbours was removed. Nasser was able to control and canalize Syrian turbulence. Hussein was able to limit the infringement of Jordanian authority represented by all the autonomous activities of the Palestinians. More generally, on the level of inter-Arab relations, each realized how futile their internecine struggles were. Verbal broadsides could shake a regime, but they could not overthrow it.

All the back-slapping and embracing in Cairo seemed to herald the opening of a new era. Nasser especially hoped that the peace which he desperately needed was now assured for some considerable time at any rate. Hussein likewise hoped for a long period of peace, and the Syrians were resigned to it. In Israel itself, Eshkol showed signs of adopting a less aggressive policy than his predecessor. Nonetheless, a chain of events, aided by the partisans of confrontation in both camps, was to bring this wise decision to nought, and ultimately, less than three and a half years later, to lead to war.

6
The Arab Circle and the World at Large

In his *Philosophy of the Revolution*, Nasser expresses with a great deal of passion and sincerity some of the ideas, doubtless not very original, which had come to guide his political conscience. Egypt was bound by the restrictions of time and space; her policy could not be determined as though she were still in the tenth century (this would appear to be a critical reference to the programme of the Muslim Brotherhood). Moreover, isolationism was futile. Every country is affected by what goes on beyond its frontiers and must inevitably take account of it,

> to find the source of the currents which influence it, how it can live with others, how ..., and how ... And no state can escape trying to determine its status within its living space, and trying to see what it can do in that space, and what is its field of activities and its positive role in this troubled world.
>
> Sometimes I sit in my study reflecting on the subject, asking myself: What is our positive role in this troubled world, and where is the place in which we should fulfil that role?*

And he discovers three circles, three zones to which Egypt must necessarily devote all her energies. Egypt cannot ignore the existence of an Arab zone surrounding it, the history and interests of which are closely bound up with her own. Nor can she ignore Africa, in which destiny has located her, nor the Muslim world, to which she is bound not only by religion but by a common history.

This clear view of Egypt's geopolitical situation (inspired, moreover, by the Churchillian idea of the three circles within which British policy was conducted) had been deliberately distorted by Anglo-French propaganda on the eve of the Suez expedition in order to justify that venture. The analysis supposedly revealed a desire to dominate the three zones in question, a desire which gave credibility to the famous equation Nasser = Hitler. Of course Nasser sought to make Egyptian influence as strong as possible in the zones in which his country was situated. But this is the programme of every political leader, and it had nothing in common with a programme of military conquest. Nasser

* Gamal Abdul Nasser, *Egypt's Liberation; The Philosophy of Revolution*, op. cit., pp. 84–5.

was enough of a realist not to harbour any grandiose and ridiculous plan of conquering the Muslim world as far as Indonesia, and Africa into the bargain! Even within the Arab world, he had had reservations over the union with Syria. In the Yemen his troops were supporting a friendly regime against the reinforcement and extension of Saudi domination (and of the American influence behind Saudi Arabia) over the entire Arabian Peninsula. It is of course true that once these regions fell into its hands the ruling Egyptian military caste exercised an unbridled authoritarianism there. It need not be supposed either that Egypt's political and military services, both public and secret, did not try to exert the maximum influence in every field of operations, sometimes using highly unsavoury methods. But this is some way from Hitler's project to enslave, in the strongest possible sense of that word, an entire continent.

At all events the Arab zone existed and Egypt could not avoid being interested in it. I have so far been referring only to Egypt and that part of the Arab countries of Asia known as the Fertile Crescent: Iraq, Syria, Lebanon, Palestine, Jordan. These are indeed the only countries directly concerned with the challenge of Israel. But the other Arab countries, especially those recently independent and hence able for the first time to decide their own policy, could not disregard the problem. The differences between the Arab states were great and their peoples had evolved in different ways; they each had their own special problems and could regard the other Arab peoples as to some extent and in a certain sense foreigners. They despised some, joked about others, while others they feared. Nevertheless, over and above Tunisians, Egyptians, Iraqis, they were all Arabs. They were all bound together by the strands of a common history and culture, and any injury done to one people from outside was sharply resented by the others.

Governments may sometimes have been contemptuous of this sentiment. But beyond a certain limit, they could not ignore it without endangering the basis of consent, however passive, on which even the most tyrannical state must in the last resort rely.

It will be enough to cast a brief glance at those Arab states on the periphery of the circle which nonetheless frequently had an important part to play in Arab affairs, and to see what had happened to them since their last mention in these pages.

Of these peripheral states, Saudi Arabia is the nearest to the central stage of the drama. This country, the birthplace of Arabism, had been transformed by the oil-extraction industry, which began its operations in 1938. The patriarchal monarchs who ruled over this vast territory, peopled by nomadic tribesmen and their camels, suddenly found themselves the owners of immense fortunes. The exploitation of the oil deposits which brought them their wealth depended on the Aramco company, a giant American trust. In 1965 Aramco paid the Saudi government 618.4 million dollars in taxes and royalties. It has been estimated that in recent years these have accounted for 90 per cent of the national budget. This has made it possible to keep up a relatively powerful army, to subsidize tribal chiefs, and to maintain the hundreds of aristocrats spawned by this polygamous society in unheard-of luxury. Oil revenues have had the usual effect of creating a closed economy, sealed off from the general economic development of the country. The archaic social structure persists. Of course a merchant class has begun to emerge, hoping for some degree of progress, which would like to make its voice heard in the councils of state. It is also attracted to Arab nationalism. King Saud, who ruled from 1953 to 1964, and his brother Feisal have been engaged in a long tussle for power, each playing a complicated game of internal and external alliances made and broken. The constant factors in Saudi politics are a vigilant conservatism more or less aware of the necessity for a minimum of reforms, the American alliance, and hostility to the revolutionary movements gaining ground elsewhere in the Arab world, with interludes of reconciliation. Israel is only of secondary interest to the Saudi monarchs. They recognize a duty to support the Arab cause, firstly because of the sympathies of their people plus some small national feeling of their own, and secondly because of Islam – they are both Guardians of the Holy Cities and leaders of a puritanical and extremist Muslim sect, the Wahhabi. But their contributions to the Arab cause are circumspect, and always made with an eye to their other interests. They prefer to give money rather than send troops, which they might have need of to maintain order at home and which, more importantly, might become contaminated by dangerous ideas. Their heart is Arab, no doubt; but their purse is American.

In the Persian Gulf and in a series of little emirates protected by Great Britain, oil resources have poured sudden immense fortunes into the pockets of a few Bedouin sheikhs. The unrest of the nascent middle class and of the population at large has led them to espouse Arab nationalist principles and follow with enthusiasm the tune called by Cairo and Baghdad. Kuwait has drawn particular benefit from the treasure trove of oil – the sovereign has reserve deposits of more than 200 million pounds sterling in British banks. The other Arab countries have suggested that this wealth might be used for other purposes than ensuring unheard-of prosperity for a tiny desert sheikhdom (6,000 square miles, 330,000 inhabitants; in 1963 the national income was 3,000 dollars per head). Kassem's clumsy and unsuccessful attempt to annex it has already been mentioned. As a contribution, Kuwait created a Development Fund for the Arab countries which has issued some considerable loans. But many Arab rulers coveted this monopoly of wealth, dreaming of the great things they might accomplish with its help.

In the south, the Yemen has for centuries been the most archaic state in the Peninsula, perhaps in the world. The revolution of 26 September 1962 was a great surprise to the Arab world, and provoked foreign intervention, as we have seen. Since that time, Royalist tribesmen supported by Saudi Arabia, Britain, the Americans and a number of neo-Fascist European mercenaries have held out against the Republic, supported for its part by the Egyptians. Egyptian aid has since turned into military occupation, partly through force of circumstances and partly because of the authoritarian bent of the Egyptian military caste, and was borne very grudgingly by the Republicans themselves. Developments in the Yemen recall the history of the 'sister republics' created by the armies of the First French Republic. From being a straight fight, the struggle has developed into a three-cornered contest, the Egyptians having fallen foul of their Republican protégés. The Egyptian troops have become bogged down in this mountainous and difficult country, with its tribal social structure of extreme primitiveness, which is only now beginning to show some signs of detribalization and the development of an urban society, including merchants and nationalist intellectuals. Nasser attempted to effect an honourable withdrawal from this hornets' nest, but his negotiations with Saudi Arabia stumbled on all kinds of obstacles. The stalemate still persisted in May 1967, and the only significant result appeared to be a worsening of relations between Nasser and the United States.

South of the Yemen, on the southern coast of the Arabian Peninsula, lay the enclave of Aden (eighty square miles), which had been in British hands since 1839, and the British protectorates of South Arabia (75,000 square miles). Historically and culturally, these territories are part of the Yemen, which has never ceased to lay claim to them. Aden, a large commercial centre, possessed ardently nationalist middle and working classes. The rest of the territory had a thoroughly primitive tribal structure dominated by twenty-six sultans, emirs and sheikhs. In the face of the rising nationalism of the region, manifested in a wave of terrorist outrages, the British created a Federation of the South Arabian emirates in February 1959 in order to appease the nationalists while at the same time retaining control of the area. The union effected between Aden and the Federation in June 1963 was designed to harness the progressive and turbulent forces in Aden to conservative structures which Britain could easily control. The protests were massive and violent, especially in the Adeni trade union movement, which was intensely politically conscious. Guerrilla warfare broke out in the sultanates themselves. Great Britain announced that independence would be granted to the Federation from 1968.* No one believed in her altruism. At all events, the Egyptians were encouraged to remain in the Yemen, if only to supervise the liquidation of the British legacy in the area. The violence of the events in South Arabia kept alive the flame of the struggle against Western imperialism throughout the Arab world.

To the south of Egypt the Sudan, which had nominally been an Anglo-Egyptian condominium but in practice a British colony, became independent on 1 January 1956. The country suffers from the very severe problem presented by the coexistence of the Arabized, Muslim north (with about seven million inhabitants) and the south, inhabited by about six million Nilotic Negroes, either animists or converts to Christianity. The Negroes of the south have for many years been oppressed by the Arabs of the north, for whom they provided the principal source of slaves. The southerners feared that independence would bring northern domination, and there has certainly been a considerable tendency towards Arabization and Islamization. From the beginning, bloody mutinies broke out in the south, denounced by the north as provoked by British imperialists with the aid of the European Christian missions. Their suppression by the north was no less bloody. Leftwing elements tried to disarm the opposition between north and south by demanding an autonomous regime for the south, and this was even accepted in principle. Civil war continued, however, and was frequently conducted with frightful cruelty. Sudanese governments, whether progressive or reactionary, have been too overwhelmed by these problems to be able to devote much attention to the far-off conflict over Palestine. They have generally assumed the role of mediators, preaching unity among the Arab ranks. Their policy towards the Western powers has oscillated considerably, according to the vagaries of internal politics.

To the west of Egypt lies Libya, a largely desert country, which had lived on Anglo-American aid (plus royalties on recently discovered oil) after the departure of the Italians. Both powers possessed strategic

* In fact she evacuated South Arabia in November 1967.

bases there, including the American base of Wheelus Field which dominated the whole of the Eastern Mediterranean. The patriarchal and conservative governments of King Idris, head of the religious brotherhood of the Senussi, had made efforts to limit the influence of the nationalist movement. The movement, which looked to Egypt for sympathy and guidance, had of course suffered oppression, but the King had also tried to disarm it by making minor concessions.

The Arab region which has undergone the most striking transformation in recent years is the Maghreb. This was divided into three countries, one (Algeria) under the direct rule of France, the other two administered under the thinly disguised form of colonialism known as the protectorate (Morocco and Tunisia). The force of the nationalist movement constrained France to grant true independence to Tunisia in 1955 and to Morocco in 1956. The long Algerian war, begun on 1 November 1954, ended in July 1962 with the granting of independence to the Republic of Algeria. Solidarity in the struggle against French colonialism could not disguise the differences and tensions between the three countries. In Morocco and Tunisia the fight for national independence was led by the middle class. But in Morocco the leadership of the movement was partly taken over by the large semi-feudal landed proprietors, who rallied to it late in the day. The movement was broadly based on small traders, craftsmen, clerks and civil servants, with a few manual workers. In Algeria, the existence of an urban proletariat in close contact with the French working class through the large numbers of immigrant workers in France created a different situation. This factor, together with the brutal break with traditional values which colonization had imposed throughout large sectors of the social structure, plus the duration and bitterness of the war and the sacrifices which it entailed, produced in the victors a more revolutionary and socialistic attitude. Ahmed Ben Bella made strenuous though not always well-directed efforts to steer Algeria's political development into radical and socialist channels. However, these efforts were largely thwarted by the resistance of a conservative middle class, traditionalist and suspicious of rapid social and cultural change. Colonel Hwari Boumedienne's military coup (19 June 1965) relied to a large extent on these classes for support. Nonetheless, Algerian politics have remained more radical in general tone than those of the two neighbouring states. The close economic links between independent Algeria and Gaullist France favoured the development of a policy of non-commitment on the part of Algeria towards American hegemony.

The three countries of the Maghreb are a long way from Israel.

Their ruling elites have frequently attempted to take up a less intransigent position towards the problem than the Middle-Eastern Arabs. They have been the bridge-builders, they have been the ones to make advances to Israel in the hopes of encountering a more flexible attitude, they have tried to establish contacts with more liberal or Left-wing Israelis. This did not mean that they renounced the cause of Arab solidarity. In Morocco, the increasingly direct pro-American bias has produced a generally passive attitude to Palestinian affairs, despite some concessions, more verbal than concrete, made to the Islamic Right. The Tunisian leader Bourguiba, the most outspokenly pro-Western and secularist Arab ruler, has boldly proposed an Arab strategy which would imply as a starting point some recognition of the Israeli *fait accompli*. As a result, he aroused terrible fury in the East. By contrast, Algerian revolutionarism has been all the more intransigent on the Israeli question for the very reason that the problem was a distant one and presented no danger to the Algerian middle class. Added to this, a complex of 'Western' superiority over the incompetence of the Middle-Eastern Arabs has arisen.

Just for the record, some mention should be made of the largely Arab and very archaic country of Mauretania at the far Western end of the Arab world. Her role in the Israeli-Arab conflict has been limited to providing a point of discord which exacerbated the rivalries between the three states of the Maghreb and made unity of action even less likely.

We may now attempt to summarize the major tendencies emerging from this brief outline. Throughout the Arab world there exists, either suppressed, tolerated or triumphant, a radical nationalist movement, which favours socialistic forms of economic organization in internal policy, and alliance with the group of socialist countries in foreign affairs. This movement has come to hold these positions through the general desire of the masses for independence, through unhappy memories of the colonial period, and through the common desire for a rise in the standard of living, which, like true independence, only seems possible through the medium of autonomous industrialization. Experience seems to show that autonomous industrialization is imperilled by the operation of free enterprise, which tends to result in American hegemony. The same factors which induce the Arab masses to support a radical nationalist ideology have produced intransigence towards Israel, a colony imposed on them by the industrially advanced West. Even the most pro-Western Arab rulers have been unable to do more than remain passive in the face of this prevailing attitude. They have not been able to repudiate it. Moreover, concessions to popular feeling on the Palestine question are easier to make and more agreeable – being mainly verbal and symbolic – than decisions to institute economic change, to revise internal policy, or review their fundamental alignments with the major powers. Thus Arab hostility to Israel is not an artificial phenomenon, a cheap cement for plastering over deep cracks. It is a necessity arising from the nature of the choices open to the Arabs in the modern world, at least as long as Israel appears as a bridgehead of the West in the midst of a profoundly committed area of the under-developed world.

Beyond the Arab world and containing it lies the world of Islam. By this is meant all the countries in which Islam is or was the dominant religion. Basically, these include Turkey, Iran, Afghanistan, Pakistan, Malaysia, Indonesia and part of Black Africa. We may exclude from consideration the Mohammedan Republics of Soviet Central Asia, whose destinies are in general inseparable from those of the Soviet Union, and whose politics are controlled by Moscow; and Albania, where the Communist regime has instituted a thorough-going programme of de-Islamization, and where in any case any feeling of solidarity there might be with other Islamic countries finds no political expression whatsoever.

It is often thought in Europe that the Muslim world is blessed with a strong sense of unity inspired by community of religious faith. This is, to say the very least, an exaggeration. In fact the Muslim world is hardly any more united than Christendom. Each country is faced with its own special problems, which arise from its geopolitical situation, and each tries to find its own solution in accordance with a number of special factors principally conditioned by the internal economic and social level of development. Moreover, even from the Islamic standpoint positions are different. The state religion of Iran is Shiism, which the other sectors of Islam regard as a heresy. Turkey, despite strong pressures in the opposite direction, has remained largely faithful to the 'anti-clerical' (but not anti-religious) secularism of Kemal Ataturk. In contrast, Pakistan deliberately sets out to be a Muslim state, a theocracy obedient to the Religious Law, although the reality is very far removed from this ideal.

Of course strong feelings of solidarity do exist between Muslims the world over. It is not the content of the Muslim faith which produces this feeling, for real faith in the religious message of Mohammed is everywhere in decline, both quantitatively and qualitatively. It is rather the feeling of belonging to a community extending over a vast area of the earth, held in contempt by the European-American world and the victim of discrimination and persecution. On the other side, there is a feeling of superiority towards infidels and 'barbarians'. This by no means excludes political and emotional attachments to Afro-Asian and Latin American countries which are, to some extent at least, in the same situation.

The Arab countries' political opposition to Israel grasped at every weapon that lay to hand. It proved especially useful to exploit the old religious antagonism between Islam and Judaism, and to quote Mohammed's military engagements with the Jews of Medina celebrated in many verses of the Koran. This kind of appeal was bound to strike a chord in the Arab countries. The Arabs then used it to try to gain the support of other Muslim countries for their anti-Israel policy. Pakistan felt obliged to support them, in conformity with her Muslim ideology, but Iran and Turkey have been much more reluctant, and for a long time maintained good relations with Israel.

The appeal to Mohammedan brotherhood is, for politicians, a political stratagem which has been used on frequent occasions to obtain specific political ends. As we have seen, Nasser did not hesitate to use it to attack his hated competitors, the secularist Ba'ath in Syria, and Kassem, allied to the infidel Communists. The stratagem had its dangers, however, since it appealed to emotions which could be most effectively exploited against Nasser by the religious fanatics of the Muslim Brotherhood. The device has most commonly been used by the reactionary regimes to over-trump revolutionary pan-Arabism, by an appeal to conservative loyalty to Islam. This Islamic loyalty was a feature of the member-countries of C.E.N.T.O., the pro-Atlantic alliance between Turkey, Iran and Pakistan. Such attempts have not, however, met with very wide success. The Arab masses, especially outside the towns, are certainly faithful to Islam, which to them means primarily traditional morality and loyalty towards a threatened identity. But they are well able to make the distinction between their faith and an allegiance to political and social objectives which have nothing to offer them and consequently do not tempt them. It should be added that the version of Islam which was often offered to them was generally highly suspect. As an instance of this, we can quote the Islamic alliance established between the Shah of Persia, a Shiite monarch and hence a heretic from the point of view of the majority of Muslims; the King of Saudi Arabia, who also belongs to a sect which, although orthodox Muslim, is not representative of the main body of Islam; Hassan II,

King of Morocco, whose assiduous respect for the ritual ceremonies has not erased the memory of his somewhat irreligious youth; and Habib Bourguiba, the very spokesman of secularism, contemptuous of ancient rites, whose Muslim faith can hardly be considered as his guiding inspiration. But if Islam is put forward as a flag under which a people can struggle to vindicate its rights, a doctrine which justifies and sanctifies this struggle, it recovers all its emotional power to mobilize hearts and souls.

Interested in the struggle against European and American domination in all its forms, Arab countries in Africa have joined the Organization for African Unity and have participated in all its efforts to coordinate the African countries' struggle to achieve autonomy. Common stands have been taken by some Arab countries with some of the countries of Black Africa when faced with similar situations. However, a hidden cleavage, never expressed, lies beneath the surface of Afro-Arab relations, which may help to explain some attitudes. The peoples of Black Africa have unhappy memories of the Arabs. Arab traders were long the main organizers of the slave traffic, delivering slaves both to the Islamic world and to white slave-masters. Not so very long ago Arabs living in Negro territories felt more community with the Europeans there than with these 'savages'. This was before Europe began to treat them as 'savages' as well. These unpleasant memories are attenuated but not altogether erased among the numerous Negroes converted to Islam. The civil war in the southern Sudan kept them alive. Distrust of the Arabs is compensated, to a greater or lesser degree depending on circumstances, by community of interest and attitude towards the European-American peoples. At the same time, the Arabs do not command the respect which is always due to the powerful. They are not the real masters.

The Arabs, for their part, still tend to regard themselves as superior to the black man. Revolutionary intellectuals are usually able to overcome these feelings, and statesmen to dissimulate them. There are still many who make their attitude felt, or even express it openly. These imprecise feelings and emotional responses do not, on the whole, play any significant part in the political decisions taken by members of one or other of the two ethnic groups. Nonetheless, one cannot be certain that they do not from time to time influence political attitudes.

Israel's attempts to exert influence on Black Africa have already been mentioned. These attempts have been successful to a certain extent. The African states have on the whole welcomed Israeli technical aid, especially agricultural aid, where Israeli experience has proved very useful to black communities. Students of agriculture have been sent to Israel on special courses. Israeli officials have been well received in African countries, as was Golda Meir on her various good-will missions. The form of micro-socialism represented by the Israeli *kibbutzim* was especially attractive to those states which could not or would not take a resolutely pro-socialist stand in the world line-up of the powers, but still needed a fashionable socialist label in order to attract sympathy and support. In 1960 Ben Gurion rather cunningly asked for United States credits to finance aid to the Africans, arguing that Israel would thus be contributing to the prevention of Communism in Africa. He also asked for a free hand in the administration of these funds. But all these strenuous efforts were to be, in the end, almost nullified by the practical cooperation between Israel and South Africa, and by all the events which seemed to confirm the Arab denunciations of Israel as a detachment of Western imperialism.

The Third World as a whole shared the embarrassment of the Africans with regard to the Israeli-Arab conflict. The Arabs' struggle against the imperialism of Europe had all their sympathy. Few could at first bring themselves to regard Israel as *only* an outpost of imperialism, as the Arabs claimed. In contrast to the Europeans, the people of the Third World are not encumbered by the age-old vision of the Jews as an oppressed race by nature, which could never be anything but the victim of oppression. It was rather Israel's small size, her social structure and her inoffensiveness beyond the boundaries of the Middle East which made other countries hesitate to copy Arab intransigence. The fact that she is recognized by the U.N. and by the vast majority of the non-Arab states made the Arab refusal to recognize her appear unreasonable. To those countries and political movements most committed to the socialist or anti-imperialist road, the Arab states' anti-Israel campaigns looked like a diversion designed to distract their peoples from an intensification of the internal revolutionary struggle. Israeli disengagement from her imperialist connections still seemed possible. But, here too, one fact after another, with a cumulative effect, gradually seemed to confirm the analysis made by the Arabs, and, more or less reluctantly, many countries of the Third World came to support their attitude.

However, in a world dominated by force, it is the powerful who deserve the most attention, and this means those states who dispose of considerable material force with which to impose their will. This does not mean that the power latent in the masses of other countries is quite without importance; merely that this form of power does not make itself felt on the world scale except in so far as it affects the decisions of the real powers, either by its support or by its resistance.

The world is dominated by the formidable power of the United States of America. Economically they far outstrip every rival, and are able to intervene anywhere with the enormous weight which wealth confers. Militarily, they possess armaments capable of annihilating the whole world in a matter of seconds. How do they use this power in their relations with the rest of the world and how does it affect the problem under consideration?

A spectre is haunting the Americans: the spectre of Communism. Communism, that demonic, protean, sophistic, elusive force, seems to them to be the very essence of evil. Such is the strange, malignant power of this monster that if it is given an inch of territory, the smallest part of a population, or even the tiniest concession in the soul of man, it quickly swallows all the rest. Unflagging vigilance is needed against such an enemy, readiness to act, to repel, to track down. Men and nations must be constantly prepared to resist the unaccountable temptations which this repellent phantom holds out. Communism is in truth the modern face of Satan.

In 1917 Satan acquired, through his foul machinations, a terrestrial base, the Soviet Union. He then subjugated and tortured the Russian people and the other races subject to the Russians. An American, Franklin Delano Roosevelt, attracted profound suspicion when he attempted to strike a bargain with this evil power – an attempt which was taken as a sure sign of derangement. He had thought it necessary to make this pact with the Devil in order to combat the monstrosity of Hitlerism, which he wrongly thought the greater evil. He had granted to Satan the power to oppress yet more peoples in Eastern Europe and had allowed him to acquire a dangerous influence in world affairs. Fortunately, Roosevelt died, having outlived his time. A true American, Harry S. Truman, then did his best to retrieve the sadly deteriorated situation, and to contain the monster until the time came to destroy it in its lair.

Of course this view of things was almost pure ideological myth. Behind it lay deeper, subconscious motives. Regrettably, however, the world is shaped by the delusions of the powerful.

From the beginning of the Cold War, the United States have been committed to the containment of revolutionary movements, always allegedly inspired by the U.S.S.R. and its diabolic nerve-centre, the

Kremlin. A military barrier had to be constructed around the U.S.S.R. and its satellites, ready to stifle any Soviet attempt to break out of its provisional limits. As has been remarked, the United States' efforts to enrol the Arabs in the coalition encircling the Communist world had in fact driven the Arab peoples, profoundly uninterested in the struggle for world mastery, into a sympathetic attitude towards the hated power.

The Americans found it difficult to distinguish between the movements and states in the Third World which for one reason or another entertained relations with the Enemy. They found it hard to determine which of a number of more or less revolutionary states, more or less rejecting capitalist hegemony both in the world and in their own country, could be saved and which could not. One certain sign of the unredeemable was any attack on major American interests; this damned the Latin American states of Cuba and Guatemala. Another criterion was quite simply membership of the international brotherhood of Communist Parties; this meant China was out. The two criteria were to some extent combined in the Philippines and in Vietnam, where an anti-imperialist movement under predominantly Communist leadership attacked a state which was practically an American colony.

Beyond these clear-cut cases, diagnosis was more difficult. It could even happen, as in the case of Titoist Yugoslavia, that a Communist state was encouraged to detach itself from the bloc, at that time still monolithic, and still keep its internal structure. Ideology, strategy and material interest combined in complex ways to formulate the judgement. Any measure of socialization was always suspect as undermining religion and free enterprise, and, more materially, as presenting an obstacle to the penetration of American capital. However, if all the other criteria were favourable, the Americans were always willing to understand that situations very different from those obtaining in the classical capitalist countries might demand different sorts of solutions. There was great understanding for the feelings of movements directed primarily against the interests of non-American imperialism – despite the fact that these were perforce the allies of the United States. The old American anti-colonialist ideology of the distant past would then be resurrected specially for the occasion.

This helps to explain the American attitude at the time of Suez. Ben Gurion had every reason to suppose, as did everybody else, that in the Eastern Mediterranean the Americans would leave the field clear for the free play of British and French policy. His agreement with the British and French ought therefore to have been sufficient protection from the reactions of the rest of the world. But the Americans were already heavily committed in the area – both in Greece and Turkey. Above all, they considered it their duty to safeguard the general interests of the anti-Communist struggle, even if this led them into conflict with their allies, blinded by their selfish imperialist interests into hasty and harmful policies. The Americans could be very perceptive of the blindness and folly of others. The British, French and Israelis threw themselves on Nasser's Egypt, hoping to overthrow Nasser by force. Nasser seemed to the Americans eminently recoverable for the Western cause. Of course the purchase of Czech arms and the nationalization of the Suez Canal had been regrettable gestures. It was recognized, however, that he had been forced into them by the attitude of the Western powers. He had been taught a serious lesson by the refusal to finance the Aswan High Dam. But he ought to have been left to digest the lesson, not pushed into a final break with the West. Above all, such behaviour was a self-condemnation before the whole Third World, proof that the imperialist bloc was unregenerate and still liable to resort to acts of brutal provocation on the nineteenth-century pattern. The French, British and Israelis had, by their action, compromised the chances of mobilizing the Arabs against the Communist menace, which the Americans still hoped to make clear to them. Despite his flirtation with the East, Nasser had never burnt his bridges to the Capitalist West, had not as yet resorted to socialist measures, and was by no means committed body and soul to the Eastern bloc. His sympathies lay with the neutralists, with Nehru, with Tito, and with Sukarno. The immorality of wishing to remain neutral between Good and Evil was deplored; but these were sensible people, and it was possible, the Americans hoped, to bring them to reason and attract them to the right side.

This train of events pushed the Nasser regime towards greater socialization and into closer relations with the Soviet Union. Nevertheless, Nasser made sure of keeping his independence of this bloc, and he kept up his relations with the Western capitalist world. Under the pressure of events, the American attitude began imperceptibly to change.

The socialist or socialistic countries slowly began to segregate, and the monolithic bloc of earlier days increasingly came to resemble a constellation of fairly independent units, each with its own interests, its own aspirations and its own policy. The U.S.S.R. began to exercise less and less control over their decisions. At the same time she made considerable strides in nuclear technology, and it became apparent that it would be impossible to attack her directly and inflict a decisive defeat without risking apocalyptic reprisals, tens of millions of American dead, even, possibly, total but mutual annihilation. The result might be an armistice in the Cold War. This is what happened, eventually, when the nuclear test-ban treaty was signed on 5 August 1963. But it was now known that the U.S.S.R. had her difficulties, in differing degrees, with socialist and even Communist states, principally China and Albania, to a lesser degree with Rumania, and still, of course, with Yugoslavia. She could not automatically protect them, and such protection as she gave would not always be effective, as was demonstrated by the trial of strength over Cuba in October 1962, and by her attitude to Vietnam.

From that time on, American policy towards the more or less socialistic nations of the Third World was given more room for manoeuvre, and at the same time became more determined. These countries' attitude towards the U.S.S.R. ceased to be a determining factor. Every movement which was in any way revolutionary might by its own dynamism represent a danger to American hegemony, and it now became possible to dispose of these movements without imperilling the world balance between the two super-powers. In October 1965 Indonesian army officers, supported as many believed by the C.I.A., overthrew Sukarno's regime, which was too prone to take socialistic attitudes and under which the Communists were acquiring too much weight. In April 1967 a similar alliance established a military dictatorship in Greece, to prevent the country from sliding towards the Left.

Nasser (not to speak of the Syrians) thus came to be classified among the irredeemables, or at any rate among those who were leading their country down a potentially dangerous road. Notwithstanding his preference for conciliation, his dislike of fanatical radicalism, and the presence in his government of notoriously pro-Western elements, he represented a danger despite himself. He had opted decisively for socialist solutions to internal problems, and had shown his hostility to Western interference in Arab affairs. In the Yemen he was in conflict with the Royalists, supported for their part by Saudi Arabia and, behind her, by the United States. Despite their mutual antagonism, not to say hatred, he supported Syrian policy in so far as it was anti-imperialist. In the Lebanon the Nasserites represented an alternative to the generally pro-Western attitudes of the commercial middle class and militant anti-Muslim elements in the Christian community. Nasser also supported Algeria's resistance to American economic hegemony, and maintained his hostility to the reactionary states throughout the Arab world, which were at the same time pro-American. He had to be got rid of, whatever his motivations. Israel did not fail to appreciate this hardening of the United States' attitude towards Nasser. This was an extremely important factor in the events of June 1967.

Of the United States' own allies, Great Britain and France had taken opposite directions. The Suez disaster put paid to all British pretensions to conduct a general independent Middle Eastern policy out of step with the policy of the United States. Great Britain now directed all her attentions to her oil interests in the Persian Gulf and to maintaining her political influence in East and South Arabia. In the Yemen her interests coincided with those of the United States, and here again Nasser was the common enemy. Obviously none of this gave her any cause to diverge from American policy, and other factors pressed her to pursue the same course in the broader field of world policy.

Israel's original attitude towards the British had been chilly. The memory of the Balfour Declaration, without which Israel could never have come into being, had long been effaced by the memory of the ill-will of British officials at the time of the Mandate, of the White Paper, of the brutality of the British army in the face of Jewish terrorism, and of Bevin's policy. This could be explained either by a deep-seated anti-Semitism, or by an infatuation for the Arabs brought on by the needs of Empire, or by both factors at once. At all events, most Israelis still thought of England as perfidious Albion. From 1958 on, Ben Gurion had followed a policy of *rapprochement* with Great Britain, making great play of the danger to British interests represented by 'revolutionary' Arab policies. This unfroze Anglo-Israeli relations, but not Israeli public opinion, which remained mistrustful. On the British side, it helped to create a pro-Israeli orientation, although still hesitant, and dependent on the attitude provoked by the various Arab policies towards the West. This attitude towards the Arabs was complex, discriminatory and fluctuating. In general it may be noted that no really major interest prevented Britain from following, in the main, the lead of her senior partner, the United States.

France pursued quite a different path. The Algerian war had provoked a wave of anti-Arab feeling among many Frenchmen. The presence of numerous Algerians and other North Africans in France forming a kind of sub-proletarian layer employed mainly in dirty, dangerous and unpleasant occupations had the kind of consequences one might expect. It is a not uncommon sociological phenomenon for a sector of the population which is placed in despicable conditions to be widely despised. Although the degree of Algerian assimilation in the

French population was relatively advanced, backwardness in catching up with French modes of living persisted and made them feel strangers. Competition from outsiders asking for little and being paid little aroused irritation in the French working class. The ill-defined but pervasive political temper and ideology of French society, strongly anti-racist in France itself at any rate, and frequently so even in the colonies, tended to succumb to a situation highly favourable to the development of racialism. It was resisted only by the liberal intellectuals, especially the Left-wing Christians and the members of the non-Communist Left, including some who left the party because of its passive attitude on the question. They embraced the Algerian cause with all the more enthusiasm in that their revolutionary ardour found little outlet in French politics themselves. They were gradually joined – though certainly without any great militancy – by elements of the Right and Centre, who were beginning to understand, as the Algerian campaign became more hopeless, the folly of wishing to maintain French domination for ever over an increasingly rebellious population. In contrast, the Socialist Party leadership did not dare to make peace and face a revolt by the French settlers in Algeria and other conservative elements; they used every conceivable Left-wing argument to justify the continuation of the struggle against the Algerian National Liberation Front. They even allied themselves with the nationalist Right in denouncing what they regarded as the root-causes of the whole problem, in the vain hope of gaining some easy victory outside Algeria. The origins of the Suez expedition lay in this attitude, which expressed itself in a general condemnation of Arab nationalism and of its figurehead, Nasser, as reactionary and even Fascist. The natural tendency of the Arab peoples to strive for a certain degree of political unity corresponding to the relative unity which existed on the social and cultural plane, was denounced as 'pan-Arabism', which had unpleasant overtones evoking the pan-Germanism and pan-Slavism of the nineteenth century (pan-Italianism was not mentioned) and had a reactionary ring. Clearly these attitudes only reinforced the anti-Arab feeling in France. From then on the alliance with Israel had a dual function: to provide military support in the East, and a justification to the liberal and Left-wing conscience. Support for a state widely accepted as socialist, support for the Jews whom Hitlerite persecution had turned into the living symbol of the minority oppressed by Fascism, all this lent the anti-Algerian faction a spurious but effective aura of militant anti-Fascism.

As usually happens, the capitulation to Algerian nationalism, so

wounding to the national pride and so harmful to the interests of a
large number of Frenchmen, could only be made acceptable by a Right-
wing government, or at least one which could not be accused of sacrificing the nation to some universalist ideology. This was the historic
role of Charles de Gaulle, who had already in a rather similar fashion
made the anti-Hitler alliance with Stalin and the French Communists
respectable in the eyes of the French bourgeoisie. Of course his personal
ambition also played its part. But once peace had been made in 1962,
the causes of conflict with Arab interests in general faded into in-
significance. For a man as detached from ideological and sentimental
enthusiasms as France's new master, the obvious policy was one of
strict neutrality in the Arab-Israel conflict, or rather of coming down
firmly on both sides. When the factors guiding his general policy led
de Gaulle in the direction of disengagement from the American bloc,
and towards a policy of support for the aspirations of the Third World,
he naturally became more favourably inclined to the Arab cause, without ever breaking with Israel. His followers, however, conservative
and nationalist and deeply imbued with the anti-Arab feeling of the
preceding period, did not relish their new role.

As for Federal Germany, her national interests and the violent anti-
Communist conservatism of her political leaders bound her to the
American band-wagon. Wishing to prove that she had broken radically
with Hitler Germany's brutal expansionism and bestial doctrines of
national purity, she was induced to make spectacular gestures of reparation to the persecuted Jews, whoever and wherever they might be.
This was the easiest, and in the long run the cheapest way of breaking
with the past. Moreover this method helped to disarm the ill-will of
the American Jewish community, a pressure-group with powerful influence on the policies of the world's dominant power. It was nonetheless necessary to maintain good relations with the Arabs, and this
sometimes led to difficulties. All these more or less contradictory needs
were classified in order of importance by reference to a compass-needle
which always pointed to Washington.

The preoccupations of the Communist states were not, in fact, at all
those attributed to them by the Americans and many others. Their
strategy was for many years wholly determined by the Russians of the
Soviet Union and by the Georgian who had paradoxically come to lead
them and incarnate them. Certainly the World Revolution was the
ultimate end prescribed by Communist ideology, and in his own way
Stalin believed in it. But very early on, while Lenin was still alive,

Stalin's solid, brutal realism led him to relegate the accomplishment of Marx's prophecies to a distant and uncertain future. For the moment, Russia was weak and backward. Within the country itself, an elite – itself not entirely trustworthy – imposed for the future good of the nation a programme of austerity unattractive to the tens of millions of benighted muzhiks and to the hardly more enlightened sons and daughters of muzhiks, who now hoped to enjoy the fruits of the revolution; but such hopes were premature. The first priority was to strengthen Russia. Severe internal and external shocks had to be avoided as far as possible. Allies had to be found – any allies, no matter who. Only after these priorities had been fulfilled would it be possible to develop, slowly, Russia's internal resources, and raise the cultural level and the standard of living. Any opportunity of recovering the territories lost to the infant Soviet Republics in the civil war and through foreign intervention had to be seized. Any opportunity of acquiring new territory would be jumped at. The new state needed room to enable it to keep any attack from outside at arm's length; it needed a sphere of influence which would act as an insulating layer. Nothing and nobody could be trusted. The Soviets would, of course, have to withdraw into their shell at the first sign of danger from the reaction to these movements. Finally the State ideology provided, in the various national Communist Parties, groups of dedicated men ready for any sacrifice on Russia's behalf, supported in their turn by a constellation of 'honest innocents', as Stalin called them. They would have to be used; but used for the benefit of the Soviet Union, and consequently in the final analysis for the good of humanity. They could not be allowed to think up and follow objectives of their own. Failing to appreciate the delicacy of Russia's situation, they might in their haste compromise the safety of the bastion of socialism for the sake of illusory gain and hence endanger the distant Millennium which they claimed to cherish.

Stalin believed in force. The powers which had to be taken into account were those which really had force at their command: the United States, Great Britain, Hitler's Germany, Japan, and, until 1940, France. The rest were a mere helpless litter of small states subject, either by right or in fact, to the decisions made by these, the great and powerful. In what was later to be called the Third World, the starving masses, possessed of only the most embryonic forms of political organization, attached themselves either to political frauds or to dreamers. At times they could be exploited to inflict insect bites on the big powers. No available weapon is ever entirely useless. But it was dangerous to over-estimate the strength of this ridiculous rabble, or the chances of success of their Communist Parties in particular.

The Arab countries and Israel were mere specks amidst the cloud of minor states. Stalin did at one time play with the idea of exploiting Israel against Great Britain, which might have caused the British Lion some embarrassment. This would have meant a complete break with all the previous theories pronounced by his movement, and amounted to sacrificing the Arab Communist Parties. These were not obstacles likely to cause Stalin any loss of sleep, as he demonstrated at the time of his pact with Hitler. But he shortly realized the pointlessness of such a move and how little he could expect to gain from Israel. The Arab states and the Arabist movements seemed just as unpromising. Apart from the Communists, the groups active in these countries were mere bands of conspirators in the pay of one power or the other, exploiting the emotions of backward masses. Thus the Free Egyptian officers were denounced, in 1952, as nothing more nor less than American agents. Even chance identity of interest with some other group and the occasional current of sympathy for the U.S.S.R. were to be exploited if possible, but too much hope could not be placed in them.

The development of the situation resulted in a corresponding change in Soviet political thinking. This change already began to show itself in the terrible Josef Vissarionovitch at the end of his life. The American attitude showed that in the face of the advance in Soviet military power, the United States would resist the temptation, however strong, to attack the Soviet Union. In 1952, in his last ideological statement, a paper on the *Economic Problems of Socialism*, Stalin considered wars between capitalist countries more likely than between the 'imperialist camp' and the 'anti-imperialist camp'. It follows from this that the latter would be able to make a free choice of allies among the rival groups of states confronting one another within the capitalist world. So far as the Third World was concerned, Soviet strategists were mostly strongly impressed by the growing force of national movements, and by the fact that countries achieving their independence under middle-class leadership did not, for all that, necessarily endorse American policy. The Bandung Conference and the policy moves made by Nasser (among others) in 1955 were proof of this. Khruschevian empiricism could not ignore potential allies of such importance. Moreover, the Twentieth Congress of the Communist Party of the Soviet Union, held in February 1956, foresaw a lengthy period of peaceful coexistence with the capitalist world, and also admitted the possibility of different roads to socialism, including parliamentary and non-violent evolution. The colonial bourgeoisie itself – subjected to intemperate abuse in the preceding period – could therefore be led painlessly on to the road to socialism. Much more important, this class could be won over as an ally, on many points at least, in the Cold War, because of its sincere desire for independence of Western, and especially American, hegemony.

Seen in this light, it became obvious that the Arab countries would be much more useful clients than Israel. Israel, armed to the teeth behind the walls of her tiny besieged fortress, was driven by factors which have already been discussed into alliance with the Western powers. The Zionist ideology could not fail to have an undesirable influence on the Jews of the Soviet Union. The Arab countries, constantly threatened by the superiority of the West in their struggle for self-determination and modernization, were peopled by masses who would long remain faithful to these objectives against Western hostility, whatever particular government they might have at any given time. The general aspirations of the people usually won in the end, or at least created powerful opposition movements if pro-American rulers remained in power. The choice was clear-cut, since the conciliation hoped for in 1947–8 had proved impossible. Respect for the U.N. Charter (which was greatly to the Soviet Union's advantage) and for U.N. decisions, fear of Jewish and pro-Jewish opinion throughout the world, and the pro-Soviet sympathies mobilized in Israel around the Communist Party and even the Mapam prevented the Soviet Union from refusing to recognize Israel's existence, as did the Arabs. But the Soviet Union affected to recognize Israel only within the limits of the frontiers granted by the U.N. in the partition plan of November 1947. The conquests made in the war of 1948 were regarded as quite without validity. Soviet schoolchildren still have to learn Israel's 'legal' area as well as her actual area (2,587,000 square miles greater) and their atlases are coloured to show the situation as it ought to have been, although some charitable cross-hatching informs them of the true situation.

For many years, the countries of the Communist bloc followed the strategic directives issued to them from the Kremlin. In Stalin's day, they were rationed to a very few decisions deviating from the strict Soviet road, and they were told what these should be. For instance, at the birth of the State of Israel, it was the Czechs who supplied her with arms, while Rumania, Poland and Bulgaria opened their gates to Jewish emigrants to the Promised Land. The Soviet Union was able to harvest some of the fruits of these policies, to observe their implementation and effects, without having to bear any of the responsibility. Only much later did Rumania embark on a distinctly independent policy.

As everyone knows, Yugoslavia broke with the bloc in 1948. The difficulties which faced Tito and his lieutenants in safeguarding themselves from possible Soviet attack while maintaining an essentially Communist system internally led them to seek alliances with the neutralist states of the Third World. More than this, Yugoslavia's leaders had to try to achieve a fairly lasting coalition, able to exert international influence as a 'third force'. Hence Tito's great personal friendship with Nehru and Nasser. For Nasser, Tito was a respected counsellor, a man of greater maturity, with long experience and a consequent thorough understanding of European affairs. This friendship was even worth the Communist hostility which it sometimes called down on Nasser. Khaled Begdash frequently denounced him to the Communist International as an accomplice in the Titoist heresy. But the same factors which drove the U.S.S.R. to support the Arabs pushed Tito in that direction too, despite his eagerness to stay on the right side of the United States. Support for the Arabs was directly in line with the political currents in the Third World. By contrast, support for Israel, closely bound up with Western policy, could have done nothing but harm without bringing any concomitant advantage.

One power remains to be discussed: China. When the new Communist power began to be able to formulate independent political attitudes, there was nothing to attract it towards Israel. Her position with regard to the Arab states was somewhat equivocal: her Communist fundamentalism made her hostile to reactionary regimes, whereas a realistic recognition of her interests as a great power often pulled her in the opposite direction. A clear example of this is provided by the coup d'état in Iraq on 8 February 1963, when the new regime celebrated its accession to power by a wholesale massacre of Communists. Relations between Iraq and the U.S.S.R. cooled markedly; but China leapt into the breach and made advances to the new regime. The Arab Communists are not likely to forget this episode very quickly.

The feelings of the Arab Left towards Communist China were fluctuating and ambivalent. The liberalism of the period of the Hundred Flowers attracted those irked by Soviet dogmatism. Development on the Chinese pattern seemed more appropriate to the Middle East's problems than the solution represented by the U.S.S.R. – too European in many eyes, and also too advanced. When the schism with the Russian leadership occurred, many at first shifted their sympathies towards Peking. But the militant extremism of the Chinese, their call to armed struggle, their mistrust, whether implicit or explicit, of bourgeois politicians were to arouse powerful antipathies. The Arab Communists themselves had been conditioned to loyalty to the Soviet Union, and had received their political education in the Popular Front era of parliamentary alliances with the nationalist middle class. They could not see themselves acting the role of subversives against their anti-imperialist allies. With regard to Israel, the Chinese counselled a war on the Vietnam pattern, without explaining precisely how this recipe was to be applied to the Middle East. They did however give warning of the terrible dangers, the great suffering and massive destruction liable to follow from such a strategy. The Middle Eastern peoples had not known a war of this nature since the Mongol invasions of the thirteenth century. The apocalyptic prophecies of the Chinese were enough to make the stoutest heart quail. The Cultural Revolution was a shock to the extreme Left, which a long period of militant nationalism had taught to respect the heritage of an ancient culture, even though they were but poorly acquainted with it. Naturally some extreme Left-wing elements were attracted, as were dissidents of every colour, including, apparently at least, the most extreme partisans of the struggle against Israel, even if they were middle class. For the moment however they were a tiny minority. Nonetheless, the intensification of the conflict and disillusionment with present ruling cliques and their Soviet ally might, in the future, attract many of the more dynamic elements to the Chinese approach in the Maoist style.

True enough, a third alternative did exist at one time – that of 'open', liberal Communism on the Castro model, which might seem especially appropriate in view of its special concern with the problems of the Third World. Ben Bella, for example, had been particularly drawn by the attractions of Castroism. However, the radicalism of the Cuban system, its unbuttoned style, and the rupture it entailed with all ancient traditions frightened off the Arab middle class, whose nationalist past, however radically anti-imperialist, had given them a profound respect for traditional values, and made them very conscious of their power. The campaign against these values, if undertaken at all, is conducted with exemplary prudence and expediency, by means of an infinite number of tiny transitional reforms. The Cubans, for their part, did not understand the Arab intransigence towards the Israelis. They were mistrustful of the bourgeois character of the Arab ruling parties, and tended to see the Israel question as a decoy, a diversion from the radical revolutionary struggle to throw off all the values of the past, which they considered just as necessary in the Arab world as elsewhere. They refused to accept that the political elimination of Israel was a self-validating revolutionary objective, even though they accepted the Arab critique of Israel. This mood was to change, mainly as a result of the same factors that changed the attitude of the whole Third World.

This, in broad outline, is how the nations of the world and their political movements were divided up. It helps to explain many attitudes and many factors influencing the struggle over the last years. But beyond these fundamental standpoints, there are further factors at work which experience has shown to be very powerful. There is the public opinion of the two world camps to be considered.

Public opinion generally moves along simple lines in problems relating to distant events which do not touch it directly. Once the public ceases to be indifferent, it tends to relate these distant problems not to the real facts, of which it is ignorant, but to facts with which it is familiar – in fact to its own problems, in so far as such identification is possible. Moreover it uses as its reference a few stereotyped images which basic education, current popular literature and the mass media have succeeded in establishing. This is obviously the cause of the gross discrepancies between the reality and its distant image. During the period we are discussing, Western public opinion knew nothing of the real Palestine. Only believers knew anything at all, and then but little: Palestine was the Holy Land. This might have had the effect of convincing some that the Christian Church had rights over some Christian sanctuaries. Others with some little knowledge of religious history (usually Protestants) knew that it was the land given by God to the Hebrews. Beyond this nothing much was known, except that the whole question had something to do with two peoples with which the public was reasonably familiar: the Jews and the Arabs.

As for the Jews, the West had good grounds for thinking it knew them well. Many people still had some notion of an old rival and accursed religion, to which belonged the murderers of Christ. The distressing notion that it was also the religion to which the founders and most highly venerated figures of Christianity – Jesus, the Virgin Mary and the Apostles – themselves belonged, and in which they firmly believed, was pushed as far back from the conscious mind as possible, like most disturbing ideas. Some innovating pioneers within the Church were forcing attention back to this unwelcome fact, and were beginning to gain a hearing among Catholic churchmen. Without realizing it, they were in tune with a widespread trend.

During the decade from 1930 to 1939, the Jews began to be violently persecuted in Germany and were the victims of more or less vexatious discrimination in Eastern Europe and the Balkans. Those who found refuge in Western Europe or America often arrived after the loss of all their possessions, wretched, supplicant and spreading uneasiness. German propaganda represented them as the children of the Devil, evil by nature, revolutionary by instinct, strangers wherever they went, ready to drain any nation of its substance, to pollute its essential nature and despoil it of its traditions. This they did from above, through the banks which they controlled, and from below, through revolutionary movements which they allegedly inspired. This fantastic picture was widely accepted, because there were a number of apparent facts which seemed to confirm it. In any case, it did not need much in the way of facts to win support, for Western opinion had a terrible grievance against the Jews. This grievance, difficult to express openly, glimmered weakly through a smokescreen of false arguments: the Jews troubled the West's self-satisfied tranquillity, and this was the best reason for mistrusting and hating them. The Germans never ceased to proclaim that they asked nothing more than to live in peace with all their Aryan brothers, that only the Jews sowed discord between them. Obsessed by the memory of millions of dead and disabled and of the enormous sufferings of the 1914–18 war, Westerners wondered if they were to be dragged once more into the same terrible cataclysm, attended by the same frightful slaughter, and all because of the Jews. Many repeated under their breath an adaptation of the terrible phrase pronounced nineteen centuries earlier by a Jewish High Priest in Jerusalem: it is better that one man should die for the people than that the whole nation should perish. Was it not better to sacrifice this group of people to the vindictiveness of a menacing neighbour in order to avoid consequences which would be disastrous for everybody? Of course a great number of justifications were adduced to show that the Jews were suspect, even guilty. They must in some way be responsible for the hatred which they aroused. Any vigorous policy towards Germany henceforth became suspect of having been inspired by this accursed group, ready to allow millions of good Frenchmen, Englishmen, Americans, Russians, etc. to die for its own interests. Governments animated by any spirit of resistance to Hitler had to forestall criticism from their own public opinion by demonstrating that their attitude was in no way dictated by any desire to placate the Jews. They had to dissociate themselves as far as possible from pro-Jewish feeling.

The war came, and persecution gave way to wholesale massacre such as had not been seen in the West for centuries. The Germans were directly responsible, but all the peoples of the West, except for a few pockets of resistance, were accomplices in the deed. The Poles, whom a hardly better fate awaited, watched the destruction of the Warsaw Ghetto as though it were a circus; French militia and police arrested Jews to deliver them up to their executioners; many moral authorities were silent; a number of bishops blessed the persecutors and mass-murderers. Even outside occupied Europe, the British and American governments resisted any energetic and effective measures against the great massacre.

When peace came and it was no longer possible to close one's eyes to the extent of the crime, when books, newspapers, films, the radio gave detailed accounts of the abominations practised on the Jews, the Western world was seized by a terrible feeling of guilt for its complicity, if only by abstention. The feeling was no more than a vague disquiet, and any straw blowing in the opposite direction would have transformed it at once into a clamour of self-justification. But everything, or nearly everything, pointed in a different direction. Western Jews were no longer pariah refugees, but, increasingly integrated into general society, they had become pillars of respectability. There was no reason to sacrifice them in any cause. Widespread prosperity gave no grounds, as poverty and fear had done, to look for scapegoats. The new Germany won a place in the community of the rich and powerful by spectacular gestures of contrition. The sum of complex forces which were driving the Catholic Church to renew its ideas and its internal structure helped it to discover, all of a sudden, the errors and misdeeds it had committed over fifteen centuries, and to seek common ground with rival denominations. Everywhere, anathema became dialogue. The Catholic Church suddenly became aware of the part it played in the development of anti-Semitism, and set out, in its habitual stately and unhurried fashion, to retrace its steps in an effort to make amends.

To the peoples of the West, the Israelis were first and foremost Jews. Unable to rid their minds of the Jewish tragedy of 1939–45, in Palestine they saw only the survivors of the massacre. This persecuted people had fled and recongregated in the land which historically was theirs, as the Bible shows; they had worked that land, and proved that they possessed the qualities which the West prizes above all: technical efficiency and military prowess. Settled in this distant country, they lost all the disagreeable characteristics (chiefly that of being different) which had blighted their life in Europe. Purified by distance and national regeneration, they now represented the quintessence of Europe amidst the dirty and backward masses of the languid and verminous Orient.

Israeli and Zionist propaganda reinforced, as it was bound to do, these images. Israel, it was said, *was* the Jewish people. The fund of good will towards the Jews was mobilized in the service of Israel. The identification of Israel with the Jews, with all the Jews, was total. The West felt bound to make good the wrongs historically perpetrated on the Jews, whether as members of the Jewish religious community or of the Jewish race, by supporting Israel, their historical representative. The history of the Jews and the history of Israel have everywhere been written from this point of view, in learned works just as much as in popularizations and vulgarizations at every level, including that of the novel (vide *Exodus* by Leon Uris, translated into every language and sold in millions of copies, in which the historical reality is carefully inflected to suit the Zionist view of things), the cinema, right down to music-hall songs. Israeli propaganda also stressed Israel's undeniable achievements, the dedication of the communities working in the *kibbutzim*, the flowering of the desert, the romance of the watch on the frontier. The Western urbanite could have his dreams of a free and healthy life fulfilled by proxy. The sympathy of the self-satisfied classes of Western society was won by developing Israel without renouncing free enterprise; the sympathy of the revolutionary or vaguely socialistic by the vision of the *kibbutzim*, representing a socialism without dictatorship, without deportations, without purges, without firing squads. Above all, none of this represented the remotest danger, the slightest threat to the masses of the West. All the disadvantages were on the other side – the Arab side.

If these pictures enchanted the non-Jewish masses, it is then hardly surprising that they should have won over all those who might in any way be termed 'Jew'. The authorities of religious Judaism had always been violently hostile to Zionism, a secular nationalist movement which wished to achieve by human strength that which belonged to God alone. Neither the Jewish community in Mandate Palestine nor the State of Israel seemed to them to resemble the messianic image of the mythic Israel which was to return to Palestine at the end of time. But the rabbis, with a few exceptions, were not long able to resist the enthusiasm of their flocks, all the more shrill and vibrant the further away they were and stayed from the new state; nor the peace-offerings held out to them by the new state itself. Non-practising Jews, for their part, did not resist assimilation with the society around them, with the culture of the country where they had found a home, of which they felt themselves to be citizens and even fully integrated members in many respects. But they attempted to combine this with loyalty to Israel, without realizing the contradiction or inconsistency this might involve. The general admiration for that country reflected on to them, and it would not have been human to reject such flattery altogether, despite the unease which many felt at their dual loyalty, and the disgust they must sometimes have experienced to hear such fulsome praise from erstwhile anti-Semites. In France, the synagogues which had been deserted by the assimilated Jews, who wanted above all to be French-men with no trace of a specific Jewish culture, were refilled by a wave of Algerian Jews of French nationality. These came from close-knit communities with their own traditions, their own way of life, their own customs and culture. Full of bitterness against the Arabs and against Islam, they were first and foremost Jews, the Jewish cause was their cause on whatever battleground it was defended. This battleground was now Israel.

As for the Arabs, the West's ideas about them were less clearcut and had less basis in experience. But at all events, they were strangers to the European world. Popular culture, compounded of half-digested history and geography lessons in childhood and adolescence, romances, and tales handed down through the ages, presented an image of half-starved and wild-eyed nomadic Bedouin on the one hand, and of harems, concubines, and lubricious and cruel despots on the other. Added to this, tales were told of the oil potentates with their immense fortunes – hardly modernized versions of the legendary Harun al Rashid. Colonial enterprise added its own touches to these pictures, to suit the predilections of the nations engaged in it. For the conservative and traditionally patriotic English, Lawrence of Arabia aroused sym-pathy towards the Arab dynasts, chivalrous allies of the Empire. Their rivals therefore tended towards greater sympathy with Israel. The French thought more in terms of the destructive Bedouin, and of the Maghreb villager buried in his archaic and barbaric traditions. The French Right and the patriotic lobby were outraged at Algerian terror-ism, and found it hard to swallow France's capitulation to this backward people. Since independence, to their mind ill-gotten, these barbarians had seemingly exhibited nothing but disorder and ineptitude. The revolutionary Left, by contrast, had been fired with enthusiasm by the Algerian cause. The disappointment was all the greater when the new Arab states proved to be very far removed from the Left's vision of a socialist society where liberty would reign at every level, and archaic values, the suffocating grip of out-dated traditions, would be thrown off. The Arab world, seen in this way, had little weight to place in the balance of sympathies against a virile, modern and forward-looking Israel, embodiment of the Jewry to which such a heavy debt was owed.

As for public opinion in the Communist countries, it tended to take the same side, despite the pro-Arab attitude of their governments, and partly because of it. Government propaganda methods had succeeded in arousing automatic distrust towards everything the government said. In the U.S.S.R. this propaganda had made strenuous efforts to represent Israel as an ordinary country, as against the Jewish religious and Zionist idealization. This was perfectly correct in principle. But it was delivered in the violent, rabble-rousing manner habitual to the Soviets. Israel was presented as a vale of blood and tears, where poverty-stricken proletarians languished under the whip of hardship and oppression. Not many believed in this grotesque image, which therefore had the effect of encouraging a boundless idealization. An ironic comment on this is furnished by the story of the reaction of Soviet Orthodox Jews when Elie Wiesel, a Western religious Zionist, showed them a Hebrew newspaper from Tel Aviv. Seeing the usual collection of daily news items, including thefts, crimes, strikes, political and social crises, etc., they immediately suspected him of being a secret government agent showing them a forgery fabricated in the headquarters of the political police. Anti-religious propaganda pamphlets directed against Judaism – similar to those attacking the other religions – were not very successful in making the radical distinction between anti-Judaism and anti-Semitism. The liberal intelligentsia spoke out against this official anti-Israeli and anti-Judaic propaganda. It seemed to them a continuation of the traditional anti-Semitism of the old reactionary governments and of Stalin's anti-Semitic machinations after 1949. They also judged the problems of distant Palestine by reference to their own problems, as is only natural, and identified Israel with the Jewish cause. They were afraid that government propaganda would reinforce the traditional anti-Semitism of the masses. It would seem, however, that this popular anti-Semitism, while it did not perhaps abate at all, was counterbalanced to some extent by an even stronger sentiment: implacable hostility to everything which emanated from the government. In addition to this, the Arabs reminded all the Balkan peoples of the Muslim Turks who had been their overlords for many centuries and for whom they had little love.

Such was the world in which the latest phases of the Israeli-Arab conflict had taken place. It is clear that the factors favouring Israel were by far the stronger. This was to have its effect on the attitudes and political decisions of both sides.

7

From Disengagement to Armed Vigil

At the beginning of 1964 the general tendency in the Arab world seemed to be towards some degree of disengagement. Nasser was visibly most interested in consolidating his rule and in promoting economic progress at home. His foreign policy was conditioned by these primary considerations, except in the Yemen, where the weight of earlier decisions, the need to avoid loss of face, and the interests of the Egyptian military caste were dragging the army deeper into the quagmire of a hopeless, costly and generally damaging conflict. However, this was a distant and secondary field of action – one might almost say colonial. Broadly speaking, Egypt was anxious for peace – and Egypt was the determining factor in the Arab world.

In March 1964 a constitutional proclamation abrogated the provisional constitution of 1958, and gave the National Assembly the power to dismiss the government. But the President retained the power to dissolve the National Assembly if it came into conflict with him. Nevertheless, the newly elected Assembly preserved some trace of the effort made to enlarge the regime's popular base. 188 out of 350 deputies were workers or peasants. But the formation of a new cadre among the lower ranks of the population desired by Nasser and the small ruling group which shared his preoccupations was continually being thwarted by the contradictions inherent in the regime. The cabinet was led by Ali Sabri, a strict Nasserite, and consisted of Vice-Presidents, almost all representing the military interest, to whom the civilian ministers were responsible. The true centre of power in the regime kept the newly-emerging cadres in leading strings, while it was supposed to be encouraging them, at a time when they were needed at the controls to effect vital economic developments.

In March the last Communist internees were freed. This was a further sign of the attempt to build up popular cadres. In May Khruschev was invited to attend and participate in the solemn inauguration of the Aswan High Dam. Nasser was proclaimed a 'Hero of the Soviet Union' and decorated with the Order of Lenin. In the course of the banquets and other festivities, the host and his guest found themselves opposed in courteous controversy. Khruschev said that he was disturbed by the nationalist tone of the movement for Arab unity, which implied conciliation towards reactionary regimes and classes. Nasser replied somewhat evasively. He was constricted by the class support to which he owed his position, and his inter-Arab policy effectively undermined the programme of radicalization implied by his ideology.

His desire to withdraw from the competitive propaganda-escalation practised by the Arab governments and to pacify the Arab front drove him to make concessions which contrasted with his ambition to lead the neutralist trend and the movements of liberation in the Third World. He bargained with the governments associated with the American bloc, while at the same time denouncing that bloc. In October 1964 a conference of the non-aligned nations was held in Cairo. At this conference, even those countries which had become more or less compromised by association with the United States were forced into a strenuously anti-imperialist pose. With the support of the Africans, Nasser affronted Tshombe by holding him prisoner in a Cairo hotel before sending him back to the Congo.

But the economic situation was grave. The government's investment effort, the massive purchases of capital equipment abroad, and the military costs piling up as a result of the war in the Yemen were draining the country's foreign reserves. The balance of payments deficit was enormous. It was becoming impossible to purchase foodstuffs, and the Nile valley was only able to produce quantities quite inadequate to feed a population which was increasing at a terrifying rate. The increase in the area under cultivation, even with the High Dam, was insufficient. Birth control was officially encouraged, but met with every kind of obstacle in such an untutored population, and in any case it would be very slow to take effect. Unemployment was endemic, and the immense mass of the destitute sub-proletariat only diminished very slowly. Egypt was reduced to awaiting anxiously the arrival of American grain consignments. The United States drove a hard bargain, supplying the precious grain only in return for arms control, economic measures and, implicitly, acceptable political attitudes. The consignments became smaller, were suspended, then started again. This was to show the Egyptians that it was in their interest to behave themselves and stop their pranks.

Although this attitude helped to weld the patriotic ruling group around Nasser, its consequences provoked growing and ever more dangerous popular discontent. While the clandestine Egyptian Communist Party, which had long since been won over to Nasser's policies, made the solemn gesture in April 1965 of formally disbanding itself, Right-wing opposition became more and more virulent. The despair and nostalgia of the dispossessed bourgeoisie found expression at the funeral of the old leader of the Wafd, Mustafa Nahas, in September 1965. The Muslim Brotherhood, a clerical and Fascist organization with a popular following, was more dangerous. In August police who tried to arrest a Muslim Brother conspirator in a village ten miles from Cairo were attacked by the local population. Four people were killed, three of them policemen, and martial law was declared in the region. A large-scale police swoop covering an entire quarter of the city of Cairo resulted in hundreds of arrests.

In October Nasser entrusted the leadership of the government to Zakaria Mohieddin, one of the leading officers. Zakaria Mohieddin was known both for his pro-Western tendencies and economic liberalism, and for the firmness of his hand. He was just the man to carry out the repression of the Right. Hundreds of Muslim Brothers were dragged before the tribunals. Many were accused of having conspired against the life of Nasser, among other things. Seven were condemned to death and three of them were executed. One of these was the ideological theoretician Sayeed Kotb, a highly regarded intellectual. Telegrams flooded in from all parts of the Muslim world pleading for clemency, but in vain; demonstrations against the execution took place in Khartoum, Amman and other places. To counterbalance these effects, some twenty pro-Chinese Communists were condemned to terms of hard labour. The goods and chattels of 169 families were seized, numerous 'feudalists' in the towns were placed under house arrest, and local government offices were purged, following two outrages against members of the Socialist Union committed in two villages at the instigation of wealthy landed proprietors.

In foreign policy the pendulum now swung towards the West. American grain consignments immediately began to arrive more regularly. Relations with France became very cordial; those with the Soviet Union remained good.

In September 1966 the 'strong man' was replaced by a technocrat, Sidki Suleiman, erstwhile Minister for the Aswan High Dam. The significance of this change appears to be that the time for repression was past, the regime was again securely in the saddle and constructive tasks were once again given priority. The economic plan was revised, and the anti-feudal purge continued. Policy towards the great powers was conducted apparently much as before, but in January 1967 a crisis arose in relations with the United States. This crisis seems once again to have been connected with grain deliveries and the Americans' demands to exercise control over Egypt's armaments and foreign policy. It seems that after the brief honeymoon of Zakaria Mohieddin's rule, the Americans had returned to their attitude of mistrust, even outright hostility, to Nasser and Nasserism.

In any case, from 1964 to the beginning of 1967 Egypt did not waver from her habitual policy with regard to Israel: verbal intransigence, and passivity in practice. Nothing seemed to be pushing Nasser to seek armed conflict; quite the reverse.

In Syria, events took a different turn. Relations with Egypt had improved somewhat, it seemed. But in April 1964 the Ba'athist government had to undergo a trial of strength. The urban tradespeople and small manufacturers on whom the Ba'ath had long relied for some of its support objected to the party's socialistic policies. Seen in terms of ethnic/religious communities, most of the members of this group were Sunnite Muslims, while the Ba'athists had many supporters – especially in the services – from minority groups, notably the Alawi. Of the thirteen members of the Central Committee of the Syrian Ba'ath Party, only five were Sunnites. An alarm-call of Alawi domination went up. Ideologically, the opposition was divided into the Muslim Brotherhood, rampart of Sunnite fundamentalism, and Nasserism, which seemed from the outside to be a guarantee of pugnacious Arab nationalism. At the same time both ideologies, however opposed to one another they might be in Egypt, seemed to offer safeguards against a too radical revolutionary policy. The respectful religiosity of Nasserism still seemed a safeguard against Ba'athist secularism. Very violent demonstrations against the regime broke out in the towns, supported by sermons in the mosques and accompanied by a strike of tradesmen and shop closures. The minority groups, the workers and the peasantry, who had benefited from the Ba'athist regime's reforms, combined in its defence and the army did the rest, i.e. the main work of restoring order. A mosque in which some members of the Muslim Brotherhood had taken refuge and which they used as a snipers' post was demolished by artillery fire. With bold but dangerous opportunism, the Nasserite press condemned the impiety of the Ba'athists, despite the fact that the Muslim Brotherhood was Nasser's most dreaded foe. Damascus made violent accusations against Cairo and Baghdad to the effect that they had supported, if not instigated, the revolt. Syria stood alone.

In order to escape from this isolation, the Ba'athist leaders were obliged to swallow their fundamental antipathy for Nasser and work for a *rapprochement* with him – a move already attempted on several previous occasions. Periods of reconciliation and renewed hostility followed one another, marked by distrust on both sides. In order to explain these changes of attitude to his followers, General Amin al Hafez, for the moment the strong-man of the Syrian regime, drew a distinction between Nasser, whom he exalted as an 'Arab hero', and his entourage, which 'often misled him into error'. In 1965 the party veered sharply to the Left and undertook an impressive series of nationalization measures. These measures were considered in many circles to have little economic justification, and to be unnecessarily provocative. They met with great resistance. The trial of strength against the urban shopkeepers, still supported by the Ulema, was won thanks to the energy of the measures taken and to the support of the groups mentioned above. An extraordinary military tribunal was set up. Fairly radical agrarian reform was undertaken, with some success it appears. Friendship with the U.S.S.R. and the other Soviet bloc countries was strengthened.

But the Ba'ath was torn with internal dissensions. A number of groups confronted one another behind the scenes, each backed in differing degrees by sections of the army. This factional struggle arose partly out of a conflict of ideologies. The old leaders of the party had based their attitude on unitary Arab nationalism, with some provision for socialist aspirations – but with the latter relegated to a definitely subordinate position. As long as the principal aim was still to overthrow the old bourgeois ruling groups and to mobilize the masses in support of traditional Arab claims and of a consistent anti-imperialist line, this ideology had been adequate. But now that the party was itself in power and confronted with the ineluctable decisions that power involved, the Arab nationalist ideology as presented in the rather nebulous theories of Michel Aflaq seemed a less certain guide. A new generation of young militants appeared, just as little attracted to institutional Communism as their elders. Many of the members of this younger generation had in the course of their studies (often in Paris) met with a form of Marxism liberated from the shackles of Communist Party dogma and the organizational bonds which this necessarily entailed. Some had lent their support to the Algerian Revolution, and had found the same ideas in some of the ruling circles of the F.L.N. Marxism, or Scientific Socialism as these young men called it, represented for them the need to integrate their own struggle in the context of the world struggle against imperialism, and to face the tasks of economic construction freed from the burden of capitalist privilege. It also entailed a refusal to abandon any universally valid principle on the pretext of an appeal to specific national or religious interests. They were just as strongly attached to national values as their adversaries; but they appreciated that although the problems facing them had an undeniable Arab or Muslim cast, this was not fundamental, and that basically these problems were the same as those faced by the peoples of other nations. This did not mean that the national question was without importance, and the Ba'ath had been right in principle to combine nationalism with socialism. However, its traditional leaders seemed to them to have sacrificed socialism to a narrow nationalism, which would in the long run prove fatal to national objectives themselves.

The active arm of this young generation of Ba'athists was a clandestine organization of army officers, the most noted of whom was to be General Salah Jedid. At the Sixth Congress of the party, held in October 1963, the 'Marxist' Left gained the upper hand. The Right and Centre resorted to underhand manoeuvres to maintain their hegemony, alliances formed and re-formed in the shadows, playing off the party's various bodies against one another. Finally, on 23 February 1966, a military putsch prepared by the Jedid group overthrew the Right-wing Ba'athist government. A new government was formed under Youssef Zuain in which two Communists figured. The Ba'athist leaders of the Right and Centre were imprisoned.

The new ruling team lost no time in making its presence felt. Nationalization was continued. An iron hand descended on those opponents who denounced the 'atheistic power hostile to Arabism and to Islam'. A military conspiracy provided the opportunity for setting up a popular militia, to which arms were distributed. Khaled Begdash was permitted to return to Damascus, and the Communist Party newspaper made its reappearance in public. But the party was still banned, and mutual distrust persisted. The Communist ministers had been appointed on their individual merits only, and Begdash's appeal for the formation of a national Progressive Front in which his party would play an open role fell on deaf ears. He denounced, in measured terms, the inadequacies of the government's social programme and pronounced his disdainful verdict on this group of young upstarts who might, at best, be credited with a few good intentions, but could not claim to hold the key to 'true' Marxism since they were not Communists.

This by no means excluded the establishment of strikingly cordial relations between the ruling group and the Soviet Union. This group had no illusions about the sentiments harboured by the C.I.A. towards it nor about American designs in general, which would only be aimed at its destruction. One of the first signs of this was, as usual, tension with Turkey. Foreign policy on several fronts was dictated by the situation. The friendship of Gaullist France was guaranteed to these French-trained anti-Americans. Among the Arabs, the choice was easy. Good relations were only possible with states which had given proof of sufficiently sincere and radical anti-imperialist intentions to alarm the Americans. This was true of Egypt, Algeria and the Yemen Republic. Consequently, a very close relationship was established with Nasser, even though the Egyptian leader may have viewed the turbulence and pugnacity of his youthful allies with some disquiet. He was at pains to exercise a moderating influence in their dispute with the mighty Iraq Petroleum Company (I.P.C.), which had given the Syrians offence. On 4 November 1966 a joint defence agreement was signed between the U.A.R. and Syria, in circumstances which will be analysed later. Naturally enough, it had mainly Israel in view. The Syrians felt themselves to be the special target of American hatred. They wondered from which direction the threatened blow would come. They took stock of all the pro-American regimes in the area: Jordan; Turkey; but above all the great military power represented by Israel. Besides, the defence agreement was in accordance with the intransigent attitude to Israel which their general philosophy dictated, as we shall see later. Also, Nasser was in a position to render effective support in case of attack. On the other side, the Egyptian leader hoped to be able to moderate and control any dangerous initiatives by his allies.

The two Middle Eastern Arab countries which took socialist anti-imperialism most seriously were thus brought together as allies by force of circumstances. Outside their immediate area they were, as has already been mentioned, decidedly sympathetic towards Algeria and the Yemeni Republicans. The latter, for their part, were somewhat torn between their anti-imperialist feeling and the difficulties they were having with the Egyptian troops, who while providing reinforcements to the Republicans, acted at the same time like an army of occupation. The other Arab governments found themselves in a delicate situation. Many were violently hostile to Syria and Egypt, whose political programme represented a grave threat to their privileges. But, with an eye to public opinion, they could not openly disapprove of all the anti-imperialist measures taken by these states, nor avoid showing some solidarity with them when such measures aroused reactions from the capitalist powers. This should be enough to demonstrate the political importance of Arab public opinion, which Western authors have often been tempted to dismiss as a myth. Within the Arab League, an unwieldy official body, conservative through sheer inertia, these rulers were in spite of everything forced at least to pretend to support the general interests of Arab nationalism. In the eyes of the masses, these interests seemed to coincide at least to a large extent with Syrian and Egyptian policies.

One means of escaping the dilemma had always been open. This entailed taking advantage of feelings of identification with the Muslim community. The remedy was well known, and, significantly, American circles interested in the Near East had long since developed a strategy for it, projecting a bloc uniting the forces of religion against atheistic materialism. I myself wrote an article as early as 1955 entitled 'Is Allah American?',* based on the ideological moves being taken in this direction. Early in 1966 King Feisal of Saudi Arabia cautiously advanced the idea of an 'Islamic summit'. The advantages were obvious. A general alliance of Muslim powers would make it possible to drown Egypt, Syria and Algeria in a gathering in which the non-Arab, conservative Muslim states, principally Turkey and Iran, would carry great weight. An appeal to Islamic solidarity would be an effective counterblast to the call of revolutionary Arab nationalism. Too radical measures of socialization could be criticized as contrary to the principles of Islam, and opposition to the capitalist West reduced to its proper proportions of a bargaining position in which the lion's share would go to the powerful Western interests. The support of the socialist countries sought by the revolutionary Arab regimes could be denounced in the name of the protest against the anti-religious attitude exhibited by the U.S.S.R. and by China in the Mohammedan areas of Central Asia. The struggle against the shackles which the West continued to impose on the self-determination and freedom of decision of the Arab world could be countered by a denunciation of Russian and Chinese oppression of the Uzbeks, Tadzhiks, Uighurs and other Muslims of that region. Among other demagogic devices used by Feisal to render his project acceptable to the Arabs, prominence was of course given to the support that the whole of Islam would give to Arab claims regarding Israel. The aim was a radical transformation of the political struggle for Palestine into a religious claim brought by Islam against Judaism. The implications of such a transformation were by no means all welcome to all the participants in the proposed bloc, notably Turkey and Iran; but things had not yet reached this stage, and initially the scheme would bring considerable advantages.

The revolutionary regimes at once understood the aims of the Saudi

* *Democratie nouvelle*, May 1955, pp. 28–37.

manoeuvre, and nobody in the Arab world was naïve enough to see in it an outburst of religious faith. The reactions of the socialistic states were violent in the extreme, despite Feisal's oratorical precautions. The Lebanon was understandably hostile, in view of its position on the duality of Islam and Christianity in the framework of Arab nationalism. Hussein of Jordan was the first and most enthusiastic convert. Ironically, and significantly, one of the Arab rulers most interested by the plan was Habib Bourguiba, who had shown the most determination (and courage) in his efforts to make Tunisia a truly secular state, in the French-revolutionary sense. Nothing could more clearly demonstrate the political nature of the project. In view of the mixed response to the plan, many even of the more reactionary Arab rulers thought it wise to reserve their opinion.

The project of an Islamic pact only accentuated the rift between socialistic and pro-Western states in the Arab world. The principal bone of contention was the Yemen. Nasser, enmeshed in the impenetrable jungle of the Yemeni conflict, had on several occasions tried to rid himself of the problem by a compromise with Saudi Arabia, which as we have seen supported the Yemeni Royalists, backed by the Americans and British. The difficulty was that since neither party had any decisive advantage, each was ready to compromise only up to a certain point. The affair was complicated by the private interests of the Egyptian military, by those of their Yemeni protégés, by the revolt of the Republicans against Egyptian authoritarianism, and by a thousand and one tribal squabbles. The Saudi Arabians could only be induced to withdraw their support for the Imam Badr in the framework of a general settlement guaranteeing them advantages elsewhere. But in fact, like their American and British protectors, they had throughout this period every reason to add to Nasser's difficulties. The latter, by contrast, appears to have genuinely desired disengagement for some time. But he would have had to obtain conditions enabling him to save face and not seem to be abandoning his protégés to the gibbet of triumphant reaction. He was subjected to powerful pressures by his own troops. Finally, the announcement by the British of their forthcoming withdrawal from South Arabia – which Yemeni nationalists call 'occupied Yemen' – made up his mind not to abandon a position which could shortly prove to be of paramount importance.

Many factors tended to push Israel into the background of the real conflicts in which the Arab countries were currently engaged. None could remove the elimination of this colonial enclave from their future programme. But whatever the solution was to be, it could be put off till a later date. This was what Nasser had wisely decided to do, as we have seen. His mouthpiece Haykal and he himself eventually came to spell it out more and more explicitly. The Arabs ought not to embark rashly on an adventurist war. The diversion of the waters of the Jordan was not a threat to the Arab world, and it was pointless to waste time and money on civil engineering works to divert the Jordan's headwaters in reprisal. In order to get the Arabs to swallow this counsel of restraint, Nasser declared that coexistence was not possible in the long term, and reminded his audience that the Muslims in the Middle Ages had waited seventy years for their first major victory over the Latin colony established by the Crusaders. The idol of Arabism was also anxious to prove his devotion to the Arab cause, but without running any immediate risks; he therefore delivered conditional warnings, threatening a preventive war if Israel began to arm herself with atomic weapons, and pledging military support to any Arab country attacked by the Jewish State.

However, two important factors – to stay for the moment in the Arab world – were working in the opposite direction. Two pressure-groups with telling motives for maintaining a state of warlike tension with Israel happened to find themselves in a position to do so. Both were very well aware that such a policy threatened to provoke a sharp response from the besieged Israeli fortress. They also knew that on their own they could never hope to defeat Israel if she decided, as she generally did, to resort to arms. But they counted on the force of Arab nationalist feeling in the masses to push the more lukewarm Arab states into supporting them. In any case, they had little to lose. These two groups were the Palestinian Arab organizations and the Syrian revolutionary Left.

The first Arab 'summit' in January 1964 has already been mentioned. This was organized by Nasser in an attempt to draw the sting of the Palestine question; the Arab governments were to be forced to face up to the responsibilities entailed by their brave words and gestures, and abandon the tiresome and dangerous game of one-upmanship so embarrassing to their neighbours. It was decided that those who were especially preoccupied by the problem should be given a bone to gnaw to keep them quiet. A united military command was to be set up, which would work, in a leisurely fashion, towards the establishment of a common military front against Israel. A 'Palestinian entity' was to be created to give expression to the desires of the Palestinians, who were the most interested party, without taking a form which might embarrass the constituted Arab states. This was with particular consideration for

Jordan, whose King, Hussein, ruled over more than one million Palestinians.

The organization of this 'entity' – which was specifically excluded from taking the form of a government – had been entrusted to Ahmed Shukairy. This individual's rise to prominence has already been traced in an earlier chapter. He was apparently Nasser's choice for the job, possibly because of the small moral influence which he wielded, which would prevent him, it was thought, from setting himself up as an independent force and taking personal initiatives which might prove dangerous. His new appointment was greeted with suspicion by Hussein and with violent protest on the part of the previous leader of the Palestinians, Haj Amin al Husseini, ex-Mufti of Jerusalem and Chairman of the moribund Palestine Arab Higher Committee. These protests were ignored. Shukairy set about creating institutions on which he could base real power. In May 1964 a Palestine National Congress consisting of delegates nominated by Shukairy met at Jerusalem and founded a Palestine Liberation Organization, electing him as President. This enabled the Arab League to rid itself of the tiresome Mufti and to confer on Palestine some international significance. In September 1964 the League appointed Shukairy Palestinian delegate at the United Nations, and from that time on the Organization had its own seat at the League. The P.L.O. decided to create a Palestine Liberation Army (P.L.A.) from conscripts recruited among the Palestinians scattered through the various Arab countries. The Organization's budget was financed by contributions from the Arab countries and by a tax levied on the Palestinians. But since it was not a government and had no territory of its own, it depended on the good will of the various Arab countries in which the Palestinians now lived.

Ahmed Shukairy could have regarded himself as the obedient instrument of the League, or rather, since the League was by no means united either in sentiment or policy, as holding the balance between the different tendencies at work within it. This would no doubt have led him to align himself with the less militant and to stir things up as little as possible. But he was a politician schooled in factional strife, rather muddle-headed, inclined to be carried away by his own words, with a taste for the grand gesture, and capable of making two equally shattering and totally contradictory pronouncements in the same breath. He had succeeded in creating a network of clients among the Palestinians and he was anxious to keep them happy in order to retain their support. Surprising as it seems, circumstances had elevated him to a position in which he was the apparent equal of monarchs and heads of state. Ambition and interest drove him to play an independent role. However, some degree of sincere patriotism cannot be excluded from the motivations acting on this Palestinian.

He therefore took his role seriously. This implied setting a course which of necessity came into fatal conflict with the desires of some of the members of the Arab League. Hussein's reservations shortly turned into implacable hostility, not unexpectedly in view of the threat which an independent Palestinian initiative represented for the Kingdom of Jordan, swollen by the annexation of non-Israeli Palestine. Saudi Arabia, Shukairy's erstwhile patron, also became violently hostile. The Lebanon, a small country already concerned to avoid an internal explosion, was not prepared to face the powerful Israeli army with its own 12,000 poorly equipped and inexperienced troops, and she refused to harbour on her territory troops answerable to a unified Arab command. Jordan followed suit. Each feared that they might be compromised by supposedly friendly troops which might take action in the interests of their neighbours.

Shukairy and the P.L.O. found their main support in the socialistic states, Egypt and Syria, although these were never prepared to give him a blank cheque. He vilified other states which expressed their reservations. Following certain declarations by Bourguiba, to be discussed later, he demanded Tunisia's expulsion from the Arab League. In September 1965 all the demands which he presented to the Arab Summit Conference at Casablanca were rejected. The League became disturbed about the running of the P.L.O.'s budget; the Organization was reproached for wasteful and purposeless extravagance. Shukairy, thwarted by the majority of the Arab states, then sought support elsewhere. He paid a visit to Kosygin; warm relations were established between this wealthy bourgeois and the Chinese, who were by definition in favour of any armed revolutionary struggle. Mao benevolently counselled him not to attach too much importance to the number of casualties to be expected from the liberation struggle.

All this drove Shukairy to take up a position of aggression, which was to remain largely verbal. The justification for the existence of the P.L.O. was the struggle against Israel, and the Palestinians were impatient for the struggle to take on some real substance. The example of Algeria was in everyone's thoughts – a country which had just won its independence through guerrilla warfare and terrorism, defeating a great nation and an extremely powerful army. Diplomacy had extracted no gains whatever from Israel. All directly concerned with the problem considered that the only effective recourse was to armed revolutionary struggle. Shukairy followed the current – or pretended to. Threats of large-scale armed raids on Israel abounded, but very little action followed. One of the major obstacles to the P.L.O. seemed to be Hussein, who refused to allow the Organization to conduct raids from his territory, since he would have to suffer the consequences. The P.L.O. made one unsuccessful attempt to overthrow him. Shukairy declared that he saw no difference between Hussein and Eshkol.

This somewhat fruitless agitation necessarily ended in splitting the Organization itself. Rivals to Shukairy appeared. Conspiracies became rife. Shukairy several times offered to resign. His 'unconstitutional methods' were attacked. Insinuations were made to the effect that his hangers-on had embezzled funds. In February 1967, his principal rival was made the object of an assassination attempt in Beirut and was taken to hospital with a bullet in his leg.

The Organization had been created to enable the Arab states, acting in concert, to canalize the claims and aspirations of the Palestinians, to keep a close watch over them and render them harmless, except when the common interest of all dictated otherwise. But the new organ had taken on a life of its own. Amongst states torn by dissension, it was able to take sides. At all events, it had brought into the foreground the Palestinian demand for energetic and immediate action, to take the form of armed intervention against Israel.

Naturally enough, those Palestinians who took this programme seriously grew impatient with Shukairy's prevarications and compromises, and with his preoccupation with the complex play of forces between the various Arab states. A clandestine 'Movement for Palestinian Liberation' had been set up some time before. This movement was determined to move into action regardless of political calculations. It took the name *El Fatah*, combining the initials of its title in the Arab word meaning 'conquest' or 'victory', which evokes for all Muslims a passage in the Koran which speaks of a 'coming victory'. It set up a commando organization called *el Asifa*, 'the storm'. In January 1965 *el Asifa* published a communiqué boasting of a raid on Israel in which 12 Israelis were killed and 18 injured. From then on, similar communiqués appeared at fairly short intervals.

The free-lancing activities of these terrorists caused official Arab bodies considerable embarrassment. In January 1966 the heads of the Arab delegations to the Arab-Israel Armistice Commission condemned them as ineffective. Shukairy announced talks to coordinate activities. Nothing further was heard of this plan. Instead, the creation of new organizations of a similar type was announced. Their relations with those already existing were obscure. In contrast to the previous situation, a full-blown movement of armed struggle against Israel was being built up, which most if not all the Arab states were completely impotent to control.

All of these movements did, nevertheless, find an ally among the Arab states: Syria. Such support was essential to make their activities possible at all. Palestinian commandos could not very well launch their attacks from Egyptian territory, which was cut off from Israel by the Blue Berets of the U.N., and the Egyptian authorities were hardly cooperative. Jordan and Lebanon, fearing Israeli reprisals, forbade the use of their territory as a base and also tried, in varying degrees and at different times, to suppress this activity. Only one Israeli frontier was left: the Syrian frontier. Instead of hostility, the Palestinians met with the warmest cooperation.

How the Syrian Left came to power and how the most radical elements, the younger Marxist or neo-Marxist generation, came to lead it has already been described. The logic of their situation drove them inexorably into an aggressive attitude towards Israel. Ba'athist governments, after a long period of wordy inaction, had finally embarked on the social transformation of their country. Whether or not such action was praiseworthy in every respect or whether it was inadequate is not the point at issue here. But in an under-developed country like Syria, dependent in many respects on the powerful economies of the capitalist world, every programme of social reform must come up against international interests. Furthermore, such a policy met with very strong opposition from inside the country, not only from the privileged classes but also from the lower-middle class – tradesmen and shopkeepers. Consequently the masses had to be mobilized if this programme of reform was to have any chance of success. The Ba'ath's vaunted secularism, its desire to transcend communal divisions which hindered all progressive action in these countries, the strong following it enjoyed (for various sociological reasons) among the non-Sunnite minorities, all dictated an attitude of pugnacious intransigence on the national level. The argument best calculated to appeal to the masses, which had for decades been committed to the struggle for national liberation, consisted in making the social struggle appear as the logical extension of the national struggle. No national struggle was possible without taking account of Israel. It should not be forgotten that in the 1920s Palestine was still thought of as a southern province of Syria, that the ties between the populations of the two areas were numerous and close, that Syria had 135,000 registered Palestinian refugees on her territory.

Also, Syria intended to uphold what she considered to be her rights over the demilitarized zones – those very areas over which Israel claimed inalienable sovereignty, and emphasized it by cultivating them from time to time. It was extremely difficult to make an appeal for mobilization against Western imperialism while at the same time adopting a soft, conciliatory attitude towards what everybody regarded as the colonization of Arab, and more specifically Syrian, territory. This colonization was itself a manifestation of Western imperialism that directly touched Syria; it had been carried out by Western elements, and was supported by the West. Conciliation would have been difficult for any Syrian government; it would have been fatal to a leadership open to charges of cosmopolitanism, one which had claimed to want to break with the purely verbal nationalism of its predecessors, and which counted among its most ardent followers many members of these minority groups which had, in the past, often been used as instruments by foreign oppressors.

All this made it impossible for any Left-wing government to obstruct the action of the Palestinian commandos; indeed it pressed it to give its active support. However, no one could afford to turn a blind eye to Israel's strength and the danger of the reprisals which this action might unleash. Everyone knew that Damascus, less than fifty miles from the Israeli frontier at its nearest point, could be bombed by Israeli aeroplanes minutes after take-off from their bases. All harboured doubts (rightly) as to the Syrian army's capacity to defend the Damascus road against Israeli tanks. The Syrian government's actions therefore showed the courage of despair, and could properly be regarded as irrational. Any counsel of moderation on the Palestinian question seemed a betrayal of the revolution. On 16 September 1965 the secretary of the Ba'ath for the region (i.e. Syria), Munif al Razzaz, said to the correspondent of *Le Monde* that his government did not consider that an armed conflict between the Arab countries and Israel was either possible or desirable in the short term. 'We do not know what the future holds in store for us,' he said, 'and whether the Palestinian question will be decided by force or not, in view of the changes which will take place in the meantime in the world situation and within Israel itself.' He showed scepticism on the usefulness of diverting the headwaters of the Jordan. Despite his insistence on the need to prepare for the worst and set up a powerful and unified Arab military apparatus, his pronouncement aroused a storm of indignation. It undoubtedly contributed to the defeat of the Ba'athist Centre and its replacement by an extremist group. In October a delegation from a 'fraternal party', the French P.S.U. (United Socialist Party), visited Damascus. An attempt was made to work out a joint declaration with the Ba'ath containing a paragraph on the Israel question which would be acceptable to both sides. The P.S.U., of course, had no intention of endorsing the Ba'ath's warlike enthusiasm. The first draft, drawn up jointly, was rejected by the Ba'athist delegates after a few hours' reflection; it could have brought about the party's fall from power. The final text, still very moderate by Syrian standards, nonetheless provoked a wave of protests from the rank and file of the French party.

From this it may be understood why the Syrian press, official publications and radio were marked by an extreme bellicosity. The Palestinian commandos of *el-Fatah*, the P.L.O. and other organizations were at the very least encouraged by this propaganda. The strict measures taken against them by Jordan and the Lebanon were not applied by Syria. They probably even received a certain amount of aid. However that may be, it did not prevent the Syrians from protesting vehemently, albeit illogically, against Israel's retaliatory measures. The Syrian government assumed a posture which was warlike in every respect. But it recoiled from the consequences of its own attitude. World opinion could, with some difficulty, have come to appreciate the merits of Syria's arguments against Israel as such. What it could not understand was how one could conduct an underground war and then protest at the military measures taken to counter it.

The Ba'athist leadership's despair went even deeper than this, at times. The total revolution which it desired was faced with obstacles which must have seemed insurmountable: the revolution had to be conducted on a restricted territory, unable to support itself, and without any realistic hope of unification to form a larger unit; Syria had no allies in the Arab world that were not at the same time rivals and competitors; and the Syrian Ba'ath's popular following was backward and intractable. Furthermore, there was the ever-present threat of action by Syria's terrible neighbour, armed to the teeth and backed by the most powerful nation on earth. At times, the governing group was tempted to embark on a cataclysmic trial of strength, in which Syria would be annihilated, but would inflict terrible wounds on her enemy; it would be a flamboyant example of life sacrificed but dearly sold, a legacy to the Arab world similar to that once given to European socialism by the Paris Commune.

Two incidents clearly illuminated for the whole world to see the absurdity of the position in which the Arabs were placed by the installation of Israel on their territory. To recognize Israel, i.e. to establish normal diplomatic relations with her, would have meant accepting the defeat inflicted by the European-American world as final, it would have meant unconditional surrender, when in fact resources for a future come-back seemed virtually inexhaustible. Just as the United States and Federal Germany could not for a long time resign themselves to accepting the *fait accompli* of a Communist regime in China and in East Germany, thereby declaring that the battle was over and won by their enemies, the Arab states could not resign themselves to announcing to their incensed peoples that there was nothing more to be done and that the struggle was being abandoned. This kind of situation might have been bearable as long as mutual hostility, institutionalized by the withholding of recognition, did not break out into actual military action. This had been well understood by Nasser, Hussein and the Lebanese – all of them directly involved. But a revolutionary regime like that in Syria, preaching the active engagement of the masses in a revolution at once social and national, would have condemned itself irredeemably if it had tried to halt the engagement on the front most sensitive to the mass consciousness. The contradiction was insurmountable.

In February and March 1965 the Tunisian President Habib Bourguiba went on a good-will tour through the countries of the Arab East. He visited every country in turn except Syria. He was everywhere warmly greeted by the crowds and by the rulers, who were willing to forget their old differences with him. In Jordan he was taken round the camps of Palestinian refugees. But on 6 March, at Amman, he made a declaration, and repeated it in substance on the 11th at Beirut, amounting to a proposal that Israel be recognized. He had been shocked by the wholly unrealistic conjunction of warlike phrases with obvious incapacity to conduct a real war. Faced with the violent reaction to his statements, he specified that recognition should be placed in the context of a negotiated settlement on the refugees and the frontiers, the frontiers proposed in the U.N. partition plan of November 1947 to be taken as a point of reference. This immediately aroused a point-blank refusal from the Israelis, who had at first been favourably impressed. Nonetheless, he had proposed at least partial recognition of the Israeli *fait accompli*, holding out at the end for the benefit of the dissatisfied the possibility of going back on this if the occasion, as yet unforeseen, should arise.

Bourguiba left for home pursued by the insults of the mob, by declarations of unalterable hostility on the part of the more committed leaders, and the rejection of all, with the exception of some Arab

Christian politicians in the Lebanon. His realism was the realism of a man not involved in the problem. No pressures drove him to commit himself to the struggle against Israel – neither Muslim fundamentalism, nor a profound sense of Arab solidarity, nor anti-imperialist revolutionary ardour. He was a man of the Arab West, and was quite unaware of the depths of passion which the problem stirred up in the East. He would have been far more careful with his words if a similar situation had arisen in Algeria, for example. The purpose of his speech was, one might think, a perfectly rational one. But diplomatically speaking, he was compromising the value of the Arab trump-card of non-recognition by announcing from the start that he was prepared to give it up; more than this, in the eyes of the masses he was proposing capitulation without compensation of any kind. Only Israel's acceptance in principle of a discussion on the basis of the 1947 partition plan and on the return of the refugees would have saved his position. The prospects of this were extremely thin. It should be added that Bourguiba's close relations with the American camp were hardly calculated to win him sympathizers or to enhance his proposals in the eyes of the Eastern Arabs, who were likely to regard them as inspired by the Western imperialism they so hated.

The international situation could not have been less favourable at this time. Rumours abounded concerning secret negotiations on the supply of American arms to Israel, compensated it is true by similar deliveries to Saudi Arabia, Iraq, Jordan and the Lebanon. In February and at the beginning of March it was learned that Federal Germany was to supply arms and economic aid to Israel, and that she was about to accord formal recognition to the Israeli state. Such recognition was a pure formality, since close relations already existed between the two states, as intimated earlier; German reparation payments constituted one of the main sources of revenue enabling the Israeli government to balance their payments. There had been massive supplies of arms and equipment to Israel from the Bundeswehr since 1960, but it seems that a threshold had been reached beyond which the Federal German government simply redirected, with United States permission, consignments of American arms. This was an expedient to camouflage American arms supplies to Israel in order to avoid Arab reactions. But word got around. The Arabs were furious and tried to exert pressure on Federal Germany. Nasser threatened to recognize East Germany, whose President, Walter Ulbricht, happened to be visiting Egypt at the time. West Germany gave way, or seemed to, on the arms question, but stuck to her decision to establish diplomatic relations with Israel.

In May 1965 this decision was put into effect. At once most of the Arab states broke off diplomatic relations with Bonn. The exceptions were Morocco, Tunisia and Libya (the German Federal Republic was the largest purchaser of Libyan oil).

Chancellor Erhard pointed out in a message to Nasser, quite logically, that seventy-eight other states maintained diplomatic relations with Israel. These included countries from the Western bloc as well as from the socialist bloc and from among the non-aligned nations. The Arab states had not broken off their relations with these states, and indeed were on extremely good terms with some. The German Chancellor might have added that the Arab states maintained good relations with states which supplied arms to Israel. Why, therefore, this sudden reaction against West Germany alone? Nasser's reply was rather laboured. He saw in the German gesture one move in a sinister large-scale operation which constituted a provocation against the Arab nations. Bourguiba, on the other hand, supported the German Chancellor's argument, showing the inconsistency of the Arab reaction.

This inconsistency was indubitable and, moreover, perfectly obvious. But the Arab gesture followed naturally from equally obvious political imperatives. Israel and the Arab states stood in a state of war, which hung fire militarily speaking except for minor incidents on the Syrian frontier. In these circumstances, the masses and the mass parties seized every opportunity for demonstrations of anger against the enemy. The news of the arms deliveries and the German recognition of Israel provided one such opportunity, among many others. The states less committed than Syria had to demonstrate from time to time that they understood and supported the aspirations of their peoples. This was an opportunity which did not cost them very much. A similar reaction against the United States, for example, would have been much more difficult and costly. Rather pathetically, the Arab governments resigned themselves to making this spectacular gesture. It meant that they lost some of the advantages of relations with Western Germany, but it was not an irreparable loss. And in any case they took good care not to press their demonstration too far, to burn all their bridges by recognizing East Germany, for instance. At least this concrete gesture added a credit to the balance of their contribution to the Arab national struggle. It may also be observed in passing that West Germany's application of the Hallstein Doctrine conformed no better with strict logic than the Arab attitude.

Another event, on a totally different plane, gave rise to similar reactions. After protracted tergiversations, the Catholic Church had decided to reconsider its traditional policy and adjust its relations with the world in a new light. As regards the rival religions, it had resolved to abandon the attitude of malignant and aggressive hostility that it had maintained for centuries and to go over to relations of peaceful coexistence, based upon mutual respect, without renouncing in the least the conviction that the Catholic Church possessed the truth. One beheld the highest authorities of this Church acknowledging, for example, that the Protestant revolt against its authority in the sixteenth century was not without justification – that the blame for it was to a large extent attributable to the Church itself. The Second Vatican Council (twentieth of the ecumenical councils), convened by John XXIII in 1962, was called upon to record this new orientation in a series of documents. When it came to adopting a 'schema' on the non-Christian religions, what was put in the forefront in each case was that portion of the truth which, according to Catholic ideas, was contained in the given religion, the validity of the worship that it rendered to God in one form or another, rather than its errors and defects, as had been the predominant treatment given until then. In relation to Judaism, it was decided to abandon, solemnly and forever, the charge of deicide which had been levelled by the Church against the Jews as a whole ever since ancient times. This had been, as no one could now conceal from himself, one of the sources from which the various types of anti-Semitism in the Christian world had drawn sustenance for two thousand years, not excluding Hitlerite anti-Semitism, despite the latter's anti-Christian orientation. To it, therefore, could be ascribed a substantial share of responsibility for the systematic massacring of millions of innocent people, barely a quarter of a century earlier, not to mention the massacres of the past, less well organized and more limited in scope. On the other hand, the very foundations of the Christian faith rested upon the thesis that, two thousand years ago, a group of Jews had urged a Roman official to condemn to death Jesus, in whom the Godhead had been made flesh.

In November 1963, the 'Fathers' of the Council had presented to them the first draft of a document which stated that responsibility for the Crucifixion could not be placed upon *all* the Jews, either those of olden times or those of today. It was therefore unjust to call 'the Jewish people', collectively, a people of deicides. It was unwarranted to feel contempt or hatred for them, and criminal to persecute them. All who were concerned with justice and peace among men could only rejoice in this removal of one cause (among others) of hatred, massacres and persecutions, whatever their attitude might be towards the Catholic Church, and whatever the latter's motives.

Nevertheless, the draft provoked virulent opposition. It came from 'integrist' Catholics who were pained to see repudiated in this way a Church doctrine which had been given expression over the centuries by innumerable Popes, members of the hierarchy and doctors of the faith, and which certain sacred texts also seemed to support. Opposition came also from many Christian prelates from the Arab world, who feared lest the rulers of their countries suspect that this was a gesture by the Church in favour of the state of Israel, and lest the genuineness of their own Arabism be once again brought into question. At the very least, they would be deprived of a specific argument which had enabled them to add their voices to the Arab choir of propaganda against Israel.

On 15 October 1965, the Council adopted, by 1,763 votes to 250, an amended document which said less than had been said by the original draft. Whereas the thesis of the collective responsibility of all Jews, past and present, for the death of Christ was explicitly condemned, the amended text omitted, for example, the repudiation of the epithet 'deicide', which was now not mentioned. On the whole, however, this was a very important step forward which no person of feeling could fail to appreciate.

Yet the Arab world was embittered by what had happened. There were many, certainly, who understood the meaning of the Council's decision, and approved of it in their heart and conscience; but only a few men of the Left, here and there, had the courage to express their approval publicly. Governments declared – it was good policy to do this – that what was involved was a purely religious gesture, having nothing to do with the Arab-Israeli conflict, and that they respected it as such. But, in the eyes of Arab public opinion as a whole, accustomed as it was to identify the state of Israel with world Jewry – as, indeed, the propagandists of Zionism also strove to do – the schema on the Jews seemed like aid and comfort given to the enemy. This public opinion thus crossed the frontier (so often hard to make out) separating anti-Zionism from anti-Semitism, since it was reproaching the Church for an act directed against anti-Semitism, that is to say, the attribution of an essentially maleficent character to the Jews as a whole. It was difficult for there to be any other reaction, in the circumstances created by the implanting of the Israeli state in Arab soil. One is entitled, though, to regret that this tendency, a normal one in the sociological sense, should have encountered so few opponents in the Arab world, and that a certain number of demagogues and publicists, both Arab and non-Arab, should have seen fit to encourage it, making use of various sophistries, sometimes of an anti-clerical sort.

What of Israel? What was going on inside the besieged fortress while its enemies were dancing their war-dance around its walls? What was her reaction to the bellicose proclamations, spectacular diplomatic gestures, to Arab arms purchases, and last but not least to the small-scale military actions of the Palestinian commandos and the Syrians?

Levi Eshkol had been in power since June 1963. This old Mapai militant, previously accustomed to the ungrateful task of treasurer, had inaugurated a policy of reaction against the frenzied activism of his predecessor. Eshkol was an Israeli patriot and convinced Zionist. But he sensed the transformation taking place within the country, its ardent desire for peace, and he was determined to explore all possibilities of fulfilling the aspirations of his people in some other way than by a permanent state of mobilization, punctuated by punitive expeditions to terrorize the enemy.

The relative security which Israel enjoyed at this time helped his plans, as well as the profound transformation which Israeli society was undergoing. Israel was becoming comfortable and bourgeois. The year 1965 saw a veritable boom in industry and commerce. The standard of living rose. The per capita income reached the level of the more prosperous European countries. Of course this meant that differences between the various sections of the population became more marked. The mass of Jews who had come from the Arab countries since 1948 provided a relatively cheap source of labour, although still better paid than in the under-developed countries, especially the neighbouring Arab states. A minor economic crisis occurred in 1966; but it was characterized by an inflationary level of activity, partly caused by the pressure for a rise in the standard of living, and only reinforced the tendency to move away from the mode of living and the ideals of the Jewish pioneers.

Israel became increasingly 'normal' as a nation. The social model inherited from the time of the colonization of Palestine before independence, with its idealization of the *kibbutz* and its soldier-monks, was gradually disappearing. The life of the upper classes, mostly 'veteran' pre-1948 immigrants, was becoming luxurious. The newcomers showed little interest in the ideologies which had animated the founders of the state. The Oriental Jews, the least ideologically inspired of all, increased in numbers, and the day seemed not far off when they would be in the majority. The Israeli people was little interested in the objectives of Zionism as such. They wanted to live in peace and live well within the limits acquired by the founding fathers. Everyone was aware of the Arab menace. But a state of mind was gaining ground which favoured concessions to buy peace from these turbulent neighbours, without worrying about maintaining or extending a base to accommodate a trickle of immigrants from the European countries or elsewhere. Nowhere, moreover, was any real wave of anti-Semitism apparent. Jews in every part of the world felt reasonably secure, and very few decided to emigrate to Israel. Those who retained any fervour in the Zionist ideal were content to express it symbolically through monetary donations, their militancy reduced to occasional evening meetings. Even this activity was gradually declining. It was easy to be a Zionist in New York, London or Paris. In Israel, those able to make the comparison were inclined to prefer a 'normal state' to a 'normal' state, and to recognize that the European-American world had many advantages over the Promised Land. Members of the upper echelons were fleeing Israel and accepting attractive posts offered to them in the United States and Europe. Immigration fell to an all-time low. The forecast for 1966 had predicted 50 to 60,000 immigrants. The actual number was some 15,000.

The Israeli people had become amenable to the prospect of peace initiatives by means other than those traditionally resorted to. An incident took place which clearly demonstrated this, by a kind of *reductio ad absurdum*. In February 1966 a one-time Israeli airman, who had become the owner of a fashionable restaurant in Tel Aviv frequented by a trendy Bohemian intellectual clique, left for Egypt in a monoplane to see President Nasser. He was forced to land at Port Said, where he was received by the Governor after spending the night in the aliens' prison. After an exchange of friendly words, gifts and other courtesies, the bold pilot was given a tank full of fuel, his machine was repaired and he was despatched back home to Israel. Some Israelis demanded that he be locked up for treason; but he was greeted on his return by a delirious crowd. This mad expedition on the part of a man who might reasonably be suspected of hankering after publicity and of being slightly unbalanced ended in a massive demonstration for peace.

There were other signs, more serious, which pointed in the same direction. Eshkol had made a great show of 'energetic' gestures, declaring that his policy was in no way different from that of his predecessor. But Ben Gurion and his clique accused him of treason for being less inclined than they to a policy of punitive, or even preventive, military raids. Dayan and Peres had been obliged to resign from their ministerial posts. The Old Man was not reconciled to finding himself put in the wrong over the Lavon affair. He was still campaigning for electoral reform to introduce a two-party system on the British model, which would place the reins of power in the hands of a strong government. He resigned from the Central Committee of the Mapai in November 1964, setting up his own parliamentary group and founding a new party, the Rafi.

The elections of November 1965 were significant. The Rafi, associated with the names of Ben Gurion, Dayan and Peres, who stood for the maintenance of Israel's security by means of 'energetic' and dazzling strokes, suffered a catastrophic defeat. It won only 10 out of 120 seats. Eshkol received his mandate; the Mapai and its ally the Achduth Haavodah (Union of Labour) returned 49 Deputies (including 4 Arabs). The Right lost ground slightly. One small event, without any real parliamentary importance, was nonetheless significant. One Deputy of a phantom party, created specially for the occasion, was elected. This was Uri Avnery, publisher of the most widely read magazine in Israel, *Ha-olam Ha-zeh* ('This Low World'). Avneri, who had an excellent service record in the fighting which had ended in the creation of Israel, had long been preoccupied with the Arab problem. He had tried various ways of establishing peaceful relations, rejecting the Ben Gurion approach. He had tried to found a movement for a 'Semitic' federation of the Middle East, in which Israel would be represented side by side with the Arab states. He preached the transformation of Israel into an ordinary Middle Eastern state, freed from Zionist ideology and from international Zionism. The Semitic Movement met with little success, and he then hit on the idea of broadcasting his views through the medium of a periodical attracting its readership by means of photographs of female nudes – condemned as pornographic by Israeli puritans and by his enemies. He also let fly against the restrictions imposed on the Israeli population by the Jewish clericalists, thanks to their privileged position as a decisive electoral pressure-group. He presented himself at the polls and, against all expectation, was elected. Indubitably, the majority of the votes cast for him were in support of his struggle against clerical tyranny and of his protest against a Libel Bill, which if passed would effectively gag all journalists not covered by parliamentary privilege. Yet everybody was well acquainted with his views on the problem of relations with the Arabs and he was still elected despite this.

The elections encouraged Eshkol to press his policies further. He replaced Golda Meir by Abba Even (or Eban, according to the usual mode of transcription). Eban, a Cambridge graduate, had violently attacked Ben Gurion's foreign policy, which he called 'adventurist' and 'bitter-endist'. He was disposed to explore new paths. From the beginning, he spoke of the need for the two peoples to modify their image of each other. This was to admit that the Israelis' image of the Arabs had as little validity as the Arabs' image of the Israelis, a sacrilegious assumption to traditional Zionism. Yet he was unable to offer the Arabs any more than his predecessors. His pet scheme seems to have been to induce the Soviet Union to intervene as guarantor of the status quo. It should not be forgotten that the U.S.S.R. had been one of the founders of the State of Israel and had never withdrawn recognition, although this was limited, it is true, to the frontiers of the U.N. partition plan of November 1947. Eban was no doubt encouraged in this by certain apparent signs of discreet Soviet support for the traditional position of the Israeli Communist Party – commitment to the existence of the state. This Party had just split into two groups. One of these was almost exclusively Jewish and more sensitive to the favourable response it could evoke from the Israeli masses by laying emphasis on Israel's right to independent existence, condemning at the same time the refusal of the Arabs to grant explicit recognition of that right. The second group was composed of both Jewish and Arab elements; it was more attentive to Arab sensibilities, pointing out the obstacles to a peaceful solution erected by the Israeli leaders, their close ties with the imperialists, their infringement of Arab rights. Nevertheless this group never repudiated the state of Israel as such. The efforts of foreign Communist Parties, primarily the C.P.S.U., to maintain the unity of the Israeli Communist movement highlighted this common loyalty to the existence of Israel, and it might be supposed, rightly or wrongly, that this was deliberate. Eban's policy broke with the pro-Western exclusivism of Israeli foreign policy by appealing to the spirit of Tashkent, where the U.S.S.R. had helped to soften the Indo-Pakistani conflict. He visited Warsaw – the first time an Israeli minister had set foot in any socialist country. Close relations were established with Rumania; Israel recognized the Oder-Neisse Line.

Eshkol also made some moves in the same direction. He suspended the raids on the sites at which the Syrians were carrying out the diversion of the headwaters of the Jordan. The name of the Histadruth ('Federation of Jewish Workers') was changed to 'Israel Federation of Labour', in recognition of the recent admission of Arab members. Arabs were finally accepted as fully-fledged trade unionists. It was announced that the military administration still governing the major part of Arab territory in Israel would shortly be abolished.

These gestures certainly fell far short of satisfying Arab claims. But they were the first steps towards the establishment of a new climate in Israel. This new climate might some day promote a new understanding between the two camps. Before this could happen, two essential conditions had to be fulfilled: the Israeli parties' policy of outbidding each other would have to cease; all apparent or real threats on the part of the Arab states would have to disappear. Neither of these opportunities for peaceful development was granted.

The new foreign policy and its approval by the majority of the Israeli people aroused the anger and indignation of the activist clique. This was the road to the precipice. The demobilization of the Israeli masses and the downward trend of immigration had to be halted. Dayan warned of the danger of 'levantinization'. The numerical preponderance of the Oriental Jews, the expected result of their greater fecundity, would have a detrimental effect on the culture of the state and on its politics. The end result threatened to be an ordinary Middle Eastern state having no use for Zionist dreams. The cultural alignment with the Middle East which these activists saw as the likely result of Eshkol's and Eban's pacifism was liable to end up as a political alignment. Ben Gurion declared: 'We do not want the Israelis to turn into Arabs. We must fight against the levantine spirit, which corrupts men and societies, and preserve the authentically Jewish values which have been developed in the Diaspora.'*

Added to these general fears aroused by the direction in which Israeli society was evolving, the old chief, full of personal rancour, suffered from a profound mistrust for the policies of his successors. At the beginning of 1966 he loudly accused Eshkol of 'irresponsible decisions' in the realm of national defence, 'acts seriously compromising the security of the nation, which could bring disaster in the four or five years which lie ahead'.† These mysterious accusations plunged the nation into perplexity. Ben Gurion sought allies to help him shake the Eshkol-Eban policy, and drew closer to his onetime hated rival, Menachem Begin, old chief of the Irgun and now leader of the Right-wing expansionist party, the Heruth. The bloody disputes of the period of struggle against the British were forgotten before the imperative need to halt Israel's current disastrous course. The Right-wing opposition joined forces and won an electoral victory, the mayoralty of Jerusalem.

* Reported by Eric Rouleau, *Le Monde*, 9 March 1966, p. 4.

† See Centre d'information du Proche-Orient et de l'Afrique, *Bulletin hebdomadaire*, no. 564, 10 February 1966, p. 10.

It cannot be supposed that the activist clan of Ben Gurionist 'Young Turks', Dayan and Peres, remained passive. They had certainly retained close relations with circles inside the Ministry of Defence, from which Peres himself had been expelled. It is thought that a 'shadow General Staff' was set up under their leadership, controlled by the Rafi. The Lavon affair (among others) had thrown light on the independent policy which various branches of the army followed when need arose – especially the Intelligence Corps. Be that as it may, pressure was certainly brought to bear on Eshkol to pursue an 'energetic' policy. He could not allow himself to be accused of softness with regard to Israel's security. It seems at least highly probable that the Army was one of the groups through which pressure was exerted.

The actions of the Palestinian commandos of *El-Fatah* and the P.L.O., more or less supported by the Syrians, were admirably calculated to further the ends of Israeli extremism. At the beginning of 1965 hydraulic engineers pointed out that even if the Arabs succeeded in diverting all the waters of the Jordan's principal tributaries, they still would fall well below the quantity which had been allocated to them by the Johnston plan. An Israeli expert further declared that the Arab project would not reach the 'operational stage' in less than twelve to fifteen years. The similarly sceptical view held by the head of the Syrian government of the time has already been mentioned. Nevertheless, Israel resumed her attacks on the sites at which the diversion work was being carried out in the spring of 1966, and the Israeli Chief of Staff, General Rabin, threatened the Syrians with full-scale military intervention. Acts of sabotage on the frontier, accompanied by inflammatory Syrian propaganda, were cited in justification of a reprisal raid on Syrian territory conducted by the Israeli Air Force on 15 July. At the same time Israel complained to Washington that she was getting fewer Western arms than the Arab countries, which already benefited from Soviet arms aid. In May a large delivery of American tactical aircraft was announced, to be supplied at very favourable prices. In June 1966 Eshkol replied to the violent attacks of the Rafi's First Congress that he had won a promise from the United States to ensure that a balance of power was maintained in the Middle East, and that this was a revolution in American thinking with regard to the problems of the area.

On 11 September 1966, in an interview given to the Israeli army newspaper, General Rabin declared:

The Syrians are the spiritual fathers of the *El-Fatah* group. . . The military engagements which Israel has to conduct in Syria in reprisal for the sabotage raids she suffers are therefore directed against the Syrian regime. . . . Our aim is to make the Syrian government change its mind, and to eliminate the cause of the raids.*

On the 18th, the hesitant Eshkol piped the tune called by his Chief of Staff, as he had often done. He declared that from now on Syria would be held responsible for all acts of sabotage committed by terrorist infiltrators from any adjacent Arab country. This seemed a direct threat against the Syrians, and they then sought to protect themselves. Talks with Nasser were begun, and on 4 November a joint defence agreement between Syria and Egypt was signed. Despite the cautious declaration made on 18 November by Nasser's mouthpiece, Heykal, to the effect that the agreement did not mean 'that the Egyptian Army would immediately intervene against any Israeli attack on Syrian positions',† nevertheless a train of events had been set in motion which was to force Egypt to take direct part in the Israeli-Syrian confrontation.

On 13 November a mine exploded on an Israeli road running along the Jordanian frontier, near Hebron, killing three Israeli soldiers and wounding a further six. Eshkol refused to apply the doctrine of reprisals against Syria, officially held unconditionally responsible for all acts of sabotage. Despite undoubted pressure from activist civil and military circles, he refused to provoke Nasser into acting on the Egyptian-Syrian pact, perhaps even the U.S.S.R. into intervention on Syria's behalf. He gave way on the principle of a reprisal operation, but it was to be aimed at an apparently less dangerous point. The operation authorized was directed against the Jordanian village closest to the place at which the act of sabotage had been committed. 125 houses in the village of Samu' (including the dispensary and the school) were destroyed after being evacuated by the inhabitants. Jordanian troops appeared on the scene, and a fight started which lasted more than three hours, until U.N. observers intervened. 18 Jordanians were killed in the operation, and 134 injured. 80 tanks and a dozen French Mirage aircraft had taken part. It seems likely that the army exceeded the government's instructions, pleading the intervention of the Jordanian troops in justification. Eshkol made efforts to minimize the casualty figures, and declared that he hoped the operation would be the last and that reprisals 'were not an integral part of Israeli policy'. Eban stated on the French radio: 'Our action was originally intended to be more limited in its scope and effects than it proved in practice.'

* See *Cahiers de l'Orient contemporain*, no. 63, December 1966, p. 43.
† *al-Ahrâm*, 18 November 1966.

The blow was a terrible one for Jordan, and had far-reaching repercussions. The Palestinians of the West Bank held violent demonstrations, complaining that they were being abandoned, demanding arms, accusing Hussein of weakness towards Israel and of betrayal. He was reproached for his refusal to allow troops of the P.L.O. and of the Unified Arab Command on to Jordanian territory. The regime came close to being overthrown. Order was restored with great difficulty by the Arab Legion, at the cost of a number of casualties, both dead and wounded, among the demonstrators in Palestinian towns. No one has ever been able to find out the exact number. To deflect the blame, Hussein accused Nasser of having remained passive. Those who spoke of Arab nationalism might at least have been principled enough not to leave him to face Israeli reprisals alone. The great Nasser could talk as much as he liked of intransigence towards Israel. The Blue Berets gave him an easy excuse for not moving on the southern frontier and for allowing Israeli military supplies to pass the Strait of Tiran unmolested.

Early in 1967 the 'energetic' measures forced through by the Israeli activist clique, thanks to the aid given them by the miniature military operations of the Palestinian commandos, supported by revolutionary Syria, had succeeded in placing the proponents of the peaceful solution – Nasser, Hussein, Eshkol and Eban – in a very difficult position. The two latter could not afford to appear to condemn action which allegedly ensured the everyday security of Israeli citizens. The parliamentary opposition was impotent; the Rafi had even split, counterbalancing Ben Gurion's move towards Begin and his 'gang of fascists', as Ben Gurion had so recently called them. Yet the Israeli rulers were subjected to a campaign of denigration which was all the more dangerous for the fact that it emanated partly from activist groups with powerful support in the army. Every cause of discontent in Israel was seized upon and attributed to Eshkol and his supposed softness. Demobilization had reached its limit, educated Jews were leaving Israel, and the economic situation was worsening. A highly popular anecdote circulating at the time ran: A notice has been put up on Lod aerodrome, saying 'Will the last to leave kindly turn out the light.' Eshkol could not allow himself the slightest 'weakness'. Similarly, the Arab leaders could not allow themselves to show too much passivity, nor too much hostility towards the militant elements which expressed in their actions the general claims nurtured by all Arabs, claims which none could afford to repudiate.

Moreover the Arabs, nervous of Israel's military strength and increasingly aware that they could not forever avoid becoming caught up in the deadly merry-go-round of frontier incidents and reprisals, were led to look for outside support, in particular suppliers of arms. Syria was driven to depend more and more on the Soviet Union, who began to find this friendly base in the region really useful. Again possibly through the influence of the military, the attitude of the Soviet Union towards Syria became increasingly protective, despite the mild anti-Communism of the Syrian ruling party.

At the same time there were rumours in Europe towards the end of 1966 that the close relations established between the U.S.S.R., Egypt and Syria had led to a 'rude awakening' in Washington. The Americans were supposed to be in the process of working out a new strategy for the 'defence of the Near East' based on the two pillars of Turkey and Israel. The Arabs also caught wind of some such development.

In January 1967 the familiar sporadic firing broke out in the region of the demilitarized zones ('seasonal', U Thant called it). But it was augmented this time by firing on the Lake of Tiberias, by acts of sabotage and various other operations carried out by *El Fatah* commandos, which grew in strength, efficiency and organization. News of troop concentrations on both sides of the armistice line filtered out. Israeli activists demanded a reprisal raid. For instance Peres, in an interview with the French Zionist newspaper *La Terre retrouvée*, observed that the Syrians were the only ones 'never to have felt any real blow from the Israelis'. 'Perhaps the time has now come,' he added, 'to teach the Syrians a good lesson.' He mocked at the 'spirit of Tashkent' to which Eban had appealed. Eshkol and Eban fought back, and made 'energetic' statements to clear themselves of the charge of softness. On 25 January the Syrian-Israeli Armistice Commission met on the bridge of the Daughters of Jacob, at the instigation of U Thant; yet Eban had in December made the startling announcement that Israel was withdrawing from this body. The two parties pledged themselves to avoid all acts of aggression and hostility. But the Syrians wanted to discuss the status of the demilitarized zones, whereas the Israelis refused to talk about anything but the cessation of frontier incidents. Israeli statements proclaimed that sovereignty over these zones was not negotiable; the Syrians tried to disarm their own internal opposition by declaring that the struggle for the liberation of Palestine would continue. A mine was discovered on Israeli territory. The discussions broke down.

Once again Eshkol was accused of weakness. The Syrian government was accused of having suspended the raids of the *fedayeen* under Egyptian and Soviet pressure. The usual pattern of events recurred in April. Eshkol gave or authorized an order that the demilitarized zones were to be cultivated. The Syrians opened fire. Before long both sides were shelling each other's positions, then Israeli aircraft intervened, shooting down at least six Syrian Migs and penetrating as far as the suburbs of Damascus. Eshkol was in practice saying to his critics: 'I am not weak. It is I who, for the first time, have brought aircraft into the reprisal raids.'

Rabin said that he hoped the Syrians would understand 'the lesson which has been administered to them'. He nonetheless considered it 'inadequate'. Israelis who were nervous of Arab retaliation were told that, as in the raid on Samu', the riposte would be a verbal one only.

The Israeli activists had succeeded in forcing Eshkol to adopt their policy, helped by Palestinian sabotage and Syrian frontier incidents. The Israeli cries of victory at the 'good lesson' which had been administered could not but incite the Arabs to revenge and banish all possibility of moves towards a peaceful settlement. Nasser in particular came increasingly under attack for remaining passive under the pretext of the curtain of Blue Berets separating him from Israel, while the Israeli generals were inflicting one 'good lesson' after another, first on the Jordanians and then on the Syrians.

Was a further 'good lesson' being prepared? The Syrians at any rate took the prospect seriously and wondered how extensive it would be this time. A flood of menacing and disquieting declarations issued from Israel. All trace of the Spirit of Tashkent had vanished. At the beginning of April Rabin declared:

> Israel, and not Syria, will in future determine the form which military operations resulting from Syrian aggression shall take. On this occasion the Israeli Air Force was brought into action as a result of frontier incidents. It might in future intervene in other circumstances, and it is in the Syrians' own interest to take heed of this warning.*

Eshkol spoke in rather less harsh tones, but his words contained the same threat. An act of sabotage committed by *El-Fatah* near to the Jordanian frontier moved him to threaten Syria. As well, he brandished the Americans' promised support for Israel, made manifest by the presence of the Sixth Fleet in Mediterranean waters.

More than anything, this last threat sounded the alarm for the Syrians. They had long been convinced – and with good reason – that they were the Americans' pet hate, and that the U.S.A. was planning

---

* *La Terre retrouvée*, 15 April 1967, p. 2.

the downfall of the Syrian regime by one means or another. The danger drew closer. On 21 April the army seized power in Greece and progressive opinion everywhere – even many other sectors of opinion – saw the hand of the C.I.A behind this coup (perhaps wrongly, but the suspicion was there). The United States, after Guatemala, Ghana and Indonesia, now turned their hand to destroying Left-wing regimes or regimes which might possibly become Left-wing in the Eastern Mediterranean. Their obstinate commitment in Vietnam, to which the U.S.S.R. submitted apparently without reaction, seemed to prove their aggressiveness and their power. The vulgar Marxist image which had taken hold of this vast sector of opinion, the image of a monolithic imperialism extending its tentacles one after the other to seize nations longing for their freedom, was all the more popular now that many facts had emerged to confirm it, its only defect being an excessive schematization. The Syrians and Nasser saw themselves as the next victims of the octopus, possibly following the Makarios regime in Cyprus. What form would the attack take? Would it come from within or from outside? If from outside, then from which direction?

General Rabin seemed to give the answer when he declared, on 12 May, that until the revolutionary regime in Damascus had been overthrown no government in the Middle East could feel safe. A few days before, the Israeli newspaper *Ha-aretz*, quoting sources in the Ministry of Defence, wrote that 'a head-on collision with Syria would become inevitable if the Syrians did not stop its encouragement of terrorist raids on Israeli territory'. On 11 May, according to the Associated Press, a high Israeli officer had threatened military occupation of Damascus in order to put an end to the acts of sabotage. The Israeli government itself advised that if *El-Fatah* raids continued it would take drastic punitive action against Syria. Press accounts of these statements also seemed so inflammatory to U.S. State Department officials that they expressed concern to Israeli authorities.*

* See Charles W. Yost, 'The Arab–Israeli War, how it began', *Foreign Affairs* , vol. 46, no. 2, January 1968, pp. 304–320.

8
Crisis

It is now understood that, at around this time, when rumours were circulating in Syrian governmental circles of an Israeli plan to launch an imminent attack on Syria, credence was given to these rumours.

On 8 May 1967 Nasser was apprised of Syrian fears of an Israeli attack. Suspicious, he demanded proof. Reports from the Lebanon, from Syria, from Soviet circles and from his own Intelligence services confirmed that there were Israeli troop-concentrations on the Syrian frontier. Rabin's statements published in the British press on the 13th also seemed to confirm it. It seems that Soviet reports were the decisive factor in convincing the Egyptian leader of the reality of the threat.

Was there any real threat? The Israelis deny it, claiming that their words were very far from becoming deeds (an argument which they reject when used by their adversaries). It has been claimed than an Israeli contingency plan, like those prepared by all General Staffs of whatever nation to cover all possible eventualities, had been stolen by the Soviet secret services and presented to Nasser as a plan for a real and imminent attack. It has also been said that some of the reinforcements sent to the north at the time of the serious April incident with Syria had been left there, giving the false appearance of an aggressive troop-concentration. Eshkol offered the Soviet ambassador the opportunity of verifying for himself that no troop-concentration existed. The offer was refused. Indeed a diplomat might not feel himself entirely qualified to spot military concentrations. U.N. observers reported that no concentration or major troop movements had been noticed. On the other hand, the Israelis are able to mobilize very quickly and invisibly, as they have demonstrated. No conclusive evidence is for the moment available, on one side or the other, as to the reality of the threat. The hypothesis has been advanced that the Israeli General Staff sought to give the Soviet Union and the Arabs the impression that an attack was imminent. To this end they allegedly made use of calculated leaks. Of course this supposition cannot be proved, but the statements made by Rabin and by other military spokesmen certainly accord with the theory. Was the desired object merely to frighten the Syrians, as the military men who hold this theory believe?

Was it hoped that by this means support for the Palestinian commando raids would be cut short once and for all? Such a hope would have exhibited a profound lack of understanding of the reactions to be expected from Syrian and Arab leaders in general – a mistake fairly common among Israeli politicians but much less likely to be made by the military, and especially not by the Intelligence services. It is difficult not to give some credit to the subsidiary hypothesis: that the situation was stirred up by the Israeli activist clique as part of a manoeuvre to provoke an Arab reaction which would force Israel to assume an 'energetic' policy and bring them back into power.

It is certain at all events that the threat to Syria was not an absurd hypothesis and that Nasser believed in it. Likewise, the Soviets undoubtedly feared an American attack (and probably a combined American-Israeli attack) on Syria sooner or later. They saw in the Israeli threats, which may or may not have been confirmed by secret information, an announcement that such an attack was imminent, and they seem to have encouraged Nasser to make some concrete demonstration of solidarity with Syria. They no doubt hoped that such a display would dampen Israeli inclinations towards possible aggression. Evidently Nasser also thought so. His solidarity had been called in question in recent months by his Arab rivals. They had all condemned his passivity at the time of the Israeli reprisal raids in November (on Samu') and April (the air-raids on Damascus). It was impossible for him to maintain this passivity. An Egyptian general was at the head of the Unified Arab Command. He had made his headquarters in Cairo, and was, in theory, responsible for the defence of all the Arab countries. At the time of the two Israeli raids, he had not lifted a finger. Nasser urgently needed to demonstrate, in some spectacular fashion, his active devotion to the Arab cause. Yet at the same time precautions had to be taken to ensure that he was not dragged into war.

On 15 May Israel organized a military parade in Jerusalem to celebrate the anniversary of the foundation of the state, at the same time demonstrating her rejection of U.N. decisions. The U.N. did not recognize any legal sovereignty on the part of the Hebrew State over the Holy City, still less the right to establish its capital or to mass troops there. Consequently the majority of foreign ambassadors boycotted this display of strength. On the same day troops, armoured cars and lorries from the south ostentatiously crossed Cairo in the direction of Sinai and the Israeli frontier. The Chief of the Egyptian General Staff was at Damascus to assure the Syrians of Egypt's support. Syria laid a complaint before the United Nations and dissociated herself from the activities of the Palestine commandos. If 500,000 American soldiers could not prevent infiltration between the two Vietnams, how was she supposed to control the Israeli-Syrian frontier better than the Israelis themselves?

However, the Syrians, Jordanians and Israelis declared themselves unconvinced by the military movements in Egypt. The old charge was levelled at Nasser once again – that he was only too grateful for the cordon of U.N. troops which prevented any Israeli-Egyptian confrontation. On the 16th Nasser made a further gesture. In the evening, a telegram from the Chief of the Egyptian General Staff, Mohammed Fawzi, was presented to the Indian general Indar Rikhye commanding the U.N. forces. This letter, which U Thant was to call 'cryptic', 'obscure' and 'unacceptable', asked General Rikhye to evacuate observation posts on the frontier. It made no reference to Gaza, let alone Sharm-el-Sheikh, which is far from the frontier. The Israelis saw in this a sign that Nasser wished to make a symbolic gesture showing his determination, but no more.

General Rikhye then declared that any decision relating to U.N. troops would have to be taken by the United Nations Secretary General. Steps would have to be taken on the political level, and it was up to the Egyptian President to make direct representations to U Thant. The latter, in New York, asked for further details. He seems to have wanted to prevent Nasser from pursuing his request – itself a bluff, to his mind. He informed him that the Egyptian President had no power to order any movement on the part of U.N. forces. All he had the right to do was to withdraw the authorization accorded in 1956 whereby these troops were permitted to be stationed on Egyptian territory. It was all or nothing. It should be recalled that Israel had always refused any parallel authorization to allow a cordon of U.N. troops to form a protective curtain on Israeli territory. U.N.E.F. had hitherto been able to function effectively only because of an informal U.A.R. agreement that its force would be held 2,000 metres back from the Armistice line in Sinai (Israeli forces patrolled right up to the line).

Nasser, after some hesitation, decided that he could not now draw back. He was still subject to continuous pressure from within and without. Jordan Radio had suddenly recalled the existence of Sharm-el-Sheikh, and derided Nasser's inoffensive moves as mere gratuitous sabre-rattling. The Syrians were also harassing him. At midday on Thursday the 18th, the Egyptian ambassador in New York presented a formal note to U Thant demanding that U.N. forces be withdrawn from Egyptian territory. The Secretary General acceded at once, for reasons which are not well understood. It is true that the Indians and Yugoslavs had threatened to withdraw their contingents from the U.N. force and that the Egyptian troops had already begun to advance on the Israeli frontier. U Thant probably thought that he would be able to defuse the dangerous train of events later, through diplomatic channels. The Secretary General received the Israeli representative, who presented his government's view that the U.N.E.F. withdrawal should not be achieved by a unilateral U.A.R. request alone and asserting Israel's right to a voice in the matter. When, however, the Secretary General raised the possibility of stationing U.N.E.F. on the Israeli side of the line, the representative replied that this would be entirely unacceptable to his government.* Egyptian units immediately took up positions on the Israeli frontier. On Friday the last observation post was evacuated. Some Palestinian units from Gaza took up positions alongside Egyptian contingents. The U.A.R., Syria and Israel placed their forces in a state of alert. The world began to be seriously disturbed. The United Nations Association in Great Britain asked Israel to accept the Blue Berets on her territory. Eshkol refused.

However, the Egyptian troop movements did not yet seem to present a grave threat. The Egyptian 4th Armoured Division had not crossed the Suez Canal. The Israelis remembered a similar military concentration in Sinai in 1960, at the time of an Israeli reprisal action against the Syrians. Nothing had come of it. Now they feared some spectacular coup by the Egyptians, like an air-raid on the Dimona nuclear reactor, perhaps to be presented as an act of reprisal, but feared no real aggression. U Thant announced his departure for Cairo. It was thought that he would try to revive the Egyptian-Israeli Armistice Commission.

As yet, peace was not threatened. The Egyptian Commander for Sinai declared that a simple incident would not be enough to unleash military action. Only an Israeli attack on Syria would produce such a result. Shukairy himself stated that he had placed his troops in Gaza under Egyptian command, and that Hussein would have to be overthrown before there could be any thought of a war of liberation against Israel.

The crucial problem was that of the Strait of Tiran. From the moment that the U.N. forces left Egyptian territory, Nasser found himself without any pretext for not reoccupying Sharm-el-Sheikh, which commands the Strait and hence the outlet from the Gulf of Aqaba to the Red Sea. On Sunday 21 May, Egyptian forces replaced the Blue Berets in Sharm-el-Sheikh.

* Charles W. Yost, *Foreign Affairs*, op. cit.

Nasser then had to make a decision on Israeli navigation through the Strait, the navigable passage of which is so narrow that the smallest fire-arm can prevent ships from passing. He hesitated, and Field-Marshal Amer told the Egyptian officers in Sinai that the Strait would not be closed. The Russians claimed that they had not been consulted. From 1948 to 1956 the Strait was controlled by the Egyptians, who in theory thus blockaded the port of Eilat at the head of the Gulf, a port built by Israel on the eight miles of beach which the Israeli army had conquered in March 1949. Israeli ships were not permitted to pass the Strait and foreign vessels had to inform the Commanders of Port Said or of Suez of the time they wished to cross. At the time of the Suez expedition the military post of Sharm-el-Sheikh had been conquered by the Israelis and then evacuated, under American pressure, together with the rest of the conquered territory; but Israeli troops had been replaced by those of the United Nations, and ships had been allowed free passage ever since. In point of fact Israeli ships passing the Strait were very rare, but foreign ships making for or returning from Eilat were fairly frequent. Only five per cent of all Israel's foreign trade was conducted through this route; at the same time the major part of Israel's oil supplies came this way. A pipeline which for the moment only reached as far as Beersheba, but which was to be continued northwards, carried the precious liquid towards Haifa. It was for the most part delivered to Eilat by ships not flying the Israeli flag. A canal had been projected which could one day enable Israel, and perhaps others also, to avoid the passage through the Suez Canal and still pass from the Red Sea to the Mediterranean and vice-versa.

In the night of 22 to 23 May Nasser made up his mind. In the small hours, he announced his intention to bar the Gulf of Aqaba to Israeli shipping. Shortly afterwards he specified that non-Israeli ships carry-ing strategic materials or oil to Eilat would also be stopped. Here at last was an action which gave the lie to all the accusations of softness and even of complicity with Zionism which had been thrown in Nasser's face or insinuated in the whole of the Arab world, even inside Egypt. The free passage of the Strait of Tiran was the only positive gain from the Suez campaign which the Israelis had been able to keep. In taking it away from them, Nasser saved Syria and at the same time won a victory – the Arabs' first victory for a very long time. He had wiped out the last trace of the Israeli victory of 1956. He had recovered Egypt's full sovereignty over the whole of her territory. None could deny it, nor continue to doubt his devotion or his contributions to the common cause.

Of course this action was fraught with danger. Nasser had weighed the risks and considered himself strong enough to face them. In March 1957 the Ben Gurion government, subject to heavy pressure from the U.N. and especially from the United States, had only agreed to evacuate Gaza and Sharm-el-Sheikh after a dogged resistance, and in exchange for the installation of the U.N. troops on Egyptian territory. Golda Meir had declared before the U.N. that Israel reserved the right to intervene militarily again if snipers recommenced their activities from their base in Gaza or if the freedom of passage to Eilat were to fall into jeopardy. Representatives of fourteen maritime powers (including the United States, France and Great Britain) had 'guaranteed' freedom of passage and proclaimed the Strait an international waterway. This might have become the object of unending and obscure controversy on a point of international law. Egypt had of course rejected this principle; at the same time she accepted the presence of the Blue Berets, so enabling it to be applied in practice. Israel delivered warnings on several occasions, stating that she would not accept that the right of free passage should ever be called in question.

No doubt Nasser thought there was a good chance that Israel would make no move – whatever he was to say a few days later. He knew that he could count on the protection of the Soviet Union and on the understanding at least of many of the nations at the U.N., and that of the Secretary General. He even had powerful friends in the State Department, and knew that Johnson, preoccupied with Vietnam, was not eager to involve himself in the Middle East. He now had all the Arab states ranged willy-nilly behind him, driven by public opinion to support him; he was in a position to drive a hard bargain. He knew that Eshkol and Eban would try to find a peaceful solution. After all, all that had happened was a return to the situation as it was before 1956.

On the 23rd he received U Thant in Cairo and concluded a secret agreement with him. No new move would be taken which might increase tension; a representative of the Secretary General would do the rounds between Cairo and Tel Aviv in an attempt to find some common ground. While waiting for a compromise to be reached, U Thant would ask the maritime powers to refrain from delivering strategic materials to Israel via Eilat. All they needed to do was use Haifa instead. Thus Egypt would be absolved from the responsibility of taking any provocative action by exercising the right of control from Sharm-el-Sheikh.

But Nasser failed to take full account of a number of important factors. He had set a mechanism in motion which was to turn on him and grind all his calculations into dust.

Up to 22 May his moves had been spectacular but innocuous. None was really liable to unleash a serious riposte from Israel. Everyone knew this very well – friends, enemies and neutrals. The situation had reached a state of tension – a commonplace occurrence. At most, all it was likely to do was to make Israel think twice before launching an attack on the Syrian regime. This had been the object of the exercise, and it was, for the moment, successful. The result was that the other Arab states and Arab movements in competition with Nasserism looked on these manoeuvres with undisguised scepticism. In their eyes this was just another Egyptian bluff, designed to polish up Nasser's image. In addition they viewed the Syrian regime with something less than warm affection and would have been delighted if Israel were to rid them of it. If Nasser were dragged down together with the Syrian Ba'athists, so much the better. Hence throughout this period Nasser and the Syrians, instead of denouncing Israel, denounced the American-Israeli conspiracy supported by the reactionary Arab states. They called for revolution against these states – Jordan and Saudi Arabia in particular. Abuse was also directed at the more distant Hassan II and Bourguiba, accusing them of being the accomplices of imperialism. Nasser rejected a suggestion to call a meeting of the Defence Council of the Arab League, declaring that Egypt was not prepared 'to reveal her military secrets to governments in the pay of the C.I.A. and the British Intelligence Service'.* On 20 May the Commander of the Syrian People's Army announced that the forces of his army 'would help to carry the war on to Palestine's usurped territory and to overthrow the reactionary Arab thrones, in particular that of King Hussein'.† On 21 May a major incident flared up between Jordan and Syria. A Syrian car blew up while being examined by the Jordanian customs. The Jordanians alleged that the vehicle was being used by the Syrian secret service, and had been intended to explode in the centre of Amman. On the 23rd Jordan broke off diplomatic relations with Syria.

All this changed the day after the declaration of the blockade of the Strait of Tiran, 23 May. No Arab government, whatever its true sentiments, could repudiate this joint victory for the Arab people. On the other hand, there was now a serious danger of a riposte from Israel.

Sure enough, the Israeli activists were triumphant and strident in their demands. This was what Eshkol's and Eban's policy of weakness had led to. It would never have happened had 'the Old Man' been in

* See *Le Monde*, 23 May 1967, p. 3.

† Quoted by *Cahiers de l'Orient contemporain*, no. 67, October 1967, p. 10.

charge, with Dayan and Peres. The press, almost entirely Ben Gurionist, kept up the refrain. Heavy pressure was being exerted on the cabinet. A renewed blockade of the Strait of Tiran had once been defined as a *casus belli*. Israel should strike back before it was too late, attack before the Arabs attacked, as they were bound to do before long. Ben Gurion would never have hesitated for so long.

The military leaders wanted to strike at once. If the Arabs attacked first, they said, the country would be in the gravest peril. Yet, in self-contradiction, they became angry when certain civilians cast doubts on the strength of the army and argued from this that the question ought to be settled via diplomatic channels. To everyone's surprise, one of these civilians was David Ben Gurion himself. The explanation lay in the fact that he felt his successors, especially Eshkol, whom he had come to detest, must have been letting this army which he had forged deteriorate.

Eshkol was forced to shift his ground. From 23 May he began to grant some responsibilities to the activist opposition. He convoked the interdepartmental Committee of National Defence, and procured the participation of Dayan, Peres and Begin, among others. The generals gave a survey of the situation. A communication was read out from the President of the United States, counselling patience.

Despite opposition from the activists, Eshkol sent Eban on a round tour of all the big powers to sound out their attitudes and ask for their aid. On the 24th, Eban saw de Gaulle in Paris, who urgently advised Israel not to attack. The General-cum-President called for a conference between the four great powers – the United States, the U.S.S.R., Great Britain and France. Eban passed on to London, where Wilson told him that he would associate himself with any American or U.N. action to reopen the Strait of Tiran. On 25 May the Israeli Minister for Foreign Affairs arrived in Washington, where the Pentagon showed itself very well-informed. It had no doubt whatever of Israel's over-whelming superiority, and confidently expected that her army was about to attack. Johnson received Eban; he begged for restraint, promising him that the Strait of Tiran would be reopened by hook or by crook.

In fact the Western powers at once accepted the Israeli thesis on the closure of the Strait. Yet Egypt could bring forward what were at the very least powerful arguments in any legal discussion on this difficult question of international law. In the absence of any specific inter-national convention, was any state obliged to grant passage, through coastal waters extending less than two miles from its shores, to strategic material intended for another state with which it was legally at war? Besides, all that had been effected was a return to the situation operating from 1949 to 1956. What precisely was the definition of an international waterway? Experts did not agree on the matter, and there was at least sufficient material for lengthy discussion before the International Court of Justice in the Hague. Yet on the evening of 23 May, Johnson had asserted that the Strait was an international waterway and that free passage through it ought to be ensured. His ambassador in Cairo proposed to Egypt a plan which would annul the effects of the latest Egyptian move. Cairo rejected the plan. Also on the 23rd Senator Robert Kennedy, speaking at a meeting of the American Jewish Association B'nai B'rith, demanded that a U.N. naval force should be sent to the Strait. On the 24th Harold Wilson, without mentioning the U.N., stated his readiness to participate in international action with the object of reopening the Strait by force.

On the evening of the 27th Eban returned to Tel Aviv satisfied with the promises made by Britain and the United States and convinced that a peaceful settlement was possible. But he found the situation at home greatly changed. The activists had gained ground – and the Arabs had given them very considerable help.

The theatrical gesture of closing the Strait of Tiran had elated the Arabs beyond all measure. This bloodless victory, representing the annulment of Israel's last gain from the Suez campaign, filled them with ardour and confidence, all the more since Israel's reaction was slow in coming and Soviet support seemed an effective counterweight to the Anglo-Saxon aid given to the Jewish State. France was a friendly neutral. Israel seemed to have been driven back into acceptance of defeat. The mob and the propagandists of the press immediately jumped from this diplomatic defeat to the conclusion that the hour had perhaps come for them to inflict the final military defeat to which they had looked forward for so many years. Their exaltation grew, expressing itself in the traditional manner of Arab prose and poetry, inspired by the braggadocio usually displayed by the fighters of the desert. The adversary was promised a thousand deaths, with the most exquisite refinements in the description of his impending annihilation, of the revenge which must surely come, of the cruelties he would be made to suffer. The caricaturists set to with relish; one would have to go back to the war of 1914–18 to find anything to compare with these vengeful drawings, in which the enemy is depicted in the most odious guise, and his forthcoming demise horribly prefigured. None could stay aloof from the general enthusiasm; even the most moderate among the Arabs were carried along by it, down to Bourguiba, so recently the apostle of peace.

Everyone was swept along by the current. The result was a sacred union based on the simplest and most universal of sentiments: the feelings of patriotism and of nationalism. Religion was enlisted in the campaign. Muftis and ulema, as well as Christian patriarchs, all called down curses upon Israel. The Arab governments could only follow the stream. Distinctions based on political and social attitudes were no longer in fashion. Only the revolutionary leaders in Damascus resisted the flow, and adamantly refused to ally themselves with the reactionary regimes.

Nasser had at first thought military retaliations by Israel unlikely, and his secret dealings had been directed towards achieving an arrangement whereby he would retain the moral benefits of his spectacular gesture, while reducing its practical disadvantages for Israel. However, the flame which he himself had fanned was beginning to scorch him. It seems that especially strong pressure was exerted on him by the officers engaged in the Yemen and by those in Cairo who reflected their attitudes. Just as in any army anywhere in the world, the Egyptian officers, engaged in a distant war against an invisible enemy, felt themselves betrayed and abandoned by the civil power – even though governed by a lieutenant-colonel – which doled out arms and reinforcements in restricted doses and seemed at times to be bargaining with the enemy. They at any rate pressed for an energetic attitude towards Israel, demanding that every advantage should be taken of the situation, in which they thought their country now had the upper hand. Their Syrian allies also urged Nasser to assume a pugnacious attitude.

In the other direction, the Soviets now began to fear a real conflict. They were afraid that a flare-up might lead to a general conflagration and end in world war. They hesitated, urging moderation on Nasser. Very likely, they used the 'hot line' to the White House. Moscow favoured joint action with Johnson, preferring an entente between the two super-powers to the four-power conference proposed by de Gaulle. After a long delay, de Gaulle's plan was rejected (30 May). Meanwhile Gromyko had meetings with George Brown in Moscow on the 24th and 25th, while the Egyptian Minister of War also held talks in Moscow with his Soviet counterpart.

In any case, Nasser sent the 4th Armoured Division into Sinai some time on the 24th or 25th. Unsure of himself, he gave increased expression to the Arab threat, both verbally and by his troop movements. He began to consider the possibility of some military reaction on the part of Israel, perhaps even of a preventive action by the Arabs. On the 26th he declared that *if Israel attacked Syria or Egypt* the war thus unleashed would become total. The objective would then be the destruction of Israel. In reality he seems at one time to have accepted the idea that if the worst came to the worst, the Israelis would attack, gaining some ground in Sinai at first, but subsequently being halted by United Nations' intervention, which would enable a final and comprehensive settlement of the problem. The Israeli service chiefs, for their part, became increasingly insistent on attack, and accused the pacifists of treason for their shillyshallying. The press depicted Israel as threatened by annihilation unless she acted at once. The threats issued by the Arab radio and press reached paroxysms of violence, mobilizing the entire Israeli population, which saw in this propaganda the promise of its approaching doom. World public opinion reached a tremendous emotional pitch. The basic sympathy for Israel, the reasons for which have been enumerated earlier, was inflamed by the prospect that this little people, including a great number of escapees from the Nazi massacre, might be wiped out in blood and flames by hysterical mobs infinitely superior in numbers and, it was thought, in strength.

On Sunday 28 May two events of major importance took place. A meeting of Israeli ministers had been called on the previous evening to receive Eban. His report was considered disappointing. There was scepticism as to the value of the Anglo-American promise to reopen the Strait of Tiran. Must they then give way to the pleas of the military and attack? The meeting was evenly divided on the question: nine ministers were in favour and nine against. This time Eshkol was for attack, together with the majority of the Mapai ministers. Was he really convinced by the military arguments? Or foreseeing that he would be forced to follow the current, did he prefer to retain some control of it? At all events, he did not put the matter to the vote, procrastinating once again. The council dispersed at one in the morning. Shortly afterwards the Soviet and American ambassadors came in turn to deliver messages to Eshkol from Kosygin and Johnson respectively. The messages pleaded for calm. At a second meeting held the same day Eshkol, convinced by these pleas, persuaded all his ministers save one that all diplomatic measures should be exhausted before having recourse to arms. This was the doves' last victory. The generals were enraged. They hurled insults at Eshkol and his ministers, threatened resignation, and spoke of a coup d'état. Rabin declared: 'It is becoming increasingly evident that the only force which can be relied upon in this country is the army.' * Public opinion was disturbed, and found little reassurance in a hesitant speech by Eshkol. Daily threatened on the air by the Arabs, the population was won over in advance to a policy of force which, it was thought, would remove the menace.

More or less similar scenes took place in Cairo. Nasser was subjected, in secret, to increasingly powerful pressures. Field-Marshal Amer and the younger officers were on the attack. They, too, desired a preventive action before Israel moved. On the other side, the emissaries from Johnson and Kosygin again counselled patience. On 28 May Nasser gave a press conference. He appeared nervous and irritable. He, too, hoped to retain control of the current by making verbal concessions. He spoke violently, enumerating Israel's past violations of U.N. resolutions. 'If Israel wants to attack us, our answer is: You are welcome!' † The Palestinians had the right to attack, to recover the rights of which they had been robbed. 'If the war of liberation becomes a total war in the Middle East, we are ready for the struggle.'

He used a phrase which recalled the principle of permanent struggle, the fundamental refusal to accept Israel: 'We shall never accept any kind of coexistence with Israel, for the very creation of this state constitutes an aggression against the Arabs.' However, he immediately followed this statement with an indication that the door to negotiation was still open. He announced that he was ready to serve again on the Joint Israeli-Egyptian Armistice Commission, if Israel would agree to its revival as asked for by U Thant (Israel had put an end to it in 1956). The condition for this was the evacuation of the al-Auja demilitarized zone, occupied by Israel in 1955, and the installation of U.N. troops there instead of the Israelis. This would mean the return of the Blue Berets to the Egypt-Israeli frontier and Israel would in practice be recognized. He also considered the possibility of an all-embracing discussion of the Palestine problem; all outstanding questions would be subject to negotiation through the intermediary of disinterested powers. In the course of the next few days, while the Egyptian head of state was delivering himself of a string of pugnacious proclamations, his own higher officials and diplomats gave peaceful assurances behind the scenes. Egypt was ready to negotiate on the right of passage through Tiran, and even through the Suez Canal, if the discussions covered the U.N. resolutions taken between 1947 and 1950 as well – resolutions

* According to Eliahu Ben Elissar and Zeev Schiff, *La Guerre israélo-arabe, 5–10 juin 1967*, Paris, Julliard, 1967, p. 97.

† See *Le Monde*, 30 May, 1967, p. 3.

which Israel had refused to apply. A really major piece of bargaining could be undertaken.

Nasser's words, the most menacing of which were picked out by the world press and by the Israelis, persuaded world opinion that an Arab attack was imminent. People everywhere took the Arabs' sabre-rattling at its face value. Of course the memory of the crushing defeat inflicted on the Egyptians in 1956 was still strong; but surely things were a little different this time? The Egyptian and Syrian armies had been well-supplied with modern arms by the U.S.S.R. Comparative tables were drawn up showing Israel at a disadvantage. Over the eleven years which had elapsed, Nasser must surely have remedied the shortcomings of his army. Moreover this time the Arabs showed a united front (or almost). Israel no longer enjoyed the advantage of the air cover provided in 1956 by Great Britain and France.

A vital element was missing from the Arab front: Jordan. Hussein was daily covered in vituperation by Cairo and Damascus, and had no desire whatsoever to join forces with his enemies; very likely he hoped they would be defeated. He had been assured that Israel would not attack him if he made no aggressive move. He had announced that he would remain neutral. But he was won over by the general confidence in an Arab victory. If war broke out, his people would never accept neutrality, and his throne would crumble. If the Arabs were victorious, he would be all the more certainly dragged down in Israel's fall. Perhaps he was also inspired by some sincere patriotism. At any rate on the morning of 30 May he took the controls of a civil aircraft and set off for Cairo, accompanied by his Prime Minister and Chief of Staff. At 3 p.m. the text of a joint Egyptian-Jordanian defence pact which had just been signed was read out over the radio. In the afternoon Hussein returned to Amman, this time taking with him an Egyptian general and Ahmed Shukairy. Until that moment, the latter had been banned from Jordan. Now there was a general reconciliation. On the following day Shukairy reopened the P.L.O. office in the Old City of Jerusalem, which Hussein had had closed down. Also on the 31st Iraq decided to send troops as reinforcements to Jordan. Algeria and Morocco also decided to send military units.

'The world will see that in the hour of need, the Arabs will unite,' Nasser had declared in his welcoming address to Hussein. It is true that the conflict had passed imperceptibly into a new phase, limited for the moment to verbal demonstrations and troop movements. This new phase was marked by the declaration of the closure of the Strait of Tiran, and was confirmed by the reconciliation with Hussein. The

Left-wing Israeli orientalist, Simha Flapan, has tried to show, as against Isaac Deutscher, that the change was from an anti-imperialist phase directed against the United States with the principal object of deflecting the threat (real or imaginary) facing Syria, to a purely nationalist and chauvinist phase in which the object was Israel's destruction. This is not the case. What is true is that Nasser widened the area of dispute. From a threat intended to dissuade Israel from attacking Syria, he hoped to be able to move on to a heavier threat which would oblige Israel to negotiate on all the problems entailed by her creation. He thought that this threat might perhaps force Israel for the first time to make major concessions on the question of the return of the refugees and of the territory conquered in 1948. Here it was no longer a question of defending the Syrian regime, but of returning to the fundamental claims which no Arab could abandon. Any alliance was worth-while if it helped to frighten Israel. Moreover if the Egyptian leader could close the ranks behind him, he would have his hands free in the final grand negotiation. But the risks were great. Israel might attack. Nasser thought Israel would feel herself at a disadvantage and would not do so. Was she really too weak? If so, why not attack himself, as his Right-wing critics, especially the military, urged him to do? The populace, unaware of the true balance of forces, also pushed him in this direction. There was, however, every indication that the Egyptian leader had no intention of giving way to the temptation.

The Syrians for their part were thinking chiefly of their internal problems and saw the Israeli-Arab conflict in terms of the struggle of the exploited Third World against American imperialism. They saw no reason to abandon this theory. To do so would have meant reconciliation with their enemies within and without, and the abandonment, at least partially, of their revolutionary programme and possibly in the end of their power as well. They had absolutely no desire for a war of the traditional type, which was the surest way of bringing Israeli tanks rumbling into the streets of Damascus. The Palestinian commandos' call for revolutionary struggle against Israel was far more to their taste. Certainly they threatened Israel. But they had no intention of letting the threat unleash a conventional war, nor obscure the revolutionary ideal underlying the struggle. They therefore bridled at the reconciliation with Hussein.

To make his deterrent more credible and to bring Israel to the negotiating table, Nasser needed American neutrality and the good offices of American diplomacy. The Soviet Union had no objections to such a course. They encouraged Nasser in his deterrent measures at the beginning of the crisis, designed to protect the Syrian regime, and were no doubt not unhappy to embarrass the United States. They wanted to give notice to the Americans that they would not sit idly by for ever and watch their friends and allies be coerced. Their pressure very likely helped to prevent the Americans from intervening and opening the Strait of Tiran by force. But now they were afraid that the Arabs were going too far, and that they themselves would be drawn into a confrontation with the United States for which they had no appetite. They pressed for conciliation. In the night of 26 to 27 May, at 3.30 a.m., a Soviet diplomat woke Nasser to deliver a message from Kosygin urging him not to give way to those who were pressing him to attack.

In his press conference on 28 May Nasser protested his good faith towards the United States. He deplored exhortations to blow up oil installations in the Arab countries, which had been common in the immediately preceding period. The Americans, in return, made a gesture of their own. On the 29th Charles Yost, a State Department adviser on Middle Eastern affairs, arrived in Cairo. He entered into intense private negotiations with the Egyptians.

The Israeli people, however, knew nothing of Nasser's private intentions or of these secret moves. Their attention had not been drawn to the prudent and responsible phrases, pointing to a way out of the impasse, which had followed all the vitriolic rantings. They heard the Arabs' threats, which now reached an unprecedented pitch; they saw themselves surrounded by a monolithic hostile coalition, and fully expected that if war came they would suffer a terrible massacre, which Shukairy was already promising them in lurid detail. The Jordanians were at their gates. The United States showed signs of weakening in their support. France had already abandoned them. The homeland was in danger. Every Israeli Jew was ready to defend it, even those who showed the most understanding for the Arabs' claims: sections of the Mapai, most of the Jewish Communists, Avneri, the Bohemian intelligentsia. Pressure from the service chiefs and activist politicians became irresistible now that Hussein had joined the Arab front. Eshkol was thought too weak and too vacillating. Pressure was exerted on him to relinquish the Ministry of Defence in favour of Dayan. The Right-wing ministers threatened to withdraw their support, the generals threatened resignation. Eshkol was ready to abandon the Defence Ministry, but did not want to see Dayan take his place, fearing that he would take dangerous initiatives. He offered Dayan a ministry without portfolio, then the Egyptian command. Dayan refused. He wanted the Ministry of Defence. On 31 May the Mapai secretariat, despite

Eshkol's and Golda Meir's opposition, decided to replace Eshkol as Minister of Defence by Dayan. On 1 June the government ratified the Mapai's decision. A Ministry of National Unity was formed. Begin, who had four days earlier been spectacularly reconciled with Ben Gurion, was made a minister. Golda Meir departed.

The activist group had won. Whatever the true intentions of either party at the time of the threats directed against Syria before 15 May, two weeks of crisis had sufficed to bring the militants to power, winning a post from which they could directly influence events. Dayan had the great majority of the population behind him. Terrorized by the Arab threat, they had faith in the determination and boldness of the victor of Sinai. They forgot the military leaders who had carefully been prepar-ing the army on behalf of this figurehead. The victory of the moderates at the elections of 1965, the divisions, the party clashes, the disillusion-ment with Zionism, all was forgotten. Holy unity was the order of the day.

This was the moment, according to Israeli sources, at which the decision to attack was taken. The only point on which there is still dispute is the precise date. Whatever the truth of the matter, by Satur-day the 3rd, in the morning, the divisional commanders received their orders to attack on the following Monday. To increase the element of surprise, many troops were granted Sabbath leave. Dayan gave a press conference on the same Saturday, spoke of patience, and said that, together with the rest of the government, he would await the outcome of the diplomatic approaches then being made.

In the Arab camp, the verbal intemperance continued. Shukairy especially distinguished himself, declaring that after the coming war there would be practically no survivors. He announced that it was possible, even probable, that the Jordanian army would fire the first shot. Hussein and Nasser, who stuck to their policy of wait-and-see, were horrified. The Jordanian press censored some of the remarks made by the head of the P.L.O. and Shukairy himself was obliged to swallow some of his words. Disunity was rife, despite the recruitment of Iraq, on the evening of Sunday the 4th, to the Jordanian-Egyptian defence pact. This same pact was still rejected by Damascus, and the Syrian press withheld announcement of it. Instead, news was published of disturbances in the Jordanian army, where revolutionary elements were said to be bridling against Hussein's hostility to Syria. The Alge-rians too denounced this alliance with a pro-Western monarch, who sullied the purity of the revolutionary Arab movement. Saudi Arabia was also upset by the pact, for opposite reasons, and suspended arms deliveries to the Hashemite king – an unreliable ally, now in league with her enemies. The United States, on whom practically half of the Jordanian exchequer depended, applied similar sanctions against Hussein.

No doubt the pressure on Nasser continued to grow. Amer and some of the army feared that Israel would strike the first blow. Hussein thought, and stated, that he was afraid the Israelis would profit from a moment's inattention. But he did not think the danger immediate, and did not therefore urge attack. The Syrians, too, thought they could make substantial gains through diplomatic action, without giving up the idea of eventual guerrilla war, and it seems that this was the burden of the Syrian Foreign Minister's discussions with Nasser.

Nasser feared an Israeli attack, and must have been tempted to launch a preventive action. He was very well aware of the Israelis' exasperation. However, he had little faith in his Arab allies. He knew that American public opinion, as well as a large part of the Administration, was hostile to him, that they would not forgive a military attack on his part. Both the United States and the Soviet Union continually urged him to show patience. Soviet diplomats must have promised that, in return, the Americans would prevent the Israelis from attacking, and it is true that both the Soviets and the Americans made similar representations to Eshkol. Nasser therefore stepped up his diplomatic activity. The crisis was so grave that Israel would surely take fright and make concessions. Nasser kept the bidding very high, but he did leave room for negotiation. In the Security Council his representative put forward a draft resolution which once again proposed to take advantage of the situation to achieve a general settlement. Israel would be enjoined in accordance with U Thant's requirements to revive the Egyptian-Israeli Joint Armistice Commission, which would have its headquarters at al-Auja in the previously demilitarized zone, occupied by Israel since 1955. This was an open invitation to return to the conditions which followed the 1948 war, including what had amounted to *de facto* recognition of Israel. At the same time it would mean ratification of the *fait accompli* at Tiran. The proposal met with Western opposition. Nasser was made to realize that he was asking too much, and that the most he could expect was an agreement which would allow him to retain some of the benefit of his gesture in blockading the Strait – viz. recognition in principle of Egyptian sovereignty.

In Cairo Johnson's envoy, Charles Yost, concluded a secret agreement in principle with the Egyptian Foreign Minister. Diplomatic channels were to remain open. Egypt would not object to the question of the Strait of Tiran being put before the Court of Justice in the Hague. Nasser's second-in-command, Zakaria Mohieddin, First Vice-President of the Republic, was to visit Washington to negotiate a compromise. Egypt was inclined to allow oil through the Strait of Tiran, limiting her controls to strategic materials. On 3 June Yost left Cairo, having given an assurance that Israel would not attack as long as diplomatic activity was maintained. Both Moscow and Tel Aviv were informed of the attempts to achieve a compromise which were under way. It seems however that Left-wing ministers were not informed, still less was public opinion. The Soviet Union was very alarmed at the prospect of war, and let it be known in the corridors of the United Nations that she might be induced to accept the four-power conference proposed by de Gaulle. They wanted to know if Israel would accept a compromise like that to be negotiated by Yost. Diplomatic circles, notably the British, turned their attention to solving the problem: to safeguard Israel's existence in return for a concession to Nasser enabling him to keep some of the winnings of his gesture and to save face.

Public opinion everywhere feared an Arab attack on Israel, while the diplomats were more afraid of an Israeli move. In London, New York, Paris and elsewhere demonstrations of support for Israel multiplied. Shukairy's threats and the cartoons in Syrian newspapers were enough to show that Israel's annihilation and the general massacre of her inhabitants was imminent.

On 2 June de Gaulle, who had just received the Syrian Foreign Minister, announced that the state which first resorted to arms would have neither the approval nor the support of France. He again put forward the idea of a four-power conference to work out solutions to all the outstanding problems concerning Palestine. He was visibly supported in this by both the Egyptians and the Syrians.

Public excitement both in Israel and in the Arab countries had reached fever-pitch. The propaganda war seemed to show that war was inevitable. Therefore why not get it over with? It was not thought necessary to inform the Israelis of Yost's negotiations nor of the Egyptian concessions then being formulated. The Israelis wanted to react to the menace hanging over them and which they thought very serious. They would win the victory, or die fighting. The Arabs, intoxicated by their own propaganda, believed in their military superiority. Therefore it was time this poisonous problem were done away with. The Arab peoples were moreover completely unaware of the sufferings which such a conflict could entail for themselves. Their armies were powerful and well equipped. They would win without any trouble.

The Egyptian and Syrian governments thought that the war of nerves and Israel's apparent diplomatic isolation would force her to yield, and prevent her attacking. The only remaining problem was the extent of the concession which could be obtained.

The Israeli government was of the same mind. The diplomatists would force them to yield up something of that which they had till then clung to with such tenacity. At most, the return of the refugees and the evacuation of the occupied demilitarized zones, possibly even more. At least, they would have to yield something of their present absolute freedom of passage through the Strait of Tiran. In return it would be possible for them to obtain some sort of *de facto* recognition, a kind of declaration of non-belligerence. But this was not enough.

Did the military chiefs and the activist clique really believe that if the Arabs struck first they had a chance of success? Not at all. The Commander in Chief of the Israeli Air Force is said to have informed Eshkol that he could take his time: whatever happened, the Arabs' air power would be liquidated in the first attack. But these elements did believe that such an attack by the Arabs would at least make their own plans for aggression more difficult to put into practice. The possible gains to be had by diplomacy did not seem to them worth the human and strategic sacrifices it would mean for Israel. Some, at any rate, thought less in terms of defence than of attack. It was an ideal point at which to strike a heavy blow and administer the promised 'good lesson' to the Arabs. After that the diplomats could have free rein. Infiltration and sabotage would be stopped; at the very least there would be some readjustment in Israel's favour of the more strategically disadvantageous sections of the frontier. At most – the sky was the limit.

Civilian leaders and the more pacific of the politicians were afraid of a kind of second Munich. They were afraid of the Arabs. Any peaceful solution without first some demonstration of force would entail Israeli concessions. The major powers would perhaps be able to enforce these concessions. Concessions are only possible between nations which have a certain degree of confidence in one another. But no Arab dared lay emphasis on the advantages which Israel could win from these concessions, on the guarantees which could be granted to her, even if secret negotiations did highlight these points, and although some reading between the lines of Arab declarations allowed them to be deduced. From that time on every concession was considered to be a dismantling of one of Israel's defences, a stage in the progress to that destruction which a thousand virulent pronouncements promised them. The Israeli population felt themselves physically threatened, and it is undeniable that the Arabs gave them some cause to feel so. Everyone remembered Munich, where the abandonment of the Sudetenland forced on the Czechs by the great powers and morally justified in the name of national self-determination led to Czechoslovakia's subjugation the moment her defences had been breached.

The installation of the Israeli colony had conditioned the Arabs' reactions. Arab reactions in turn affected Israeli attitudes. The Arab position of moderation in practice could not carry the day, given the obligatory verbal intransigence imposed on every Arab ruler, and the signs of impending guerrilla warfare. The Israelis did not, in such conditions, have enough reason for confidence in the safety not only of their state and institutions but of their very lives. No one in Israel had arguments strong enough to maintain against the activism which believed in safeguarding the state by demonstrations of force, by rebuilding the country in the shape of a modern Sparta, hard and pure. On Monday 5 June, at 7 in the morning (Israel time), the Israeli air force left the tarmac. Less than two hours later, the Arab air force had to all intents and purposes ceased to exist. The war, which was to last another six days, was virtually won.

Another victory, another conquest, but no peace.

9
The Palestinians Take Over

We shall not here go into the details of the military operations: hundreds of publications have dealt with them. As everyone knows, the war of 5–10 June 1967 was, from the technical standpoint, a notable success for Israel. Just as in 1948 and in 1956, proof was given of the striking superiority of a people possessing many technical cadres, with an army organized in ultra-modern fashion, united by a common will or a common fear, rich in skill, talent and enthusiasm, and organically linked with the advanced industrial world, over states in a condition of under-development, deeply divided in spite of their momentary agreement on a common strategy, and poor in cadres capable of making proper use of modern equipment and coordinating the actions of soldiers who were docile, and often zealous, but often also (especially the Egyptians) poverty-stricken, ignorant and resigned all their lives to submission to an adverse fate.

Israel's triumph, so complete, so quick, so impeccable, inaugurated a new period. The respective situations of the contending parties, their internal dispositions and the way they saw themselves, all underwent change. Within each camp a process began which was to alter profoundly the conditions and even the prospects of the struggle.

The two-sided conflict between the Arab states and the Israelis quickly became three-sided. The Palestinians, who until then had played only a minor role, soon became an essential participant in this tragic game for which, seventy years earlier, Theodor Herzl had signalled the start without suspecting all its implications.

Two of the three participants found themselves strengthened in a self-confidence that was dictated, in each case, by diametrically opposed attitudes of mind. The Israelis and the Palestinians alike thought that they had the movement of history with them. But their conceptions of history were quite different. For the Israelis it was a question of that history which has always justified the strong, which, as Jesus of Nazareth put it, gives to him that hath, and which maintains those who are stable in their stability, the rich in their riches, the powerful in their power: the conception, in fact, held by the persecutors of the Israelis' own fathers and forefathers. For the Palestinians it was a question of that history which overthrows empires that seem to be at the height of their strength, which enjoys humbling the pride of the powerful and gives victory to the oppressed and humiliated – in short, it was a question of revolutionary history. Without knowing it, they adopted for themselves the outlook of the Hebrew prophets of ancient times – their bitter exultation in predicting the collapse of the Colossus with feet of clay, the destruction of Babylon the Great – just as they resumed the denunciations, full of confidence in the future, uttered by the numberless successors of those visionaries of olden times – the Christian heresiarchs or Muslim rebels who rose against the established order – and, later (the guarantee of a deified History having replaced that of the divine will), by the revolutionaries of the modern age. Millennial prophecies of apocalypses of vengeance, lit by the red glow of the conflagrations of proud cities, inspired their struggle, idealizing in the usual way factors that were a great deal less uplifting.

Both sides were to learn, to their great detriment, slowly and painfully, that nothing was as certain as they expected. To be sure, nothing is stable, victories have to be paid for, powers collapse; but the experience of the apocalypse, as Malraux said, is also strewn with countless disappointments, the weak and the rebellious triumphing only under strict conditions which render their victory ambiguous, to say the least; and often, moreover, they taste the bitter salt of defeat. Perhaps it is always right to rebel, but the outcome of rebellion frequently disgusts the rebel, when he is allowed the favour of retaining his capacity to feel disgust.

As for the Arab rulers, the assurance that certain of them might once have felt was dead indeed. Some might, for a time, share the Palestinians' confidence in the future. But that future was put off further and further, which is usually the way in which one eventually forgets the hopes originally placed in it. They initiated more or less quickly (when this had not begun much earlier) that process of reconciliation with reality once celebrated by Hegel and which has always sickened revolutionaries. Soon, a substantial section of the Palestinians themselves would follow them along that road.

But the reality with which one seeks reconciliation is often only the reality of yesterday: rebellion is never overcome without having left its mark. Our descendants will know, perhaps, who was right and who was wrong and, much more probably, in what ways the same persons were at once both right and wrong.

The external world, too, was divided into a world of stable states and a world consisting of forces of contestation. The latter was bewildered, because the revolt in the Middle East was not its own revolt, and to some it seemed, in a way, to be in opposition thereto. Nevertheless, the rebels gradually rallied to the side of the rebels. This process had hardly been accomplished when the former began to wonder whether the latter, who were now sobering up, really deserved their support. As for the states, they appreciated to an increasing degree that stability would not be maintained without making some concession to the demands of the rebels. Some of them, which had recently emerged from revolutions, were soon to learn, contrariwise, that contestation itself had to become reconciled with a certain reality.

A general consensus thus began to take shape, the only elements unaffected being those most deeply committed to total victory – through, on the one hand, stubborn persistence in opposition to the wave of revolt or, on the other, rejection of any compromise with a reality regarded as unjust: that is to say, the majority of the Israelis and the extremist minority of the Palestinians. Even the clearest-headed of their leaders, being their leaders, had to follow them.

Thus, Israel had triumphed once again, and in a way that was more brilliant, more assured, more masterly than ever. The Israeli empire extended to the Suez Canal and to Sharm-el-Sheikh at the tip of the Sinai Peninsula, to the Jordan on the east, and, in the north-east, to the Golan Heights, from which it was possible to make out Damascus. Jerusalem was, as the Israelis put it, reunited: that is, Jewish Jerusalem, the modern suburbs which had proliferated since the nineteenth century, had annexed the Old City, surrounded by the wall of Suleiman the Magnificent, or Arab Jerusalem. The whole of the former British mandated territory of Palestine had been reunited under the rule of the Israeli authorities. All that remained, in order to reconstitute ancient Israel in accordance with the Zionist vision, was the rest of the Kingdom of Jordan, the former Transjordania. But only the most 'integrist' still dreamt (or dreamt already?) of annexing that to the new state

What was to be done with this victory? What was the precise role to be played in political plans by these conquered territories? At first it had been indicated that Israel did not wish to annex anything. Had not Hussein been assured, during the war, that his kingdom's integrity would not suffer, provided that he remained neutral? Only Arab Jerusalem was formally incorporated into the state of Israel by a vote of the Knesset. It was explained that the ancient city which all the languages and literatures of the world treated as the symbolic and sacred centre of Israel, with all its memories accumulated above and below ground, with the parvis of the Temple of Solomon and Herod (which, all the same, they did not dare wrest from Islam), could not be allowed to fall again under non-Israeli authority, that it was inhuman to cut in two a town, an historic capital, a sacred centre.

And that final peace with the Arabs which had always been proclaimed as the ultimate aim of Israel's efforts? Some leaders doubtless thought that attainment of this aim was worth the cost of giving back the occupied territories, as outsiders suggested. There was now in hand a means wherewith to bargain for full and complete recognition of Israel as it had been constituted twenty years before, including acquisitions which even then went beyond what the United Nations had laid down and had been agreed upon. Some thought for a moment that, as outsiders were suggesting, a solemn offer in that sense would have a chance of getting acceptance, at a time when the Arab states were cast down by the burden of defeat. Is this not what wars are for, in principle – to compel the side that is defeated to accept something it had rejected when there was peace? To liquidate the conflict, to end the Arabs' rejection of Israel, was it not worth while to give back territories that were incongruous, either consisting of desert or inhabited by a hostile population? Such an offer might have been rejected; but no one can prove that, because the offer was not made, either in an all-embracing way or even at this time in the form of exchanging for definitive peace with Egypt or Jordan, the states most ready to make concessions, the lands which had been taken from them.

On the contrary, Israel showed very quickly that it preferred to keep the lot. Sinai was stated to be essential in order to provide a protective space that would guarantee Israel's cities against direct attack. Conquered Golan safeguarded the villages of Galilee from being bombarded from Syrian gun positions. As for the West Bank, those areas were given the historic names of Judaea and Samaria, which clearly demonstrated that they formed part of the Jewish homeland. Considerations were added concerning the disadvantages of the frontiers of before June 1967 from the military standpoint. The old frontiers, thus criticized, had not, to be sure, prevented Israel gaining the victory. But the new cease-fire lines, by ensuring that Israel's losses in the event of another war would be fewer, and those to be expected by the enemy more numerous, would have the effect of discouraging attacks. Experience was to show, in 1973, that this was not so at all. That time, though, had not yet come; and anyway, that experience would be disregarded in its turn.

However, within the leading group, those personages who had the clearest views about the future, and who were also in closest touch with economic realities, could not but be alarmed at the consequences of the state of permanent latent war, the sacrifices it imposed on Israel, the dependence on foreign aid that it entailed, and the barriers it set to the country's development. A certain number of these leaders, who were called, following American usage, the 'doves', were therefore inclined to sacrifice something – but not too much – for the sake of peace with the Arabs. In contrast to them, the 'hawks' preached a hard line, the policy which, it seemed to them, had succeeded so often in the past: hang on to as many as possible of the positions won, and make them serve as the basis for possible further territorial gains in the future, and surrender nothing except under the most pressing constraint, and then only in exchange for the maximum of concessions from the Arabs and the outside powers. The most prominent spokesman of the hawks was Moshe Dayan, with the glory of victory about him, a romantic hero whose language was simple, tough and straightforward, the man who 'knew how to talk to Arabs'. He did indeed conform closely to the ideal type of the 'strong man' towards whom peoples have always turned in times of distress or danger.

The fact was that, despite the intoxication of their triumph, the mass of the Israeli people, in the depths of their hearts, were well aware of how precarious their position was. Their country was still a besieged fortress, even if brilliant sorties had annexed a substantial glacis, and even if the besiegers were for the moment suffering from the consternation caused by their defeat. These besiegers were still numberless and irreconcilable, dreaming only of 'the next time'. Fear continued to inspire, at the very bottom of their unconscious, deep beneath the intoxication of victory, the reactions of the masses and of the elite. No confidence could be placed in the Arabs. They would see any concession as a sign of weakness, a weakness of which all possible advantage should be taken: they would accept it only so as to use it as a basis for more decisive victories, until they achieved the total destruction of the stronghold under siege.

Indeed, did they not proclaim this themselves? Was not any declaration from their side that was even slightly moderate quickly contradicted or counterbalanced by explicit threats? In the usual way, specialists reinforced these fears by attaching the prestige of their special knowledge to the feelings and the implicit considerations of the masses. A general who was an expert in Arab affairs, Yehoshafat Haskavi, acquired in this way a substantial measure of fame by giving to the popular fears the endorsement of a pseudo-scientific analysis of the motivations of 'the Arab soul'.

The hawks were real hawks, but the doves were only semi-doves. A compromise between them was possible, and was realized. As most frequently happens when this type of split occurs, if the situation is not immediately threatening and no strong man has inspired by his prestige or his power a decision that bears hard upon many, the compromise inclined towards 'no change', while creating situations that mortgaged the future.

Thus, they behaved as though Sinai might one day, in exchange for substantial concessions, be given back, at least in part. In the case of the West Bank, where the doves also contemplated a possible amputation of territory some time in the future, but which the hawks were unwilling to let go, it was agreed that Jewish settlements would be established on selected sites. As the doves saw the matter, these strongpoints might (some of them at least) be withdrawn into the territory to be retained by Israel, in the event that a peace treaty required restitution of the zone in which they were situated. From the hawks' standpoint, the settlements were, as Dayan said openly, so many 'accomplished facts'. As in the past, their Jewish character would be used as an argument against any cession of the territory concerned, which would thus be contrary to the rights of nations. As for the Golan Heights, in view of the military threat that they constituted, everyone agreed that annexation was irreversible, and the settlements planted there were seen by all as permanent.

The planting of the settlements followed the lines of considered plans which had been worked out at governmental level. Here and there at the start, and then frequently as time went by, the authorities found their hand forced by religious or extreme nationalist groups who were indignant that Jews should be forbidden to settle on land which had been granted them by God, that the Jewish settlements of the Mandate period had been uprooted, that ancient Israelitish cities like Hebron had become wholly Arab, and that there was delay in establishing Jewish fortresses in territories conquered at the cost of Jewish blood. The Government sometimes briefly resisted these encroachments upon its authority, but usually ended by ratifying the accomplished fact. The application of its own plans went ahead, moreover, with material and legal resources that were much more substantial. Thus, it was not content with occupying Jordanian crown lands, or land the owners of which had fled. Land was confiscated, and chemicals were used to destroy the crops in those fields whose occupiers were unwilling to get out. In the north-east corner of Sinai thousands of Bedouin were expelled by force. Those dispossessed in this way might sometimes be granted the favour of a job for wages; for example, as watchmen employed on lands which had once been their own. In Jerusalem and Hebron Jewish quarters were created. This Judaization, sometimes openly paraded and sometimes sly, either brutal or shelter-ing behind legal subtleties, was vaguely concealed under pretexts intended to disarm international opinion and serve as a case for the defence before the United Nations and other organs which might notice that what was happening was a flagrant breach of the principles recog-nized by the regulation annexed to the fourth Hague Convention of 1907 and the rules laid down by the Geneva Convention of 12 August 1949, which had been countersigned by Israel. These documents of international law actually prohibited the making of such changes in occupied territory. The Israeli Government's quibblings might well enable mystical Judeophiles like Maurice Clavel, in France, to burn with anger that anyone should dare to blame Israel for Judaizing places as clearly Jewish (the Bible, or the 'sacred history' learnt in their youth, testified to this) as Jericho and Hebron. But they could not delude peasants or shepherds who had used these lands as their own, like their ancestors since time immemorial, who had been born there, had lived, worked and begotten children there, whose joys and suffer-ings these lands had witnessed, and whom their eviction doomed to worse misery, to a proletarianization or semi-proletarianization that they had in no way chosen for themselves.

Yet their reaction was slow to get going, sporadic, easily damped down. In the euphoria of their triumph, many Israelis and foreign Judeophiles could imagine for a long time that, by grace of some strange phenomenon rarely witnessed before, the people of the West Bank were happy to see their territory occupied by foreigners who did not hide their desire to subject them or to drive them out. Intelligent measures, liberal in appearance but intended to hoodwink outside opinion while preparing the way for annexation and disarming potential opposition, comforted the naïvety of those who, here and there, believed in this unexpected rallying of the West Bank's population to Israel.

Moshe Dayan, who in practice wielded sovereign power over the occupied territories, kept an eye on everything, as a pragmatic soldier, contemptuous of 'humanistic' considerations, and alternating in a masterly way the iron hand with the velvet glove. Admired by all, reconciled with Golda Meir, his former enemy who was thenceforth to give him her support, and seeing that even violations of Israeli law were tolerated with a kindly indulgence, he acted in accordance with the regular philosophy of the Right. The Arabs would yield only to force, concessions would merely encourage their hope and their determination to destroy Israel: the Jews must continue to dominate at least the entire territory of the Palestine of the Mandate, and the Arab inhabitants of the occupied territories must either submit or emigrate. Vigorous measures would crush any inclinations to resist. The guilty, or the suspect, would be interned, compelled to stay in an appointed place, subjected to severe penalties of imprisonment or expelled. Their houses would be demolished by dynamiting. Recourse was had even to collective punishments.

The basis of Dayan's policy, backed by successive governments, was to stake out the West Bank for annexation without annexing its inhabitants. Indeed there was no Israeli, or hardly any, who did not shiver at the latter prospect.

If the whole of the dominated territory became, in its existing condition, a Greater Israel, if its inhabitants all became Israeli citizens with full rights, it was obvious that the state would cease within quite a short space of time to be a Jewish state. Together with the Arabs of pre-1967 Israel, they would have a bloc of 1,500,000 Arabs confronting 2,800,000 Jews. Everyone knew that population increase among the Arabs was greater than among the Jews, and the prospects of Jewish immigration were limited. No new Hitler was in sight anywhere in the world, and all the vigour of the Zionist ideology, proclaiming the ignominy of 'Exile' in the lands of the *Goyim*, the imperative duty of *Aliyah*, of 'going up' to Jerusalem, was clearly incapable of persuading more than rather small minorities to prefer a hard life, under constant threat, in the historical 'homeland' to an existence free from major difficulties in Europe or America.

Some drew the conclusion that it was necessary to give back as soon as possible, in exchange for substantial concessions from the Arabs, these burdensome alien-inhabited territories. The conclusions drawn by Dayan and the uncompromising nationalists were quite different. The West Bank people must be encouraged to remain alien to Israel and to link themselves even more closely with the Arab countries not under Israeli domination, the countries where they would eventually find their true place of settlement. Did not the West Bank people retain their Jordanian nationality? Everything was done (to Hussein's great satisfaction) to enable them to participate in the political life of the Kingdom of Jordan. Circulation of persons and goods between the two banks of the Jordan was facilitated to the utmost extent compatible with the interests of Israel. Eventually, it was hoped, the last memory of Palestine would fade away, and there would no longer be on the soil of Greater Israel anyone but Jews and Jordanian aliens.

These aliens, who would certainly abandon in the end the absurd notion that they were the native inhabitants of a land that was Jewish by divine decree, must not risk infringing the rights of the people who wielded the hegemony. Jewish settlements would gradually Judaize the West Bank, and, despite an official prohibition, sales of land to individual Jews were allowed to continue. But there was no question of seeing a parallel process of Arabization of the territory of pre-1967 Israel, where the Jewish population was heavily predominant. Furthermore, the Arab minority living in that territory, more or less resigned to Jewish hegemony, or at least accustomed to it, often speaking Hebrew and without any visible hope of self-determination, must not be contaminated by contact with the newly annexed element, who were still living in a completely Arab environment and still confident of a liberation guaranteed by the international authorities. While the cheap labour of the occupied territories was certainly not a negligible consideration for the Jewish enterprises of 'old' Israel, these numerous 'alien' workers were not to be allowed to establish themselves on its soil even for a single night. Coaches took them back every evening to their villages or towns on the occupied West Bank.

However, although the problem of the occupied territories is central to the theme of this book, and although it was among the major concerns of the Israeli leaders and of those politicians of the outside powers who were specialists in international relations, it did not greatly preoccupy the people of Israel except in moments of crisis. Every people tends to be interested, first and foremost, in its everyday life and in what obviously affects this in a direct way. Like all other peoples, the Israelis aspired to live a normal life among themselves and to be troubled as little as possible by others. External problems that threatened the normality of this everyday life were 'forgotten' as much as possible, put between parentheses, so to speak, and entrusted to specialists whose task it was, precisely, to relieve the mass of the people of concern about them. It was the misfortune of the people of Israel that these external problems were unwilling to let themselves be forgotten, in the way that usually happens in the case of other peoples, that they were constantly knocking on the window or at the door. It irritated the Israelis when attempts were made to get them to realize that this disagreeable peculiarity of their situation resulted precisely from Zionism, that it was inherent in what the Zionists had chosen to do. They found it easier, and more convenient, to explain it as the result of an essential curse, a misfortune associated with the Jewish condition, a consequence of historical persecutions and the irremediable wickedness of the Gentiles.

They wanted to live normally, and nowadays, for all peoples, a normal life, the life one ought to have, is that which is led, according to the radio, the television and the cinema, by the prosperous peoples of Western Europe and North America. This applies even more than ever in the case of a people whose essential component, the one that sets the tone and holds the dominant position in the social hierarchy, has come from these prosperous countries, has regular family and cultural links with their inhabitants, and regards itself as being at one with them.

It was irritating to find the road leading to this normality constantly blocked by a single obstacle – stubborn refusal on the part of the people who had been conquered, and who were therefore despised, to accept defeat. Yet this obstacle was a sizeable one, and also made itself felt day after day. The new nation had to be constantly on guard, arms had to be bought and maintained, an army kept ceaselessly on the alert. That was expensive, very expensive, in money and in the use of man-power. Every Israeli had to pay very heavy taxes for the upkeep of the army and its armaments, and everyone had to devote a considerable part of his time to military training and military service, to attending the constant refresher-courses needed because modern military technique is always changing.

These military exigencies weighed heavily on the economy. Since 1967 the Israeli economy has undergone fluctuations which I shall not try to trace and analyse here: my aim is not to write a history of the state of Israel. From the standpoint of this book it will suffice to draw attention to certain facts of major importance, which are, moreover, merely a continuation of phenomena observable before the Six Day War. Israel's economic progress has often been impressive. Production has increased, industrialization has advanced, the national product has expanded rapidly. One of the factors in this progress has been immigration, which was still quite substantial in the first years after 1967, despite its slight amount when seen in relation to the mass of Jews who prefer to live in the Diaspora, and despite its inadequacy in relation to the population increase among the Arabs. But this progress was costly. Combined with the huge military expenditure, it fuelled an inflation which attained extreme rates of increase. The rise in prices as followed only at a distance by a rise in wages. The trade union centre, the Histadruth, whose somewhat curious features were noted earlier and which was closely linked with the ruling Labour Party and put the unity and strength of the nation in the forefront, helped a great deal to hold down wage demands. Strikes broke out, nevertheless – those which the Histadruth thought could not be held back without incurring danger, safety valves for labour unrest; or else, and more and more frequently, wild-cat strikes. The appetite for modern consumer goods swelled the volume of imports to a dangerous level, whereas, despite marvellous feats of international marketing, exports remained limited. This meant a deficit in the balance of trade and of payments which often became unbearably large. Foreign currency was in short supply. Remedies were sought in draconic measures: forced austerity, increased taxation, all manner of restrictions on imports and on the export of currency through trips abroad, and so on. The comfort and opportunities of the citizens of Israel thus came to be restricted more and more severely.

Here it is necessary to emphasize again that an outcome threatening the very survival of Israeli society has been avoided only through external aid of impressive dimensions. International institutions, organs of the governments of the United States and some other powers, and the richest Jewish communities (that of America first and foremost) pour unceasingly a river of money into Israel. Entreaties, collections supported by all kinds of pressure, go on without stopping, conducted by Zionist organizations. The most eminent leaders of Israel put in requests for subsidies when they go on lecture tours and visits to the leaders of other countries, mingling, so as to stimulate generosity towards Israel, references to the sufferings of the Jews and to the authority of the Bible with an appeal to Western solidarity against the Communist menace, against the menace of the Third World in revolt, and against the menace of the Arabs, turbulent, disturbing and considered to be accomplices, actual or potential, of the Soviet empire. The result of this perpetual asking for alms is substantial. The citizen of Israel is the person who receives by far the largest amount of foreign aid of anyone in the world. In 1980 each Israeli must have received $528 from the United States Government alone.*

* This aid is not, of course, confined to government funds. Total American aid to Israel could be calculated, for the year 1977, as $2,995 million – that is, altogether, $1,198 per individual Israeli – on the basis of documents quoted by Samir A. Rabbo ('American Aid to Israel: Patron-Client Relationship', *The Search: Journal for Arab-Islamic Studies*, vol. I, no. 1, Miami, 1980, pp. 22–38). For aid from private sources Rabbo refers, in particular, to

A highly skilled workforce is one of Israel's major advantages, contrasting markedly in this respect with its Arab neighbours and the underdeveloped countries. This workforce is kept renewed, of course, by the Israeli educational system, which is expensive. But it also increases through immigration. Since 1967 immigration has had its ups and downs. From the rich countries have come a certain number of young Jews who were stirred by the danger that threatened Israel in 1967 and thereby won over to the Zionist ideology. Some precious skills have also come from that quarter, though the numbers of persons concerned are limited. But the biggest immigration has been that of the Soviet Jews, who in many cases possess high- or medium-level qualifications. The Soviet Government has allowed this emigration to take place despite the principles of its general policy, which keeps Soviet citizens firmly inside the frontiers of the U.S.S.R. This was a matter of getting rid of elements irreconcilable with the state's ideology, actual or potential dissidents. There were also other factors at work, of secondary importance. Naturally, the brutal, stupid and mean methods of the Soviet bureaucracy resulted not only in restricting the volume of emigration but also in vitiating the moral profit which the U.S.S.R. might have made out of this exceptional act of 'liberalism'. The Zionist movements were thus given excellent arguments with which to denounce the intolerable vexations inflicted by the Soviet administration. Persons of principle could not but join with them in condemning such conduct. Thus, paradoxically, whereas the other Soviet nationalities envied those who were being allowed to leave, and whereas the Arabs were indignant at the complaisance shown by their Soviet 'friends', which helped to strengthen the human and technical potential of their Israeli enemy, the democrats and liberals of all countries were compelled to denounce the restrictions and extremely disagreeable methods which accompanied the granting of permission to emigrate!

A split which had long existed in Israeli society was gradually to assume a certain political importance. The number of Jews who had come to Israel from the Arab and Muslim world had, as we have seen, grown considerable with the passing of time. They had increased enormously the numbers in Israel of the Sephardim, that is, the Mediterranean Jews, as distinguished from the Jews of Eastern Europe, who are called Ashkenazim. (These epithets are derived from the highly

---

the data given in Alfred Lilienthal's book *The Zionist Connection*, New York, Dodd and Mead, 1978. American investment in Israel should also be taken into account (cf. S. A. Rabbo, 'American Investment in Israel', *The Search*, vol. I, no. 2, 1980, pp. 113–34).

audacious geographical interpretations given by medieval rabbis to the names of peoples which appear in Genesis x.) The Ashkenazim had founded the state and for a long period had provided its cadres. They monopolized posts of responsibility and decision-making functions and constituted, by virtue of their comparative seniority in the country, an 'Establishment' which possessed power, prestige and higher education, together with the advantages, both material and moral, that these confer. Many of them were imbued with the humanitarian and socialist ideologies current in Eastern Europe at the beginning of the twentieth century, melded in a synthesis (having little coherence logically, but all the more convincing for that) with the dogmas of Zionist nationalism. They were the pioneers of this nationalism, to which they had often sacrificed positions or prospects in their countries of origin. The immigrants coming from the Arab countries were welcomed warmly, to be sure, in the name of this same Zionism, but the warmth was somewhat forced. It seemed to the Ashkenazim that these people had waited for a very long time before making their *aliyah*; had waited, in fact, until they were practically driven to it by the climate of opinion in the Arab countries after the formation of the state of Israel. It looked to many as though these immigrants wished to benefit, on the cheap, from facilities that had been prepared for them by the sacrifices of the pioneers. As a whole, their level of qualifications and education was below that of the Ashkenazim. A numerous proletariat among them appeared capable only of menial tasks, and was disquieting in its turbulence and its remoteness from respectability as measured by Western criteria. What was most repugnant was that their habits of everyday life bore the mark of that 'Levantinism' which horrified the Ashkenazim, fearful as they were that this might be the end result of Israel's evolution. In short, they looked on their Mediterranean brothers as semi-Arabs.

Tension increased between the two elements in proportion as Israel's triumph seemed to render less immediate the Arab threat which cemented national unity. Incidents became frequent and were occasionally serious. Some young Jews from North Africa, inspired by the revolt of the Negroes in America, formed a group which called itself the Black Panthers. This group succeeded from time to time in drawing a section of its mass basis into violent demonstrations, or mobilizations of a more peaceful kind. Sometimes, though rarely, there was collusion between them and Israeli Arabs demonstrating in support of economic demands. But these second-class Jews were still Jews, broadly privileged by the state and, moreover, full of bitterness against the Arabs. In grave situations they could not fail to unite with the Ashkenazim to defend (and with even a special aggressiveness) this threatened state which, after all, was theirs.

This state continued with, at the top, a body of leaders which underwent very few changes. The national unity, which had been sealed on the eve of the war of June 1967 by the formation of a government bringing together representatives of all the important parties, remained in being for a long time after. The death of Levi Eshkol on 26 February 1969 brought Golda Meir back to the head of affairs, at the age of 70. Not until August 1970 did the bloc of the nationalist Right, Gahal, withdraw its ministers. Gahal reproached Golda Meir for accepting the American Rogers Plan, which envisaged the possible evacuation of the West Bank, and which will be discussed later. Yet this acceptance was a forced acceptance, in words only, with many reservations and stipulations which (along with the difficulties on the Arab side) postponed indefinitely the realization of the Plan. While the Labour Party, in power, tacked between the requirements of Zionist ideology and those of that minimum of socialist ideology which had to be preserved, the pressures from its mass basis seeking assurance that they would be guaranteed both well-being and state security, and, finally, the constraints of international high politics, the heirs of Jabotinsky and the terrorist Irgun, rallied behind Menachem Begin, made sure, for the record, to consolidate their reputation for flawless intransigence by engaging in criticism, which is always easy, of the ruling party. Such a position generally proves profitable in the long run.

Faced with Israel triumphant, the defeated Arab states found themselves before a hard choice. Contrary to what had happened in 1949, the cease-fire was not an affair of bilateral agreements (on the military plane) between all the belligerent Arab states on the one hand and Israel on the other, but a decision taken by each separate state in the light of its own military situation, in obedience to the injunctions of the United Nations Security Council. The more distant Arab states, not directly affected by the fighting, refused to terminate the conflict. Iraq and Algeria, in particular, declared that, so far as they were concerned, the state of war continued. The Algerian masses, proud of having overcome the powerful French Army after a bloody and exhausting struggle lasting seven terrible years, were indignant at what seemed to them a cowardly surrender after only four to seven days of fighting. On 9 June the Egyptian embassy in Algiers was attacked by angry demonstrators. Recalling the folklore of the French Army in

which many of them had served, they shouted: 'Nasser, march or die!'
[The watchword of the French Foreign Legion was: 'March or die!' –
Trans.]

The belligerent states themselves had been very badly shaken.
Nasser, in distress and accepting responsibility for the defeat, resigned
on 9 June. An immense wave of popular feeling in Cairo, the other
towns of Egypt and elsewhere in the Arab world, made him take back
his resignation on the following day. People were unable to endure the
thought of being left without this guide, whose goodwill, sincerity and
devotion to the Arab cause, at least, could not be doubted. His departure would have been a symbolic crowning of the defeat: it would have
meant total victory for Israel. But Nasser's prestige was irrevocably
compromised and his political weight greatly diminished. Hussein was
given credit for the courage he had shown, but Jordan, deprived of its
acquisitions of 1948 and reduced once more to the desert emirate of
Transjordania, invaded by a horde of refugees both old and new, was
placed in an unstable situation. There was vigorous criticism of the
Syrian Government, which, despite its extremism in words, had preferred to keep its best troops in the heart of the country to protect the
regime, rather than use them for resolute attack (or defence) on the
front against Israel. Finally, though Lebanon had kept itself intact by
de facto abstention from any action during the war, that country's
young generation found it hard to accept the shame of what for them
amounted to an act of desertion. The tension between Muslims and
Christians, always latent, became worse. The former suspected the
latter of lacking enthusiasm for the Arab cause and perhaps even of
secretly rejoicing in the presence of Israel, through obsession with the
possibility of a Muslim hegemony. As for the Palestinians, even if they
could not be blamed for this, it had to be acknowledged that their
contribution in the war had been practically nil.

Powerful reasons, to be sure, urged the belligerent Arab states to
admit their defeat and sanction it by a treaty in due and proper form,
while hoping for a return match in the more or less distant future, like
Thiers at Frankfurt, or Lenin at Brest-Litovsk. Nasser and Hussein
had, in any case, long been aware of the need to arrive one day at a
compromise with Israel. But many factors were at work to postpone
once again the date for such a compromise. The intervention of the
Great Powers – and that alone, the leaders were quite convinced –
prevented the Israeli Army from crossing the Jordan and the Suez
Canal and occupying Amman, Damascus and Cairo. That being the
case, it was possible to go on remaining in the ambiguous situation of

theoretical or virtual war, with a complete, or almost complete, absence of military operations which nevertheless did not mean peace, while waiting and preparing for a situation in which real peace could be purchased at a lower price. As we have seen, the Arab world as a whole vehemently condemned anything that might look like surrender. Any Arab leader who agreed to that would be denounced everywhere as a traitor, and might expect to share the fate of Abdullah, Hussein's grandfather, who had been murdered in front of the mosque of al Aksa. The Arab countries as a group were still rich in a potential strength that might one day turn the scale the other way. The Soviet Union did not want Israel to disappear, and was doubtless unwilling to equip the Arab belligerents with too great an offensive power. But it had to preserve its protégés from sinking into an excessive weakness which would put them at the mercy of Israel and its American protector. The Soviet Union was ready to make up by arms deliveries the losses in material they had suffered, to help the Arabs at least to present themselves at a possible negotiating table in a less disastrous position, and in the meantime to support them on the diplomatic plane.

The Arab leaders could take the tremendous risk of agreeing to a genuine peace only if, at the very least, the conditions of this peace were not too severe, only if Arab opinion could be shown that it offered definite advantages – in short, only if it did not look too much like a surrender. But Israel was less disposed than ever to make concessions. The victorious outcome of the demonstration of strength which it had undertaken, together with the backing of the United States, led Israel to believe that the defeated Arabs would have to put up with whatever conditions Israel might impose. The public opinion of the developed capitalist world encouraged the Israelis in this belief. It was said that they were awaiting, in Jerusalem, a telephone call from Nasser or one of his colleagues. They gave it out that they were ready to hold negotiations anywhere at all. But it very soon became clear, as we have seen, that Israel meant to keep at least a large part of its new conquests. Israel agreed only to bilateral talks with each of its adversaries taken separately. Under these conditions, the first state to sit down at the negotiating table would be branded by the others as a traitor who had broken the Arab front. Immediately, by the very fact of such conduct, a master card would have been thrown away without anything to show for it: namely, non-recognition of the Jewish state. The Arab states had long realized that this card was undoubtedly the principal weapon at their disposal. Many a time before, and now again, it was even their *only* card.

Israel claimed to be offering negotiations without conditions, but it was plain that there were implicit conditions: recognition of Israel and acceptance of annexations which, it became increasingly clear as the days went by, in the light of declarations by Israeli leaders, would be substantial. Given the state of Arab public opinion and of the economy, the armed forces and the international relations of the Arab countries, these conditions were unacceptable. Two paths were left.

First, there was the one advocated by Syria, Iraq and Algeria, re-commended by China, extolled by the Left-wing tendencies and which could not but be chosen (publicly, at least) by the Palestinians: that of revolutionary total war, in the style of the Vietnamese and the Alger-ians, among others. Whatever the cost, resume hostilities at once, mobilizing not only the conventional armies, hastily restored to health, but also people's militias involving the entire population. Accept the price which would evidently have to be paid: millions of dead and wounded, destruction without foreseeable limit, the occupation of ex-tensive territory, complete rupture with the West and perhaps even with the U.S.S.R. At this price, after many years and vicissitudes that were unpredictable but must certainly be disastrous in many ways and many times over, one might hope one day (far in the future) to finish off Israel and hoist an Arab flag (which one, actually?) over the whole of a reconquered Palestine. That would also imply, as everyone was well aware, a profound upheaval in all the structures (economic, politi-cal, social and ideological) of the countries involved. Issuing arms to the poverty-stricken masses and giving free rein to popular organiza-tions which would have to be allowed a certain autonomy, or which would take it for themselves, might have unforeseeable consequences, dangerous for the power, the privileges, the very way of life of the dominant social strata, including many persons who considered them-selves revolutionaries.

It was therefore towards the other path that the leaders were thrust, by their gut fears and class interests as well as by a rational view of the hazards to which the revolutionary alternative was subject, and even by moral revulsion in the face of the enormous sacrifices which that alternative would entail. Besides, they knew well that the attractiveness of the revolutionary alternative for many resulted, in part, from their unawareness of these hazards and sacrifices, from their irresponsibility or cynicism, their confidence (justified or not, plausible or not) that they themselves would be sheltered from these consequences. This other path consisted, as in the past, of not finally shutting the door on any possibility, of continuing as far as possible to refuse to surrender to

Israel's demands, of raising the bidding by means of every form of struggle that was still available without plunging into the experience of the apocalypse, and in this way bringing pressure to bear on the world powers and on Israel. It was necessary to be ready to compromise when the conditions of such a compromise were acceptable, without ceasing to wield that threat of total war which would help, precisely, to ensure that these conditions were indeed acceptable. It was necessary to go on playing off against each other the powers whose help was needed. To make this threat plausible, one must not discourage the revolutionary forces, while at the same time keeping them under supervision and limiting any too dangerous effects of their actions. Nor must one rule out the possibility, even if this was only slight, that unforeseeable circumstances would one day make total victory possible; it was imperative not to seem to exclude such an eventuality, but to remain in a position to claim the credit of having prepared for it.

Hence the need to keep up ambiguities which demanded a capacity for verbal invention that exasperated minds inclined to favour logical rigour, but which was politically indispensable. The extension of Israel's authority beyond the area assigned by the United Nations in 1947 and the conquests of 1948 actually facilitated ambiguity. A formula as vague as could be wished was thought up: the aim (the immediate aim, at least) was said to be to 'liquidate the consequences of aggression'. Did the Arab states mean by this expression that they would be satisfied with recovering the territories occupied by Israel in June 1967? Or did they mean to carry through the total reconquest of the territory taken by Israel from the Arab world? Were they distinguishing between a legitimate Israel (within what frontiers?) and a blameworthy expansion of this state? Or was the state of Israel as such fundamentally illegitimate? What mattered was: not to speak clearly. In this way everyone could contribute to the Arab struggle, encourage it, exert pressure on Israel, while having in mind either the one prospect or the other. It mattered little that all this confused potential friends, embarrassed the outside powers, and somewhat discredited Arab propaganda abroad. It mattered little that it greatly helped Israeli and Zionist propaganda to denounce the aims of the Arabs, to convince the Israeli people and their friends that any concession made to the Arabs would merely encourage them to attempt thereafter a further advance towards the total destruction of Israel. The disadvantage was a real one, but it was only slight when compared with the immense advantages conferred by ambiguity. Besides, there were abroad plenty of people with muddled minds or who were so soaked in ideology that they either did notice this obvious ambiguity, or else justified it with the aid of illogical reasonings such as the partisan-minded have always found it easy to produce.

Adjustment of a common position, along lines that were verbally ambiguous but politically clear-sighted, was effected by a conference of Arab sovereigns and heads of state held at Khartoum between 29 August and 1 September 1967. The concluding resolution was naturally the outcome of compromise. They declined to follow Bourguiba, who proposed to recognize as Israel's legitimate frontiers those laid down by the United Nations in 1947. But they also declined to endorse Shukairy's proposals, made in the name of the P.L.O., which ruled out any negotiation, even indirect, with Israel, 'any settlement which might affect the Palestinian cause'. Shukairy left the conference. They refrained from condemning the idea of a 'political solution', a term put forward by Egypt and Jordan. On the contrary, while they spoke of 'unifying the efforts' of the Arab states, this unification was situated exclusively 'on the plane of international and diplomatic policy'. The purpose of this united action by the states was defined as 'liquidation of the results of aggression' (a formula of remarkable haziness) and 'withdrawal by the Israeli troops from the Arab territories occupied after 5 June'. It was proclaimed that 'the occupied territories are Arab, and the task of recovering them is incumbent upon all the Arab countries'. The principles, 'recognized by all the Arab states', which must serve as a basis for these actions were: 'no peace with Israel, no recognition of Israel, no negotiations with Israel, action to safeguard the Palestinian people's right to its homeland'. It must be noted that the Arabic word here translated as 'peace' refers to a total peacemaking, a reconciliation. That ambiguity, the profound reasons for which have been indicated above, concerned the 'homeland' of the Palestinian people, to which it had a right. Did this mean the whole of Mandate Palestine? And, if so, why the emphasis placed on the Arab character only of the territories occupied in 1967? While the recovery of these territories was demanded, nothing here proclaimed the need to reconquer likewise the Palestinian territory on which Israel had constructed its state since 1948.

The refusal to break with the West was marked by the decision to resume the pumping of oil, which had been interrupted by several countries during the war. All these decisions were seen in the West as pointing to an uncompromising extremism. The Arabs, together with those few Western observers who were aware of the difficulties, the subtleties and the distinctive style of Arab politics, were struck, rather, by the moderate attitude which was implicit behind the fanfare of formulas. Syria refused to take part in the conference, and Algeria stayed in the background.

The consequences of the defeat as they affected relations between the Arab states now began to be revealed. The belligerents were exhausted, especially Egypt and Jordan, who had given most and lost most in the battle. These countries had the most urgent need of massive aid. This meant making an appeal to the oil-producing Arab states, which happened to be also states that were despotic and reactionary, opposed to any policy that was even slightly socialist, nay, even democratic where internal affairs were concerned, and states that, in external affairs, favoured alliance with the U.S.A. For Nasser this appeal implied a marked variation in his policy. Already at Khartoum Saudi Arabia, Kuwait and Libya had decided to give £135 million per year to Egypt and Jordan, whereas Syria's revolutionary character made it unworthy of such bounty. In exchange, an agreement between Nasser and King Feisal of Saudi Arabia provided, under the chaste covering of a peace commission, for the withdrawal of the Egyptian troops who were helping the Republic of Yemen against the 'royalists' supported by the Saudis. Nasser had thenceforth to set a limit to his ambitions.

On the other hand, the U.S.S.R., which had broken off diplomatic relations with Israel at the end of the war, soon set about re-arming Egypt and Syria, while both denouncing the pro-American lobby which was active in Cairo and criticizing the 'hysterical' slogan of the wiping-out of Israel. This Soviet effort was to be developed cautiously during the months and years that followed. Harbour facilities were granted, in exchange, to the Soviet fleet, which made up somewhat for the considerable harm done to it by the closing of the Suez Canal. Military advisers came with the arms. Their presence had the great advantage of enabling the Soviets to control the use made of the arms they were supplying, and to nip in the bud, if need be, any adventurous warlike decisions that might prove tempting to those who were still, in a broad sense, their allies.

The mechanism of the United Nations had been set in motion. The Americans and the Soviets, equally anxious not to let war break out again and not to intervene in a direct way, were agreed, at least, in leaving to the authorities of the international organization the responsibility of sorting out the problem of ending the hostilities of June 1967, if possible along the line of a definitive settlement.

The General Assembly agreed on hardly anything except condemning Israel's annexation of Arab Jerusalem (July 1967). The Security

Council took several months to approve a compromise document put forward by the British. This was the famous Resolution 242 of 22 November 1967, which still constitutes the only document, theoretically binding on the parties concerned, that lays down the conditions for an advance towards peace. It states that it is inadmissible that territories be acquired by war, that the Israeli forces must withdraw from the territories ('*des territoires*' in the French text) occupied during the recent conflict (the English text says 'from territories occupied . . .') and that every state has the right 'to live in peace within secure and recognized boundaries'. It affirms the necessity of guaranteeing freedom of navigation through the international waterways of the region, of 'achieving a just settlement of the refugee problem', and of creating demilitarized zones to protect each of the states from aggression. The Secretary-General would be required to designate a special representative to go to the region and promote agreement. Next day, U Thant announced the appointment, to play this role, of the Swedish diplomat Gunnar Jarring.

Egypt and Jordan accepted the United Nations resolution after some hesitation. This meant a concession on their part, since they were agreeing to begin indirect negotiations *before* the occupied territories had been evacuated. Over several years Jarring had to make repeated visits to the states concerned and carry on discussions with their rulers and their diplomatic representatives. He got nowhere. The Israelis agreed only to direct negotiations with each of their adversaries separately, even if these negotiations should take place in the same building. The Arabs wanted a general conference. In the end the Swede had to give up.

Skirmishes between the armies on the cease-fire lines (and especially on the most conspicuous of them, the Suez Canal) continued and developed. The Israelis were unwilling to let the Egyptians clear the Canal of the ships held up there and get it back in working order, unless they were sure that their own ships would be allowed to sail through the Canal like those of other countries. At the very least they wanted to have the cease-fire line run down the middle of the waterway and to utilize the eastern side of it. Naturally, the Egyptians rejected these demands and tried to get support, from the powers interested in reopening the Canal, to prevent the Israelis from firing on the men who were at work getting it in order again. The powers did nothing, the Egyptians continued to reject the Israelis' conditions, and the Israelis continued to shoot, despite the presence of observers from the United Nations. Egypt gave up trying to unblock the Canal at the beginning of 1968, but artillery duels continued to set ablaze both banks.

All these clashes, on that front as on the others, were due, over and above particular circumstances and mutual charges of 'odious and un-justifiable acts of aggression', to a common underlying cause. Israel wished to show the Arabs that it was still strong and determined, and that it would be better for them to negotiate peace as quickly as possible on Israeli conditions. The Arabs wanted to make clear that, while for the moment they were not resuming the war, they were resolved to raise the bidding as high as they could, to accept Israel only subject to strictly defined conditions – in the first place, evacuation of the territories occupied in 1967, a condition recognized as just by the powers and by the international authorities. Above all, what had to be avoided was letting the situation become frozen, so that the cease-fire lines came gradually to be seen as definitive frontiers not to be brought back into question. It was already quite enough that a similar process had consecrated the cease-fire lines of 1949 which enclosed Israel's conquests in 1948, extending beyond the frontiers laid down by the United Nations' partition plans. Hardly anyone (not even the Soviets, who had been the keenest supporters of the idea for twenty years) spoke now (for the time being) of going back to those 'legal' frontiers drawn in November 1947.

The escalation of dogfights and artillery duels, together with landings of Egyptian commandos in Sinai and of Israeli combat and even sabotage teams in Upper Egypt, was accompanied by the construction by Israel, along the shore of the Canal, of a line of strongpoints which was called 'the Bar-Lev Line', after the general in charge of its establishment. On the other side, the Egyptian towns adjoining the Canal, which had suffered much bombardment and were to a large extent destroyed, became uninhabitable and were evacuated. In Egypt the military, the Left and the Right-wing opposition grew furious at the inadequacy of the country's retort to the Israeli actions, and demanded warlike initiatives, together with arming of the people and increased civil liberty. In very serious riots in November 1968, at Mansura and Alexandria, students battled with the forces of law and order. Nasser took note, moreover, that the diplomatic activity which he was still carrying on, in combination with military exertion, was bringing no result. He decided to intensify pressure, which would at the same time satisfy Egyptian public opinion. On 23 July 1969, he solemnly proclaimed that the cease-fire agreements were henceforth null and void when, in fact, they had been continually violated for over two years. A protracted 'war of attrition' was begun, in which the Israeli Army in Sinai was to be harassed, so as to compel it to mobilize a large proportion of its resources and prevent it from transforming the cease-fire lines into permanent frontiers.

Was this just another risky wager, aimed at getting out of an intolerable situation in which every day that passed consolidated Israel's conquests, or had Nasser foreseen all the consequences his initiative would bring? In any case, the immediate result was that Israel hit back strongly, intensifying the incursions by its aircraft and landings on Egyptian soil. It was quickly made plain that Israel was the stronger antagonist. The Egyptians' anti-aircraft rocket and gun positions were soon incapacitated, together with most of their radar stations, and their artillery reduced to quasi-impotence. Deliveries of the first U.S. Phantoms increased still further, at the end of 1969, the capacities of the Israeli air force. On 7 January 1970 a series of raids in depth was launched, with as targets the army camps and strategic centres in the heart of Egypt, starting with those quite close to Cairo. Once again, the Israeli leaders hoped by means of a major blow to force the Arabs to submit and, first and foremost, to force Nasser either to give in or to go.

Nasser turned to Moscow. He went personally, in secret, to the Kremlin to plead his cause, on 23 January 1970. He asked that, in order to be able to outdo the weapons possessed by the Israelis, or at least to resist them, he be given the highly sophisticated weapons which were used by the U.S.S.R. and its allies but which the Soviet military had so far been reluctant to entrust to combatants of whose reliability they were not too sure. The Soviet leaders agreed in part to the requests of their Egyptian client, sending him Mig 21s of a more modern type and Sam 3 ground-to-air missiles, for which they installed launching ramps. Soviet technicians, whose help was needed if only for learning how to operate these sophisticated weapons, arrived in rapidly increasing numbers along with the *matériel*.

The protective cover of the Soviet weaponry was first of all given to Cairo, and then gradually extended to other places. What was constantly feared was a collision between Israeli and Soviet crews, the consequences of which might prove tremendous. Dayan published in April, in the weekly paper of the Israeli Army, an article in which he said that he hoped the Soviets 'would establish themselves in places where we shall not be obliged to attack them' and would 'leave clear a strip wide enough for us to defend the cease-fire line and carry out a number of other essential operations'. What would happen if Soviet protection was extended to the Canal Zone? Israel discreetly suspended its raids in depth. Diplomacy became very active. The Soviet leaders, having protected and strengthened their ally, had no intention of risking conflict with the United States. They preferred to settle, during the period of relative peace, a problem that would prove to be extremely dangerous in the event of a crisis. They certainly discussed with Nasser, who was in their power, the conditions for making peace, and dealt in secret with Nixon, who had been President of the United States since January 1969. Nixon, who followed strictly the policy of *détente* with the Soviet partner, had rejected Israel's suggestions that he exert pressure on the U.S.S.R.

Previous peace plans, both American and Soviet, had for two years past been rejected by Israel and Egypt alike. This time the plan announced by Secretary of State William Rogers, on 25 June 1970, had better success, despite an initial avalanche of indignant reactions. Nasser spent three weeks discussing it in Moscow, and then, evidently encouraged to do so by the Soviets, announced on 23 July his acceptance of the plan, to the amazement of almost everyone. Hussein, in his turn, accepted it on the 26th. Already on the 24th Nixon had written to Golda Meir, urging her to accept the plan. She eventually yielded on 31 July, with the result that the Israeli cabinet of national unity broke up. The six ministers from the nationalist bloc withdrew, despite the Prime Minister's efforts to minimize the consequences of her acceptance: Resolution 242 would not be applied until all the points in dispute had been settled through direct negotiations with the Arab states, and there would never be a return to the frontiers of 1967.

The Rogers Plan was indeed aimed at securing the application of Resolution 242, and consequently proceeded from the principle of evacuation by Israel of the territories (or of territories) occupied in the 1967 war, coupled with recognition of the Jewish state by the Arab states. Meanwhile, a fresh cease-fire was to be concluded for a three-month period, and negotiations were to be resumed under the auspices of Gunnar Jarring, with a view to arriving at 'a just and lasting peace'. By 7 August operations along the Suez Canal had, in fact, come to an end, but it was quickly to prove as difficult as ever for Jarring's mission to succeed. Grave events soon diverted attention from it.

While the Suez Canal, Egypt and Sinai were the scene of these battles and truces by means of which each of the adversaries hoped to get the other to accept its own conditions, the Jordanian and Syrian fronts also saw plenty of clashes, which it would be tedious to recount

here in detail. Despite the disaster of June 1967 and Egypt's dependence on the finances of the oil-producing states, Nasser's energetic
attitude towards the Canal enabled him, in the main, to preserve his
prestige. The Arab world seemed to be evolving in the direction of
what was called Nasserism, a middle-of-the-road political line which
sought to combine the necessary ties with the West on the one hand
with, on the other, a cautious appeal for Soviet aid. Tacking between
the two shoals of total subordination to the interests of capitalism and
the Western states and submission to the Soviet bureaucracy, the
Nasserite ideology stressed the 'revolutionary' struggle against
'imperialism'. To the latter force – real enough, but turned into a
myth – was attributed unity of leadership and an infinite capacity for
Machiavellian conspiracies. According to circumstances, 'imperialism'
was either diversified or reduced to American capitalism alone. This
myth made it possible to keep up a revolutionary tone, a mobilizing
élan which reproduced – helped by the persistence of the irredentist
demand for Arab Palestine – the enthusiasm of the struggle for
independence. Inside Egypt, this policy and ideology required strong
state control of the economy, but also an ostentatious fidelity to the
traditional values (religious, or treated as sacred by religion) which
were upheld by the social strata backing the state power.

Two *coups d'état* had ensured the triumph of a more or less Nasserite
orientation on Egypt's western and southern flanks. In the Sudan,
progressive military men overthrew (on 25 May 1969) the Right-wing
rulers and set up a government which followed the Nasserite line, with
participation (until November 1970) by the Communists. In Libya the
clandestine organization of young nationalist officers overthrew (1
September 1969) old King Idris, who was moderate and pro-Western.
These soldiers in power demanded and obtained the evacuation of the
American and British bases in Libya. Their leader, the young Colonel
Gaddafi, looked on Nasser as his hero and model. He advocated return
to a pure and hard form of Islam, and displayed a virulent anti-
communism motivated by the official atheism of the Communist
movement. Using his wealth in oil to win support, he set about preparing organic unity with Egypt.

In Syria and Iraq, Ba'athism (in different forms which were to
become increasingly antagonistic) represented a tendency parallel to
Nasserism, from which it was divided by rivalry between party apparatuses and by a difference of tone. As we have seen, since February
1966 a Left-wing Ba'athist government had been in power in Syria, in
which extreme revolutionists coexisted with some elements that were a

little more moderate. In Iraq two coups in July 1968 gave power to the Ba'athists, who launched a savage campaign of repression aimed especially against the Right. They sought support from the Communists and friendship from the U.S.S.R. On 11 March 1970 a pact with the Kurds seemed to have settled that crippling problem once again.

Thus, events following the war of June 1967 appeared to reinforce the Nasserite and Ba'athist orientation in the Arab states. In reality, as was only gradually to be revealed, it had been profoundly weakened. The deep shock of defeat helped to ensure both the growing supremacy of the Right (which took a long time to affirm itself decisively) and the development of revolutionary tendencies which outflanked on the Left the apparatuses that held power. These two processes strengthened each other. The helplessness and connivance of the apparatuses in relation to the Right embittered the revolutionaries, while, as the menace from the Left made itself felt, this stimulated the Right's planning to put an end to it.

As usual, it was in the most militant and ardent quarter that the new tendencies were to develop. Ever since the morrow of the first defeat, in 1948, a clandestine movement of young people had been formed around a nucleus educated at the American University of Beirut, bringing together elements from all the Arab countries. This gradually acquired a structure, and took the title 'Movement of Arab Nationalists' (*ḥarakat al-qawmiyyîn al-'Arab*). Its central slogan was Arab unity, and for a long time the dominant tendency in it was pro-Nasser. But doubts gradually arose and an opposition took shape, especially from 1964 onwards. The authoritarianism of the Nasserite cadres had been displayed in a particularly glaring way in North Yemen. The Egyptian troops who came to the help of the Yemeni Republicans against the Royalists supported by Saudi Arabia ended, because of this, by being detested by those whom they were 'protecting'. This experience gave rise to salutary reflections on the inadequacy of pure nationalism to promote equality and freedom everywhere among the sons, so different from each other, of one and the same nation.

Disillusionment was intensified after June 1967 when necessity compelled Nasser to reach agreement at Khartoum with Feisal, upon whom he was now financially dependent for survival. Nasser withdrew his troops from Yemen, having, in any case, grave need of them in Sinai. A 'good story' circulated in the Arab world in those days (the Arabs, and especially the Egyptians, have a great liking for these anecdotes which, though imaginary, are significant). It was said that while the first Moses (the prophet) had succeeded in bringing the Jews out of Egypt, the second (Moshe Dayan) had brought the Egyptians out of Yemen. The Yemeni Republicans soon got rid (in November 1967) of the pro-Egyptian fanatic Sallal, who was now deprived of support, but a split soon appeared among them. For at least three years past the Left, organized in a branch of the Movement of Arab Nationalists, had been criticizing the Egyptians' policy, which allowed no possibility of development to local autonomous and progressive forces but, on the contrary, strengthened the tribal chieftains, and obviously sought an advantageous compromise with Saudi Arabia. Yet the tribal chieftains took arms and money from all sides alike. The united Republicans succeeded in withstanding the disunited forces of the tribal Royalists who laid siege to San'a from December 1967 to 8 February 1968. Soon after the siege had been raised, the victors split and the tribalist Right attacked the Left. The Arab Nationalists, clear at last about the mystifications of national unity, broke with their centre in Beirut, which still lingered amid the Nasserite ideology. They announced that they were going over to what they called 'Marxism–Leninism' (June 1968). Despite an heroic struggle and desperate efforts to achieve organization, they were defeated. The Right, in power, was then in a position to negotiate with Saudi Arabia and become reconciled with the Royalists, in March 1970. North Yemen became, for practical purposes, a satellite of the Saudi kingdom, but underground revolutionary forces continued to be active there in spite of repression. Above all, this experience had taught important lessons, extremely useful ones, to the entire Arab Left.

An evolution of quite a different kind, but which led to the same conclusions, had proceeded in South Yemen. Since 1964 the British had been preparing to get out, leaving behind a South Arabian Federation in which the conservative sultans of the countryside would dominate the trade-unionist and nationalist elements that were strong in Aden. They had been forced to undertake this decolonization by the resistance, both violent and non-violent, put up by the population, by means of strikes, demonstrations and terrorist actions in Aden, and rebellions in the countryside. The local supporters of the Movement of Arab Nationalists had joined with other organizations to found a National Liberation Front in June 1963. A clear-cut criticism of Nasserism and of the equivocal policy followed by Nasser in North Yemen was very soon heard among them. They began to study Marxism–Leninism and to take the path of radicalization, while still for a time keeping up contact with the Nasserite apparatuses. Impatient with these aspirations to independence and worried by this Leftward tendency, Nasser and the Nasserites had stimulated a split in 1966 and set up an apparatus, F.L.O.S.Y. (the Front for the Liberation of Occupied South Yemen), which was wholly under their control. Despite all manner of manoeuvres (frequently of a brutal and bloody kind) in favour of F.L.O.S.Y., the N.L.F. succeeded in preserving its autonomy and orientation. It won a striking degree of supremacy in the resistance to the British, which became extremely violent, and also within the native army hastily formed by the British. The defeat in June 1967 helped to weaken the Nasserite tendency. Impatient to get rid of the burden of this awkward and expensive colony, and moved also by their profound hatred of Nasser, Britain's Labour rulers proclaimed the independence of the People's Republic of South Yemen on 30 November 1967.

This meant leaving the country in the hands of the National Liberation Front. Within the Front a struggle at once began between the Left and a Right which was itself subject to attacks by reactionaries who were either pro-Saudi or more narrowly Nasserite. In June 1969 the Left gained the upper hand. It put into effect a revolutionary policy, inspired by Marxism, which was more radical than any before seen in an Arab country – even hindered as it was by lack of resources, the dramatic decline of Aden as a port after the closing of the Suez Canal, and the ceaseless attacks aimed at it by the neighbouring Arab states, the capitalist powers and their supporters inside the country.

These events, in which factors external to the Arab-Israel conflict made themselves felt and which happened more than two thousand kilometres to the south of the battlefields, had consequences of capital importance for the evolution of that conflict. They contributed strongly to a movement towards the Left, and even more towards an independent orientation on the part of the Palestinians and their friends. These events dug a chasm between the latter and Nasserism – or, more broadly, the ruling circles of the Arab states most closely engaged in the struggle against Israel. The Movement of Arab Nationalists, whose local followers had wielded such influence on the destinies of southern Arabia, included among its members many Palestinians, who may even have constituted the majority. Some of these were to become well known throughout the world: notably, Nayef Hawatmeh and George Habache.

The shock of the defeat of June 1967 had put in question in a profound way the situation of the human basis of the Palestinian movement, the place of this movement in the order of battle of the forces hostile to Israel and, consequently, the movement's own internal structure and orientation.

Nearly 400,000 Palestinians had fled from the West Bank and come to swell the mass of refugees. Some of them were persons who had already, in 1948, fled from the territory which became Israel. The majority chose to go to the Transjordanian part of the Kingdom of Jordan. A new bitterness and wretchedness were added to the old. It is true that the shock of this third defeat had affected all the Arabs. All, whatever their moderate attitude in the past, felt deeply wounded, not so much by Israel's direct attack, its success and its vengeful acts, as by the ostentatious bias of the European and American world in favour of Israel, by the hatred, or at least contempt, for the Arabs which burst out everywhere in May and June 1967 and then in the succeeding months. The misery of the refugees increased considerably without the world showing much concern. The Israeli troops had used towards their Arab prisoners and Arab civilians measures that were humiliating, brutal and sometimes cruel. Many of those in the Arab countries who had not hitherto felt that it was their business now wanted to do something for the common cause. However, this was naturally truer of the Palestinians than of any others. Even those among them who had made for themselves, here and there, a new life that was peaceful and sometimes enviable felt impelled by a pressing duty to join in the fight.

It seemed now to have been proved that the Arab states, their regular armies and their diplomats were incapable of waging an effective struggle. More than ever the Palestinians were convinced that they must themselves, independently, take over the leadership of the struggle. The Arab masses regarded them as the spearhead of a common resistance and combat. The movement had to re-examine in this light its organization, methods, structures, aims, strategy and tactics.

Supporters and fighters flocked in but the movement was divided into many different groups, coordination between whom proved difficult and always subject to revision, precarious and temporary. The Palestine Liberation Organization, created and recognized by the Arab states, was not at all seen by the Palestinian militants as an organ that could lead and unite them. Its president, Ahmed Shukairy, had been widely discredited long before June 1967. The leadership of the P.L.O. was even challenged, to start with, by the Palestine Liberation Army, which it had itself formed. Shukairy was forced to resign in December 1967, and arduous bargainings were undertaken with a view to improving the way the Organization functioned, and securing, if not an illusory unification, at least a minimum of coordination between the dozen or so organizations which existed already or which emerged under the impact of the defeat.

This process was hindered by the manoeuvres of the Arab states, each of which tried to get control of one or more groups, or at least a certain amount of influence over them, and also by divergent ideological tendencies and the persistence of traditional divisions in Palestinian society in exile. No group was willing or able to apply the brutal methods of unification that Algeria's F.L.N. had employed. The fragmentation of the movement had its advantages, moreover, when it came to mobilizing fighters with different orientations; and the Arab states did nothing to facilitate a unification which might prove a danger to them. It was easier to influence (and even to corrupt) small groups.

The principal group was *El Fatah*, which enjoyed a deserved reputation for uncompromising activism, had a purely nationalist orientation, possessed quite varied support among the rival Arab states, seemed fairly independent, and had an ideology vague enough not to turn away any militant. As early as August 1967 it had decided to continue armed action against Israel. On 21 March 1968 an Israeli column of considerable size, with tanks and aircraft, crossed the Jordan to carry out a reprisal operation. At the village of Karameh the Jordanian troops and those of *El Fatah* accepted battle and resisted the invaders for twelve hours, inflicting substantial losses. Armoured vehicles and aircraft were destroyed, yet Israel considered the outcome of the operation as being positive. However, for the first time the Palestinians had held their ground honourably against the Israeli Army in a real battle. This partial success from the tactical point of view showed that it was possible to resist Israel in arms: that was something tremendous. It acquired considerable symbolic value in the eyes of the Arab world. *El Fatah* saw its prestige increase and recruits flow in.

While the pure nationalism of *El Fatah* and its neutral position amid the conflicts, ideological and social, among the Arabs attracted many militants, these features hardly satisfied those who looked critically at Arab society and suspected that Israel was not the only enemy needing to be fought; that Israel's successes even resulted, to some extent, from unconscious complicity on the part of the Arab states and their allies or, in any case, from defects in the structures of these states which must first and foremost be put right. We have seen that the Movement of Arab Nationalists was the scene of questioning of the tendencies of this Arab nationalism itself, despite the dominance of Nasserism among its members. Some groups broke away from it and others were formed parallel with it, among those who thought that a social revolution must accompany, and must even be the condition for the success of, the national struggle. In December 1967 they merged with the Palestinians of the Movement of Arab Nationalists to form the Popular Front for the Liberation of Palestine (P.F.L.P.). The dominant figure in this was a Palestinian Christian doctor of forty-one, George Habache, who had been a leader in the M.A.N. for fifteen years or so and was beginning to modify his original anti-Marxist outlook.

The Left in the P.F.L.P., which managed to make itself heard within the group but not to impose its views therein, seceded in February 1969, under the leadership of a Transjordanian Christian named Nayef Hawatmeh, to form the Democratic Popular Front for the Liberation of Palestine (D.P.F.L.P.). Having already been won over to a Marxist critique of Arab and Palestinian nationalism, Hawatmeh had set off to South Yemen to take part in the struggle of the Left in the N.L.F. of South Yemen in 1967–8. It was in the D.P.F.L.P. that thinking went furthest on the way in which the problem of Israel and Palestine was rooted in the relation of forces on the international scale, the wave of colonial expansion and the struggle of the Third World against capitalist imperialism, as well as in its relation, much more hypothetical, and in any case indirect, with the class struggles inside the states of Europe and America. The movement devoted a lot of time to the political education of its members, practised a discipline less based on respect for hierarchy and blind obedience than in the other Palestinian groups, and endeavoured to enter into relations of trust with the peasantry. From this orientation there resulted a quite different view of the enemy, of Israel itself. The enemy was not the Jews of Israel or elsewhere as, in practice, most Arabs supposed, but the baneful social structures of which the Jews themselves were victims. It was possible to conceive of an alliance with Israeli revolutionaries inspired by the same ideas. There even began to emerge within the D.P.F.L.P. the beginnings of an appreciation of the actuality of the Israeli nation, of the fact that (even if this was to be regretted) the Jews of Israel now constituted a new nation with a Hebrew culture and not a religious denomination, and that one had henceforth to reckon with it as such. But this last idea was still taboo in the Arab world through fear of its logical consequences, and even those who were convinced of its validity did not dare to give open expression to it.

Of the other Palestinian organizations we shall here mention only Sa'iqa ('the thunderbolt'), which had been formed in 1968 by the Ba'athist government of Syria. This was an organization which strictly

observed the rules of military discipline, with members who were relatively well paid and were equipped and trained by Syrian army officers.
It followed, of course, the orientations of Syria and reflected the splits
and conflicts that took place within the Ba'athist leadership in Damascus, which did not mean that members of its leadership did not themselves sometimes try to utilize and influence the Ba'ath party. Ideologically, Sa'iqa emphasized, along with the Ba'ath party, Arab unity as
the aim of which sight must never be lost, linking it indissolubly with
the liberation of Palestine, all this being spiced with socialist and even
'proletarian' phraseology.

The old P.L.O., though scornfully regarded by the activists of *El
Fatah* as a gathering of 'armchair revolutionaries', was still needed as a
framework for indispensable dealings with the Arab states and the
outside world. The Palestinian notables and their Arab friends had
grasped the necessity of renovating it and making it really representative. This was a long and difficult process, in which the eviction
of Shukairy in December 1967 was only the first step. The executive
committee appointed in his place Yahya Hammuda, a personage
slightly Left-inclined, with the task of working for the unification, or
at least the coordination, of the various movements. The former 'Palestine National Council' was done away with, and a new assembly of
one hundred members, considered as representing all the Palestinians,
of every tendency, was chosen after difficult negotiations with the
groups. This assembly met in Cairo in July 1968. It did not prove
possible to reach agreement on the composition of a new executive
committee, and so the old one was reconstituted for the time being,
even though it had resigned, for lack of any better solution. But a
national Charter was adopted, by re-working and adapting an earlier
text which had accompanied the foundation of the P.L.O. in 1964.

The document, which has not been revised to this day, defined the
character and objectives of the struggle. It was a national struggle with
two stages (in space, not in time), the Palestinian level being part of the
general Arab destiny. Palestine was defined as an integral part of the
great Arab homeland, and the Palestinian people as a section of the
Arab nation possessing a specific identity, to be preserved, at least in
the present phase, until the epoch of Arab unification. The only means
of liberation was armed struggle. The liberation of Palestine, for which
it was every Palestinian's duty to sacrifice himself, was the 'principal
contradiction', in the face of which all internal divisions must be suspended – these being regarded, moreover, as divergences between political groups and not between functional strata of society. The Pal-

estinian movement, although the vanguard of the Arab nation, was independent, rejecting any interference from other Arab states or forces and itself refraining from intervention in their internal affairs. The aim was the complete liberation of Palestine, without making any concession to accomplished facts or to decisions by the League of Nations or the United Nations, these being considered illegal and invalid. An article of the Charter defined Judaism as a revealed religion, and opposed the conception of the Jews as constituting 'a people with an identity of its own'. The Jews were citizens of their respective countries. Zionism was denounced as 'fascist in its methods', racist and fanatical in its nature, aggressive, expansionist and colonialist in its aims, an agent of world imperialism against the Arab nation. It was accepted that 'those Jews who had normally resided in Palestine before the beginning of the Zionist invasion will be considered Palestinians'. This 'Zionist invasion' would appear from the context to be dated from 1947: other indications point to 1917 as the crucial year, but subsequent interpretations were to bring this date nearer the present. In any case, it is clear that the Jews in question would have to be, or become, Palestinian Arabs of Jewish faith.

This document marked a stage in the Palestinians' awareness of the conflict to which what they called 'the Zionist invasion' had committed them, and in their conception of what it meant. Or, more precisely, it registered one of the conceptions at which the Palestinians had arrived, the conception held by an elite who nevertheless had reason to suppose that the masses following them were, broadly speaking, close enough in their outlook to this conception not to be shocked by it. Under the influence of events, of the reflections provoked by them, of the evolution of the world-wide configuration of political forces and ideologies, and, finally, of suggestions contributed by faraway analysts, the vague notions of an earlier period were more or less abandoned. Those notions had tended to see in the conflict a struggle by the Arabs against the Jewish invaders, and in support thereof one could mobilize all the imagery, hostile or disparaging, passed on by tradition concerning this conquered and dominated religion, this perverse people who had opposed the Prophet of Islam, the unifier of the Arab nation. Another aspect of the same tradition was now preferred, according to which Judaism was to be seen as a religion worthy of respect. The enemy was not Judaism or its adherents as such, but Zionism, a doctrine of colonialist aggression which, for greater clarity, was identified with the Fascist doctrines of which the Jews had themselves been victims.

The dichotomy, thus so clearly emphasized, between Zionism and

Judaism made it possible to shake off the accusation of essentialist Judeophobia (or, to use the inadequate term traditional in Europe, anti-Semitism) which was aimed by the world of Europe and America against the movement and against the Arabs in general. It was based upon the traditional conception of religious denominations in the Near East, which, indeed, more or less corresponded to that of the ideologies current up to that time, but in the process of withering away, of the orthodox religious and the assimilationists among the Jews. It perpetuated, in proclaiming it the only proper and necessary one, a situation which was precisely on the way to becoming (temporarily?) something of the past. It denied a new reality, that of a new people, recruited, to be sure, among members of the Jewish faith or their descendants and officially identified with these members by the Israeli authorities, but the bond between whom was thenceforth quite a different one. It was no longer a question of persons of the Jewish faith gripped by the unnatural desire (somewhat like the Protestants of France in the sixteenth and seventeenth centuries) to build a state for their religion, but of a new Israeli nation, with its own culture, newly constituted on the basis of the revived Hebrew language. At the outset, only the leaders of the D.P.F.L.P. had shown some degree of understanding of this new phenomenon. The time had not yet come for them to be followed along this line of thought.

The Charter was, all the same, a step towards unity, and its adoption was a subtle sign of the influence of the new activist resistance. This influence, and above all that of *El Fatah*, was to intensify as the process of unification went forward. In January 1969 partial agreement was reached on the number of seats to be allotted to each movement at the fifth congress of the Palestine National Council. *El Fatah*, which obtained the largest number, was thus enabled to be in the majority in the new executive committee of eleven members elected by this congress in February. The president of *El Fatah*, Yasser Arafat, became president of the P.L.O.

The P.L.A. (Palestine Liberation Army), the P.F.L.P. and the D.P.F.L.P. (which broke off at this time from the previously named group) had protested against the share-out of seats and had not taken part in the congress, which was dominated by *El Fatah* and Sa'iqa. Small groups continued in their marginal existence, sullenly preserving their independence. However, the common problem created by the activity of all these organizations in Lebanon and Jordan, and by the reactions of the governments of those countries, impelled them to accept a certain amount of coordination. In April 1969 a Palestine

Armed Struggle Command was formed, to coordinate to some extent the activity of the major movements, without reference to the P.L.O. framework. The P.F.L.P. of George Habache declined to enter it and boycotted all the joint organs. The D.P.F.L.P., on the contrary, participated, in an attempt to spread its ideas: it failed to get acceptance for its conception of the problem of the Jews in Israel but nevertheless succeeded in exercising some influence, despite the hostility of the other groups to what it called its Marxism-Leninism. All the groups that were active in Jordan joined together in February 1970 in a United Command to which even the P.F.L.P. adhered. The effort towards unification resulted in the setting up of organs of coordination, in principle transcending the P.L.O. and in which the leaders of the latter were present as members. However, the P.L.O. was later to absorb these organs. The Jordano-Palestinian crisis of summer 1970 and the plans for a political solution to the conflict worked out by the Arab states were bound to favour coordination within the formal framework of the P.L.O. This framework was also modified so as to restrict the proliferation of organs duplicating the same task and to rationalize the mechanism for arriving at decisions. This relative unification placed in command a centrist group dominated by Yasser Arafat, but this succeeded in getting a relative alignment on its own positions only by tacking between tendencies and organizations and negotiating with them. The fragmentation of the movement obliged the P.L.O. to take up positions which were often ambiguous and frequently contradicted by the actions of one part of its basis which world opinion might regard as initiatives coming from the top. Along with obvious disadvantages, this state of affairs could present the advantage of giving satisfaction to external forces that were divergent or opposed to each other (such as the U.S.S.R. and China), sufficient to persuade them to go on supporting the movement as a whole.

The groups formed with a view to carrying on a military struggle, and the movement as a whole, having been reorganized in reaction to the inactivity of the P.L.O. in Shukairy's time, had to prove their existence, to justify it, to acquire political weight through independent actions. They had been organized in order to react against the monopolizing of the Palestinian cause by the Arab states, which they mistrusted and which nevertheless they could not do without. They also suspected the Arab states, and rightly, of trying to rid themselves of this interminable conflict which was so costly to them, if need be by sacrificing the Palestinians' aspirations to a large extent. Actions against Israel carried out by Palestinians from bases which were necessarily on the territory of Israel's neighbours had the effect of committing the latter, whether they liked it or not. Israel could be relied on to hit back so as to harm them. While actions inside Israel and the occupied territories were very difficult, the constitution of actual bases there soon proved practically impossible, for the time being at any rate. The Israeli forces were too vigilant and enjoyed too much corrupt collusion, and the country, by virtue of its very small size (the area of three large French *départements* or of Wales), its relief and the way the population was distributed, did not lend itself to the establishment of zones safe from control by the authorities. The only exception was the Gaza Strip, where camps sheltering more than 300,000 Palestinian refugees were crammed into a small space. But a series of measures taken by the Israeli authorities, combining police supervision, repression, expulsions, demolitions and town-planning, succeeded after a few years in rendering this centre of opposition relatively inoffensive.

In spite of everything, sabotage, attacks and ambushes were organized, sometimes with success, in Israeli territory, usually from Jordan. Some installations and a certain number of individuals, military or civilian, were struck at by means of booby-trapped cars, delayed-action bombs and so on. But these losses inflicted on Israel remained tiny, and the Israelis consoled themselves by making the usual comparison with the number of victims of motorcar accidents, or the numbers, out of all proportion, killed in actual wars. It was clear that something more had to be done to get at the morale of the Israelis and attract the attention of the outside world.

Whereas *El Fatah* envisaged a patient, long-term strategy proceeding by stages, the less important groups, which were also less concerned with respectability and little bothered about safeguarding the reputation of the Arab states in international affairs, wished to assert straightaway their existence, their determination and the revolt of their human basis, by means of spectacular actions, wilfully challenging the laws of war both implicit and explicit. The technique of hijacking an aeroplane was used for the first time on 23 July 1968 by a group of the P.F.L.P., led by a former officer of the Syrian Army, Ahmed Jibril, which was soon to split off under the name of P.F.L.P. General Command. The first attempt made by Jibril's group went off without bloodshed. They forced an aircraft of the Israeli airline *El Al*, which was flying from Rome to Lod, to change course to Algiers. The passengers and crew were kept at Algiers for five weeks, then released, and the aircraft was handed back. There had been pressures from both sides, and indirect negotiations. Not long afterward, the Israeli Government released sixteen Palestinian convicts. On 26 December two Palestinians belonging to the same group attacked at Athens airport an aircraft belonging to *El Al*: one Israeli passenger was killed, a hostess wounded and the aircraft damaged. The Greek authorities sentenced the two men responsible to seventeen and fourteen years' imprisonment respectively.

It was Israel's doctrine to hit back in reply to all attacks. The problem was to know which of the country's numerous enemies should be 'punished'. Already before June 1967 some odd choices had been made. The problem was even more difficult when the attacks were made by Palestinian groups with no homeland and dependent on no particular state. It was necessary to strike, but where? As regards the hijacking of the Israeli aircraft from Rome to Algiers, Eshkol had said: 'Cairo is the centre of all terrorist activity, and so Cairo is really responsible for it.' When the Athens affair occurred, it emerged that the terrorists had come from Beirut. Israel declared that the Lebanese Government was responsible.

Two days after the attack, on 28 December 1968, Israeli commandos landed from a helicopter at Khalde airport, which serves Beirut. They destroyed thirteen aircraft belonging to the Lebanese civil airlines before re-embarking and withdrawing without difficulty. The Lebanese police and army waited patiently for them to get away before making any move. Lebanon had hardly participated at all in the wars with Israel, having neither attacked nor been attacked. Its army was weak and, above all, its people were gravely divided. The least move by the authorities might be denounced as communally inspired, a blow struck by one of the religious groups in rivalry with another. Hence the extreme caution and, in most cases, inactivity shown by them. The Muslims and the Left suspected, and not without reason, that the Christian hierarchies, especially the Maronites, were lacking in zeal for Arab causes, and in particular for the Palestinian cause, and sometimes even revealed a complaisant attitude towards Israel.

Israel's action was openly stated to be aimed at forcing the Lebanese Government to expel the Palestinians from its territory, to do away with their bases and to abandon their cause. Actually, this could not happen (more or less) until after an internal struggle such as was to break out seven years later. The other states (except for Jordan, on which more anon) did, of course, supervise the *fedayeen* strictly and restrained their initiatives. But this was infinitely harder to do in Lebanon than elsewhere, owing to the country's liberal structure and especially its division between rival communities. The slightest sign that the Palestinians were being persecuted was bound to evoke protest, a flood of denunciations and acts of violence incompatible with the country's political equilibrium. In fact, the Israeli attack sowed the seeds of civil war and the break-up of Lebanon.

This attack was subjected to an international censure which worried Israel very little. It was unanimously condemned by the United Nations Security Council. France, which saw herself as the protector of Lebanon, denounced 'this attack out of proportion to the pretext cited and liable to expand the area of conflict'. General de Gaulle, who still had four months to go as President of the Republic, denounced as 'an exaggerated act of violence' this action 'which has just been committed by the regular forces of a state against the civil airport of a country at peace which is also a traditional friend of France'. At the beginning of January 1969 he announced an embargo on France's deliveries of arms to Israel. This was the first time that a liberal Western state had taken up (running ahead of its public opinion) such an unfavourable attitude towards Israel.

The year 1969 and the first half of 1970 marked, as a result of these events, a decisive development towards a new stage in the struggle and, even more so, in the way this struggle was *understood*. A new phase was entered. In the usual way, many people throughout the world thought that, because this phase was new, it was definitive and final. The passage of only a few years was needed to show that this was not the case at all – which does not mean, of course, that this phase failed to produce lasting consequences.

It was in this phase, indeed, that the Palestinian movement was to rise to the position of essential protagonist in the conflict between the Arabs and Israel, and to do so in the eyes of everyone, regardless of Israel's increasingly virulent and unrealistic denials. Not only had Israel failed to get Lebanon to expel the Palestinian commandos, but the Beirut airport operation had not discouraged the latter from their activities, which were merely intensified. True, direct attacks on Israeli territory and the occupied territories, the armed actions, attempts at sabotage and the like carried out there, were not numerous. Despite the dramatic nature of some of these (a booby-trapped car exploding in the middle of a market-place, and so on), the intervals that elapsed between them prevented a real feeling of insecurity from becoming widespread among the Israelis. It was rather the skirmishes along the frontiers and, especially, the 'war of attrition' in Sinai (between July 1969 and August 1970) that caused losses of Israeli soldiers which soon exceeded (taken with those resulting from the operations of the *fedayeen*) the numbers of the Israeli dead in the Sinai campaign of 1956 and the Six Day War of June 1967.

But what most attracted the attention of the outside world, as well as the Arabs and the Israelis themselves, were the terrorist operations of the Palestinian commandos, in particular the hijacking of aircraft and taking of hostages. Such operations became more and more numerous, usually being carried out by small marginal groups rather than by *El Fatah* and the centrist nucleus of the P.L.O. However, in accordance with the process common to all struggles in which terrorism figures as one element, the more moderate were unable to dissociate themselves completely from those who were fighting for the same cause, even if they used methods that the more moderate condemned. Those against whom the attacks were directed were all the less disposed to distinguish between different categories and shades of opinion among their attackers.

Hijacking of aircraft and taking of hostages provoked general censure in the world outside the conflict, at least in those states where the public was informed about them and was able to give expression to its reaction. Anybody might one day find himself in the situation of the victims of these operations and could not be happy about them, even if, perchance, he sympathized with those responsible. Israel could not fail to profit from this censure and gain sympathy by contrast, and yet the effect of the operations was, on the whole, beneficial to the Palestinians. A large section of the revolutionary groups who, throughout the world, had declared war on the capitalist society in which they lived, denouncing daily its evil deeds, among which figured everything tending to dispossess, put down and subordinate the peoples of the so-called Third World, inevitably recognized in these guerrilla fighters a band of brothers in arms. This happened even though the contradiction with the image, dominant in Europe, of the Jews as classical victims of that same society caused difficulty for many. Above all, though, the publicity necessarily given to these operations had to include at least a minimum of explanation of their causes. Even in unsympathetic accounts it still emerged that the Palestinians existed and had at least some reason to revolt against the situation that had been imposed on them. Before 1967 the world at large was unaware of the Palestinians, and nine tenths, if not more, of opinion in Europe and America accepted only the Israeli version of the facts, without any preliminary examination – naïvely, in fact. At the price of the blood and tears of innocent people it became clear to the majority that this conflict had two sides to it, and that the total culpability of the enemies of Israel was not an obvious and simple fact. It was possible to see – a quite new phenomenon, unthinkable before 1967 – books in the bookshops, films on the cinema screens and reports on television which admitted at least some degree of validity in the grievances of the Arabs in general and the Palestinians in particular. Soon it was to be only Israel and Israel's unconditional supporters who would continue to proclaim that those who made war on the Jewish state were criminals and outlaws by virtue of the fact that they were attacking Jews. They had always thought in that way, but they were now able to add a supplementary justification, which soon became the main item in their case, namely, that Israel's enemies were using abominable means, the methods of terrorism, voluntarily killing innocent people. They had apparently forgotten that the state of Israel itself owed its establishment essentially to the vigorous use of terrorist methods against the British.

The growth of the Palestinian movement, the attention which it received from now on all over the world, and its popularity in sectors of world opinion which, though limited, expressed themselves very volubly, resulted, as we have seen, in a diversification of views that was soon carried to extremes, but also had consequences that were even more important. It became much harder for the Arab states to exercise strict control over a movement of this kind, and it was absolutely impossible to extend this control to all its branches. Yet such control became more and more necessary. The actions of the *fedayeen* compromised the states which gave them shelter or provided them with facilities. Israel did not fail to emphasize this and to carry out reprisals – selective, and not always based on direct responsibility – which proceeded from this principle. What was even more serious, though, was that the political decisions of certain Palestinian groups might, at the very least, run counter to those of their host state, and it might be inevitable that this should happen in certain cases, given the diversity of the positions of the states and groups concerned. Finally, the Palestinian troops, together with the mass of the Palestinians now organized around well-structured formations, had attained a scale, an independent importance, which was bound to turn them into political and military pressure groups within the Arab states.

These were new circumstances to which each state had to respond according to its own situation. The states that were distant from Israel had comparatively few Palestinians on their territory, and the organizations of these Palestinians did not take up a position of combat to be waged therefrom. Relations were in these cases quite relaxed. The states so situated were able, in the main, to indulge themselves in the luxury of supporting the Palestinian movement, and even the most extreme and uncompromising tendencies in it, without risk to themselves.

It was quite a different matter for the states which had a common frontier with Israel, those which it had become customary to call the 'front-line', 'confrontation' or 'battlefield' states. Here, the Palestinians who, being ignored as a political entity by the United Nations, had not had to agree to a cease-fire in June 1967, claimed to continue their fight against Israel across those frontiers, those cease-fire lines which they were tempted to try and break through. The majority of the population, convinced of the justice of the Palestinians' cause and the basic guilt of Israel, which had forced them into exile, and fraternally distressed by their misfortunes, were fully persuaded of their right and even their duty to attack, at least as long as they themselves did not have to put up too seriously with the consequences of these attacks. But the host states themselves, however understanding they might be where the Palestinians' motives were concerned, had to take account of these consequences, that is, of the Israeli reprisals, which grew increasingly dangerous to the persons and property of their citizens and to the integrity of their territory. Stirring up moral indignation at these Israeli reprisals, or even obtaining solemn condemnation of them by the United Nations, did not suffice to eliminate their effects. Every government functioning under such conditions had to endeavour either to prevent attacks being launched from its territory or at least to control them carefully, in view of the consequences that might be expected to follow from them.

But this control, however necessary, was not possible everywhere. Given the strength that the Palestinian groups had acquired and the complicity they naturally enjoyed among the Arab population, they could be bridled only by a strong state able to make itself obeyed, a state backed by at least a large section of its citizens or by a military and police authority powerful enough to subdue the Palestinians and their active friends. These conditions existed in Egypt and Syria. The rulers of these countries were able to express, whether sincerely or not, their deep sympathy with the Palestinian cause while at the same time subjecting to discipline the initiatives taken by their organizations, limiting and, if necessary, forbidding them.

This was not the case in Lebanon or Jordan. The former was almost the only Arab country living in accordance with the rules of the parliamentary pluralist regime and the liberal capitalist economy. Newspapers could be freely published there, different opinions voiced and associations formed. The Palestinian movement could therefore set itself up and find expression. Yet even liberal pluralist regimes hardly tolerate, as a rule, a situation in which certain organizations formed on their territory acquire there an almost total degree of independence in relation to the state power, create an army and a police force of their own, not under state control, utilize the country as a base for attacks on a neighbouring country, even if the latter is hostile (but theoretically in a state of peace with them), and thereby provoke counter-attacks the burden of which has to be borne by the host state. Conditions that were quite special to Lebanon were needed for such a situation to arise.

These conditions included, in addition to freedom of expression and association, the profound division of the country (as has been mentioned more than once already) into communities distinguished by religion, recognized by the state as being more or less autonomous and enjoying the primordial allegiance of most of the country's population, individually and by local groups. These communities, although sharing a common culture, are quasi-nations which constantly tend towards forming quasi-states or sub-states. Every Lebanese is classified from the cradle to the grave as regards his identity card, the way he votes, his chances of acceptance for public or private employment, public opinion in general, and his own estimation of himself, as either a Sunni Muslim, a Maronite Christian, a Shiite Muslim, a Druse, a Greek Orthodox Christian, etc., even though he may lack any religious feeling and take part in no act of worship. Each denomination has its own hierarchical organization, its cadres and even, to some extent, its own judiciary. The consequence is that the state is weak in relation to these communal affiliations and has to take most careful account of them before making any decision, so that it is often compelled to do nothing. Lebanese patriotism exists, but it is a delicate flower which has only recently bloomed; it is constantly being overborne by communal patriotism, or else taken over and compromised by the latter, being very unevenly distributed, in accordance with these communal affiliations and the orientations imposed by them.

What is most serious for the unity of this state, which was formed only recently, although it possesses partial roots in two of the communities (the Maronites and the Druses), is that communal affiliations are more or less firmly linked with orientations concerning the nation to which supreme and legitimate allegiance must be given. The Sunni Muslims are, in theory, supporters of Arabism and cannot openly repudiate supreme allegiance to the great Arab nation, an allegiance which in their case tends to become exclusive. This is so even though many of their cadres have, for their own reasons, rallied in practice to the concept of the Lebanese nation, and though a large section of their masses are susceptible, given favourable conditions, to Lebanese patriotism. However, it is the case that many of them, having been joined to the Lebanese state by others' decisions, have kept up their hostility to this annexation and to this state. The Maronites, who are often in a privileged position in relation to the Muslims and even to the other Christians, cling to the Lebanese state, which protects their particularism, because they are afraid of being completely absorbed in a great Arab state dominated by Islam. The majority of their cadres had rallied to Arabism, which was prompted by their culture, under conditions such that their own particularism seemed safeguarded by special structures – first and foremost, by the independence of the Lebanese state. These structures seemed to many (with a good deal of hesitation) to include also the Lebanese system under which political responsibilities were shared out in a balanced way (but to the Maronites' advantage) among the different communities.

The Lebanese Left had the usual illusions of the Left in every country: in the first place, that it represented the popular will, transcending the archaic structures which it imagined were on their way out. An evolution which was real, but which fully affected only some sections and was hindered by many contradictions, was gratuitously supposed to be close to completion. The revolutionary prestige of Arabism, more or less well-deserved, stimulated the Left to adhere to it and perhaps to subordinate to it the very existence of the Lebanese state. This was all the more the case because the Lebanese state was extremely inegalitarian, bound up with world capitalist economy, with the consequences that this implies in the domain of international policy, and because the cadres leading the communities were, for the most part, reactionary in the strictest sense of the word, and the communal structure seemed itself to be archaic, conservative and helping to protect acquired situations. The Left was, of course, favourable to the Palestinian cause, seen as the spearhead of a major challenge to established structures throughout the entire Middle East.

What resulted from all this was a condition of permanent suspicion between the communities of Lebanon, the vitality of which structures was maintained by the surrounding circumstances. A vicious war was soon to furnish sad proof of it even to the blindest observer. This suspicion paralysed the state and its organs. The army, which was in any case not strong, was dominated by the Maronites and suspected, not without justification, of acting in the interest of that community.

Any movement in the direction of Arabism could be suspected by the Maronites and some others of preparing the liquidation of the safeguards enjoyed by their community. The Maronites themselves, on the other hand, were often suspected, and again not without justification, of relying upon Israel as a very useful counterbalance to the threatening weight of an Arabism whose designs for unity must operate to their disadvantage – of seeing Israel, perhaps, as a potential ally, though they were without any great sympathy for that state or for Jews in general.

The Palestinians made the fullest use of the facilities offered them by the situation in Lebanon. The refugee camps and other installations became for them something in the nature of strongholds. Their armies and the political structures which organized them, growing in size, coherence and strength, gradually became quite independent of the Lebanese authorities. Part of the southern region of the country, adjoining Israel, became a territory under their absolute and exclusive control, to which Israeli journalists gave the name 'Fatahland'. In order to consolidate this situation they made use of the support given them by the Sunnites, the Left and others, of the revulsion that every Arab might feel, when meditating whether to put some restraint on their actions, at the idea that he was thereby objectively helping Israel, and last but not least, of the somewhat hypocritical support rendered by some Arab governments. These, which had to deal, on their own territory, only with Palestinian propaganda bureaux, and which limited very severely the activity carried on by the Palestinians in their countries, were able to acquire at very low cost the laurels due to uncompromising defenders of the cause of the Palestinians, by protesting against any move made to control them by the Lebanese state, which was already subject to suspicion *a priori* because of its structures and its orientation.

Incidents became frequent, from August 1969 onward, between the Palestinians and the forces of order in Lebanon, which claimed the right to enter their camps – not without ulterior motives, moreover, especially on the part of the Christian heads of the army. Dozens of people were killed or wounded, *El Fatah* called on the Lebanese people to rise in revolt, Syria closed its frontiers with Lebanon, punishing that country as a demonstration of solidarity with the *fedayeen*, and the latter seized control of part of the town of Tripoli. In October the President of the Lebanese Republic, Charles Helou, appealed to Nasser to mediate. On 4 November an agreement was signed at Cairo, under Nasser's auspices, between Yasser Arafat, now president of the P.L.O., and the commander-in-chief of the Lebanese army, the Christian general Emile Boustani, who apparently had some secret plans of personal ambition which made him wish to become *persona grata* with the Muslim communities. A significant, astonishing and perhaps unique feature of this Cairo agreement was that its terms were revealed only to the military commanders. The Lebanese cabinet and Parliament, or at any rate most of their members, had to ratify it without knowing what it provided for. It was clear, however, that in exchange for certain conditions (kept secret), the agreement left the Palestinians free to continue actions against Israel from bases in Lebanon.

The Cairo agreement did not prevent incidents from continuing between the Lebanese and Palestinian forces. However, the Prime Minister, the Sunnite Rashid Karame, who was concerned to defend the sovereignty of Lebanon, had been clever enough to entrust the Ministry of the Interior (on 25 November 1969) to the Druse leader of a Socialist party, Kemal Junblat, whose sympathies lay with the Palestinians. But it was not possible even for him to ignore the rights and interests of the state that he represented. The matters in dispute related to the right of the Lebanese forces of order to intervene in the Palestinian camps, and to firing across the Israeli frontier by the Palestinians who were established in the South. Negotiations and clashes ended for the time being – until fresh incidents should occur – with the fixing of a new date for full implementation of the Cairo agreement, which still remained secret!

While conditions were different in Jordan, they nevertheless led to the same result as regards the relative weakness of the state and the nature of the relations consequently established between this state and the Palestinian forces. The authority of King Hussein had been under attack from the start. Heir and relation of rulers whose complaisant attitude to Britain had been looked on with mistrust by the Arab masses, the intransigence of his nationalism doubted, suspected of an inclination or a desire to compromise with Israel, he alone continued in his person that epoch, now left behind, in which the Arab national movement had been headed by the Arab aristocracy. He had tried to move with the times, to take up positions more consonant with the dominant mood, but being a realist, aware of the strength of Israel, concerned not to compromise by chivalrous initiatives the material progress of his kingdom, and to safeguard his throne, and linked with the Western powers by his cast of mind and his interests, the King failed to disarm suspicion even when he struck the most nationalistic attitudes. His subjects wavered between suspicion and hostility, resulting from the same factors which influenced the other Arabs, and a certain respect, due principally to his personal courage as well as to the memory of his great-uncle Feisal, the hero of the Arabs' fight for independence. For the most part they were capable of being mobilized against him by active minorities waving the banner of the Arab nation. His last resort against this possibility was his Bedouin army. The Bedouin, still loyal to tribal fealties, despising the settled population of the countryside and the towns, and often filled with hatred of the ideologists who guided the thinking of the latter, remained closely bound to their lord by ties of quasi-feudal personal allegiance and the behests of tribal honour.

Between 1967 and 1970, even if Hussein regretted having let himself be drawn in June 1967 into that war which had cost him the better half of his kingdom, he tried not to lose the laurels he had won during the conflict. He sought to safeguard his reputation and not to appear in the eyes of the Arabs as an enemy of the Palestinian struggle. This was made very hard for him, on the one hand through the exigencies imposed by the need to preserve his authority – indeed, to preserve any kind of Jordanian state conceivable in the situation of that time – and on the other, through the activities of the Palestinians.

Hussein therefore undertook to reconstruct and re-affirm his state, and his own authority in the state, in the tragic situation in which it had been placed by the outcome of the conflict of June 1967. The financial aid granted him by the Arab oil states at the Khartoum summit helped him in this task to some extent, but it was insufficient. In the course of much journeying, he solicited additional help in money, arms or technicians from the widest variety of sources. Though by tradition a friend of the West, he travelled to Moscow (in October 1967), where this aristocratic monarch spoke in praise of the Great October Revolution. The realism of the Soviets responded to his own. The men in the Kremlin wanted, at least, to make good the losses suffered by their Arab protégés and not to leave a hostile Israel in a position of hegemony. In conformity with the tradition established under Stalin, they ignored, in the sphere of international relations, all differences of an ideological kind and based themselves on the established powers. They went so far as to carry out soundings and approaches among the Palestinians, but the extremism that was widespread among the latter, the challenge inherent in the Palestinian movement to the territorial status quo that they wished to uphold everywhere, caused them disquiet.

Hussein thus reinforced his economy, his army (which he purged) and his weaponry. He also strove to disarm the hostility of the Arab states whose orientation was more or less revolutionary and which disapproved of his moderation and pro-Western sympathies, so as not to give opportunities to those who might, though themselves moderate, forge a reputation of unyielding nationalism by condemning him. He held his ground against the Israelis' reprisal attacks, denouncing such methods of theirs as the use of napalm, and demanded that the United Nations condemn Israel. At the same time, however, he was sounding Israel about the possibility of an honourable peace that would enable him to recover the part of his kingdom he had lost. There were rumours of secret meetings with the Israeli leaders, but these contacts or sound-ings proved disappointing. In Israel the will to annex the West Bank was less and less concealed. Besides, the status of Jerusalem remained an insuperable obstacle, despite the efforts made by some to find a solution satisfactory to all parties. Israel had annexed that part of the Holy City which had been Jordanian between 1948 and 1967, the Old City enclosed within the Ottoman walls. Israel proclaimed loudly that never again would the ancient capital be divided. Despite the decisions of the United Nations from 1947 onward, and even the line taken on this matter by Israel's best friends, it refused to share in any way whatsoever sovereignty over David's City.

However, the ascendancy of the Palestinian movement inside the Kingdom of Jordan steadily increased. The Palestinians had their own army, their own gendarmerie and police, their own official services, which behaved with even greater impertinence than in Lebanon to-wards the authorities of the host state, in spite of the prudence of that nucleus of their leadership which realized that it was necessary to keep on the right side of the King. On the roads, in the streets, armed Palestinian patrols were active as well as those of the Jordanian Army. The latter tolerated less and less patiently this rivalry, this permanent challenge which restricted their own actions. Behind the Army was a whole anti-Palestinian aristocratic clique dominated by the King's uncle, Sharif Nasser ben Jamil, which, relying on Bedouin support, urged Hussein to subdue these 'foreigners', these troublesome revolu-tionaries. Hussein was indeed thinking of doing just that, but still continued to temporize. He tried to compromise with circumstances by propounding a doctrine according to which the Palestinian com-mandos and the Jordanian troops would share their functions. He wished to retain, as well as supreme control in his kingdom, the ex-clusive right of attacking directly the territory now under Israeli rule only as and when he saw fit.

Arafat and the centrist nucleus of the P.L.O. were able to appreciate

the King's anxieties and resolved not to undermine an authority which
was useful to them and which their allies and sleeping partners, Arab
and non-Arab, wished to uphold. But they found it hard to resign
themselves to the prospect of not being allowed to retain and develop
to the full this Jordanian base of theirs where they were so strong. A
minimum of armed actions against Israel was also needed in order to
maintain their own credibility. But their desire to reach a compromise
with the Jordanian monarch was constantly shaken by the logic of their
struggle, undermined by the reactions of their troops and, even more,
by the actions of the extremist organizations, either more or less integrated in the P.L.O. or remaining outside it – first and foremost the
P.F.L.P. led by George Habache. A theory had been developed in
these groups and among their Arab friends which influenced even
those sections least inclined towards extremism. The new conception
of the Arab-Israeli conflict treated it, as we have seen, as one element
in a world-wide revolutionary struggle against the dominant capitalist
powers and the order they imposed, against what was called, in all
those circles, 'Imperialism'. Consequently, the fight against Israel
implied equally a fight against all the Arab regimes which seemed to be
accomplices or elements of this world-wide structure. For some of the
groups the struggle against these Arab states ought even to be given
priority, a conception given practical reinforcement by the difficulties
of the direct struggle against the Jewish state. The Palestinians, having
nothing to lose, forced by their very plight to be revolutionaries, seemed
to be the spearhead, the detonator of the general Arab revolution. A
slogan circulated: 'The road to Jerusalem runs through Amman.'

This was a strategical prospect which possessed coherence but which
was not shared by more than a minority among the Palestinian cadres.
This minority sought to compromise the forces of the majority by
means of actions which they could not refuse to approve, thus dragging
them on to a road that they did not want to take. This is a tactic that
has frequently been used ever since there have been revolutions. In
this case, however, the organizations and cadres resisted being dragged
where they did not want to go, using a combination of flexibility and
determination. What resulted was an apparent lack of consistency at
the level of events. At the beginning of 1970 it seemed obvious to many
observers that the Palestinians were in a position, should they choose,
to get rid of Hussein, seize power in Amman and at last acquire a safe
base where they would be the masters, in a sizeable territory which,
after all, had been part of historical Palestine and detached from it only
by an arbitrary decision of the British between 1921 and 1923. The

majority of the cadres of the P.L.O., however, and even some elements among the revolutionary groups, refused to pursue this line, despite its apparent logic and advantages. They realized that the new Trans-jordanian Palestine would be unable to do other than follow, in large measure, the same policy as Hussein. The new authorities, once saddled with responsibilities, would have to be much more circumspect before launching operations against Israel, because the consequences of such operations would now fall upon themselves and the country ruled by them. This would mean, as the *Fatah* cadres in Amman put it, in a roundabout way, in 1970 to an Italian Communist official, 'falsifying our character as a liberation movement by subjecting us to a logic of state which is not for us'.* Furthermore, it was necessary to reckon not only with Hussein's Arab and international backers but also with the reaction of Israel, which would very probably reply to the King's fall by launching a large-scale invasion of the country across the Jordan, supported by the American Sixth Fleet.

The majority of the Palestinian cadres were much happier with the ambiguous situation in which their troops were free to act while the consequences and responsibilities were borne by Hussein, whose atti-tude could easily be stigmatized. But every situation of dual power is doomed to precariousness, as Nayef Hawatmeh saw clearly, comparing it directly with the conditions in Russia between February and October 1917.† Hussein could not put up with it for long, and the extremist groups did all they could to make it daily more intolerable for him.

The moves made by the authorities and the Jordanian troops to assert some degree of control over the Palestinian armed forces and camps, between 1968 and 1970, led to fights and acts of destruction, with hundreds dead and wounded. Each clash was followed by a com-promise agreement which was barely observed, and hostilities were resumed on the slightest pretext. Hussein retreated, sometimes ap-pointing pro-Palestinian ministers, but conditions remained the same and the situation became more serious and more strained each time, without being cleared in favour of one side or the other.

This could not go on forever: a showdown could be foreseen. That prospect impelled the Palestinians to strengthen their structures and their unity. The seventh session of the Palestine National Council took place in Cairo between 30 May and 5 June 1970. A Central Resistance Council was appointed, in which all the organizations and all the mem-bers of the P.L.O.'s executive committee were represented. Also set up

* Romano Ledda, *La Battaglia di Amman*, Rome, Editori Riuniti, 1971, p. 38.
† Ibid., p. 36.

was a Joint Resistance Command, with Arafat as chairman, and a Jordano-Palestinian Committee for joint action. They had realized (rather belatedly) that it was necessary not to look like a foreign body in Jordan. However, the P.F.L.P. insisted on specifically reserving its independent freedom of action.

During June and July 1970 tension became acute. Hussein had long been urged to react against the Palestinians by the group hostile to them led by his uncle Sharif Nasser ben Jamil, who organized a Hashemite Movement with its own armed militia. In June 1969 the King had appointed him commander-in-chief of the Army and carried out a ministerial reshuffle which resulted in members of his group taking over key positions. In February 1970 pressure from the Palestinians, backed by demonstrations in the towns, and from Parliament, obliged the King to dismiss the Minister of the Interior, an arch-enemy of the Palestinians, and in April he had to appoint as the Army's chief of staff a pro-Palestinian, Mashhur Haditha. In June his uncle was dismissed and a government favourable to the Palestinians, led by 'Abd al-mon 'im Rifa'i, was formed. But Hussein remained quite determined to recover his full authority.

The trial of strength became more or less inevitable when, on 26 July 1970, as mentioned above (page 208), the Jordanian Government accepted, three days after Nasser, the Rogers Plan, which implied recognizing Israel as a legitimate state that would enjoy permanent existence within reduced frontiers and with which a lasting peace should be concluded. All the Palestinian organizations could not but protest against this attitude, which ran counter to their official line and the demands of the masses, even if many of their leaders thought that they would one day arrive at that same position. Even these leaders considered that their possible acceptance of the Plan ought to be negotiated with them in return for substantial benefits, of which there was no sign in this position taken up by two established Arab states with the backing merely of a few others – Lebanon, Libya, Sudan. The Palestinians were stimulated by fear, constant since then and to this day and constituting the principal reason for their attitude, that an agreement might be concluded without them, between the Arab states involved in the conflict and Israel, which would ignore their demands and even their existence. They had to react.

All the organizations promoted protest demonstrations in Amman at the end of July, in which Jordanian townspeople took part, together with actions by the Palestinian forces which sometimes provoked soldiers and officers of the King's Army. On these occasions Nasser was vilified, treated as a defeatist and quitter. Egypt retorted by closing down the Palestinians' radio station in Cairo, and Heykal, Nasser's spokesman, emphasized the minor and casual role which was all that the Palestinians could play in the conflict with Israel. Hussein felt encouraged, and resolved to attack. He got ready by reinforcing his Government with a Crown Council dominated by his uncle Nasser ben Jamil and appointing (on 9 August) as assistant to the pro-Palestinian Chief of Staff a reliable officer, Zayd ben Shaker. The personalities of the anti-Palestinian group who had been unwillingly removed in June were now back in positions of power.

Preparations for struggle went ahead on both sides during August, punctuated by hesitations and incidents, with an eye kept on the attitude of the outside world, especially the U.S.A. and Israel. Arafat went to Baghdad, where the Iraqi Government announced that it was putting at the disposal of the Palestinian Resistance the 12,000 Iraqi soldiers who had been stationed in Jordan since 1967. This was the moment when Israel protested against Egypt's installation of rocket-launching ramps in the Canal Zone after 7 August, the date of the last cease-fire agreement. On 30 August the Israeli government decided, in consequence, to pull out of the negotiations with Jarring which had been resumed on the 5th. After some beating about the bush, the American State Department agreed with Israel's denunciations, despite the denials and attempts to justify themselves put forward by the Egyptians. This was interpreted as meaning American support for Israel in applying a hard line, and implementation of the Rogers Plan was thereby hindered, to say the least. Hussein had reason to fear that the plan might be dropped, and with it all hope of one day recovering the West Bank. He would deduce from this that he must demonstrate his power and capacity to contain the Palestinians, so as to be able to appear as a credible partner in the peace negotiations that would certainly be held. On 27 August the Palestine National Council assembled in Amman under the protection of its armed militias. It adopted resolutions rejecting the Rogers Plan and any solution that fell short of destruction of the state of Israel, and proclaiming the absolute independence of the Palestinian movement. This looked like a challenge thrown down to the Jordanian monarch.

He replied, two days later, with a solemn and unequivocal warning to the Resistance. It must stop confronting the King's Army, thus challenging his authority and disrupting the national unity of Jordan, and obstructing negotiations along the line of the Rogers Plan. Next day his artillery opened fire in all directions to show its presence and its strength. The *fedayeen* did not reply. Their Syrian and Iraqi protectors, alarmed, threatened to intervene on their behalf. Libya suspended its subsidies to Jordan.

A compromise might still have been arrived at, and the P.L.O. nucleus made efforts in that direction, since it wished to retain its positions but also to avoid giving pretexts for the attack which now obviously threatened. But that was not at all the way that George Habache and his P.F.L.P. saw the situation. They suspected that within the Central Committee of the P.L.O. there were leanings and even definite intentions towards conciliation, in spite of its vigorous proclamations. That meant a conciliation with Hussein – and on this point their suspicion was to a large extent correct – which could lead (after some considerable time, to be sure) to acceptance of the Rogers Plan or of a similar project recognizing the legitimacy of some Israeli entity, even though Israel's attitude had just deprived the Rogers Plan of most of its chances of success. Habache wanted to nip in the bud any move of that sort, to dig an impassable gulf around the Resistance, to make its opposition to Hussein, Nasser and other 'quitters' irreconcilable, and to urge the P.L.O. towards the conquest of Amman. His scheme succeeded, with tragic consequences for the Palestinians.

On 6 September Palestinian commandos attacked four aircraft. One of these attempts, made in London against an aircraft belonging to the Israeli company *El Al*, failed to come off. One of the guerrilla fighters was killed and another, Leila Khaled, was taken prisoner. But three other aircraft (belonging to Panam, T.W.A. and Swissair) were captured in full flight. The Panam plane was taken to Cairo and blown up after the passengers had been allowed to leave. The two others were taken to a makeshift airfield held by the Palestinians at Zarka, in Jordan. On 9 September another plane, belonging to British Overseas Airways, was also taken to Zarka. Four hundred passengers became hostages of the P.F.L.P.

Great was the enthusiasm throughout the Arab world. The masses saw in these actions, which had been very well organized from the technical standpoint, above all a retort to the industrial world which applauded Israel and showed indifference to the fate of its Arab victims. The political leaders, however, were frightened by the foreseeable consequences, including the leaders of the P.L.O., against whom (as the cadres of the P.F.L.P. said in so many words to Romano Ledda) the coup had been also, and even mainly, directed. The European states and the U.S.A. protested with the greatest vigour, encouraged by their indignant public opinion, and the possibility of American

military intervention was allowed to appear. The U.S.S.R. also disapproved. The only politicians to be happy at what had happened were
the Israelis and the Jordanian camarilla around Hussein.

Israel saw itself relieved of the hesitations on the part of international
public opinion which might have been caused by its withdrawal from
the talks with Jarring. In comparison with 'the Arabs' at large, to
whom the coup was generally attributed, Israel's image improved still
further. The Security Council unanimously demanded unconditional
liberation of all the hostages. Hussein saw his authority flagrantly
flouted in his own kingdom. He could no longer be considered a valid
interlocutor in international discussions: he would be thought incapable of imposing respect for his own commitments. It was impossible
for him not to react. The Central Committee of the P.L.O. tried to
defuse the imminent conflict by pressing the P.F.L.P. to free the
hostages, but it also declined to allow a wedge to be driven into the
Resistance by participating in a struggle against the P.F.L.P., or even
by seeming to authorize such a struggle. Clashes continued: attacks by
Bedouin troops on Palestinian positions; an attempt (faked, perhaps)
on Hussein's life; efforts at appeasement by the Rifa'i Government and
the Central Committee; a cease-fire that was not respected.

On 16 September Hussein dismissed Rifa'i, formed a new government composed exclusively of military men, and replaced the commander-in-chief of the Army by General Habes al-Majali, an adherent
of the hardest line. Martial law was proclaimed. On the morning of the
17th the Jordanian guns bombarded the Palestinian camps in Amman
and practically the entire capital. The P.L.O. closed ranks, with all the
groups now accepting (in principle) the authority of the Central Committee and of Arafat, who was appointed supreme military commander.
But it was too late.

Hussein and his general staff apparently thought that they would be
able to restore Jordanian authority quite quickly through the sudden-
ness of their action. However, this did not happen, which made their
task more difficult. Without bothering about details, the Jordanian
Army bombarded the Palestinian bases. This meant, in practice, that
hell was let loose in the camps where thousands of refugees were sheltering in sordid hovels. The very centres of the towns were not immune.
The Bedouin hurled themselves upon the Palestinians, whom they
hated, and committed atrocities. The towns were deprived of water
and food. But the townspeople, whether organized or not in militias,
mobilized themselves on the Palestinians' side. The defence they put
up was effective. The troops were able to bombard and destroy the

towns, but not to control them or win a decisive victory. The Palestinians and their allies blocked the troops' advance, while themselves remaining incapable of launching a decisive counter-attack.

Feeling among the Arabs was too much exacerbated by the wretched fate of the Palestinians to tolerate in silence what looked like a deliberate massacre of these last victims, as they saw them, of the colonialism from which the whole Arab nation had suffered. Even beyond the Arab world information about the refugee camps had become widely known during the three previous years and had touched a wide section of world opinion, including those minds most sympathetic towards Israel. As for the extreme Left, they could have no doubt of the justice of the cause of a people decimated by a reactionary monarch. Amman in flames recalled the Commune and Paris bombarded by the armies of Thiers.

The Arab governments, the sincerity of whose concern cannot be denied out of hand, were unable to remain indifferent to the pressure of their peoples and the heart-rending appeals of the Palestinians. From the very first day Nasser got together with Gaddafi and the Sudanese. He sent his Chief of Staff to Amman, to confer fruitlessly with Hussein, who prevented him from meeting Arafat. The attitude taken up by Nasser and the Arab rulers throughout the crisis clearly revealed the ambiguity of their position. Most of them were disgusted by what Hussein had done, deplored the fate of the Palestinians and, on a more political plane, wished to conserve for the Palestinian Resistance a certain amount of strength – as much, at least, as they thought would be useful to them, on condition that its attitude was 'reasonable', which was guaranteed by the positions of Arafat and the leading nucleus of the Central Committee. Nobody, however, wanted to see Hussein fall from power; apart, that is, from the Palestinian extremist minorities, along with Habache, and inexperienced enthusiasts like Gaddafi, who was being described as a 'boy scout' in power (later he was to be called mad) because he took seriously the slogans that were put out officially in the Arab world. Arafat never ceased offering the King ways of escape, and disavowed the foreign bureaux of the P.L.O. which were issuing statements calling for his overthrow. Furthermore, the threat of American intervention became clearer, even though Europe declined to join in and Israel eventually decided that it was more expedient to let the Arabs exterminate each other than to attempt a show of strength that might weld them into unity. Accordingly, Nasser and those who followed his line treated the two contending parties as being on the same footing and preached moderation to both. It is true that expressions of indignation against Hussein became increasingly severe, but this left the Jordanian monarch cold, perfectly well aware as he was of how hard it would be for his Arab colleagues to take effective action, and firmly resolved as he was to make maximum use of the opportunity offered him by the situation to re-establish his authority.

The concern for the Palestinians felt by the Arab masses found expression at state level only in diplomatic pressure and verbal denunciation. To this there was only one exception. Syria sent in two divisions of tanks and heavy artillery officially composed of Palestinians embodied in the Syrian Army. They engaged the King's forces, but without penetrating further than the 'liberated zone', the enclave in the north of Jordan where the Palestinians had, at the beginning of the attack by the King's men, arrested the military governor, handed over the administration to Jordanian personalities sympathetic to their cause, and nominated four local politico-military chiefs. Abroad, it was feared that the Syrian intervention might serve as a pretext for interventions on the other side, especially by the U.S.A. and Israel, with unpredictable consequences, perhaps world war. Contacts between Israel and America with a view to such action did indeed take place. Nixon deployed American troops and warships and declared his readiness to intervene. He called on the U.S.S.R. to restrain the Syrians, threatening 'serious consequences' if they did not. The U.S.S.R., France, Great Britain and some Arab countries all exerted pressure on Syria. Heated discussions took place within the Ba'ath Party in Damascus. Israel mobilized and concentrated forces against the Syrians. General Hafez Assad, Minister of War and commander of the Air Force, won the day against the Left wing led by Salah Jadid, the advocates of intervention. The Syrian troops (or the troops which had come from Syria) withdrew on 24 September. As for Iraq, from which country had come the most violent invective against Hussein and the most eloquent declarations of support for the Palestinians, its 12,000 soldiers who were already stationed in Jordan and had no frontier to cross not only gave no aid to the *fedayeen* but apparently facilitated the movements of the King's forces. In any case, they allowed themselves to be easily blocked off by the Jordanian Army. Gaddafi proposed joint military intervention by Algeria and Libya, but nothing came of this.

Under these conditions it was clear that Hussein had won the upper hand. The only obstacle to total victory for him was the revulsion of Arab consciences at the crushing of the Palestinians and the atrocious character assumed by the operation. It was the most moderate of the Arab leaders, Bourguiba, who proposed, on 19 September, a meeting of chiefs of state with Hussein and Arafat present. Six Arab chiefs of state and the Tunisian Prime Minister Bahi Ladgham assembled in Cairo on 22 September, without the Palestinians and with, as sole representative of Jordan, that country's Prime Minister Mohammed Daud, a person without real power. All that was agreed was to send to Amman a peace mission headed by the Sudanese President Nemeiri. Hussein prevented him from seeing Arafat, and put him in touch with four Palestinian leaders whom he had taken prisoner and with whom he had concluded an agreement, which was immediately repudiated by the Central Committee. A completely factitious cease-fire agreement was concluded on 23 September.

When the Arab mission returned to Cairo it soon realized how it had been deceived. The struggle on the spot was continuing and the country's situation getting worse. Arab anger mounted and, here and there, rather more effective measures were contemplated. The journalists from all over the world who were at last able to leave Amman published details of the atrocities they had witnessed. Mohammed Daud, whose daughter was fighting alongside the Palestinians, took advantage of his stay in Cairo to resign. On 25 September Nemeiri, back in Amman, succeeded in getting a second cease-fire signed, this time with Arafat's concurrence, but the Jordanian troops at once renewed their attack. The Bedouin slaughtered a large number of wounded in a hospital.

Nemeiri and Bahi Ladgham publicly denounced Hussein, Gaddafi threatened him and Nasser became pressing. At last, on 27 September, Hussein resigned himself to going to Cairo to confer with the assembled Arab leaders, who were joined by Arafat. Hussein was received like an accused person appearing before a tribunal of his peers. The tone of the discussion was extremely rough. The Jordanian King's proposals were dismissed out of hand, and the plan prepared by the P.L.O.'s Central Committee was taken as the basis for discussion. Gaddafi, it appears, drew his revolver and wanted to shoot down Hussein 'the butcher'. Nasser managed, with great difficulty, to calm him, and exerted himself so much in order to secure an agreement that he died the next day, from a heart attack.

The agreement, once more, could only be a compromise. Nobody wanted to see Hussein fall, especially as Dayan threatened to intervene if that should happen. The contending forces were required to call off their operations and withdraw from Amman and the situation that existed on 17 September was to be restored. Internal security would be ensured by Jordanian troops. An Arab Higher Commission chaired by Bahi Ladgham, provided with full powers, was to supervise the process of peacemaking and prepare a detailed agreement, which must accomplish the feat of safeguarding both Jordanian legality and freedom of action for the Palestinians, who had to be able to continue their struggle.

The reconciliation was spectacular. Before the photographers, Hussein shook hands with Arafat. This photograph was for a long time to serve as a weapon in the hands of the Palestinians and others who denounced the crypto-moderate line they attributed to the leader of the P.L.O. For the moment, however, all the groups rallied in support of the agreement. Besides, George Habache had chosen this month of September to be away from the Middle East.

The reconciliation was artificial. The Palestinians congratulated themselves on having acquired decisive political weight and made Hussein give way, while the King's extreme supporters blamed him for having capitulated. But this was only the outward appearance of things. Hussein retained power, and the preservation of legality could only favour him in the long run. His Army had stayed loyal. The Palestinians had suffered a formidable bloodletting and had not managed to get the better of him on the ground. Amid the widespread emotion surrounding the death of Nasser and his dramatic funeral, the problem slipped for the moment into the background. While the Palestinians would not forget that 'black September', the other Arabs returned to their own concerns. Many Egyptians were heard to call down curses on these quarrelsome Arabs for whom they had fought, who had caused them to lose part of their national territory, who had subjected them to a burdensome state of war, and who had just practically caused the death of their benevolent, wise and well-beloved leader. This mood was to persist and develop, culminating seven years later in major initiatives.

Hussein lay low, but had no intention of refraining either from exercising his full powers or from quelling the Palestinians, which he could only do, as events had just shown, by expelling their organization. He merely hesitated between brutal methods and a gradual gnawing-away. In any case, he knew that he held the major trumps in his hand. The succession of events was to prove this soon enough. After a few months, no traces were left of what had been the parallel power in Jordan. The historical law of which Nayef Hawatmeh had spoken was confirmed: any coexistence of two powers in one state is precarious. This time, however, it was not Lenin who had triumphed.

The panorama of the Arab world at the beginning of October 1970 showed that a phase had ended. Nasser was dead and the Palestinians had been beaten. Israel seemed stronger than ever and the American power which sustained it had shown its redoubtable effectiveness. The hopes of the most extreme revolutionaries in a radical transformation to be brought about by the dynamic of the Palestinian movement, the struggle against Israel, had been frustrated. They had lost a battle, but clung to the hope that they would win their war. They still possessed bastions and forces, but practically none on which they could absolutely rely, except perhaps in South Arabia. Algeria, Syria and Iraq had shown that their own concerns took priority at the decisive moment, and the revolutionary *élan* proved to have sobered down considerably. Gaddafi was as zealous as ever for the Arab cause, but his conception of it was far from clear and his political methods were muddled. His antipathy to atheistic communism kept him aloof from the only superpower whose alliance might be advantageous, the U.S.S.R.; which, moreover, did not seem to be disposed for its part to provide him with reliable backing. The middle road of Nasserism was itself seriously put in question. One could see that the outpourings of black gold were already strengthening and would strengthen still further the conservative influence of Saudi Arabia, which was now in a position to weigh heavily in the decisions taken by nearly all the Arab states.

The future might well look dark for the more clear-sighted of the Arab revolutionaries. Some of them began to suspect that the linking of their aims with struggle against Israel as the first priority might not be wholly advantageous. But militantism presupposes optimism. Past instances, in Vietnam and Algeria, of victories won over European and American imperialism encouraged them to hope. The struggle continued.

10

The Intoxication of Victory: and a Desperate Remedy

I shall retrace in less detail the events which occurred between 1970 and 1979. The important changes in the situation had been made, in fact, in the preceding period. The factors then introduced continued thereafter to make themselves felt, only with increased and cumulative effect.

Israel continued to enjoy the intoxication of victory, further strengthened by the defeat which had just been suffered by its most determined foes. Moreover, this defeat had been inflicted by fellow Arabs! It confirmed the idea that one could rest confident that the divisions among the Arabs would make unlikely any coalition that might spell danger for the Jewish state. Yet no Arab state had agreed to make peace on the Israelis' conditions. Consequently, the state of war persisted, and with it the need to obtain increasingly costly armaments.

Although growth continued and the Israeli economy could be considered prosperous by the usual standards of the capitalist world, this prosperity had its dark sides, which were greatly aggravated by the usual impediments: the burden of war expenditure, which meant very heavy taxation, and Israel's isolation in the region, which was mitigated by the policy of open bridges over the Jordan, enabling Israeli products to reach the Jordanian market and, from it, the markets of some neighbouring countries. Inflation was severe and poverty the lot of large sections of the population. These difficulties, added to the absence of any serious threat from the Arabs, caused or intensified some cracks in the nation's unity. Strikes became frequent. As the most underprivileged sections were often 'Arab Jews' and, more broadly, Oriental Jews (Sephardim), the latter complained more and more loudly about the conditions provided for them in this society created and dominated by the Western Jews (Ashkenazim). In Israel the Sephardim figured as sub-proletarians, whose way of life was regarded as backward and who attained only slowly the required level of technical skill and the jobs associated with prestige and privilege. The protest of these 'black Jews' often took vehement and even brutal forms. A 'Black Panther' movement developed among the youth, inspired by the movements of the Blacks in America.

Contrary to widespread illusions on the subject among the Arabs and in the European and American Left, this situation rarely caused these Oriental (often Arabic-speaking) Jews to sympathize with the demands of the Israeli Arabs or the people of the occupied West Bank. They had suffered, in the countries they came from, at the hands of the local Arabs or Muslims. Their expatriation had made them more bitter. Yet a few youngsters, Sephardim and Ashkenazim alike and sometimes even Sabras, Jews born in Israel, impelled by the world-wide and national climate of contestation, have on a few (a very few) occasions taken a stand against the Jewish state itself. There is a general wave of horror when a spy network is discovered, perhaps one that uses terrorist methods, and it is found to include young Jews.

In the political class the conflict between strategical orientations, which began with the very beginning of the Zionist settlement in Pal-estine, continued and intensified without coinciding precisely, as the naïve Left in Europe supposes, with the split between Left and Right. Financial and economic difficulties, Israel's increasing international isolation and, above all, the serious problem presented by the West Bank territories conquered in 1967 worried many thinking people. Ought one to go on showing contempt for world opinion and counting on constant American support, despite half-hearted expressions of dis-approval from the American Government, or ought one, on the con-trary, to try and achieve a *rapprochement* with the forces in the world that challenge American hegemony, first and foremost the Soviet Union? Ought one, above all, to safeguard the possibility of using partial withdrawals from the West Bank as a bargaining point and, therefore, not go too far in the Judaization of that territory, or on the contrary, ought one to encourage Jewish settlement there so as to use this as an argument for keeping hold of the territory, in spite of every-one? Ought one to yield to the pressure of the religious elements who, along with the extreme nationalists, believe in the inalienable right of the Jewish people to these ancestral lands and who, in addition (but all this is interconnected), demand full application of the archaic require-ments of Jewish religious law? Or ought one to resist them and move towards a secularization of the state and (a distinction can be made here) allow the West Bank to preserve a certain Arab character, which would be rather useful if cheap labour, profitable to the Israeli econ-omy, were to be drawn from there? Be it noted in passing that the logic of the theory of religious rights (the divine promise about Canaan) and historical rights would lead to a demand for the East Bank of the Jordan, Hussein's kingdom, no less than the West; but a last-moment spasm of realism causes all Israelis, apart from a few fanatics, to 'forget' that vision.

Only a few on the fringe of politics strive desperately to make contact with the Palestinians and advocate a complete, or practically complete, withdrawal from the occupied territories, in exchange for an all-round and lasting peace. As usual, their position is rendered unrealistic by the Arabs' refusal, ostentatiously maintained (even if it accords less and less with the deep-down thinking of the leaders concerned, who drop hints to this effect), to recognize the state of Israel as a legitimate reality within certain limits.

The political class which has some actual influence on the state's choice of policy is therefore divided into 'doves' and 'hawks'. This division is often hesitant, it runs through nearly all the parties, and it is not consistent but varies in relation to different problems. Old David Ben Gurion, in his retirement, declared in favour of the doves, and from time to time denounced the futility of the attitude of 'no compromise'. But the hawks saw in this only the senile ramblings of an historical personage who had outlived his time. He died on 1 December 1973 without having been listened to.

On 4 August 1970 the Government of National Unity broke up. The Right-wing bloc Gahal, led by Menachem Begin, withdrew, unwilling to approve Golda Meir's acceptance of the Rogers Plan, even though this was reluctant and subject to reservations. The aged leader seemed, to the religious elements especially, too ready, despite her rigidity, to agree to concessions. Besides, the old team around the Labour Party, Mapai, which had been running the country for so long, was increasingly discredited. People were tired of its internal squabbles, of the favouritisms which operated as a matter of course as in every 'Establishment' of this sort, and of its incapacity to cope with the economic difficulties. There were revelations concerning war and armaments profiteers. In September 1973, in the Histadruth elections, the governmental front lost the support of about 4 per cent of those who had previously voted for it and the Panthers won 2 per cent of the votes, an obvious sign of discontent among the Sephardim. Elections to the legislature, fixed for October 1973, were drawing near. All the politicians were taken up with pre-election agitation. General Ariel Sharon, commanding the Southern Front, who was famous for his boldness and for his brutality towards the Arabs (the notorious Unit 101 which he led after 1952 engaged, among other things, in murders of isolated Arab shepherds on Jordanian or Egyptian territory, on the pretext of carrying out reprisals), furious at not being appointed Chief of Staff, resigned with a bang from the Army in July 1973 and openly joined in the political game. Popular as a 'strong man' and for his energy, he succeeded in adding other Right-wing groups to the Gahal coalition dominated by Begin's Heruth. It was under his auspices that Likud was born, the Right-wing bloc which would soon reveal its power to attract the Israeli masses.

The predominant sense of security had complex and contradictory effects. It produced expressions of delirious optimism, with contempt for the Arabs and their military capacities reaching its apogee. Details of this can be read in the fine book written by the Israeli journalist Amnon Kapeliouk, which is based on extensive documentation.* Here I can only summarize his analyses. The death of Nasser, to whom Israeli opinion, like a substantial section of world opinion, falsely ascribed a decisive and diabolical role in the mobilizing of Arab energies against Israel, contributed much to the genesis of this feeling. The Palestinians' attacks from Jordan had ceased after the 'black September' of 1970. The people of the West Bank seemed calm and more or less resigned to their situation as victims of colonization. The eviction from Egypt in July 1972 of the Soviet technicians and advisers made complete the Israelis' confidence that Egyptian threats were meaningless. The hawks, with General Dayan at their head, felt encouraged to give clear utterance to their ambitions, their plans to perpetuate this favourable situation, to pursue with determination the Judaizing of the West Bank and to present Israel as the gendarme of the Near East, capable of countering any move on the part of the neighbouring countries which might in any way challenge its supremacy. In agreement with Golda Meir and the very influential minister Israel Galili, Dayan caused to be adopted, on 3 September 1973, by the leadership of the Labour Party, with a view to improving this party's position in the coming elections, a plan which was called the Galili Document. This provided for all sorts of measures aimed at intensifying Jewish settlement in the West Bank and in north-east Sinai. The doves were afraid of arousing popular hostility if they opposed it openly. Few voices were raised against it.

The Palestinian terrorist attacks on Israeli territory which developed in this period, as will be seen, appeared mere pinpricks, exasperating and painful to be sure, but of minor importance. They increased the hatred and contempt felt for the Arabs, but people trusted in the state's special services to discourage them and, in any case, they were unable to affect general security except in a very slight degree. They

* Amnon Kapeliouk, *Israël, la fin des mythes*, Paris, Albin Michel, 1975.

were desperate actions which bore witness, in their own way, to the Arabs' inability to resist effectively the triumphant strengthening of Israel's position. Israel's arrogance and assurance attained extreme levels at this time, with expressions of self-satisfaction which an Israeli writer has associated with pathological manifestations of the form of madness called autism. Contempt for the capacities of the Arabs, encouraged by a team of orientalists, self-styled specialists on the so-called 'Arab soul', attained proportions that were dangerous to Israel itself. All warnings about Arab preparations for attack were rejected, for these preparations, if, at worst, they proved to be real, could only be ineffective and come to nothing: Israel was invincible and had only to wait, without offering the slightest concession, for the Arabs to recognize and surrender to her, accepting all the facts that had been accomplished to their detriment. What else could they do, since they were already beaten in advance? Besides, as General Ezer Weizmann said, war was not a game suitable for Arabs.

The decline of the Palestinian Resistance seemed to support these contemptuous conclusions. It was soon made clear that the Cairo agreements between Hussein and the Palestinians, despite appearances to the contrary, constituted only an armistice which left the Jordanian monarch wielding military superiority and a monopoly of political legitimacy in his kingdom, with every possibility of carrying through to completion the task he had set himself – to destroy the power of the Palestinians in Jordan. He was not slow to apply himself afresh to this task. Headship of the government was entrusted on 28 October 1970 to a tough man, Waçfi Tall. Clashes between Palestinian guerrilla fighters and Jordanian soldiers had ceased for no more than a few days. They continued regardless of the exhortations of the Arab Higher Commission chaired by Bahi Ladgham, the many and always futile local cease-fires concluded under its auspices, the protests of Arab opinion and the offers of mediation. It soon became clear that George Habache was right when he declared, in an interview in January 1971, that Hussein was 'determined to crush the Palestinian resistance movement' – inside his own kingdom, at any rate. But Habache's call to overthrow the King no longer had any hope of being realized, any more than Gaddafi's exhortation in the same sense addressed to the Jordanian Army. In January 1971 Iraq withdrew its troops which had been stationed in Jordan. Waçfi Tall moved methodically, troubling less and less to preserve appearances, the Army remained loyal, the Jordanian masses remained passive, the protests by the Arab countries remained verbal.

In vain did a conference of nine states, assembled in Cairo in April, denounce the plan to suppress the Palestinians. In vain did Libya and Kuwait suspend payment of their subsidies to Hussein. In vain did Syria attempt to mediate in April, setting up a fresh committee to supervise the cease-fire. In vain did Bahi Ladgham resign, accusing the Jordanian Government. The Palestinians' offices were closed, their popular militias disarmed, the P.L.O.'s newspapers banned and the commandos forced out of the towns.

In July 1971 the situation was ripe for the final blow to be struck. The last of the Palestinians' strongholds, in the north, was surrounded and attacked. The last members of the Resistance were killed or taken prisoner. A hundred or two of them sought refuge in territory occupied by Israel, a symbolic paradox that gave much pleasure to the Israeli press. The reaction of the Arab countries was feeble. Some neighbouring states closed their frontiers to road and air traffic with Jordan and broke off diplomatic relations. Sadat eloquently stigmatized Hussein. Gaddafi proposed that military action be taken against him, but nobody followed his lead.

Hussein had too much experience of Arab politics to worry a great deal. He knew that all this excitement would last for a short time only, and that its practical effects would be limited. The Palestinians sabotaged the Tapline oil pipeline on three occasions in September 1971. Plots were hatched and thwarted. In November 1971 the *fedayeen* assassinated Waçfi Tall in Cairo. In April 1972 the P.L.O. called for Hussein to be brought before a People's Court. In February 1973 a commando got into Jordan with the intention of taking hostages from among the leading personages of the kingdom, but was exposed. Hussein pursued his course regardless. He kept on with his approaches to the powers, which, indeed, he had not interrupted even while his troops were dismantling the Palestinian organization in Jordan. America enabled him to renew his armaments and make up for the losses due to trade embargos by his neighbours or the interruption in the transit of oil across his kingdom. The U.S.S.R. maintained and developed good relations with him.

At the same time, the Hashemite monarch made known his peaceful intentions towards Israel, while maintaining a firm position on the rights of the Arabs. On 15 March 1972 he published a 'Hussein Plan', which was circulated with much publicity. This was a draft for a new status for the West Bank when the long-awaited day should come for Israel to set it free. Instead of forming just a few districts amongst others in the Hashemite kingdom, the West Bank would become an autonomous province with Jerusalem as its capital. Along with the autonomous province of the East Bank, each of these having its own legislative assembly, executive and judiciary, it would enter into the framework of a 'United Arab Kingdom'. The federal kingdom would also have an executive (the King's), a unified army, and a central legislative assembly and supreme court. What was intended, above all, it seemed, was to win over the people of the West Bank (whom Israel was about to invite to participate in municipal elections), to detach them from the P.L.O., and make the unpopular Jordanian regime more attractive to them. Hussein was accused of having secretly come to an arrangement with Israel and of preparing, by means of his plan, for acceptance of the Allon Plan by which the West Bank would receive a certain degree of autonomy under the supervision of Israeli troops, who would remain as a compact cordon along the Jordan. In any case, Israel rejected Hussein's scheme and showed no sign of giving up its desire to keep hold of the whole of Jerusalem.

One of the aspects of the Hussein Plan was implicit recognition of the legitimacy of the state of Israel within frontiers corresponding more or less to those of before June 1967. There was nothing new in that. Hussein had long since openly proclaimed this recognition, and even let it be known that he might agree to frontier rectifications. But his plan re-emphasized this, and that was what earned him reproaches from the Arab world: Hussein's gaze was directed more towards the West. He seemed to be the only Arab ruler ready to agree to the only peace that would be acceptable to the outside world, apart from the extremist regimes, namely, a compromise peace with Israel. Having learnt from the bitter experience of June 1967 the strength of the Jewish state, he knew well that only American pressure could make Israel accept such a compromise. He hoped to be the first beneficiary thereof. Meanwhile, he launched a three-year plan of economic development, and soon observed that he had been right not to worry too much about the Arab sanctions imposed as a result of his rough dealing with the Palestinians. At the end of 1972 and during the first half of 1973 these sanctions were lifted, one after another. Kuwait even paid him the arrears of his interrupted subsidy, and Saudi Arabia increased its aid to him.

All that was left to the Palestinians who had been driven out of Jordan was one single country bordering on Israel where they were still free to move, free to constitute a really independent force, and comparatively free to launch attacks against the enemy state. This was Lebanon.

The divisions in the movement continued to bear very negatively on its activities and attitudes. However, efforts at unification continued, although with only limited results. The crisis of September 1970 had forced the groups to draw together, but the divergences between them were quick to re-emerge. The disaster naturally entailed a torrent of self-criticism and, above all, of mutual criticism between groups and leaderships. The 'moderates' and centrists criticized the adventurism of the Left-wing groups, which had led them blindly into a trial of strength under unfavorable conditions. The Left perceived, rather late in the day, some of the causes of its defeat. It had been presupposed, on the basis of sloganizing, that unity existed – a unity which was in fact non-existent and which no attempt had been made to bring about in practice – between the Resistance, the Jordanian masses (especially those in the rural areas) and the Army. The myth of the revolutionary determination of the masses had been taken for reality. The problem of the Bedouins' hostility had been overlooked.

But it was difficult, as it is always difficult for a revolutionary movement, to escape from myth. Any movement which sets itself the task of overthrowing an existing situation in order to realize a political and social aim which has been defined ideally has a tendency to talk in the future perfect tense, as Abdallah Laroui puts it. The requirements of mobilization naturally foster exaggeration of the prospects of success. Those who develop this kind of intellectual and verbal logistics tend to convince themselves that it coincides with the facts of a situation. It is for those who preserve a more realistic view to be accused by the more 'faithful' of a certain softness, or even of treachery, so that they are obliged to 'go further', to display a confidence and conviction that they do not really possess. This entire mechanism operates to the detriment of clear-sightedness. Paradoxically, some conditions needed for success may thus become factors of defeat.

Criticism and polemic concerning the technical and strategical errors committed had serious repercussions on the plane of organization. They served as reasons, or pretexts, inside the group for conflicts between tendencies which in some cases went as far as to split them asunder. They served as ammunition in the conflict between groups whose common aim only sharpened and emphasized their rivalry. The numerical superiority of *El Fatah* encouraged it constantly to try and dominate and control the other movements. The latter resisted this pressure and denounced it, striving to defend their independence to the utmost. The Palestine Liberation Army, which was, in theory, the military arm of the P.L.O., continued to criticize the military defects of the other organizations and to demand a monopoly of the struggle on that plane, without, however, submitting unconditionally to the decisions of the congresses and higher organs of the P.L.O. Its alternation of attacks on *El Fatah* and reconciliations with it were coupled with internal conflicts that were sometimes grave.

Plans for unifying and rationalizing the movement succeeded only in part. In 1971 a new group was accepted into the movement: the Ançars (helpers, supporters). Essentially, they represented the Communists, who possessed a substantial mass basis on the West Bank and also the backing of the Soviet Union. In return for their acceptance, they expounded, cautiously, the thesis of a political solution, which, though denounced officially, was winning more and more supporters, clandestine or semi-clandestine.

In the usual way, the young generation attacked the leaders, who had now been in office for a very long time. But the leading nucleus held its ground. Arafat, though attacked from several sides, particularly for the tendency to compromise which was ascribed to him (not without reason from this time on), managed to keep his post by tacking between the tendencies, giving pledges successively to this one and to that. He succeeded, nevertheless, by means of a great deal of patience and tenacity, in gradually promoting his own ideas and those of the centrist group around him. But in doing so he was often compelled (and this is still the case today), as a result of one vicissitude or other, to make temporary retreats, going back to positions which he had supposed (and which one might have supposed) had been left behind. He was obliged, at all costs, not to sever contact with the political networks which were his only source of strength, even when they criticized him. He was able to guide them a little only by appearing to follow them, and often by following them in fact.

Besides the divergences caused by differences in ideology, and sometimes in combination with these differences, the choices to be made as regards relations with the various Arab states provided other occasions, reasons or pretexts for divisions in the movement. Each state aimed, of course, to have its supporters therein, motivated either by conviction or by payment. Correspondingly, each tendency, even if it was only embryonic, had to define its attitude to the various regimes under which the Arab countries lived, and was tempted to seek support among them. The Palestinian Resistance, with its entire original territory occupied by its opponent, was from the start, structurally, so to speak, doomed to constant dependence in highly concrete and practical forms – financial and military – upon the Arab states, each of which

defended, first and foremost, its own interests. The only way to preserve a considerable margin of independence was, as everyone knew, to
tack between these states.

Hussein's brutal reaction disposed, at least, of the problem of relations with Jordan, now settled by means of a total rupture. But this
rupture could not be final and, besides, it was necessary, even so, to
define what these relations were to be in the future. Syria, which
wielded that effective instrument of pressure, Sa'iqa, itself defined, in
accordance with the fluctuations of its internal politics, its relations
with the various groups. Iraq sought allies, and found them, in the
groups that rejected the other choices made. Saudi Arabia and the
Arab oil-producing states provided finance and were naturally concerned, at the very least, to ensure that their investments did not
subsidize actions contrary to their own interests. Egypt, despite the
loss of Sinai, the decline since Nasser's death in the leading role the
country played, and its refusal to permit armed groups on its territory,
continued to be a factor of major importance. It still possessed the
strongest Arab army, the largest population of any Arab country, and
that incomparable centre of culture and propaganda, Cairo. One of its
most powerful means of pressure was constituted by the radio trans-
mitters which it either allowed or refused to allow the Palestinians to
use, depending on the state of its relations with the P.L.O.

Using these means, Anwar El-Sadat, who had become Egypt's
master, exerted pressure on the movement in pursuit of his long-term
aims. The Arab world knew well that Egypt's permanent objective was
peace, with recovery of its territory lost in June 1967. Nasser himself
had proved that by accepting the Rogers Plan. This was what any
rational government of Syria would have to aim for, too, but it was
much more difficult to get the idea of peace accepted by the Syrian
masses and political groups, which were deeply susceptible to the ideology of Arabism, than by the Egyptian masses. Did this idea of peace
not imply acceptance of the accomplished fact of Israel, in its solid
nucleus, since a decisive victory over Israel was out of the question for
a long time to come?

The specific patriotism of Egypt, surrounded for decades past by
Arabism, was indeed much more inclined to distance itself from great
Arab causes when serving the latter proved to affect harmfully the very
serious problems which daily confronted the average Egyptian. That
was so whatever might be the illusions of the Left and the nationalist
ideologists on the banks of the Nile.

Sadat knew well that one of the conditions for acceptance of the idea

of peace by the Arab masses was a certain amount of satisfaction to be
given to the Palestinian demands, which no Arab could entirely disavow.
He knew, too, that a limitation of these demands by accepting the fact
of Israel was necessary, and that this limitation could be imposed on a
decisive proportion of the Palestinian masses (since there would always
be some bitter-enders) only by a Palestinian authority that was strong,
coherent and responsible. It was with this aim in view that he urged
the setting-up of a Palestinian government in exile. But the Palestinian
leaders, as a whole, were loath to take that step, and they remain so at
the time of writing. The reasons they give publicly in order to justify
this refusal, when they are questioned on the subject, are rather flimsy.
They are obviously mere secondary rationalizations produced to explain an attitude which is due to profound reasons, conscious or unconscious, that those concerned are unwilling or unable to express
publicly.

Here is how, in my opinion, these profound reasons are to be seen.
The more a central organ is endowed, in the eyes of the outside world,
with power over a given set of individuals and subordinate groups, and
the more this power is marked by the symbols which are its usual sign
(and the title of 'government' is at the very least a supreme symbol of
power), the more is it expected to take far-reaching political decisions,
to assume responsibility for them, to cause them to be accepted, along
with their consequences, by those who are supposed to be its subjects,
and to answer also for the actions of the latter, when it has not ordered
these actions or disapproves of them, by taking measures to compensate
the third parties they have harmed and to punish the transgressors. If
the central committee of a party or of a movement is not obeyed by a
considerable number of members of the organization concerned, if
these members openly and actively contradict the decisions it has taken,
and if measures are not taken against them and reparation is not offered
to their victims, that is, of course, unfortunate, detrimental to the
reputation of this central organ and of the movement itself, reducing
its weight in the game of politics, but it is seen as something that does
not transcend the frontiers of normality. But if a *government* reveals
similar impotence and incapacity, that is regarded as something much
more serious: it runs counter to the normal working of international
relations and discredits the government in question, with all sorts of
consequences, frequently of a dramatic nature.

A government, even a government in exile, has to behave differently
from a national movement. It is expected to set its signature to precise
agreements, conventions and treaties, and to honour them. It has to

enter fully into the game of international relations, to apply for admission to the United Nations and accept the conditions for membership thereof. Now, the present state of the international game requires that Israel's existence be accepted, even if the extension of its frontiers be regarded as illegal. The People's Republic of China was able to demand the expulsion of Taiwan from the United Nations as a condition for joining that body, and succeeded in getting its demand accepted. It seems out of the question that a similar demand put forward by the Palestinians in relation to Israel could meet with success – not for a long time yet, anyway. Israel occupies the entire territory of Palestine, whereas it was the state making the demand, People's China, that occupied the entire territory of China apart from the 0·37 per cent constituted by Taiwan. Members of the United Nations Organization undertake to 'settle their international disputes by peaceful means' and to 'refrain in their international relations from the threat or use of force against the territorial integrity or political independence of any state' (Article 2 of the United Nations Charter). States are admitted to the U.N.O., in principle, when they accept the obligations imposed by its Charter and 'in the judgement of the organization, are able and willing to carry out these obligations' (Article 4, paragraph 1). These are conditions which it would be hard for a movement to satisfy when its *raison d'être* is, precisely, to fight against a member state, and when its programme lays claim to the entire territory of that member state.

One cannot apply for admission to the United Nations without accepting Israel. One cannot adopt the mode of operation of a state without claiming the right to join the United Nations. If a fresh conflict with Israel should erupt (which cannot be ruled out), a constituted government, even if it has no territory, may be called upon to sign an armistice which will inevitably imply recognition of the Jewish state.

All these considerations, and doubtless others as well, account for the P.L.O.'s unwillingness to agree to the suggestion made by Sadat and by many others that it should form a proper government. Above all, it is known that this government would not be recognized and obeyed by all the groups – that they would denounce it and make a mockery of it. The P.L.O. would have to give up numerous facilities it enjoys at present: profiting from the initiatives taken by certain groups without clearly taking responsibility for them, or leaving that question in an equivocal haze, and, especially, permitting, allowing to go forward, and even directing certain warlike initiatives without reckoning with the possible reprisals which may ensue and affect, primarily, the host countries. Even if the exiled Palestinians were sometimes victims of the bombs dropped in reprisal by the Israelis, it was the governments – Jordanian, Lebanese, Syrian – that had to cope with the political repercussions of these actions by the enemy, to appease and indemnify the surviving victims, allow the zones affected or threatened to be detached, in many respects, from their national territory, and put up with the international complications that resulted from this. Furthermore, they were often denounced for their passivity and weakness, and even insulted for their treachery, whereas the Palestinians were accorded the laurels due to heroes.

Arafat and the centrist nucleus of *El Fatah*, while politely rejecting Sadat's suggestion, tended to lean for support upon Egypt. Besides its demographic and military power, Egypt had to offer a 'reasonable' government which no longer brandished those socialist and revolutionary claims which, even though mainly verbal, were as repugnant to the conservatives among the Palestinians as to their Saudi and other paymasters. Egypt gave hardly any facilities to the Palestinian armed forces, but, on the other hand, it did not have in its service within the movement a shock-troop as important and potentially dangerous as Sa'iqa. This was why *El Fatah* showed an understanding attitude even towards Sadat's declarations in favour of a 'political solution' (the euphemism for a peaceful solution). It was explained that the Egyptian leader's diplomatic efforts were complementary to the Palestinians' military pressure. True, this left in the realm of night and fog the nature of the aim pursued: reduction or destruction of the Jewish state? True, this theory of complementarity made it easy for the Israelis to denounce before world opinion the hypocrisy of the peaceful solution being offered to them. Did it not amount to admission that this solution was merely a stage on the road to that destruction of their state which the Palestinians had not abandoned as their ultimate aim? In this way one could be fuelling the fear felt by the Israeli population, which united them with their government, the solidarity of the Jewish Diaspora with Israel, and the sympathy of the masses in the West for this country under threat. However, here as elsewhere, considerations of internal politics took precedence.

The *raison d'être* of the Palestinian movement was to fight against Israel. Now, the defeat suffered in Jordan in 1970–71 had reduced still further the possibilities for this struggle. A total cessation of operations would be seen by the whole world as a decisive victory for the Jewish state. To the activists it was clear that the struggle must be continued, using every means available.

Since Clausewitz, everyone has known that war is only the pursuit of politics by other means. Let us understand this as meaning external politics, that is, the relations, rivalries and conflicts that take place between communities which are more or less independent, or wish to be so. The aim of compelling the adversary to behave as we wish is pursued, in this case, by means of force, by violent means. But war, in the currently accepted meaning of the word, is a specific and particular form of violence, a form that is regulated, canonized, ritualized, and thereby legitimized – and there are other forms. Only independent communities (and above all those which are widely recognized as such, namely, states) are considered to possess the right to try and attain their political aims by using force, and then only in the canonical conditions of war. Since long ago, states have found it on the whole to their advantage to conform to these conditions, even if their irresponsibility, their complete independence and their will to win have frequently led them to commit more or less numerous breaches thereof. A codification of the rules of war has even been adumbrated. Parallel with this situation, in contests and conflicts between groups, classes, sections of society and organizations inside states, when the aim of these adversaries is not to break away from the state or to destroy it, violence is excluded on principle. Peaceful forms of struggle have been elaborated, even though these sometimes border closely on violence: election campaigns, demonstrations, strikes, etc.

But the desire to overcome drives people constantly to overstep and transgress the norms which custom has legitimized through experience of the disadvantages that result from their violation. Inside states, everyone knows that forms of peaceful struggle often lead to violent incidents or developments: brawls, riots, revolts, revolutions. As between states and communities that wish to be independent, actions are frequently carried out in the course of regular warfare which are infringements of these norms. Sometimes even, especially when the contestants are not recognized states, war is quite simply replaced by other forms of violence.

These transgressions of the normal forms of conflict consist, in the first place, when there is a struggle inside the state, in resorting to the methods of warfare – methods which are normally reserved exclusively for struggles *between* states. When there is a struggle between states, these transgressions consist in the use of forms of violence that do not fall within the definitions and criteria of 'normal' warfare. In all these cases, one transgression which is generally stigmatized is that of applying in these collective conflicts those methods of violence between individuals which are ordinarily described as criminal and punished by law: the murder of non-combatants, that is, persons who do not belong to the more or less regular forces of the contenders. Murder is considered legitimate only when performed collectively. Soldiers or policemen can fire on rioters, revolutionaries can kill members of the 'forces of order', two armies can exchange shots – all that is accepted, or more or less excused. General censure comes when one side or the other kills 'women and children', those who have been by their very nature, throughout the ages, the symbolic representatives of the persons excluded from actual combat.

While most states, authorities, organizations, groups and even individuals try to avoid this censure and to give 'the public', or even history, a good image of themselves, they are impelled in the opposite direction by the will to achieve their aims as quickly and efficiently as possible, at the least cost to themselves. Terror injected into the heart of an enemy, actual or potential, has always been recognized as a generally effective means of dissuading him from continuing, or even from manifesting, his opposition to the aims one seeks to realize. This method is also suitable for subduing that permanent, sullen, 'creeping' opposition which every ruling power encounters, to one extent or another, among the masses of those who are subject to it. The less closely these 'subjects' are controlled by means of regular institutions of constraint, the less the administration of persons is developed, the more does resort to terror seem necessary in the eyes of the rulers. Hence the barbarity of the penalties laid down in the states of olden times, in which administration was underdeveloped. The same applies in conflicts both internal and external, when victory seems hard or slow to attain by the canonical methods of struggle, when the authority, the state or the group engaged in combat seems to be on the brink of defeat, with its very existence threatened by the enemy's action, or when the forces at one's disposal seem inadequate in relation to those of one's opponent.

Thus, Clausewitz's disciple Helmuth von Moltke, Chief of Staff of the German Army between 1858 and 1888, using arguments that were even, in a way, humanitarian, wrote that, the greatest good in war being to get it over with quickly, 'for that purpose all means are valid, not excluding the most blameworthy'.* In the Second World War the Allies accordingly bombed the cities of Germany, just as the German air force had, in 1940, destroyed 50,000 houses around the factories of

* *Moltke in seinen Briefen*, Berlin, 1902, vol. II, p. 271, quoted by Colonel Eugène Carrias, *La Pensée militaire allemande*, Paris, P.U.F., 1948, p. 238.

Coventry. In 1793 the French Jacobins made large-scale use of the guillotine in order to discourage the innumerable enemies of their regime. The Fenians and other groups fighting for the independence of Ireland resorted to murders of British officials and to dynamitings which made Britain tremble. When the Jews of Palestine wanted to drive out the British and establish the Jewish state at the end of the Second World War, they used the method of armed attacks on the soldiers, officials and installations of the forces of occupation (as they called them) of the United Kingdom. I have mentioned earlier that these methods were first used by clandestine extremist organizations, and then eventually adopted by the official, or quasi-official, military force of the Jewish Agency.

Militants who are convinced of the justice of their cause and who, rightly or wrongly, do not believe in the effectiveness of a struggle waged in accordance with the laws of regular war or of 'normal' internal struggles, embrace a special morality in which almost every, if not every, means is legitimized by the greatness of the end served. Among other examples, here is a faithful definition of their cast of mind given by a woman militant of the Jewish terrorist group known as the Stern Group. The writer later became a member of the Israeli parliament, and has continued loyal to the most extreme nationalist ideology, accusing in 1978 the former terrorist leader Menachem Begin, now Premier, of betraying the national aims, whereas the entire world was, on the contrary, deploring his intransigent attitude.

This is how she describes her mind's working in the days of her terrorist activity: 'In the Lehi [the acronym for 'Fighters for the Freedom of Israel', alias the Stern Group] we didn't conduct examinations or have prearranged discussions ... The questions themselves had been asked and answered for us long ago – at the moment we went underground, in fact. And just as none of us asked whether it was permissible to flout the laws of the British Government (who was there to give us permission?) or whether it was morally desirable to ambush the enemy if you had a chance, so none of us requested a special dispensation for burglary. How could you question whether a particular means was more or less valid than another when the basic question – the legitimacy of the underground itself – went so much deeper and was so much more intractable? The very fact of going underground created a new set of laws, and above all one prime law which bestowed on the underground its authority to legislate and to judge.'*

* Geula Cohen, *Woman of Violence: Memoirs of a Young Terrorist, 1943–1948*, London, 1966, p. 55.

The Palestinians, in their turn, entered into the logic of that form of struggle its special rules of behaviour. Some of them, at least, carried this to the limit, going beyond not merely the canonical rules of classical warfare but also the restraints which some terrorist movements had imposed on themselves. Since it was difficult to attack the Israeli soldiers and their installations, some of them resorted to attacks on civilians and civilian enterprises, doubtless justifying their actions to themselves by the fact that the individuals and enterprises concerned were subject to mobilization against them. Since Israeli territory was closely guarded and hard of access, they attacked, abroad, the offices of the Israeli official services and those of the Israeli airline *El Al*. The technique of hijacking aircraft having become widespread, they turned their attention in this direction. Since the aircraft belonging to *El Al* were closely guarded, they hijacked those of foreign airlines flying to Israel, or attacked *El Al*'s aircraft when they landed at European airports. Bombs were set off on board.

Such actions as these became increasingly frequent after the end of 1968. We are not yet in a position to know what sort of discussions led to the decision to undertake them, or who was, in each case, in favour and who against. The first of the attacks which violated most outrageously the usual norms of struggle were attributed to extremist Palestinian organizations, or else they themselves claimed responsibility for them.

While one essential motive for the resort to terrorist activity was to demonstrate to Israel and to the whole world that they were not giving in, that the fight was still going on, they wanted more especially to shake up Arab opinion. It was necessary to rouse this opinion, to call upon it to mobilize in support of the cause of the Palestinian Arabs, to denounce before it the tendency of the Arab rulers to seek a peace which would ignore the war aims of the Palestinians, sacrificing them to one extent or another to a settlement with Israel: the tendencies of these rulers towards moderation, tendencies which, though camouflaged, were becoming clearer and clearer, had to be unmasked.

Since they were behind the most traumatic manifestation of this trend in the movement, the 'black September' in Jordan, it was a terrorist group calling itself Black September which was the first to organize, or to claim authorship of, these attacks, endeavouring in this way to remind the Arab peoples incessantly of the Palestinian cause. It was already Black September that had murdered in Cairo in November 1971 the Jordanian Prime Minister Waçfi Tall, and had tried in December to murder Jordan's ambassador in London. But they soon went beyond action aimed directly at the Jordanian authorities.

The years 1972 and 1973 were thus filled with Palestinian terrorist operations, carried out in various parts of the world, which were particularly precise and calculated to produce spectacular effects. In February 1972 a Lufthansa aeroplane was hijacked to Aden with 172 passengers, for whom the Bonn Government had to pay a ransom of two million pounds. On 8 May a Belgian aeroplane was hijacked on its way to the Israeli airport of Lod, in order to secure the release of 317 Palestinian guerrilla fighters from Israel's prisons: the Israeli Army succeeded in killing or wounding the terrorists. On 30 May at the same airport, three young Japanese extremists (belonging to the United Red Army) who had been trained by the P.F.L.P. in Lebanon, disembarked from an Air France aeroplane and opened fire on the crowd. Twenty-six people were killed and about seventy wounded, among the victims being a number of Israeli passengers.

In September 1972 the world was given its greatest shock yet when Black September struck again, during the Olympic Games at Munich. The seizure of Israeli athletes as hostages ended in the deaths of eleven of these, five Palestinians and one German policeman. Letter-bombs arrived at various Israeli embassies. In December 1972 Israel's embassy in Bangkok was attacked. It was soon the turn of the 'moderate' Arab states. Palestinian commandos struck at the Saudi embassies in Khartoum (1 March 1973) and Paris (6 September 1973). In the first of these attacks the men of Black September killed the American ambassador and his deputy and also the Belgian *chargé d'affaires* (a man of Lebanese extraction). On 20 July 1973 a Palestinian commando, disavowed by the recognized organizations, hijacked a Japanese aeroplane with 145 passengers, taking it first to Dubai and then to Libya, without getting what it wanted. On 5 August two Palestinian guerrillas who were preparing a similar operation at Athens airport opened fire, killing three persons who were on their way to Tel Aviv and wounding about fifty.

Where Palestinian terrorist actions were concerned, Israel had adopted two rules of behaviour which often brought it into conflict with the policy of other states. In the first place, it refused to yield to the demands of the attackers, however tough the consequences might be – for hostages, for instance. This Spartan attitude was indispensable, in the opinion of those who decided on it, in order to discourage, in the long run, the *modus operandi* in question. But the governments on whose territory the hostages were taken found it difficult to agree to adopt this attitude when the lives of their own nationals were at stake. In the second place, the Israelis intended to give back tit for tat. On the military plane, this meant operations by the Israeli Army on the frontier with South Lebanon, where the Palestinian guerrilla fighters were concentrated. But Israel went further than that, by launching commando operations in the very heart of Lebanon which imitated those carried out by its enemies. On 8 July 1972 an explosive device placed in his car killed, in the middle of Beirut, Ghassan Kanafani, an outstanding member of the P.F.L.P. and a writer of worth, together with his young niece. Letter-bombs had also been sent to him and to other Palestinians in Lebanon. One of these severely wounded, on 19 July, Anis Sayegh, director of the Institute of Palestine Studies in Beirut. During the night of 9–10 April 1973, the Israeli Army launched an undisguisedly military operation against installations and offices of the Palestinian Resistance at Saida and on the outskirts of Beirut. At the start of this, a commando, which was awaited by 'tourist' accomplices in several hired cars, had killed three well-known Palestinian leaders in the flats where they lived. The Israeli secret services murdered activists and officials of the P.L.O. in Europe. Among others, the head of the P.L.O. office in Rome, Wa'el Zu'ayter, was killed on 16 October 1972, the head of the Paris office, Mahmud Hamshari, on 8 December, and their colleague in Cyprus on 25 January 1973.

One incident in particular clearly revealed the contradictions produced by these operations and counter-operations, against a background of deeper-lying contradictions. For some time past, the Soviet authorities had decided to allow a certain number of their Jewish citizens to leave the country. This was an exceptional departure from a fundamental rule of the regime, banning all emigration. The principal motive for this was doubtless a desire to get rid of some noisy dissidents who were able to arouse an echo in the outside world owing to their family connections. At the same time it was an attempt to disarm the hostility of an influential section of American opinion, channelled by the efficient Jewish lobby in the U.S.A., towards any decision that seemed in any way to the advantage, or in the nature of 'appeasement', of the other superpower. Even if this permission to emigrate was accompanied by difficulties and unpleasantnesses and restricted by a severe process of selection among those wishing to leave, it was envied by Soviet citizens of other 'nationalities'. (In the U.S.S.R. the Jews are considered as forming a Yiddish-speaking nationality, alongside others such as the Uzbeks, the Letts and the Russians, all of them possessing Soviet 'citizenship'.) Demands by Soviet Jews for visas poured in. In 1971 authorizations to leave the U.S.S.R. numbered 13,000, and in 1972 and 1973 there were about 30,000 in each year. The procedure followed was and still is rather curious, being due, doubtless, to some mysterious preoccupation of the Soviet bureaucracy. In contradiction to the anti-Zionist attitude maintained in principle by the Soviet state, visas are granted only for emigration *to Israel*, despite the indignation this causes among the Arabs, whose astonishment is easy to understand. In practice, those seeking to leave the U.S.S.R. are sent to Austria, from which country the Zionist organizations take responsibility for conveying them to Israel. Many of the emigrants prefer, however, to proceed to other countries. The proportion they constitute has increased as the idealizing of Israel (the reasons for which have been explained above, page 131) has diminished among Soviet Jews. Already in 1975 almost half of the emigrants avoided going to Israel.*

In 1973 the relay station in Austria consisted of a transit camp at Schoenau, controlled by the Jewish agency. On 28 September two Palestinians seized four hostages in the train taking the Soviet Jews from Prague to Vienna. The head of Austria's government, the Socialist Chancellor Bruno Kreisky, quickly secured the release of the hostages in exchange for a promise to close the camp at Schoenau, which was to be replaced by a camp under the control of the Red Cross. There was great indignation in Israel. Bruno Kreisky had a bad name there. Of Jewish origin, he had chosen to identify himself with his Austrian homeland, and did not conceal his remoteness from Zionism. But it had not been expected that he would go so far in what Zionist ideology regarded as 'treason to his own people'. Golda Meir hastened to Vienna in order to remind the Chancellor of his alleged duties as a Jew. Their meeting was anything but cordial, and Kreisky held firmly to his position.

From now on, the confrontation between Israel and the Palestinians on the military plane took place on the soil of the Lebanon. For the reasons which have been explained above, in Chapter 9, the Lebanese Army intervened neither against Israel nor against the Palestinians' armed organizations. As has been said, Lebanese opinion was divided, and this division was becoming intensified. Nevertheless, the Israelis' night raid of 9–10 April 1973 produced a brief outburst of indignation which was very widespread. So, then – the Israelis were able to operate with impunity in the capital of the Lebanon, and the Lebanese Army waited for three hours, until they had left, before showing that it was there? Tens of thousands of Lebanese (but not the government) took part in the funeral of the three Palestinian victims.

* See Hélène Carrère d'Encausse, *L'Empire éclaté: la révolte des nations en U.R.S.S.*, Paris, Flammarion, 1978, pp. 212 ff., and her sources.

The Palestinians reacted mainly by strengthening the autonomy and defence capacity of their camps, which became independent zones, so to speak. Everything pointed to the prospect that the dual power situation which had developed in Jordan in 1968–70 would now become established in Lebanon. From now on, the Lebanese Army, just as formerly the Jordanian, abandoned its (at least apparent) attitude of passive neutrality, and turned against the Palestinians, with the backing of the Maronite President of the Republic, Suleiman Franjieh. There were violent clashes in which even the Lebanese air force took part. It was a foreshadowing of the Lebanese civil war that began in 1975/6. Representatives of the various Arab countries hastened to Beirut in order to try and put an end to the fratricidal struggle, but it was Syria that finally imposed a provisional pacification. It 'allowed' Palestinian elements of the Palestine Liberation Army, based in Syria, and especially Sa'iqa, the Palestinian organization which it controlled, to intervene in Lebanon. The leader of Sa'iqa, Zoheir Mohsen, played a key role in the negotiations which accompanied Syria's pressure, which was both military and economic (Syria closed its frontiers). On 17 May the Hotel Melkart Protocol, signed by the Palestinians and the Lebanese, brought the fighting to a conclusion. The Palestinians obtained a reaffirmation of the Cairo Agreement of 1969 (which had been published, though unofficially, in the Lebanese press in April 1970), with some amendments which were kept secret.* This was a victory for the Resistance, but one obtained at the cost of submitting to intensified Syrian control. Behind Syria loomed the moderate Arab block formed by the 'confrontation' states and the oil-producing monarchies. This bloc had now decided to move towards a political solution. An international peace conference was to result from the military offensive which was already being prepared for October 1973.

Syria had seized the opportunity of the events set in motion by the Israeli raid in April. Its strengthened control over the Palestinians, exercised mainly through Sa'iqa, freed it from all fear of rash initiatives on their part. It had resumed relations with Jordan, terminating the reprisals taken against Hussein. An agreement with the U.S.S.R. enabled it to benefit from supplies of arms without falling into complete dependence. Its relations with the Egyptian President Sadat were close. Syria had its hands free and its rear covered.

There had been much laughter in many places at midnight on 31

---

* On the events in Lebanon during this period, the most reliable guide is the conscientious work by René Chamussy, *Chronique d'une guerre: Liban 1975–1977*, Paris, Desclée, 1978.

December 1971. In Israel it was touched with triumphant confidence, and in Egypt with bitter irony. Five months previously, on 23 July, President Anwar El-Sadat had delivered a solemn speech. He had declared that the year 1971 would be a year of decision. It 'would not end without the conflict with Israel having been settled', either by peace or by war, even if the latter should cost the lives of 'a million martyrs'. The year 1972 had dawned without anything having happened that resembled either a war of reconquest or a peace settlement.

Sadat explained on 13 January that he had not been able to put his plans into effect owing to the war between India and Pakistan, in December, and the repercussions this had on America's attitude. He compared this conflict to an artificial fog which, in July 1967, had prevented Egyptian aircraft from bombing an Israeli battalion in Sinai. This fog made the Egyptians laugh a lot, while the Israelis and many others were not behindhand with their gibes.

Sadat gritted his teeth and let go by 'this ferocious campaign of sarcasm' as he was later to call it. He had his own ideas and plans. Already he had been an object of banter by his colleagues in the Revolution Council and by Nasser himself. 'Why did they attack and ridicule me . . .?' he wrote in his memoirs.* According to his own account, though he was the actual founder of the Free Officers, he had been eclipsed by Nasser while he was lying in prison. Of peasant stock, child of a numerous family, and having had to get through his studies under hard conditions, in poverty, he knew how to bear with slights, preparing and patiently awaiting his chance to get his own back.

It was precisely his relative self-effacement, his apparent lack of ambition, waiting in patient expectancy, that had caused him to be chosen by his peers, in October 1970 after Nasser's death, as Egypt's head of state. As often happens in successions of this sort, recourse was had to a collective leadership with, as nominal arbiter between the tendencies, a man of second-rate standing. And, as also often happens, this calculation proved to be ill-founded.

Sadat had begun by ensuring his own popularity through measures for reducing prices, raising wages and restoring the legal safeguards of the rights of the individual. This enabled him to manoeuvre along the line of his own ideas. He was surrounded and watched over by two groups which may be broadly categorized as a Right and a Left. The Left was, in principle, for a 'socialist' structuring of society, that is, in practice, for a managed economy, for alliance with the U.S.S.R., for

* Anwar El-Sadat, *In Search of Identity*, London, 1978, p. 122.

permanent preparation for war with Israel, and for an orientation towards the ideology of Arabism. The Right was for a liberal economy, for alliance with America, for an orientation towards a political solution of the conflict with Israel, and for subordination of the Arabist ideology to the realistic interests of each of the Arab states. Sadat was definitely inclined towards the second of these tendencies but, like all those in the ruling team who favoured it, he had faithfully followed Nasser's directions which, though fluctuating, had as their axis both Arabism and an economy that was, at any rate, vigorously planned from above.

Religious without being fanatical and lacking any ideological leaning towards socialism, Sadat had little sympathy with the U.S.S.R. As a realist, he was very well aware of the misery into which Egypt had been plunged and which continued to get worse. From experience, the results of Nasser's regime on the economic plane seemed to him at the very least unconvincing. His inclination towards economic liberalism won him sympathy from all the social strata that had been victimized by Nasserite socialism, as well as those who regretted their past privileges, and all who now aspired to a privileged existence within a structure typical of the European and American capitalist world. Like these groups which supported him and urged him forward, Sadat was convinced that, first and foremost, it was necessary to shake off the unbearable burden of the state of war with Israel. Considerable sums were swallowed up by that situation, 800,000 men had to be kept under arms, all progress in respect of a number of problems was held up, the Suez Canal stayed closed, and Sinai, part of Egypt, was under alien occupation. The new President had no liking for the idea of permanent revolutionary war going on for decade after decade and bringing into action forces whose reactions were unpredictable. As a realist, Sadat knew that total victory over Israel as a result of a conventional war was not possible – for a long time yet, at any rate. Like Nasser, he understood that the only conceivable solution was a peace to be obtained through making concessions sufficient for Egypt to be able to live in less abnormal conditions, for Egyptian patriotism to be given at least the minimum of satisfaction, and, if possible, for disarming the certainly foreseeable attacks from the less virulent of the Arab nationalists, and perhaps even for getting support from the largest possible grouping of Arab political forces.

But how was he to obtain these concessions when Israel clung to all its gains of June 1967? The United States would never permit total victory over the Jewish state. Rogers and the State Department were devoted to the idea of a compromise based on Resolution 242 of the

United Nations, which meant concessions by Israel that were more than satisfactory from Sadat's standpoint. But it was increasingly plain that they either could not or would not bring the supreme decision-makers of American policy – who were at that time Nixon and his adviser on questions of national security (since December 1968) Henry Kissinger – to exert sufficient pressure on Israel to compel the Israeli Government to agree to this compromise, which they then looked upon as disastrous. As for the Soviets, they openly supported that same compromise. They reinforced the military power of the Arabs, but they clearly subordinated this aim to their game of mingled threats and inducements aimed at getting the United States to agree to an advantageous *modus vivendi* known as '*détente*'. They would not risk becoming involved in a major conflict with the United States just for the sake of the Arabs. Moreover, they paid out their military help in such a way that no Arab state could take ill-considered steps which might put them in an embarrassing position on that plane. They were unable to impose anything whatsoever upon Israel, which was protected by their rival.

The most that the Arabs could hope for (which was also the least that would allow them to go for a peaceful solution) was that the Americans would bring such pressure to bear on Israel as to compel that state to make concessions that would have to suffice for want of anything better. Nasser had fully appreciated this, at a time when concessions by the Israelis, always needed by any Arab leader in order to justify his making peace with them, would have been a much more serious matter for Israel than after its conquests of June 1967. Nasser had aimed to secure that American pressure on Israel by means of permanent blackmail, ostentatiously aligning Egypt with the U.S.S.R. – an alignment he was quite ready to abandon if only the Americans would show signs of doing what he wanted. However, the Americans were not very much encouraged by his constant and virulent denunciation of American imperialism, which resulted from his view of the world situation and the role he sought to play as supreme guide of Arabism. In May–June 1967 he had hoped to get the superpowers to exert the pressure on Israel he wanted, by himself taking measures that threatened Israel and then actually mobilizing. The outcome was disastrous. But at least he had shown that war was a radical means (and doubtless the only means) of getting decisive reactions from the U.S.A. and the U.S.S.R.

Sadat now adopted the same line of policy, but he was free from any ideological inhibition in seeking American support and did not feel required to remain faithful to the role of Arab revolutionary leader.

With remarkable perseverance he undertook a long march, a series of manoeuvres that seemed disparate and even contradictory. However, these manoeuvres all tended towards one and the same aim: to obtain, at the end of the day, American pressure on Israel that would ensure a relatively acceptable peace settlement. If, at one moment or another in his moves, Sadat was tempted to prefer a different solution in order to achieve the same purpose, experience soon showed him that this was impracticable.

He had, first of all, to convince American opinion, and world opinion at the same time, that at least Egypt was seriously disposed to acknowledge the legitimacy of a state of Israel, even if only within contracted frontiers. In order to do that, he had to abandon the usual ambiguous formulations, the semi-official statements to journalists or diplomats which were denied as soon as published. All that sort of thing could only undermine belief in the sincerity of any promises the Arabs might make, and Israel would not fail to exploit it. Once Arab recognition of Israel became credible, everyone would be able to judge Israel more critically if it were to persist in rejecting acceptable conditions attached to that recognition. This was the only way.

Sadat began by taking up an idea put forward during the late summer of 1970 by Dayan. The latter had suggested that they start with a limited withdrawal of Egyptian and Israeli forces from the Suez Canal, so as to make fresh negotiations possible without fear that war would start up again. Actually, as Kissinger notes, Israel's idea was in this way to eliminate a risk, after which negotiations might be dragged out indefinitely.*

The cease-fire provided for by the Rogers Plan, which Nasser had accepted (see above, page 208) and which had already been extended by three months in November, was due to expire on 4 February 1971. That very day, Sadat announced in Egypt's National Assembly that he was extending the cease-fire for another thirty days. If Israel would take the opportunity thereby afforded to carry out a partial withdrawal in Sinai, leaving both banks of the Suez Canal under Egyptian control, he would undertake to reopen the canal to the world's navigation, so greatly wished for by the Soviets and the Europeans alike.

Golda Meir responded by demanding, once again, all-round negotiations. She remarked that the Egyptian President had not spoken of peace with Israel. Sadat was not slow to react. On 15 February, replying to a questionnaire from Gunnar Jarring, Egypt declared that it was ready to join in a peace agreement with Israel provided that the latter

* Henry Kissinger, *The White House Years*, London, 1979, pp. 1280–81.

withdrew from the Arab lands occupied in June 1967. This was a date of capital importance. For the first time since the birth of the state of Israel an Arab state (and, as it happened, the most important of them) agreed to enter into relations with it, not in the forced and furtive form of cease-fire agreements but in that of a genuine peace agreement. This meant openly recognizing that a Jewish state had the right to exist, and accepting the accomplished fact of the alienation of a piece of Arab territory.

Sadat must have expected stormy protests from his Arab colleagues. The attitude of the Israeli Government spared him any anxiety on that score. The leaders of Israel replied that the Egyptian initiative was positive in character, but that they absolutely refused to return to the frontiers of before June 1967. Nixon recorded this refusal and took note of it for the future. He had fully understood the factors in the long-term problem. On 25 February, in his message on the state of the world, he declared that no lasting peace could be attained without satisfying 'the legitimate aspirations of the Palestinian people'. The Arab Governments would accept nothing short of a settlement that ensured recovery of the lands lost in the war of 1967. 'Without such acceptance, no settlement can have the essential quality of assured permanence.' Nixon realized that the situation in the Middle East was the biggest threat to world peace since he had taken office. However, the United States, bogged down in Vietnam, Cambodia and Laos, had no intention of intervening more effectively in that region for the time being, despite the opinion of some high officials, in the State Department especially, who would already have liked to force the Rogers Plan on Israel. Nixon, clear in his long-term view, thought that it was possible to wait and that, for the moment, it was necessary at least to refrain from weakening Israel, a reliable and powerful ally.

Sadat made moves, at the same time, in all the different directions he had in mind. While carrying on close negotiations with the Soviets (he made several trips to Moscow) in order to obtain arms (he obtained some, but always in insufficient quantity and subject to conditions which made their use dependent on Soviet agreement, so that he was constantly angry), he won freedom of movement for himself inside Egypt. In May 1971 he dismissed and arrested the members of the so-called Left group (they were, at any rate, anti-American and more or less pro-Soviet) which formed the majority in the Supreme Executive Council and the Central Committee of the Party. Led by one of the two Vice-Presidents of the Republic, Ali Sabri, this group disapproved of Sadat's overtures to the United States, his moves towards peace, and the federation agreement he had just concluded with Libya and Syria. The group was conspiring against the President. On the morrow of these arrests, he cordially received William Rogers, who agreed with his ideas. With the exception of Dayan, however, the government of Israel was unwilling to allow Egyptian soldiers to cross over, in no matter how small numbers, to the Sinai side of the Canal, or to allow to be contemplated the slightest linkage between a movement of this sort, should they come round to agreeing to it, and the overall compromise indicated by Resolution 242 and the Rogers Plan. Now, Sadat would not be able to get a limited agreement accepted at all widely unless he could persuade Arab opinion that this was only the first step towards an overall agreement which this opinion would find more satisfactory. The American government was not ready to follow Rogers. Inevitably, Sadat was greatly disappointed.

Then it was that he began to threaten war, and thought to put the two superpowers and Israel on the spot by announcing (23 July) that the year 1971 would not end without a settlement, either peaceful or military. The contempt felt for Arab military capacities and for Egypt's political weight was such that this made no impression on anyone. The last day of 1971 was awaited without excitement, and no surprise was felt in noting that on 1 January 1972 the situation had not altered in the least. Sadat's most bellicose declarations reduced neither the universal scepticism nor Israel's arrogant self-confidence. Neither the Soviets nor the Americans showed themselves ready to engage in vigorous measures.

The former were worried by the arrest of their friends in Cairo in May 1971. They had immediately sent Podgorny to sign a treaty of friendship and cooperation with Sadat, which reassured them somewhat. All the same, they did not yield to Sadat's reiterated requests for sophisticated weapons, which he could use without Soviet control. They were content to discuss the problem bilaterally with the Americans, bringing in their grievances on other matters, first and foremost the presence of American advisers in Iran. With a view to bargaining on a world scale, they gave up none of their demands in the Middle East that favoured the Arab cause, but it was well understood that this was just a position taken up at the beginning of negotiations, and that gains made elsewhere might lead to concessions here. The Soviets found these world-scale negotiations too intense, too important, to be ready to allow the Arabs to intervene in them independently. It was enough for the Arabs to know that Moscow had their interests at heart and that they could hope to receive one day some benefit from these dealings on the part of their protectors.

This attitude infuriated Sadat. In spite of all his visits to Moscow and the other steps he had taken, he was not being given the arms he asked for and he was being made to wait a long time for those he was given, while substantial deliveries of arms from the U.S.A. to Israel continued. The 15,000 Soviet experts controlled the entire life of Egypt, where revolt was rumbling. He was only a pawn in Russia's game, a pawn that the Kremlin made use of in order to show its strength and to try and wrest concessions from Nixon.

The world's grand manoeuvres went ahead without any concern being shown for the Arabs. The situation of 'neither war nor peace' which suited everyone (especially Israel) except the Arabs was allowed to continue indefinitely. At the end of May 1972 the Moscow summit between Nixon and Brezhnev clearly revealed this. The two superpowers arrived at a *modus vivendi* on a number of points, and in particular on limiting those of their armaments that were mutually most threatening. This happened even when Nixon had just drawn close to China, a move full of danger for the U.S.S.R., and while American planes were subjecting to massive bombing the capital of the Soviets' ally Vietnam. On the final afternoon of the summit meeting, Gromyko and Kissinger were given the task of drafting a statement of principle regarding the Middle East. This statement confirmed the previous positions taken up on the bases for a solution with all their vaguenesses, equivocations and implications.*

Sadat was severely shocked by this 'bland' document, as Kissinger called it. It confirmed that Moscow was, in practice, satisfied with the status quo. The Soviets took more than a month to give Sadat the analysis of the post-summit situation which they had promised him. They said nothing about the delayed deliveries of arms, which had been finally promised for this period.

Sadat reacted at once: he had made his preparations. On 18 July 1972 he expelled the 15,000 Soviet experts from Egypt. Everyone was taken aback, starting with the Americans. Many thought that it must be an impulsive act on the part of the Egyptian president. Should he not, following the proper rules of international politics, have haggled, demanding assurances and substantial advantages from the United States in return for deserting the camp of their powerful rival? It was not good procedure to give something for nothing.

But Sadat knew what he was doing. He was now at last convinced that only military operations could compel the two superpowers to give up their preference (in practice) for the status quo. Military

* Ibid., pp. 1246–7, 1294 and 1493–4.

operations alone could enable him to get something out of Israel. The expulsion of the Soviet advisers enabled him to go ahead without taking account of Moscow's cautious control. It would also make the Americans realize that they were not dealing with an enemy, which was indispensable for the negotiations that would put an end to the crisis to be opened in this way.

All that remained was a matter of military, political and diplomatic preparation, with, even so, some last disillusioned attempts to explore other avenues. It had been thought that Nixon's situation in the midst of an election campaign might be what was preventing him from going further in seeking a solution in the Middle East. But although he was triumphantly re-elected in November 1972, this changed nothing. He received Sadat's envoy Hafez Ismail, on 23 February 1973, in friendly fashion, but had nothing new to say to him. On the other hand, Golda Meir, who came to Washington a few days later, on 1 March, went away with the assurance, soon to be confirmed, that a fresh delivery of Phantom aircraft would be made to Israel, and with a declaration by Nixon that he would continue to support Israel to the end.

The Soviets did not seem to take the expulsion of their advisers too tragically. It even had some advantages for them in committing them less closely to the Egyptians in any conflict that might break out * – a conflict which everyone at that time, the Soviets included, thought would be disastrous for Egypt. All the same, the Egyptians had to be strengthened so as to preserve the possibility of influencing them and saving them from too complete a defeat. It would be better to act as Egypt's protector on the diplomatic plane and draw some benefit from that. Accordingly, the U.S.S.R. ended by responding favourably to fresh advances from Sadat and delivering a substantial quantity of arms to him at the beginning of 1973. Nevertheless, reproaches and a cautious coolness predominated in Soviet–Egyptian relations.

On the Arab plane, Sadat had succeeded in retaining friendships more or less everywhere. Gaddafi was the exception. Still remaining faithful to his line of Arab unity, he had wanted to establish, in August 1972, a merger between Egypt and Libya, to be achieved by stages, but to be pursued seriously. Surprised, Sadat had acquiesced, while being firmly resolved to keep this merger void of any concrete content. In July 1973 Gaddafi had tried to force his Egyptian colleague's hand by sending tens of thousands of Libyans to march on Cairo. Sadat took it very badly, and used military force to drive back this 'spontaneous'

---

* Cf. Hélène Carrère d'Encausse, *La Politique soviétique au Moyen Orient, 1955–75*, Paris, Presses de la Fondation Nationale des Sciences Politiques, 1975, pp. 226 ff.

horde. He had shaken off the initiatives, always to be feared, however good their intentions, of a man he looked upon as a dangerous lunatic who had tiresomely retained in maturity and in power impulses that would be understandable in an enthusiastic young militant.

On the other hand, Sadat was able to count on the serious and fundamental support of a very rich friend, and a most reasonable one, namely, King Feisal of Saudi Arabia. The King directed his policy, and that of the no less oil-rich emirates of the Gulf, along the same line as Sadat. Owing to his financial power, his influence was very great throughout the Arab world and beyond. From the military point of view one could not count much on Jordan, weakened as it was by the crisis of 1970 and with its problems with the Palestinians not settled. But Sadat could fully rely on Syria. In September 1970 the Jordano-Palestinian crisis had blown apart the compromise which had been realized, with much grinding of teeth, between the two tendencies that were in conflict at the top, in the Ba'ath party and the government. The political leadership was dominated by a radical and even extremist group, which tightened to the utmost the authority exercised by the Ba'athist cadres inside Syria, was against any compromise with Israel, resolved to support the Palestinians to the end (or almost) and to go so far as to wage mass revolutionary war against Israel, and which was determined to seek, first and foremost, support from Moscow, since the Soviets were the only power (the Chinese not being very 'operational' at this time) which, these ideologists thought, one might hope to win over to such a policy, or which might give it backing for a time. Over against them, a group led by General Hafez-el-Assad, Minister of Defence, was well rooted in the Army. This group advocated (at that time!) greater caution and more discrimination in actions projected against Israel and in support for the Palestinians, more moderation in the application of the socialistic laws and in the way the party held control inside the country, and, above all, an attempt to diversify Syria's external alliances, so as to avoid too close, exclusive and re-stricting a relationship with the Soviet Union.

In September 1970 the radical wing was ready to brave the most precise threats from America by allowing the armoured brigades which had entered Jordan to continue their advance in support of the Pal-estinians against Hussein. Assad refused to support the advance with his air force, and secured the withdrawal of those tanks which had come from Syria and were officially part of the Palestine Liberation Army under Syrian control. At the end of October a congress of the Syrian Ba'ath party reviewed the situation. Assad, finding himself in the minority, had the leaders of the radical tendency arrested and dismissed on 13 November. Systematically he consolidated his power by getting himself appointed general secretary of the Ba'ath party, Prime Minister, and then President of the Republic, elected by universal suffrage for a seven-year term. Inside the country he made the controls over the economy more flexible, and formed a 'Progressive National Front' in order to support the government by uniting, along with the Ba'athists, various nationalist elements and also the Communists. While not repudiating support in principle for the Palestinians, he tightened control over their activities. They were strictly forbidden to carry out unauthorized operations against Israel from Syrian territory, certain elements were made to leave Syria for South Lebanon, and there were even confiscations of arms intended for them. Good relations were maintained with the Soviet Union, but Assad declined to sign a treaty of friendship and alliance, despite the Soviets' importunity. They did not hold this against him. They needed to have in the Eastern Mediterranean area an ally more reliable than Sadat, who had expelled their advisers. They showed generosity in helping to finance major public works in Syria and sent in a large quantity of arms, receiving in exchange 'facilities' in the Syrian ports of Lattakieh and Tartus. However, in practice, these privileged relations came up against the same difficulties as in Egypt. The Soviet experts in Syria obeyed only Moscow's instructions, and the Kremlin leaders refused to send their allies their most sophisticated and effective weapons. Like Sadat, Assad resorted to threats in order to obtain aid better adapted to the intended war against Israel and allowing him greater independence of decision. At this time, that war against Israel was about to break out.*

On the purely military plane, Sadat had belatedly observed that his army possessed only a purely defensive plan, bequeathed by Nasser, and even this had serious deficiencies. He had been obliged to apply the spur to his military chiefs, and to remove those who lacked confidence in the outcome of a warlike operation, before he could get an offensive plan drawn up and serious preparations undertaken. Coordination was easily achieved with Syria, which favoured the same designs. Everything combined to confirm Sadat and Assad in the decision they had taken. In June 1973 Brezhnev spent a week in the United States and, as a result, nine agreements were signed between Washington and Moscow. There was nothing in these conversations and agreements

* Ibid., p. 244 ff.: Ph. Rondot, *La Syrie*, Paris, P.U.F., 1978 (Coll. 'Que sais-je?' No. 1704), pp. 45 ff.

that indicated anything, as regards the Middle East, that went beyond maintenance of the status quo and the situation of 'neither war nor peace'. In August 1973 the Galili Document was made public in Israel, and the ruling Labour Party ratified it on 3 September. This was a plan put forward by the minister Israel Galili (see above, p. 246). Moshe Dayan had expended great efforts to get it adopted, using his prestige and threatening to leave the electoral bloc that included the Labour Party, which would certainly have meant depriving it of many votes. The Galili plan provided for intensifying colonization of the occupied territories, in pursuit of a policy of *de facto* annexation. On matters affecting the interests of Egypt and Syria, provision was made for the establishment of a veritable industrial city in north-east Sinai and another of the same sort in the Golan.* It was clear that, unless something was done, the territories conquered in 1967 would slip rapidly into a condition of annexation pure and simple, with the tacit consent of the powers.

The war preparations had to be kept secret. Sadat and Assad were able to maintain this secrecy, confusing the calculations of outsiders by means of false information. Ostentatious troop movements were carried out, accompanied by press and radio campaigns aimed at arousing the Israelis' suspicion that something was up, so that they took certain emergency measures. When the threats came to nothing, and the pointlessness of these highly expensive measures became apparent, the Israelis felt reassured. Confirmed in their contempt for the military and political capacities of the Arabs, for their Oriental vaingloriousness, fertile in bluster without any intention or power to pass from words to deeds, the Israelis' calm arrogance rose to dizzy heights.†

Nothing could now shake this assurance on the part of the political and military authorities, as of the entire population. The clearest warnings given encountered, down to the last minute, only scornful smiles. In such an atmosphere of triumphant intoxication it was obviously futile to ask for any concession whatsoever to be made. Precautions, it was felt, were hardly needed against these verbose and inefficient foes. Examples of negligence grew more and more numerous, breaking the rules of the most elementary prudence.

Besides, the whole world, including, probably, many Arabs, shared

* Cf. Kapeliouk, op. cit., pp. 19, 30, 42 ff. The document mentioned is given in full on pp. 296–9.

† Many eloquent examples, taken from the Israeli press, will be found in the remarkable book by the Israeli journalist A. Kapeliouk, op. cit., p. 66 ff.

this certainty that if, by some extraordinary turn of events, certain states were to attack Israel, they would once again be beaten, promptly and completely. Nobody believed the slightest Arab success to be possible. Jokes about the pitiful performance of the Arabs, when confronted by the strength and efficiency of Israel, flourished in all the newspapers and in all the radio and television broadcasts in which they were allowed. In private, many of the Arabs themselves did not refrain from such comment. As for the Soviet 'allies', their behaviour in the matter spoke volumes. When warned three days ahead, by Sadat and Assad, of the imminent attack, and asked what their attitude would be, their only answer was to send aircraft to evacuate urgently the families of their experts. A Soviet ship carrying supplies which were to be landed at Alexandria was ordered not to head for that port but to cruise around in the Mediterranean while waiting on events.* Since the Arabs had been so rash as to pass from words to deeds, the Soviet authorities obviously thought, they might expect to see Egypt and Syria very soon engulfed in flames and blood and invaded by the forces of Israel.

On Saturday 6 October 1973, the day of the great Jewish fast Yom Kippur, corresponding to the tenth day of the Muslim fast of Ramadan, at 1400 hours, waves of Egyptian soldiers swept across the Suez Canal and attacked the Bar-Lev line, which was alleged to be impregnable. In reality it was defended by only some 600 men, who were supposed to occupy thirty strongpoints, of which only sixteen were actually operational. Down to the last moment the Israelis had refused to believe in imminent danger. By nightfall the 'impassable' barrier had been passed. Similarly, on the Golan Heights, Syrian tanks advancing in successive waves had crushed and overwhelmed the feeble anti-tank obstacles of the Israelis, dominated the Israeli armoured vehicles stationed there in greatly inferior numbers, seized a fortress of capital strategic importance on Mount Hermon, and rapidly recovered a large part of the territory taken from Syria in 1967.

The whole world was incredulous. Could it really be that the invincible Israeli army had been beaten and was retreating? That was inconceivable. Many people imagined that it must be a cunning manoeuvre, to let the enemy advance so as all the better to beat him. Indeed, Israel was to pull itself together and, in the end, to get the better of the attackers. But its initial reverses were anything but deliberate. For the first time, the drift of things had been switched, for a few days at any rate. For the first time, the Arabs had given proof of

* Anwar El-Sadat, op. cit., p. 247.

their capacity in the domain of modern warfare. For the first time, their arrogant foe had felt the breath of defeat upon him. Nothing could wipe out that experience.

11
Steps Towards Peace?

by Olivier Carré

The war of October 1973 was a bloody semi-victory won by the Syrians and Egyptians with the support of the oil-producing states of the Gulf and the (prearranged?) passivity of Jordan. The Palestinian units played some part in the battle for the Suez Canal and in the battle for Mount Hermon in Syria. But the Palestinian cause as such was abandoned. The proclaimed objective of the offensive was to recover certain Egyptian and Syrian territories which Israel had occupied since June 1967. This limited act of recovery was to provide an honourable basis for comprehensive negotiations with Israel.

On 6 October the Egyptian and Syrian forces launched a concerted offensive against the Israeli troops in Sinai and Golan. Jordan refrained from attacking the occupied West Bank. The crossing of the Canal, which made it possible to take by surprise the Israelis' Bar-Lev Line on the eastern side, was a remarkable success for the Egyptians. The large-scale offensive continued, without overspilling a consistent width of front of about fifteen kilometres, in accordance with the limited objectives aimed at. The Syrian troops similarly cut off a substantial section of the Golan area. The Israelis' counter-offensive did not begin until 8 October – in Syria first, where they reoccupied the Golan Heights and even pressed further, to take in the Syrian peaks of Mount Hermon, while Israeli aircraft bombed Damascus, Homs, Tartus and Lattakieh. On the Egyptian front the war of position in Sinai assumed a different aspect after 17 October, when an Israeli bridgehead was established on the western side of the canal and gradually expanded until some 25,000 men were lodged in a pocket between Suez and the southern approaches to Ismailia, so as to cut off supplies from the Egyptian Third Army shut up in Sinai. This effect was actually achieved on 23 October.

The United States and the Soviet Union were unable to get a cease-fire resolution through the Security Council before the night of 21–2 October. This was Resolution 338: 'The Security Council (1) calls upon all parties to the present fighting to cease all firing and terminate all military activity immediately, no later than twelve hours after the moment of the adoption of this decision, in the positions they now occupy; (2) calls upon the parties concerned to start immediately after the cease-fire the implementation of Security Council resolution 242 (1967) in all of its parts; (3) decides that, immediately and concurrently with the cease-fire, negotiations start between the parties concerned under appropriate auspices aimed at establishing a just and durable peace in the Middle East.' Meanwhile, from 10 October onward the Soviet Union had organized systematic replacement of the stocks of arms held by Egypt and Syria, and the United States had done the same for Israel. Kosygin was in Cairo on 15 and 16 October, and Sadat, in conformity with the planned scenario and strong in his limited military victory, proposed, in the evening of 16 October, an immediate cease-fire, to be followed by Israeli withdrawal to the lines of 5 June 1967. That same day, the Arab states of the Gulf decided to raise the price of crude oil once more, and on the following day they undertook to reduce their production by 5 per cent every month until the Israelis withdrew from all the territories occupied since 1967. Kuwait and Saudi Arabia even decided to reduce production by 10 per cent per month and to stop exporting to the United States and the Netherlands. Golda Meir, who already knew about the Israeli bridgehead established in African Egypt (whereas Sadat, apparently, did not), at once declared that 'there will be no cease-fire until the Egyptian and Syrian troops have been defeated'. Kissinger visited Moscow on 17 October and Israel on 22 October. The cease-fire Resolution 338 was recognized by Israel and Egypt late on 22 October, and on 24 October by Syria, but the Israeli forces continued their advance in Egypt until they had occupied the road linking Cairo with Suez and the town of Suez itself. A second Security Council Resolution on 23 October and a third on 25 October had to be passed, requiring withdrawal of forces to the positions of 22 October at 1650 hours G.M.T. On 24 October, indeed, Egypt asked for joint American and Soviet intervention on Egyptian soil to ensure application of the cease-fire. American intervention being ruled out, but not intervention by the Soviet Union, the United States decided to put their forces on minimum nuclear alert, so that the Soviet-American agreement of 22 June 1973, by which no local conflict was to be allowed to develop into a nuclear war, was endangered. Eventually, an emergency force of United Nations troops went to Egypt and sponsored an agreement between Israel and Egypt, signed on 28 October, to allow the Egyptian Third Army in Sinai to receive supplies under Israeli supervision.

From then on the process of negotiation was begun, but not in the way that Sadat, Assad and Feisal had intended. The war had, in fact, turned to Israel's advantage, in a process interrupted on 25 October by the United States and the United Nations. Any settlement ultimately depended, therefore, on the United States and on Israel, the only party which, in the end, was in a position to grant concessions. Thus, on 11 November came the agreement signed at Kilometre 101 on the Suez–Cairo road, by which the supplying of the Egyptian Third Army was to be supervised by the U.N. forces and no longer by Israel. Exchange of prisoners was also arranged. Finally, a beginning was made to the application of Resolution 338 as a whole, that is, to the organization 'under appropriate auspices' of a peace conference with a view to 'the implementation of Security Council resolution 242 (1967) in all its parts'. The summit meeting of Arab heads of state held at Algiers on 26–8 November gave the green light to Egypt and Syria to go forward to this peace conference. The P.L.O. was not yet, at this summit meeting, recognized in a written resolution as the sole legitimate representative of the Palestinian people: this was so as not to offend Hussein of Jordan. The peace conference opened in Geneva on 21 December in the presence of the Secretary of the United Nations Organization, at the invitation of the Soviets and the Americans, between Israel, Egypt and Jordan. The table reserved for the Syrian delegation stayed empty. This meeting, a very short one, was intended to be the first in a long conference: but no more meetings took place. The Syrian Government had, in fact, accepted the cease-fire Resolution 338 only on condition that the Israelis began withdrawing from the territories occupied since 1967, and that the legitimate rights of the Palestinians were safeguarded.

The negotiations which had begun became more and more clearly an affair regulated by the United States, in accordance with Kissinger's 'step by step' policy. Instead of an overall settlement there were successive applications of the cease-fire, first between Israel and Egypt, then between Israel and Syria. Complete evacuation by the Israelis and the solution of the Palestinian problem were, however, left, so far as possible, to be dealt with later. It was thus a matter of agreement for gradual disengagement of the military forces – Israeli and Egyptian, on 18 January 1974, on the eastern side of the Suez Canal; Israeli and Syrian, on 31 May 1974, on the Golan Heights; and Israeli and Egyptian again, on 4 September 1975, in Sinai. By these three agreements, sponsored by the United States and guaranteed by the United Nations Organization (which provided the appropriate buffer zones, manned by 'Blue Berets'), Egypt recovered sovereignty over the whole of the Suez Canal (which was restored to normal working in June 1975) and subsequently over the oilfield of Abu Rodeis, while Syria recovered the mountainous area conquered by the Israeli troops in October 1973, together with a narrow strip of Golan with the town of Qunaitra. Furthermore, the interim agreement between Israel and Egypt in September 1975 reinforced the 'Blue Berets' (U.N.E.F.) with 200 American 'civil personnel' who were to be responsible for supervising a highly technical warning system installed in the Sinai passes of Mitla and Giddi.

This interim agreement aroused the anger of the Syrians, the Palestinians and the Soviets. It was felt to be separatist in character and not at all an 'interim' arrangement on the road towards an overall settlement, and also to be exclusively American. The moderate Arab bloc was consequently split for a time, with Saudi Arabia continuing to support Egypt. Eventually, in October 1976, through the good offices of Riyadh, Syria forgave Egypt the 'treacherous' and solitary agreement, while the P.L.O., faced with the mounting Syrian offensive in Lebanon, had become reconciled with Egypt at the beginning of May. The bloc was thus reconstituted. Its only impenitent enemies among the Arabs were Iraq and Libya, as uncompromising in their hostility towards Syria as towards Egypt. The moderate Arab bloc seemed to be so solid, since the eve of the war of October 1973 (owing, in the final analysis, to the Saudis' bounty), that even in the autumn of 1979, after the Arabs' almost unanimous rejection of the Camp David agreements and the treaty of peace between Israel and Egypt, it did not appear to have been finally broken up. The experience of inter-Arab relations since November 1973 would seem to show that this bloc will re-emerge. In any case, at the end of 1976, despite the passing tactical divergences between Egypt and Syria, their essential objective remained the same: to achieve an honourable settlement with Israel, while controlling to the utmost the actions and aspirations of the Palestinians. The objectives of the October war were still in force, and the post-war years have shown that they were, in the end, more anti-Palestinian than anti-Israel – not, perhaps, in the realm of sentiments and beliefs, but in the actual implications of the facts and forces involved. There is no essential difference between the Jordanian offensive of 1970–71 against the Palestinians, the Lebanese offensives of 1973 and 1975, followed by the combined Syrian-Lebanese offensive of 1976, and, finally, the Egyptian peace offensive of 1978–9.

It was doubtless awareness of this conspiracy of the Arab *states* against the Palestinian *revolution* – not formed as a state, and even, by its make-up, actually 'anti-state' – that led the P.L.O. to assume, starting in 1974, a markedly more realistic position, which would eventually prove acceptable to the states.

The evolution of the Palestinian movement since 1973 is closely linked both with the consequences of the October war and with the civil war in Lebanon that began in 1975–6. The contradiction between the Palestinian resistance movement and the Arab states developed in such a way that the cause of preserving the states seemed to be winning. After October 1973 the Resistance could find no refuge in the contradictions between the host states themselves, such as it had found previously. It was therefore obliged to align itself, as honourably as possible, with the bloc of Arab governments seeking a rapid all-round solution. This marked the Palestinians' turn towards realism. Only the Egyptian initiative of 1977–9, taken in isolation (and no longer in combination with Syria and Saudi Arabia, as in October 1973), towards comprehensive and definitive negotiations with Israel, under American auspices, gave the Palestinians the chance to proceed any further in the path of realism, thanks to a fresh split between the Arab states. Nevertheless, an overall negotiated peace remained, more than ever, the objective of Syria, Jordan and Saudi Arabia, since there were no means of waging war without Egypt, and resort to a general guerrilla struggle was still ruled out by the states. The Palestinians' turn towards realism could not actually be reversed. Any alternative solution to the Camp David agreements (September 1978) that was put forward would have indeed to follow the line of *accentuating* this realism, for the very purpose of increasing the credibility of such a solution.

With the attack, on 10 April 1973, by an Israeli commando on three leaders of *El Fatah* in their own homes in the heart of Beirut, not to mention the Israeli Army's operations in South Lebanon throughout 1972 and 1973, the conflict between Israelis and Palestinians was now taking place on Lebanese territory. For reasons already mentioned in Chapter 9 (page 221), the Lebanese Army had not intervened so far, either against Israel or against the armed organizations of the Palestinians. The popular demonstrations in Beirut during the funeral of the three victims of the Israeli raid brought to the forefront, as we have seen, the profound division of opinion that existed in Lebanon where attitude to the Palestinian Resistance was concerned. The dual power which had emerged in Jordan in 1968–70 seemed now to be establishing itself in a similar way in Lebanon. In May 1973 the Lebanese Army abandoned its passive neutrality and turned, like the Jordanian army earlier, against the Palestinians. These were premonitory symptoms of the Lebanese civil war that began in 1975–6. The crisis was settled, for the time being, only through Syrian mediation, both military (Sa'iqa and the Palestine Liberation Army, both based in Syria) and diplomatic (the Melkart Protocol of 17 May). The Palestinian Resistance came out victorious through the revival of the Cairo agreements of 1969, but, as has been explained (page 263), only at the price of subjection to intensified control by Syria, with behind it the moderate Arab bloc, which was resolved upon seeking a political solution through an international peace conference to follow the limited military offensive already planned for October. The Lebanese civil war was essentially a confrontation between the Maronite nationalists and the Palestinian Resistance concentrated in Lebanon. The offensive launched by the former, and the counter-offensive, on a large scale and extremely risky given the regional situation, with which the latter replied, led to a Syrian military intervention against the Palestinians resulting in the establishment of strengthened Syrian control over all the Palestinian centres, with the sanction of the Arab League. The Palestinians' military adventurism in Lebanon actually ran counter to the decision for realism taken by the centrist nucleus of the P.L.O.

The twelfth meeting of the Palestine National Council (1–9 June 1974, in Cairo) had in fact defined the national rights of the Palestinian people as meaning the right to establish an 'independent national authority' in 'any liberated portion of Palestinian territory'. This signified acceptance of a Palestinian territory confined to the West Bank and Gaza, once these should be evacuated by Israel. While the term 'Palestinian state' was not yet employed (it would be at the thirteenth meeting of the National Council, 12–20 March 1977, in Cairo and again at the fourteenth meeting, on 15–23 January 1979, in Damascus), the choice had been made. The idea of a unified democratic and secular Palestine, between the Mediterranean and the Jordan, was left for later – perceived as a dream, as Arafat put it in his address to the United Nations Organization on 13 November 1974. The utopia was replaced by a demand for a Palestinian state which would exist alongside the Israeli state, though this concept was still expressed in a somewhat unclear way. At the same time, the P.L.O. declared its readiness to attend the peace conference in Geneva 'as an independent entity and on a footing of equality'. The National Council of 1977 even gave full powers to act in this matter to the Executive Committee, without any preliminary meeting of the National Council being required.

These were the two questions that the Palestinian organs discussed on the morrow of the October war: the Palestinian state and Geneva. The centrist nucleus of *El Fatah* and of the P.L.O. succeeded in pro-

moting a positive response on both points. Abou 'Iyad, *El Fatah*'s
Number Two, describes the difficulty he had in voicing these new
ideas in the refugee camps in Lebanon at the beginning of 1974,
surrounded as he was by banners proclaiming: 'No to negotiation, no
to a Palestinian state, no to capitulation.' Incidentally, he claims * that
this realistic idea, 'putting an end to the policy of all or nothing', had
already been advanced among the leaders of *El Fatah* in July 1967,
when it encountered lively opposition from the higher cadres of the
movement. If he is to be believed, the idea had thus lain dormant since
then. When one thinks about it, that seems very regrettable, because
the demand had at that time a better chance of being honoured, or at
least approved, by world opinion than it had seven years later. The
programme of the unified, democratic and secular state of Palestine
announced in 1968 was unacceptable to all tendencies in Israel, because
it necessarily presupposed and, indeed, logically implied such a radical
alteration in the existing state of Israel as would amount to destruction
of the latter. Thereby the Palestinians lost the advantage contained in
the idea, which their stand was beginning to suggest to Arab opinion,
that an Israeli nation really existed and that it was necessary to coexist
with this nation. Hawatmeh had carried his analysis so far as to envisage
a bi-national state. Abou 'Iyad explains that the idea of the democratic
state had been put forward in 1968 in place of that of the Palestinian
mini-state, whereas in 1974 the opposite change was made. This change
entailed a split, important though not complete, within the Palestinian
movement.

Whatever Abou 'Iyad may say, it seems unquestionable that the tendency towards moderation in the P.L.O. came about under the increasing pressure experienced from the Palestinians of the interior, the
inhabitants of the occupied territories. They were mobilized by the
Communists, the successors of the Communist Party of Jordan, whose
Transjordanian detachment, the Ançars, had recently been admitted
into the P.L.O., as has been mentioned (page 251). In this way there
was formed, in August 1973, a clandestine Palestinian National Front
(P.N.F.) of the occupied territories, which at once proclaimed its allegiance to the P.L.O. The reticence shown by the latter towards the
Arab Communist Parties and the movements inspired by them resulted
from their alignment with the Soviet Union and, consequently, their
acceptance, announced at the end of 1947, of the partition of Palestine
and the state of Israel which followed therefrom – not to mention

* Abou 'Iyad, *Palestinien sans patrie: entretiens avec Eric Rouleau*, Paris, Fayolle, 1978,
p. 209.

Soviet disapproval of the Palestinians' terrorism and of the 'Leftism' of some of their organizations. The P.N.F.'s campaign in the P.L.O. in favour of a realistic line, which began during 1973, was greatly helped by the October War, for several reasons. The P.N.F. had succeeded, during the war, in launching a strike movement that involved many of the more than 70,000 Palestinian workers from Gaza and the West Bank who go into Israel to work each day. Several demonstrations against the Israeli Army also took place in the West Bank area. On the other hand, King Hussein's non-participation in the Arab offensive (except by sending Jordanian troops into Syria) lost him a good deal of support among the West Bank's population. Finally, the feeling that the Arabs had won a victory and the invincible Israeli Army of occupation had suffered a serious defeat prompted confidence in the peace conference to be held at Geneva.

Following this war between states, and in view of the forthcoming peace conference to be held within the concert of states-members of the United Nations, it was important to ensure that, for once, the Palestinian people should be recognized and listened to: they therefore assumed the style of a state, a Palestinian state taking its place alongside other states, including the state of Israel, and not in substitution for the latter. All through the years 1974–9 the question of a Palestinian Government in exile was under consideration (and Sadat had called for this as far back as 1972). Up to now, all that had been said was that the P.L.O. acted in lieu of such a state: its executive committee served as a ministry, its central council as a small chamber of parliament always ready to meet, its national council as a national assembly – not to mention the planning centre, the research centre, the Palestinian Red Crescent, and the Palestinian National Fund, as well as, of course, the Palestinian army with its various organizations dependent, in principle and ultimately, on the executive committee and the security forces (the Armed Struggle Command).

But the base of this leading organization remains, to this day, fragmented into several tendencies which are often acutely hostile to each other. We have just mentioned the P.N.F., which represents the dissident Palestinian population of the West Bank and Gaza, especially since the municipal elections of April 1976 produced a large majority of pro-P.L.O. municipalities. The executive committee of the P.L.O., as formed in March 1977 and provisionally reconvened in January 1979, contains three members of the P.N.F. The second tendency, undoubtedly the oldest (it goes back to 1958) and by far the most numerous, is *El Fatah*, an organization which itself includes, between a purely Palestinian nationalist trend and a pro-Soviet revolutionary and socialistic trend, a centrist nucleus where Arafat holds his ground, aided by a marked talent for bargaining. The third tendency is that of the Popular Front for the Liberation of Palestine (P.F.L.P.), which emerged from the Movement of Arab Nationalists mentioned above (page 210). This tendency is revolutionary and opposed to any compromise with bourgeois governments, whether Israeli or Arab. Thus, Habache openly opposed the turn of *El Fatah* and the P.L.O. towards realism in 1974 and subsequently. It is the P.F.L.P. which has been, since the summer of 1974, the centre of what is known as the Rejectionist Front.

In addition, there is Hawatmeh's Democratic Front (D.P.F.L.P.) which, though of similar origin to the P.F.L.P., has since 1971 associated itself with the centrist line of *El Fatah*. And there remains Sa'iqa, created and wholly directed by the Syrian general staff, which enables Syria to align, without much difficulty, the policy of the P.L.O. with its own, in conformity with the Ba'athist conception of the single Arab nation, and in the service, also, of the Syrian state's strongly anti-Iraqi policy pursued since 1966. It is certainly one of the mistakes of the Palestinian movement to have tolerated groups which are wholly dependent on particular Arab states, while constantly striving to ensure its independence of all the states. It must be added that even the Palestine Liberation Army (P.L.A.), the P.L.O.'s own military organ, is pro-Syrian in Syria (the Hittin Brigade), pro-Iraqi in Iraq (the Qadisiyya Brigade), and pro-Jordanian in Jordan (the Yarmuk Brigade), with only the brigade based in Egypt ('Ayn Jalut) being unconditionally pro-P.L.O.! It is easy to appreciate the difficulty in such circumstances of arriving at a uniform policy and line of conduct.

Thus, since the summer of 1974, the Rejectionist Front has not only opposed the 'capitulationist' demand for a Palestinian mini-state, but also the P.L.O.'s diplomatic successes in the United Nations Organization. In fact, the two operations are connected. The more the Palestinian cause is accepted in the United Nations, the more precise, and consequently moderate, does the Palestinians' demand become. The Arab summit at Rabat (26–8 October 1974) at last proclaimed publicly that the P.L.O. was 'the sole legitimate representative of the Palestinian people in any liberated Palestinian territory' – which ruled out the Jordanian claim, traditional since 1949, at any rate for the period after Israeli evacuation. And in the following month Arafat was invited to the General Assembly of the U.N.O., where he gave a moderate address in which the unified democratic state was referred to only as a dream. The P.L.O. was then invited to accept the status of 'observer' in the

United Nations Organization, while the General Assembly proclaimed the 'inalienable rights of the Palestinian people in Palestine including: (a) the right to self-determination without external interference, and (b) the right to national independence and sovereignty' (Resolution 3236, 22 November 1974). In January 1976 the P.L.O. was even invited to take part as a full member in a meeting of the Security Council to discuss the Palestine question. The document put forward at that meeting, with the P.L.O.'s approval, came up against the American veto, because it mentioned the Palestinians' right to 'establish an independent state in Palestine', while at the same time affirming respect for the sovereignty and territorial integrity, within certain and recognized frontiers, of all the states in the region. Thus, at last, the P.L.O. expressed openly, in the United Nations, its demand for a Palestinian state alongside the Israeli state. Within the U.N.O.'s new committee on the inalienable rights of the Palestinians, the P.L.O. agreed in November 1976 to a precisely formulated plan. This provided for evacuation by the Israelis, to be followed by U.N.O. supervision until a Palestinian Government could be established, and finally, arrangements for the integration of the Palestinians displaced since 1948. In January 1977, in a letter to Austria's Chancellor Kreisky, the P.L.O. made it clear that the Palestinian state would cover the West Bank of the Jordan, the Gaza Strip, and the enclaves of Hamma (in occupied Syrian territory) and al-'Auja (in occupied Egyptian territory), and that this state would be in a relationship of mutual non-belligerence with its Israeli neighbour. The Secretary of the United Nations Organization passed this proposal on to the Government of Israel. In May 1978 the centrist P.L.O. launched a great offensive for the concept of a Palestinian state. It would be guaranteed (and supervised) jointly by the U.S.A. and the U.S.S.R. (Arafat, 1 May). It would be a state, and no longer a revolution or a guerrilla struggle, and Israel would be recognized *de facto* (Tarzi, the P.L.O.'s representative at U.N.O., 5 May). It would be a non-aligned state, on the Austrian model, guaranteed by a pact between the United Nations Organization and the Arab League: not wholly demilitarized, owing to the danger from Israeli extremist groups, but with U.N.O. troops on its frontiers and in its ports and airports, with an Arab Jerusalem not separated from Israeli Jerusalem, both being headed by a unified municipal authority, and also with a corridor linking Gaza and the West Bank. It would, finally, be a state with, most probably, a government drawn from the centrist nucleus of the P.L.O.*

* Walid Khalidi, *An-Nahar*, 17 June 1978 (in *Foreign Affairs*, July 1978: 'Thinking The Unthinkable: A Sovereign Palestinian State').

It was at this point that there was, for a moment, a split in *El Fatah* itself, and that the opposition of the Rejectionist Front was joined on this issue by that of Hawatmeh. Arafat was accused, at the end of May 1978, of behaving autocratically, and of a Rightist deviation, pro-Saudi and pro-Egyptian. This accusation had not entirely faded away at the end of 1979, even after a unity commission and a programme of Palestinian national unity adopted by the fourteenth National Council (January 1979), because the election of a new executive committee, which was the principal purpose of the meeting, did not come off.

On the eve of the Camp David agreements, therefore, the moderate policy of the P.L.O. had been defined and confirmed: Sadat was to try to get it included in the agreements.

The October war and its consequences had thus brought about a major turn in the Palestinian movement towards a demand for a mini-state alongside Israel, and no longer for a unified state in place of Israel. This turn was accompanied, however, by armed actions of the terrorist type inside and outside Israel – most of them, to be sure, the work of small groups of the Rejectionist Front, sometimes directed by Iraq or Libya. There was the massacre at Rome airport (17 December 1973), individual attacks in Israel in December 1973, the deadly attack on civilians at Kiryat Shemona in April 1974, at Maalot in May, at Nahariya in June, and at Beit Shean in November, the hijacking of aeroplanes and an attack at Orly airport in January 1975, the attack on the Egyptian Embassy in Madrid in September, the assault on members of the O.P.E.C. conference in Vienna in December, the hostage-taking at Entebbe (Uganda) in July 1976, and still other operations in 1977–8 (in particular, the attack on a bus on the Tel Aviv to Haifa road in April 1978, which acted as catalyst for the series of Israeli offensives in South Lebanon). In most cases the purpose was to offer a violent challenge to the centrist decision taken by the P.L.O. These were so many stabs in the back which reduced, on the international scene, the capital of sympathy which the new realism of the P.L.O. had slowly built up and consolidated. The contradiction between the Palestinian movement and the Arab states was reflected from now on inside the Palestinian movement itself, between the revolutionary tendency and the nationalist tendency. The civil war in the Lebanon was due, to a large extent, to this conflict among the Palestinians themselves.

The Lebanese civil war, which we can only touch on here, was first and foremost an armed confrontation between the Maronite Right and the Palestinian Resistance established in Lebanon. The Lebanese Left, grouped around Kemal Junblat, thought that it could turn this confrontation to its own advantage, so as to create and develop a genuinely Lebanese revolutionary movement. On the other hand, the Palestinian movement considered that it ought both to support and to utilize the insurrectionary initiative of the Lebanese Left, if only to ensure the survival of its armed bases in Lebanon. As we have said, however, the Palestinians' revolutionary conviction had by now definitely been reduced to a point where it was merely marking time. To an even greater extent than in the Jordanian affair of 1970–71 it was pressure from the extremist groups (since 1974, the Rejectionist Front) that aggravated the crisis. During the first phase of the civil war (April–December 1975), although this began with street fighting in Beirut between militiamen of the Lebanese Phalange and Palestinian units, the Palestinians, apart from the extremist groups, stayed out of the positional warfare between the forces of the Left (generally supported, if only for geographical reasons, by the Muslim population, whence the expression 'Islamo-Progressives') and those of the Right (which were basically Christian, and mainly Maronite). The Lebanese Army itself intervened for the first time only in December, when the war became acute in the mountains. The second phase, in January 1976, was a concerted offensive by the Maronite forces, with the aim, declared at Baabda on the preceding 31 December, to bring about partition of the country, because the Palestinian *fedayeen* had put an end to the coexistence between Muslims and Christians. It was a matter of wiping out the Palestinian and Shiite Muslim enclaves in the midst of Maronite Lebanon, which more or less coincided with the autonomous province (*mutassarifat*) of Mount Lebanon that had existed in the Ottoman Empire towards the end of its days (1861–1914). Hence the sieges and bombardments of Palestinian refugee camps and the Shiite quarters in East Beirut and near Jounieh – in particular, the camp and quarter of Tell al-Za'tar. This Maronite frenzy to get rid of the Palestinians, even if it meant breaking up the Great Lebanon of 1920, forced the Palestinians of all tendencies to intervene in order to defend themselves, with the help, discreet but effective, of Syrian forces, including Sa'iqa and the P.L.A., which were concerned above all to prevent partition.

The third phase of the Lebanese civil war corresponds to the increasing Syrianization of the internal conflict, from the end of January 1976 onward. When, in March, the Lebanese Army split, as was bound to happen, a counter-offensive by the Lebanese Left became possible, thanks to the Army of Arab Lebanon (A.A.L.), which brought together more and more units that were opposed to the Maronites' policy.

Naturally, the Palestinian forces linked up with this A.A.L. and with the militias of the Left-wing parties. Sa'iqa alone, at the end of March, called for an end to the offensive. The P.F.L.P. then publicly mended its quarrel with *El Fatah* and the P.L.O. After a Syro-Palestinian agreement, signed in Damascus on 15 April, which established, in principle, a state of peace in Lebanon in accordance with Syria's wishes, the P.L.O. executed a total swing-round on 14 May, and took up a position opposed to Sa'iqa and Syria, alongside the Rejectionist Front. After that, one could forecast the massive armed intervention by Syria which started on 31 May, with the aim of restoring order in Lebanon by stopping the offensive of the 'Palestino-Progressives'. Syria could not permit in Lebanon, any more than the partition for which the encircled Maronite community was again striving, the creation of a 'Palestino-Progressive' Lebanon obviously supported by Iraq. That would have meant the failure of all Syrian policy since 1970, and especially since October 1973. It would have constituted a serious threat to the policy followed by the moderate Arab bloc (Egypt, Syria, Saudi Arabia and Jordan) since 1973. Besides, after the Sinai agreement of September 1975, Syria had been left alone, with Jordan and the P.L.O., to face the Israeli Army. No split in the Eastern front could be tolerated, nor any sort of adventure.

The Syro-Palestinian agreement of 29 July 1976 confirmed that of 15 April. The Palestinian adventure in Mount Lebanon and the Syrian response had therefore served no purpose, apart from the total destruction of the Palestinian and Shiite enclave of Tell al-Za'tar by the forces of the Maronite Right, with indirect help from Syria. Order was re-established in Lebanon thanks to the Syrian Army, transformed into an Arab Deterrent Force by the mini-summit at Riyadh (18 October) and the Cairo summit (26 October), 'with a view to giving emergency assistance to the Lebanese Government and to the P.L.O.' [*sic*]. As for the withdrawal of armed men and the stacking of their heavy weapons, provided for by the Riyadh resolution, neither had been accomplished at the end of 1979. The Syrian occupation therefore continued, in order to ensure almost complete control over the Palestinian forces, except in the south of the country.

South Lebanon is, indeed, the arena in which an endemic conflict is being fought out between the Palestinian forces (about 15,000 men plus some 2,500 Arab volunteers, mostly Iraqis) on the one hand, and, on the other, the Israeli forces, acting through or alongside some units of the Lebanese Army. The latter have since 1977 formally taken their stand with Israel against the Palestinians and the Syrians, with the aim of reconquering Lebanon. Evacuation of South Lebanon by the Palestinian forces is the *leitmotiv* of the policy of the Syrians, the Maronite Right and the Israelis alike. This is true of the Shtaura agreement of July 1977, the large-scale Israeli offensive affecting the entire south (March 1978) which failed to rout the Palestinian units, Resolutions 425 and 426 of the Security Council, the repeated pressure on the Palestinians by Syria and by the local Muslim population (Sunnite and Shiite) grouped in a Committee for the Defence of the South, and also the combined pressure, inspired by anti-Egyptian fervour, of Iraq itself, Saudi Arabia, Kuwait and Syria in February 1979. The centrist element in the P.L.O. is also prepared to appease the south and stop the fighting with Israel and the Maronites, and a Palestine security force has even been formed to bring this about. Down to the beginning of 1979 this force encountered opposition from the forces of the Rejectionist Front, enlarged by Iraqi 'volunteers'.

This, then, in broad outline, is how the Palestinian side in the struggle has evolved during the period following the war of October 1973. There has been a remarkable turn towards realism, which has been accompanied, however, by an adventure costly to Lebanon, which was plunged into civil war. We will now add some points concerning the evolution of the Arab states and will indicate how Israel has evolved, before ending this review with an examination of the Camp David agreements and the peace treaty between Egypt and Israel.

The Arab solidarity between states with varying regimes and orientations which took shape in the 1970s has remained one of the features of the evolution of the Arab Near East. We have mentioned the Palestinian movement's need to reckon with this development. The failure of recent attempts at federation or union made by Libya in relation to Egypt, Syria and Sudan (1971–3) and even Tunisia (1976) has shown how anachronistic is the Arab nationalist model of a merger of all the Arab countries under an Egyptian, Syrian or Libyan hegemony. The concept of an Arab nation which is to be unified in the way that Prussia united the German nation or Piedmont united the Italian nation no longer finds an echo even in Ba'athist or Nasserite circles. A sort of ideological temperance has become established. The interests of the separate states take precedence over the interest of the Arab nation. There is at one and the same time a certain degree of cohesion, safeguarded, above all, by the financial power of Saudi Arabia and the Gulf States, and, on some occasions, tension between states. The principal aim of the cohesion between the Arab states is to bring about a comprehensive and final settlement with Israel under American and United Nations patronage. The rapidity with which Egypt has acted to advance this process of peacemaking, from 1975 onwards, has given rise to the principal tension between the states, and a split seems even to have been consummated, in 1979, between Egypt and the rest of the Arab world, once Saudi Arabia, not without hesitation, aligned itself with the position of the Steadfastness Front at Baghdad in March 1979. Is this really a split, or merely a rejection for appearance's sake by Saudi Arabia and Syria? Temporary rejections by some states of the bloc actually form part of the fundamental solidarity of the bloc in its tactical adaptations to international and regional conjunctures.

It is, in any case, a striking fact that since 1975 there has been a regular and certain development towards increasing solidarity between Syria and Jordan. Everything has proceeded as though Damascus, supported financially to a much greater extent after 1975–6 by Saudi Arabia, has taken care of the eastern phase of the Arab-Israeli negotiations (after the Sinai agreement, on the western front in September 1975) in such a way as to ensure that the P.L.O., essentially not itself a state, has been absorbed into a Syro-Jordano-Palestinian federation. Forthwith, Hussein's 1972 project of a United Arab Kingdom has resurfaced, with the formal modification demanded by the Arab summit at Rabat (October 1974) and supported, above all, by Syria and Saudi Arabia. The very notion of a Palestinian state in the West Bank and Gaza is thus nipped in the bud. Everyone is aware, indeed, that, as Hussein said at Rabat, Jordan alone would, so far as Israel is concerned, participate in any general Arab-Israeli negotiations as the representative of the Palestinian cause against Israel. A plan for federation between Syria, Jordan, Lebanon and Palestine (West Bank and Gaza) was discussed in the summer of 1976. In November Syria urged the Palestinian authorities to 'exclude the fighting forces' from the next Palestine National Council, so that it might at last be able 'to take up a position in favour of the peace of Geneva and the Palestinian state' (the newspaper *Al-Ba'th*, 24 November 1976). In June 1977, in the same stride, King Hussein revived the plan for a United Arab Kingdom, in which the Palestinian province would be autonomous, under the control of a unified Jordano-Palestinian army. The Syrian aim seems clear, especially if one does not forget that, since the summer of 1976, the Syrian Government has exercised almost complete control over the movements and orientations of the Palestinian Resistance in Lebanon. Reconciliation between Jordan and the Palestinians has been under way since 1978: it was implicit in the resolutions of the Palestine

National Council of January 1979. On the Saudi side, it was only in June 1979 that Saudi Arabia urged the U.S.A. to enter into direct negotiations with the P.L.O., even if the latter still rejected the United Nations Resolution 242; and in July a linkage was proclaimed for the first time, by the oil minister, Yamani, between Saudi Arabia's future oil policy and 'the solution of the problem of the Palestinian people'. These were pretty definite signs that the moderate Arab bloc wanted to proceed, basically, in the same direction as Egyptian policy since the interim agreement of September 1975, and even since the framework agreements of Camp David, in September 1978.

With or without Egypt, officially, the bloc was greatly embarrassed by the Palestinians. A Palestinian state was, on the whole, as little wished for by the bloc as by Israel. Unlike Israel, however, the bloc could not, publicly at least, repudiate the Palestinians' demand in the minimal form obtained from the centrist nucleus of the P.L.O. Even after Camp David, even after the treaty between Egypt and Israel, Saudi Arabia and the bloc which it inspires do not renounce the possibility of a compromise peace with Israel. The Palestinians cannot divert them from their aim, which is moderate and pro-American, and in any case anti-Communist and as little as possible dependent on the Soviet Union. The Palestinian 'revolution' is no more acceptable to the bloc than the revolution of the Front for the Liberation of the Gulf and Oman, in Dhofar. Now, the rebellion in Dhofar, supported by South Yemen and also by Iraq, organically linked with Habache's P.F.L.P. and Hawatmeh's Palestinian Democratic Front, had been by December 1975 almost totally suppressed, thanks to military aid from Britain and Iran and also to the reconciliation between Iraq and Iran (March 1975) and the moderate attitude of South Yemen after 1976, under Saudi economic pressure. The basis of support for the P.L.O. in South Arabia, mentioned above (page 242) thus disappeared almost completely: and the fate of the Front for the Liberation of the Gulf and Oman showed what might happen to the P.L.O. itself. Thus, the pro-Saudi Arab bloc, far from wanting a revolutionary war waged by the Palestinians to counter the Israeli-Egyptian bloc now being formed, envisaged, on the contrary, a peaceful and anti-revolutionary solution – in other words, an improved version of Camp David. The break with Egypt seems to testify to these tactical tensions which have been mentioned, within and at the service of the solidarity between states.

The strength of this bloc, whatever the occasional splits in it, lies in the oil revenues of the monarchies and principalities of the Gulf. The Right-wing orientation of this same bloc is based on the alliance between, on the one hand, their dominant social stratum, which has become tremendously powerful since 1974 as a result of its investments throughout the world in finance, commerce and industry, and, on the other, the well-established middle classes in the countries of state capitalism – Egypt and Syria, and even Iraq and Algeria. A revived Islamic political ideology, fostered by Riyadh, may help to strengthen this alliance. These are doubtless the three aspects of the solidity of this pro-Saudi bloc.

As for the oil revenues of Saudi Arabia (which produces 43 per cent of all Arab oil), and of Kuwait and the United Arab Emirates, the two biggest oil producers after Saudi Arabia and Iraq, they surpassed, in 1974 alone, in absolute figures, the total amount of revenue for the years 1960–72. The announced prices for crude oil were, in fact, quadrupled at a stroke, confirming a tendency which had begun in 1971. As we have seen, the war of October 1973 provided an excellent occasion for this confirmation. The increase in prices, together with a cut in oil production, was decreed by the Organization of Petrol-Exporting Countries (O.P.E.C.), in which, since 1973, the Arab oil-producing countries have played a leading role. The mass of finance thus multiplied and concentrated alters considerably the world's economic configuration, even though it is invested, first and foremost, where it is most profitable, that is, in the zone of 'central capitalism'. The enrichment of the Middle-Eastern 'periphery' of the Gulf thus necessarily benefits the centre, though in a different way from before. It is this power of what has been called the 'petrodollar' that gives Saudi Arabia the hope that it may be able to pressurize its American friends to lean sufficiently hard on Israel to make that state withdraw to its frontiers of 1967, so as to defuse completely the Palestinian revolutionary threat. This is, indeed, the role and the capacity of a power acting as a relay station for world capitalism. The Saudis' regular and substantial financial aid to the P.L.O. (channelled through *El Fatah* exclusively) has, ultimately, no other purpose that this. And it is in this way that, with the help of diplomatic pressure from Egypt and military pressure from Syria, the P.L.O. has been brought to line up with the pro-Saudi bloc, alongside Syria and Jordan. Indeed, Egypt and Syria have been more and more firmly in the grip of Saudi finance from 1967 onwards and especially since 1974.

The 'confrontation countries' are, in fact, situated in the poor zone of the Arab world. Syria's and Egypt's oil resources, only recently brought under exploitation, are not to be compared with those of Iraq or Algeria, two countries which, like those of the 'confrontation' group, are faced by immense tasks of economic development. Saudi financial aid to Egypt and Syria is thus modulated in accordance with the good or bad political conduct of these two countries, and is, in any case, limited in its absolute amount so as to ensure that neither of them shall possess an independent capacity of decision rivalling that of Riyadh. In this way Saudi Arabia gets its own back for the Nasserite leadership of the Arab world in the 1950s and 1960s. There is still no question of an integrated economic development of the Arab world based on the capital resources of the Gulf.

Instead, there is an alliance between the capitalists of the Gulf and the middle strata of Syria and Egypt. The latter make up for their glaring financial inferiority by their skills and, above all, by the experience of an economic liberalism of which they were deprived, both in Damascus and in Cairo, until 1971 or 1974. State capitalism, dressed in the robes of 'Arab socialism', provided substantial advantages to several sections of the middle strata. They have no intention of losing these advantages. They now link up, in their class interests, with those sections of the middle strata which had been thwarted by the state-socialist measures – internal trade, foreign trade, small and medium enterprises.

Today these different sectors, newly united, offer a broader basis (potential, or at least sought after) to the established authorities. Economic interest determines to a large extent and, in the long run, completely, civic and political attitudes. While Israel was seen in 1948 as a society that would compete with this bourgeoisie just freed from British control, today that bourgeoisie's views are modified. Why not balance the domination of the Gulf financiers with that of the Israeli entrepreneurs? The failure of Nasserite socialism, alongside what has to be admitted as the success of the Israeli economy, has for years provided food for thought. At any rate, there is certainly a desire to get rid of the burden of the Israeli-Egyptian war. The progress of negotiations between Egypt and Israel since November 1973, though seen outside Egypt as being too rapid, has inside Egypt been considered too slow.

Do the conditions of the Syrian state bourgeoisie and the other sections of the middle strata differ to any marked degree? Apparently not. The temptation to create a commonwealth of all the countries of the Eastern seaboard of the Mediterranean will become still stronger, to counterbalance the dependence of these countries on the Gulf states. As for the popular strata, those on whom the costs and sacrifices of the wars bear hardest, their demands are domestic and social. Hence the troubles in Egypt in January 1977 and in Syria during that same year.

The time (1968) has passed when workers, peasants and students demonstrated in the streets of Cairo to oppose Nasser's capitulating attitude! Nevertheless, the popular hostility towards Sadat and his economic policy may, in the near future, become associated with hostility to his foreign policy.

The middle strata we have mentioned, and even those sections of them which have been favoured or created by the 'revolutionary' regimes, are not as 'new' as is sometimes claimed. Structurally, they are in large degree descended from earlier, traditional middle strata of Arab societies. They are new in respect of a certain acculturation. But only rarely are they uprooted, or, let us say, completely Westernized. This is why, in general, in one and the same person we find two contradictory systems of values jostling on more than one point. It is not enough to have become, in the course of a few years, a technocrat educated in the United States and familiar with the laws of marketing, to be *ipso facto* emancipated from a traditional culture deeply imprinted by Islam. The continuance in force, unchanged, of the old traditional rules governing family matters and the status of women is an eloquent indication of this truth. The same social groups that were formerly enthusiastic for Arabism, socialism and secularism may today, if their class interest prompts this, be enthusiastic for Islamization and economic liberalism. Having often been disappointed in their expectations by the socialist regimes, they are easily captured by the Islamic populism which has taken root so strikingly since the 1970s.

This Islamic card may be important in the game of the pro-Saudi bloc, especially as it is backed by the finances of the Gulf. But it may also prove the destruction of the bloc, if it falls into the hands of a revolutionary Islamism on the Iranian model.

In Israel great excitement was caused by the first week of the Yom Kippur War of October 1973. The Prime Minister, Golda Meir, and the Minister of Defence, Moshe Dayan, had to apologize orally to Israeli public opinion and to the new generation of the Labour coalition. In May 1974 the government team had to be changed, and the new cabinet headed by Rabin, was, *a priori*, more dove-like than Golda Meir's. An Israeli peace plan was produced, following the already familiar line laid down by Yigal Allon, the new Minister of Foreign Affairs. This was to clash with territorial ambitions (backed by mystical justifications) in the territories occupied since 1967: the question of the Zionist settlements which multiplied, sometimes illegally, after 1973, was the second important point in Israel's evolution. The victory of the nationalist and religious Right, Likud, in May 1977, crowned these two developments. The third important point was the recent evolution of the Arabs of Israel, that fraction of the Palestinian people left in Israel since 1948 which was gradually re-establishing its links with the fractions living on the West Bank and in Gaza.

The Allon plan* consists in the restoration of 'a single Jordanian-Palestinian state', with Gaza (which, later, Allon was to prefer to exclude, for security reasons) as 'that state's Mediterranean port'. This state would be completely demilitarized. Sovereignty would be Arab almost everywhere, but Israel would retain some zones of defence in depth: the south of Gaza, Sharm-el-Sheikh and some other points in Sinai, the defence line in Golan (Syria), Jerusalem, and an arid and almost uninhabited strip along the River Jordan. This plan proposed that certain and recognized frontiers be fixed by negotiation. The Labour Party's idea was to give back some Arab territories in exchange for guarantees of security and treaties of peace. Prolonged occupation of the Arab territories seemed to be dangerous, and annexation still more so, because of the Arab demographic majority with which the Jewish state would have to cope in future decades. A Palestinian state was also regarded as a dangerous idea. The example of South Lebanon was quoted to show the danger of a Palestinian terrorist base adjoining Israel. On this point Israeli opinion was almost unanimous. The Allon plan envisaged a solution of the Palestinian problem within Jordan. Although opposed by Jordan, it was sufficiently comparable to Hussein's plan for a United Arab Kingdom to serve as a basis as soon as the moment should arrive for negotiations to begin between Israel and Jordan. This was all the more so because the Arab states of the moderate bloc favoured different schemes for representation of the Palestinians – as part of a federal Syro-Jordanian delegation, or as part of a delegation from the Arab League, or, again, as part of a unified delegation of the three 'confrontation' states.

Some who followed the line of the Allon plan, or that of what was to be the Begin plan, even though their orientations varied, declared bluntly that it was King Hussein who constituted the obstacle to a settlement, and that a negotiated solution on the West Bank and Gaza would be possible only with the Palestinians, even if this should mean with Arafat – but only after they had taken power in Amman. This was the view expressed by Yadin, the founder (in May 1976) of the Democratic Movement for Change, and by Sharon, leader of the ultra-nationalist Shlomtsion party, founded in November 1976.

* Cf. Y. Allon, 'Israel: The Case for Defensible Borders', *Foreign Affairs*, October 1976.

The tendency of Likud and the Religious Party is quite different from that of the Labour coalition. The demographic problem is not seen by them as being of dramatic significance. The occupied territories are regarded as liberated Israeli territory over which Jewish sovereignty is historical and even sacred. The 'Arab population of Eretz Israel' is invited to live there as guests, in a climate of peaceful coexistence between Jews and Arabs, like the Arabs of Galilee, the Triangle and the Negev. The security of Israel is not seen by them as ensurable by evacuation of territory but rather by allowing a limited autonomy of the Arab inhabitants, under the 'protection' of the Israeli armed forces. This view is broadly similar to that of Dayan who, since 1967, as we have said, has been preparing the Arabs of the West Bank to live in their provinces as guests enjoying both employment in Israel (one third of the working population of the West Bank and Gaza)* and civic and political rights in Jordan, with constant traffic across the bridges over the River Jordan. For this reason Dayan found no difficulty in joining the government led by Begin in June 1977, after Likud's success in the legislative elections of 17 May.

Begin's doctrine on the West Bank territories includes a juridical preamble according to which Resolution 242 of the United Nations does not apply to Israel where the concept of occupied territory is concerned. Apart from the mystical justifications regarding 'Eretz Israel', this doctrine holds that, on the one hand, the West Bank belongs legally to no state, so that it has not been 'occupied' by Israel since 1967, and, on the other, the West Bank is not affected by any of the U.N. resolutions previous to Resolution 242, since Arabs and Israelis alike, it is said, rejected both the partition resolution (No. 181, November 1947) which provided for a Palestinian Arab state, and the resolution on the return of the refugees (No. 194, December 1948).† Consequently, it is concluded: first, the Geneva Convention on occupied territories does not apply in this case; second, Resolution 242 implies neither total evacuation nor respect for a Palestinian entity; and third, Jewish settlement and the agricultural colonies planned for the West Bank area (which is called Judaea and Samaria) are legal. This juridical preamble is not at all to the liking of the United States, or even of American Jewish circles. How can Carter manage to get Resolution 242 accepted by the P.L.O., which he has been trying to do since 1977, when

* Report by the International Labour Organization. Cf. *Arab Report and Record*, no. 10, 1978, p. 393.

† Cf. *Arab Report and Record*, no. 10, 1977, p. 423. Compare Israel's Declaration of Independence, 15 May 1948, which is based upon Resolution 181 (22 November 1947).

Israel voids it of its substance? And the United States, while they have never talked of an independent Palestinian state (but only of a 'homeland' for the Palestinian refugees), have, at the same time, always been against Jewish agricultural colonies or settlements in the occupied territories.

However, the drive for Jewish settlements has only intensified since the Yom Kippur War, so that in 1979 Israel controlled between 25 and 35 per cent of all the occupied West Bank, 90 per cent of the land affected being held privately and 10 per cent by the state. What is involved is not only Crown lands of the Jordanian state but also lands belonging to Arab owners who have been absent since the conquest of 1967 and whose names are inscribed in the registers of the Israeli police controlling the Jordan bridges and the frontiers, so that they may be prevented from re-entering the West Bank in order to claim their property. To this must be added the procedure, tried out long since in Galilee, of expropriation for military or security reasons or for the public interest. There are thus today 66 centres of colonization in the occupied West Bank, including Jerusalem and its environs, together with 29 on the Golan Heights (Syria) and 19 in the Gaza Strip, the Rafah gap and Sinai. In 1976 the Bloc of the Faithful (Gush Emunim) and in 1977 the Jewish Defence League of Rabbi Meir Kahane promoted marches and 'wild-cat' settlements which were illegal until Begin came to power. Nevertheless, contrary to what might be supposed, the number of Israeli Jews settled in these centres is quite small, except in East Jerusalem and its immediate environs, where there has really been a plan for Jewish settlement ever since the summer of 1967. Leaving East Jerusalem out of account, there are 4,700 settlers in the West Bank, 3,700 in the Gaza Strip and Northern Sinai, and 4,000 in the Golan Heights.* The repatriation of these few thousand persons, in the event of a settlement between Israel, Jordan and Syria, would not present a serious problem from the technical standpoint.

The movement of opinion opposed to the settlements and in favour of negotiation with the P.L.O. and for a Palestinian state, a movement which, though affecting only a minority, is not of negligible importance, has been unable to hinder this wave of settlement to colonize 'the Land of Israel'. The movement includes the party known as Shelli, a coalition of the New Left (Moked, the former Communist Party called Maki) and the Israeli Council for Peace between Israel and the Palestinians,

* Cf. *Arab Report and Record*, no. 8, 1978, p. 317, quoting an article in *Ha-aretz*, 19 April 1978; also Ann Mosely Lesch, 'Israeli Settlements in the Occupied Territories, 1976–1977', *Journal of Palestine Studies*, vol. VII, no. 1(29), 1977, pp. 26–47 and 'Israeli Settlements in the Occupied Territories', ibid., vol. VIII, no. 1(25), 1978, pp. 100–119.

led by Uri Avnery and Arie 'Eliav, which arranged, in Paris and elsewhere, meetings that, though nominally secret, were actually semi-
public, with certain leaders of the P.L.O., after the latter's change of
policy in 1974.

There is also the orientation of the Arabs within Israel, frequently
mentioned in this work, who voice their demands in an increasingly
massive way through the Israeli Communist Party called Rakah. The
latter, allied with part of the Black Panther movement (Oriental Jews),
formed for the elections of May 1977 the Democratic Front for Peace
and Equality, which won five seats (one more than Rakah had won in
December 1973). At the same time, Rakah advocated an orientation
favourable to the P.L.O., which had not been the case before 1973.
Thus, the Palestinians of Israel – some 500,000 in 1978, with an
annual demographic increase of 3.3 per cent – are becoming more
radical, while the P.L.O. (which represents the Palestinians of the
Diaspora) is becoming more moderate. It is this very evolution in
opposite directions that has made possible a regrouping of the Palestinians in face of Israel's anti-Palestinian policy. The 'Day of the
Land', 30 May 1976, in protest against vast expropriations of Arab
land in Galilee, was also observed in the West Bank and in Gaza, just
as throughout the whole Palestinian Diaspora. And while the Palestinian population of the West Bank elected municipal councils (often
Communist) which were mostly favourable to the P.L.O. (April 1976),
the 18th Congress of Rakah, held at Nazareth, declared the P.L.O. to
be the sole representative of all Palestinians for the Geneva Conference
(December 1976). In February 1978 a petition was even signed by
several Israeli Arab mayors and intellectuals declaring that the 500,000
Arabs of Israel are an integral part of the Palestinian people and that
the P.L.O. is the legitimate representative of the entire Palestinian
people. A delegation of the P.L.O. met representatives of Rakah for the
first time officially in Prague in May 1977, applying Article 14 of the
political programme of the 13th Palestine National Council, which
recommends dialogue with the progressive forces of Israel. Finally, in
January 1979, again for the first time, Rakah sent to the 14th Palestine
National Council a peace plan involving mutual recognition by two
independent states – Israel (with its Palestinian minority) and a
Palestinian state – within the framework of the Geneva Conference, as
a counter-proposal to the Camp David agreements.

This development, however, took place outside the evolution of
Israeli opinion, in the strict sense, as the Rakah party is of only very
marginal interest to non-Arab Israelis. It is the opposite of a pressure-

group. Its rallying to the P.L.O. serves rather to provide the extremist Zionist tendencies with an additional argument. The Begin plan concerning the future of the occupied territories, with its juridical preamble already mentioned, giving the green light to Jewish colonization, coincides with these tendencies. What is proposed is that 'administrative autonomy' be granted to the inhabitants, with the military government abolished, but not Israeli responsibility for security and public order. An 'administrative council of eleven members', which is to be elected by the inhabitants for four years, will sit at Bethlehem and concern itself with various sectors of the administration, including finance, the integration of refugees and local police arrangements (all matters, be it noted, dealt with by the present municipal councils). The inhabitants of these autonomous territories would be able to opt either for Jordanian citizenship (and secure representation in the Jordanian Parliament) or for Israeli citizenship (and secure representation in the Knesset). They would also be represented both before the Israeli Government and before that of Jordan. The Israelis would possess complete freedom to acquire land in these territories. Israel claims sovereignty over Judaea, Samaria and Gaza, but leaves this question open 'in the knowledge that other claims [to sovereignty] exist'. This system of administrative autonomy would be subject to review after five years.*

It was this Begin plan that served as basis for the framework agreement concluded at Camp David concerning the West Bank and Gaza, with some notable modifications to which the Americans had got their Israeli partner to agree between December 1977 and September 1978.

The Camp David agreements (17 September 1978) and the treaty of peace between Israel and Egypt (26 March 1979) were the culmination of the process of peacemaking undertaken between the Arab states and Israel after the war of October 1973. The Geneva Conference which opened in December 1973 was backed – some would say betrayed – by the American initiatives, usually approved *post factum* by the Soviet Union, in 1974–5.

The Geneva Conference properly so called was to have resumed its meetings in the year 1976–7, but the new Israeli Parliament and the Begin Government complicated matters. A fresh adjournment seemed inevitable, despite a joint Soviet-American declaration (1 October 1977) followed by an Israeli-American working paper (13 October), which both (despite certain divergences) prepared the way for partici-

* *Arab Report and Record*, no. 23–4, 1977, p. 1018.

pation by all the parties concerned, including representatives of the Palestinians. There was no question of a Palestinian state, nor was the P.L.O. named. It was then that Sadat sought to get things moving faster, deciding, unlike Nasser in 1955 and Hussein on several occasions before and after 1967, to do this in a public and even spectacular way. This took the form of his visit to Jerusalem and his speech to the Knesset on 20 November 1977. Direct negotiations between Israel and Egypt were put into gear, but they could not get started without a serious shove from the Americans, because the United States became parties to both treaties. Basically, it is hard to suppose that Soviet mediation added to American mediation, within the framework of the U.N.O. at Geneva, would have provided anything tangibly better than this, as regards Palestinian national rights. But what was unacceptable to Moscow was the involvement of the U.S.A. in the very terms of the agreements and the letters annexed thereto, and consequently in the affairs of the whole region. The rejection of the agreements by Syria, followed by all the Arab states with few exceptions, was obviously made possible owing, in large part, to Soviet support for such an attitude. Hence the Arab rejectionist meetings at Tripoli (as early as 2 December 1977), Algiers (4 February 1978), Damascus (September 1978) and Baghdad (5 November 1978 and 27 March 1979). Up to now, these gatherings have done no more than recall certain principles, without managing to propose any different procedure for negotiation. What is fundamentally involved, it would appear, despite the arguments put forward in public, is opposition to Sadat's taking the lead on the Arab side, rather than to the actual content of the agreements.

The two documents secure the restitution to Egypt of the whole of Sinai in a period of three years, together with the establishment, along with this gradual evacuation, of a 'self-governing authority', defined as an 'administrative council', in the West Bank and Gaza, for an interim period of five years 'in order to ensure a peaceful and orderly transfer of authority'. This is to happen after negotiations, begun in the third year of the interim period between Israel, Egypt, Jordan and Palestinian representatives, have succeeded in defining 'the final status of the West Bank and Gaza', a status which will then be submitted to the vote of elected representatives of the two territories. These were considerable results, if compared with those obtained by the previous disengagement agreements. Furthermore, a formal treaty of peace between Israel and Egypt, with all the peaceful relations implicit therein, is gradually taking effect. A similar treaty is envisaged, between Israel and Jordan, at the end of the five years of administrative autonomy in the West Bank. Syria is invited to follow Egypt's example in order to obtain the evacuation of Golan and the establishment of peace, with participation by the U.S.A. and backing from the U.N. Security Council.

The framework agreement on the West Bank and the Gaza Strip differs from the Begin plan on two important points. On the one hand, it is aimed at securing 'the resolution of the Palestinian problem in all its aspects', with involvement of 'representatives of the Palestinian people', who are to be brought into negotiations concerning the forms to be assumed by the Administrative Council. In this way, 'the Palestinians will participate in the determination of their own future', in the various phases of the application of the framework agreement. It is this mention of Palestinian self-determination that has aroused opposition in Labour circles in Israel. The framework agreement will lead inexorably, they say, to a Palestinian state, and that is something to be avoided at all costs. For the same reason, Uri Avnery's group is, on the contrary, pleased that Palestinian national rights have at last been recognized, officially and in the texts of treaties, by Israel. It therefore begs the P.L.O. and the Palestinian councillors in the occupied territories not to reject this agreement, but rather to demand its full application, so as to bring about, in actuality, a Palestinian state that would be not a puppet state but a genuine expression of the Palestinian nation. The Palestinian interim administration, and the Palestinian representatives entrusted with negotiating the final status of their territory three years later, will indeed be puppets if the P.L.O. and its local sympathizers boycott the elections to be held for this purpose.

Up to now, however, it is that negative attitude that has been taken up by the P.L.O. and by nearly all the Palestinian leaders in the West Bank and Gaza. The moderate P.L.O. has been outflanked by the tendency of the Rejectionist Front. It is interesting to note that the first resolutions adopted at Tripoli and Baghdad rejected the concept of any Palestinian state or authority if this was to be obtained at the price of recognizing Israel and renouncing all claim to the rest of Palestine. This meant abandonment of the realistic position assumed by the P.L.O. in 1974 and 1977. The second Baghdad summit (5 November 1978) was much more moderate, since it referred to Resolution 242 and to the rights of the Palestinians, which constitute the basis of the framework agreements of Camp David and the peace treaty between Egypt and Israel. What, at bottom, embarrassed the P.L.O. was the provision for establishing a 'strong local police force' linked with the Israeli, Egyptian and (in principle) Jordanian forces entrusted with the preservation of security. Abolition of the Israeli 'military government' (which was to be replaced by the elected Palestinian Administrative Council) was to be balanced by 'a redeployment of the remaining Israeli forces into specified security locations'. These arrangements were obviously aimed against possible operations by armed Palestinian units. The P.L.O. seemed unready to move from a military to a civil footing, especially in a context in which it had gained no substantial and immediate diplomatic victory. The administrative autonomy conceded seemed to fall so far short of its minimum objectives that it saw this as just another form of Israeli occupation with as end-result a disguised annexation, and not Palestinian national independence.

Begin's pronouncements brought grist to the mill of the rejectionists, since, as he saw it, the military government would be transferred, not abolished, and he proclaimed that the establishment of Jewish colonies would not be interrupted in any way, but could and must be continued, since Israeli sovereignty over the *land* of the West Bank and Gaza was still insisted on, with autonomy applying only to the Arab *inhabitants*. A more realistic tendency within the Israeli Government itself takes a more serious view of the matter (Weizmann, Dayan), and many consider that negotiations on Arab Palestine will not be able to produce results until Begin has been removed. It is not surprising, given these conditions, that the 14th Palestinian National Council (January 1979) firmly recalled that the P.L.O. alone represents the Palestinians, that the armed struggle must continue and increase, especially in the occupied territories, and that the autonomy plan must be rejected because it 'consolidates Zionist colonialism on our land and denies the rights of our people', its 'unconditional right to establish an independent state on its national soil'. The Palestinians' interpretation of the Camp David agreements is, as will be seen, that they are plainly unfavourable to the Palestinian cause – a tendentious interpretation inspired by the intention to reject. The most favourable interpretation possible, supported by a movement of opinion of the Palestinian masses, especially in the occupied territories, and backed by the principal Arab states, would completely change the factors in the current negotiations. Sadat would then be in a much stronger position, in relation to Begin, to defend his idea of interim autonomy for the Palestinians, which he wishes to be provided with legislative, political and governmental powers and accompanied by a complete Israeli evacuation of the whole area including East Jerusalem and the settlements. The calendar for application of the peace treaty between Egypt and Israel, which includes the establishment of Palestinian autonomy, is so spread out that one may suppose that the pro-Saudi Arab bloc – Syria, P.L.O., Jordan and Saudi Arabia – will eventually take an honourable part in the negotiations that are under way. These negotiations exist, they are in progress, they are, henceforth, an essential element in the entire Near Eastern question. How, in face of this fact, will Saudi Arabia evolve, and what will be the evolution of opinion amongst the Palestinians most directly concerned?

It is, of course, the Palestinians of the West Bank and Gaza who are primarily concerned, and whose conduct will determine the outcome of the current process. Three attitudes are to be found in these territories. The attitude which is favourable to administrative autonomy and to Sadat's initiative since December 1977 is rather rare. The delegations of support from Gaza and the West Bank which came to Cairo in December 1977 followed several demonstrations against the P.L.O., and against Arafat in particular, during 1977. After the two treaties had been signed, the P.L.O. itself declared that it would take steps to ensure that this tendency in favour of interim autonomy was eliminated in the territories concerned, and certain personages accused of collaboration with Israel and Egypt were, in fact, assassinated during 1979. The power of the P.L.O. – moral, but also exercised through guerrilla actions – makes it difficult to escape from the terror which it intends to impose in this way. This is the meaning, first and foremost, of the decision of the 14th Palestine National Council to support and strengthen the resistance in the occupied territories.

An intermediate position was expressed particularly well by Shawa, the Mayor of Gaza, who, after some hesitation and even after announcing, on 11 March 1979, his support for Sadat, declared that limited autonomy would be acceptable only on condition that genuine and complete self-determination for the Palestinians would be ensured after the interim period had expired. For him, as for the Mayor of Bethlehem, Elias Freij, even an independent Palestinian state of Gaza and the West Bank is Utopian (a pro-Jordanian attitude) and administrative autonomy quite inadequate. Even such intermediate positions as this had to shift towards the hard line, that of the P.L.O., supported by important demonstrations organized, in some cases, by the mayors themselves – as, for example, the demonstration at Nablus on 17 June 1979, which led to the trial of fifty notables, including the mayor himself, and the shopkeepers' strike launched by the municipalities themselves on the 'Black Day', 26 March 1979.

However, as is known, rejection of the initial proposal forms part of all bargaining. If the P.L.O., acting through the West Bank municipalities and the Palestinian National Front of the occupied territories, were to succeed in this way in excluding anti-P.L.O. candidates from the proposed Administrative Council, that might well lead the P.L.O. to put forward its own candidates: those who took part in, and won, the municipal elections of 1976 – to the chagrin of the Israelis. Furthermore, Dayan was seeking, at the end of 1979, Palestinian interlocutors from outside the ranks of the well-known 'collaborators'. The independent power of decision which the P.L.O. fought for in the blood of Lebanon ought, logically, to be exercisable so as to establish peace in Palestine even against the ill will of the Syrians, Jordanians and Saudis.

The texts of the framework agreements and the treaty between Egypt and Israel were such as to irritate Syria, to whom they taught a lesson in the matter of negotiation, and also Jordan, whom they committed without obtaining that state's previous consent. This was the case to such a degree that one would not be surprised if there had been some secret understanding beforehand between Cairo and Amman. Until better information comes to hand, however, we must suppose that there was no such understanding. Nevertheless, Jordan's rejection was gradual. First, there was refusal to take part in the Camp David meeting (August 1978); then came a wait for tangible results to follow from the agreements signed (September 1978); then a demand for explanations from the U.S.A.; and, finally, adoption of the Arab rejectionist standpoint. Jordan's ultimate position was dependent upon Syria and even more upon Saudi Arabia. The latter state did not align itself with the anti-Egyptian economic and financial decisions taken at Baghdad on 26 March 1979 until after attempting to negotiate between the Arab Rejectionist Front and Egypt (messengers sent from the Baghdad summit to Cairo, November 1978), and after the Saudi royal family had decided against convening an Islamic summit meeting on the Palestinian question, to which Egypt and the U.S.A. would be invited (an idea of Prince Fahd's rejected by the family council, which preferred the more Arabist position of Prince Abdullah). The role played by the Saudi kingdom in the Arab world demands that it adopt a pro-Palestinian attitude, somewhat in the same way as the United States of America has to maintain a pro-Israeli position. The anti-Egyptian measures were doubtless required as a first stage. They would make it possible subsequently to modify, in the way desired by Riyadh, the position of its allies in the moderate bloc – Syria, Jordan and the centrist P.L.O. That is to say, Egypt found itself completely deprived, from June 1979 (but not yet in April), of financial support from Saudi Arabia and the Gulf States. It had to turn to other sources of finance – to the U.S.A., to the World Bank and to other industrialized countries, in which, however, the banks were subject to considerable pressure from Arab investors. Would it be to the Saudis' interest to push Egypt into total dependence on Israel and the U.S.A.? The Saudis hoped, no doubt, to get their American friends to exert sufficient pressure upon Israel to ensure that the terms of the Camp David agreements affecting the Palestinians were honoured, with a view to arriving at additional assurances. Begin's hard-line interpretations actually furnish Saudi Arabia with good reason to appeal for American pressure on Israel in the name of the agreements negotiated by the United States.

The situation in the Near East at the end of 1979 marked, even more than that at the end of 1970, the conclusion of a period and the beginning of a highly important turn. The Right-wing Arab bloc, guided by the influence of Saudi finance, clearly directed the policy of the Arab states, and even that of the Palestinians, in the confrontation with Israel. The joint offensive by this bloc, military and by means of the oil weapon, in October 1973, led logically, as the inspirers of this offensive themselves said, to the Camp David agreements and the peace treaty between Egypt and Israel. Prince Fahd, the Saudi Minister of Foreign Affairs, had declared in March 1978, that is, in the midst of a diplomatic struggle to ensure that Sadat's visit to Jerusalem was transformed into an all-round agreement, that his country was ready to recognize Israel as part of a comprehensive settlement, so long as evacuation by the Israelis and Palestinian rights were provided for, and that the Arab states had a united position (meaning that they agreed to come under the Saudi aegis). 'No war is possible without Egypt,' he added, 'but it is not possible for Egypt to make peace alone.'* This is true. Thus, contrary to what is said by Arab opponents of the Camp David agreements, a situation of peace has been established in the region, and *not* the threat of another war. And while Egypt has, so to speak, broken the rules of the 'Arab cold war', it nevertheless remains true that it has brought nearer, rather than contradicted, the objectives of the pro-Saudi Arab solidarity of 1973. The simple fact is that, unfortunately, it is easier to agree on waging war than on proposing peace. Sadat's peace possesses the disadvantage of being an 'accomplished fact', but it also

---

* *Al-ra'y al-'amm* (Kuwait), 9 March 1978. Prince Fahd repeated the substance of this declaration in an interview with the *Washington Post*, published on 25 May 1980.

possesses the advantage which this implies – at least for those who see peace as an advantage, rather than the total victory of one side – namely, that it exists, that it is a fact. Arab rejectionism has at last been clearly ruled out by the most important Arab state.

Israel tried to make the most of its incomplete military victory of October 1973 so as to restrict the subsequent negotiations to military disengagements and to confine them, so far as possible, to Egypt. The peace of 1979 can be seen as a victory for Israel, and, more profoundly, a victory for the Zionist entity and for the activism which always comes to the fore in Israel at difficult moments. It was the culmination of the uncompromising stubbornness of a colonial entity transformed into a state reality which had at last been recognized, officially and solemnly, by the head of the most important Arab state. However, for the first time since 1956–7, Israel was obliged to evacuate, even though very gradually, the whole of Sinai, including the recently established Jewish colonies, agricultural or urban, together with the airfields, in exchange for an increase, on an equally large scale, of American arms supplies. The present government of Israel is doing all it can to burke the framework agreement so far as the Palestinians are concerned, and to thrust Egypt into the isolation of a separate peace. By doing this it hopes to strengthen its position in relation to its other Arab neighbours and to force them to initiate separate negotiations. The continued settlement, carried out with impunity, of Jewish colonies in the West Bank, Gaza and Golan, contrary to the provisions of Camp David – as, at any rate, these were understood by the U.S.A., Egypt, and persons of goodwill throughout the world – is also regarded as a victory, and a pledge of victory, by Begin, though not by the Labour opposition or, of course, by the 'Peace Now' movement (Avnery, Eliav and others). The present uncompromising attitude of the Israelis regarding the territorial and national rights of the Palestinians, together with the similarly uncompromising attitude of the Arab rejectionist states, has produced considerable disenchantment among the Israeli people, after the great hopes aroused by Sadat's visit to Jerusalem and the beginning of peace negotiations. The continual offensives launched by the Israelis in South Lebanon, in conjunction with the extremist Maronite forces of Major Haddad, show that the war is not over. The repression of Palestinian demonstrations in the West Bank, and even in Gaza, confirms the view that peace between Israelis and Palestinians is not to be expected tomorrow.

Finally, the Palestinians have certainly won some prestige victories on the international stage as a result of their decision for realism since

1974, and especially since 1977; but their involvement, which was perhaps inevitable though certainly adventuristic, in the Lebanese civil war and in opposition to the state interests of Syria and, more broadly, of the Arab states in general, has had to be paid for by their present dead-end situation. They have, in fact, lost almost completely the small degree of independence of action and decision that remained to them after they had been liquidated in Jordan in 1970–1. In Syria and in Lebanon Assad controls them practically one hundred per cent, yet without protecting them against Israeli offensives such as those of spring 1978 and those, limited but continued, of 1979. This refusal by Syria to intervene militarily in support of the Palestinians is an element in the strict Syrian control to which they are subject. The ephemeral union between Syria and Iraq, for tactical and military reasons if not for political ones, in the spring of 1979, obviously strengthened the Arab states' grip on the Palestinian resistance. What some have described as the Palestinians' victory at the Arab 'Steadfastness' summit meetings in Baghdad is a matter of pure form.

It would appear that no Arab state (apart, doubtless, from Libya) really wishes, any more than Israel does, to see the eventual establishment of an independent Palestinian state. This was said privately by Carter not long ago – and he was probably right – when he summed up his recent talks with all the Arab heads of state. Iraq itself, by presiding over and signing the decisions of Arab conferences which were anti-Egyptian but, ultimately, pro-Saudi, thereby took up a position much more moderate than hitherto. In addition, the Palestinians have been invited to reconcile themselves completely with Hussein of Jordan, which they are in the process of doing, this intention being written into their latest political programme (January 1979). From the independent Palestinian mini-state they will have to go over to the old Palestino-Jordanian idea of 'unity of the two banks' of the Jordan. It seems that, despite present appearances, the Palestinians will be obliged by the Steadfastness Front to submit, *de facto*, to the provisions of Camp David, or something very similar, even if they do not accept them in so many words. They would retain a great deal more of the independence they have been demanding since 1967 if they were to play the card of Sadat and Camp David against the ill humour of Syria, then of Jordan and ultimately of Saudi Arabia. This is more or less what some Palestinian leaders themselves perceived at the end of 1977: for example, Isam Sartawi, who was Arafat's confidential agent during the Palestinian drive for dialogue with Israeli Zionist pacifists in 1976–7;

or the Mayor of Gaza, until the beginning of 1979, when he went to consult the P.L.O. in Beirut and Damascus. The Palestinian decision to oppose Egypt and Camp David, alongside Syria, seems to be an adventure just as pregnant with consequences as the one in Jordan in 1970 and in Lebanon in 1976. Each time that the centrist P.L.O. has lined up with the policy of the Rejectionist Front (Habache) it has had to pay the price of increased dependence on the Arab states and of substantial losses of Palestinian lives. The fact is that the P.L.O. wants less than ever the 'protracted revolutionary war' that the P.F.L.P. conducts: any alliance with the P.F.L.P. – necessarily provisional and adventuristic in relation to Arafat's centrist norms – is thus paid for in the shape of unavoidable Arab reprisals, resulting in increased dependence.

At least the Palestinians have acquired since 1970 one weighty argument in relation to Israel, namely, a kind of (unorganized) front of solidarity between the Palestinians of the West Bank and Gaza and – something new and extremely worrying for Israel – of Israel itself, that is, of the legal Israel, within the frontiers of 1967. The fact that 13 per cent of Israeli citizens (the Arabs of Israel) recognize the P.L.O. as their representative will be an important card in the hands of the latter when it takes its place at a negotiating table. The status of the recently installed Jewish population of East Jerusalem (some 90,000 persons) and of the West Bank (a very small number) will be negotiable against that of the 500,000 Palestinians in Israel. The P.L.O. does not, in fact, demand any longer the whole of Palestine, or even those parts of Israel with an Arab majority, on the basis of the partition plan of 1947, but it can claim the support of the Arab minority in Israel. This argument seems all the more plausible in that the Palestinians in Israel and in the occupied territories are, in the main, not at all disposed to welcome the revolutionary war of unlimited duration advocated by George Habache. So there is no alternative to negotiation, or, in other words, Camp David *at least* as starting point, as a basis for a process leading towards peace, given due supplements and adaptations. There is no other possibility open to the Palestinians of the West Bank and Gaza: willy-nilly, Camp David is gaining ground among them.

Conclusion and Prospects (*summer 1980*)

The evolution of the last eleven years in the Near East seems to confirm some points in the conclusion published in 1968, but also to require their modification. The Palestinians have acquired armed forces of their own and also a national and 'revolutionary' prospect of their own. Thereby they have confirmed that the conflict is essentially a struggle against an unaccepted foreign occupation, which was colonial from the start and is such even on a permanent basis, as we see from the Israeli policy of settlement in the territory occupied since June 1967. After 1967, as after 1948, the Arabs' rejection of Israel was asserted, but this time it was confirmed by means of an organized Palestinian resistance. However, this rejection already left room for a certain compromise, since the struggle envisaged a democratic and secular coexistence between Jews and Arabs in a unified Palestinian state. This objective, unacceptable to the great majority of Israelis, would have been just as unacceptable to Arab opinion in the late 1960s, for which the formula: 'Drive the Jews into the sea!' corresponded to a feeling of uncompromising anti-colonial struggle. On the other hand, it was the Palestinian Resistance, living in the interstices of the Arab states, that took over the line of rejection of Israel when these states – Egypt and Jordan from summer 1967, Syria after 1970 – began to seek an honourable political solution. Thus, compromise drew nearer on two planes. The states agreed to negotiation, in accordance with a variety of successive formulas, while covering themselves, in the eyes of Arab opinion, with the heroic struggle of the Palestinian people. For its part, the latter was led, through military and political pressure from the states, to compromise increasingly with these states and, consequently, with Israel. In this way the rejection of Israel disintegrated, through successive adaptations to the reality of this region of the Arab world. In the case of the Palestinians, the transition from the unified democratic state to the Palestinian mini-state, and from revolutionary war throughout the region to diplomatic struggle in the United Nations and in relation to the U.S.A., with a view to being present, directly or indirectly, at the peace conferences, was a transition that was rather remarkable for a national movement. Israel's Arab neighbour states, on the other hand, can argue from their relative military victory of October 1973 in favour of abandoning, clearly and irrevocably, their traditional rejection of Israel, as Egypt did in 1977–80. A dynamic of acceptance of the accomplished fact of Israel is thus under way. This Egyptian position is not the beginning of it but rather the end-point of a process which goes back at least to 1970. Consequently, the Palestinians have been required to make fresh and substantial concessions. The independent Palestinian mini-state must be put off till later, in favour of, on the one hand, a limited amount of internal autonomy, and on the other, an organic link with Jordan.

Palestinian rejection of these new forms of compromise can find support in their rejection by the Arab states, which were in 1979 almost all opposed to Egypt. Thereby, however, it becomes still more dependent on their goodwill. Revolutionary war is less than ever in favour in a bloc which is supported by Saudi finance, and the dynamic of which has been moving for ten years past towards a final settlement with Israel and the Palestinians, to be guaranteed by America. Thus, contrary to what it was possible to foresee in 1968, no Arab state (not Syria, any more than Jordan) has agreed for any length of time to be drawn into the Palestinians' armed rejection of Israel. This rejection had, and still has, before it the barrier constituted by the states concerned, both Israel and Israel's Arab neighbours. Thus, all the Palestinians' revolutionary undertakings, inspired by the extremists of the movement, were, are and will be so many adventuristic enterprises – very heroic, to be sure, but always bringing results disadvantageous to the Palestinian cause. The contradiction between the Palestinian Resistance and the Arab states having proved to be essential, the contradiction between the increasing ideological moderation of the centrist P.L.O. and the warlike adventures of that same P.L.O. is both understandable and painful. The balance-sheet of these adventures, whether in the form of international hijacking, terroristic military operations inside Israel, or conventional military operations in Jordan in 1970 and in Lebanon in 1973 and 1975–6, is not at all favourable to the Palestinians' political position, contrary to what many believe and to what was believed by the Palestinian 'martyrs' of the camps that were bombarded in reprisal. Absolutely the opposite is the case, and the imposition of this sort of heroism, either on or by the base of the movement, seems to the greater part of world opinion to be absurd and revolting.

The peaceful Palestinian state demanded is, indeed, not very credible in such a context of violence, and the Israeli concessions, which have been important in relation to Egypt, are as though killed at birth where the Palestinians are concerned, so long as the latter fail to adjust their military conduct to their political objectives. We even think that, in face of the inner dynamic of the activist political Zionism which has dominated Israel since May 1977 somewhat more than previously, the Palestinian cause should react as one reacts in order to dam up a disaster such as a flood, a tidal wave or a volcanic eruption. Under such circumstances he would indeed be mad who demanded a comfortable house in the best part of the town when it is only with the utmost difficulty that he will be able – while waiting for something better, and in order to avoid something much worse – to preserve his life and that of his family in a makeshift shelter which he will have to keep repairing. The limited internal autonomy provided for by the Camp David agreements in order to prepare for definitive Palestinian self-determination certainly falls far short of an independent Palestinian state on a territory wholly evacuated by Israel. It is, nevertheless, for Israel, a first step along the path of compromise. The Palestinian state may be implicit there, though on one condition – that the Palestinians grasp the hand held out to them, in accordance with abandonment of their line of refusal to compromise with the states of the region. In this matter, too, their recent negative attitude, if it were to be prolonged, would, in our view, constitute a costly adventure, in contradiction with the P.L.O.'s turn towards realism since 1974 and 1977.

The sentiment we are expressing here runs counter to the opinion which is most widespread in the French Left and, especially, in those groups which want to support the Palestinian cause and all good Arab causes. Yet it seems to us to be well founded in, on the one hand, the analysis which we have attempted in these pages of the facts of the conflict and, on the other, an urgent desire to promote peace in the Near East. It is indispensable that Palestinian national rights be satisfied. This can be achieved on the peaceful basis provided by the agreements of 1978 and 1979, if the initial minimum be not rejected. To encourage the process (disastrous for the Palestinians, as we have insisted enough) of Arab rejection, especially rejection by the Palestinians, means hindering the advent of peace. That is what we do not want to happen, even if the peace in question be a *pax Americana* – which would, anyway, be merely the fruit of what was called the *pax Sovietica* of 1967–73. To indulge in militant talk is, in this case, to incur responsibility for blood which is to be shed by others.

As for the Levantinization of Israel, its transformation into a state like all the others in the Near East, this has certainly not made much progress, and we do not think that it will happen principally from within. We have said – and here again in opposition to a naïve view which is found rather comforting – that the demands of the Oriental Jews contribute very little to the orientalizing of society and the state in that country, and still less to moderation towards the Palestinians or integration in the Arab Middle East. The electoral victory of Likud in 1977, crowned almost at once by an unprecedented diplomatic victory in relations with Egypt, shows the contrary to be true.

There is, above all, the weight (not economic but political and psychological) of that million of Palestinians who are treated, day after day, as a colonized people, in the West Bank, in annexed East Jerusalem and in the Gaza Strip. An everyday relationship of colonial domination has been established since June 1967. Here we have Arabs – neither Jews nor Israelis, and all, *a priori*, 'terrorists' who endanger the security of Israel – who come to work in Israel as unskilled or poorly skilled labour, and who are also subject to a military control which is constant and armed with its own laws. The entire process of defence against terrorism, appropriate to a prolonged occupation of conquered territory which is hostile and with widely diffused resistance activity, a process which could be foreseen in 1968, has developed with all the abuses that could be expected. To this process has been added an enterprise – at first timid and formally illegal, but then made official, subjected to regulation, and calculated in accordance with long-term plans – for the Israelization of the occupied lands and their settlement with agricultural colonies, using the juridical instruments and methods of confiscation long perfected in Galilee. This side, inglorious and contrary to human rights, of Israel's defensive colonialism, is the absolute opposite of Levantinization. The latter will, however, perhaps be favoured in the long run by internal reaction against these excesses which are the shameful side of colonialism, and we, outside Israel, have to take our stand in such a way as to foster and encourage that sense of shame. But the wished-for results will come slowly.

As against that, the establishment of peaceful relations with Egypt in the months that lie ahead should make possible a gradual acclimatization to the Arab environment, outside the immediate relations of domination. In this connection those Israelis who come from Arab countries will indeed be able to play a distinctive role. To be sure, this will mean, in a sense, an external expansion of the internal colonization, which is itself a two-storey affair – over the Oriental Jews, and over the Arabs of Israel and the occupied territories. But – and this is a quite new and decisive factor – it will be, first and foremost, an opening towards an independent Arab state. This is a beginning, just a beginning. And even as war breeds war, so does peace breed peace – even though much more slowly.

12

Conclusion: on the General Nature of the Conflict

The aim of this book has been to give the reader a picture of the broad outlines of the Israeli-Arab conflict. The study has been historical in essence, with a few fundamental sociological observations included here and there. Some of the assertions made may appear astonishing, since they go against widely held opinions. Nonetheless they have in every case been scrupulously documented, and in other works which, unlike the present study, demand the deployment of an academic armoury I have quoted the arguments and references which support them.* Of course this does not mean to say that the arguments which I have advanced are irrefutable. I am no more infallible than anyone else in the selection and evaluation of facts. I merely wish to point out to those disposed to contradict me that their criticisms will have to be more firmly based than on assertions which they believe to be undeniable simply because they are current in their milieu or country. They will likewise have to bring forward attested facts, supported by serious documentation.

The facts in themselves are of course numberless. Like every historian, I have had to be selective in recounting them. I have chosen those facts which seemed to me to illuminate aspects of the conflict which are fundamental. Here again it is possible that I have made mistakes. But those who would contradict me will have to show that the facts which they adduce – given that they are well-attested – will throw light on an aspect which I have overlooked and which refutes one of my conclusions.

Such observations may seem self-evident, and so they are. A historical or sociological analysis can usually dispense with them. But the problem with which this book deals has aroused an unusual flood of passion. Rarely has opinion been so one-sidedly informed; the information available to it further reinforced an already strong tendency to make judgements favouring one particular side of the question. It must be admitted moreover that these tendencies partially sprang from

* See particularly M. Rodinson, 'Israël, fait colonial?', *Temps Modernes*, no. 253 bis, 1967, pp. 17–88 (translated by D. Thorstad as *Israel: A Colonial-Settler State?*, New York, Monad Press, 1973).

highly honourable, even praiseworthy motives. Unusual precautions have therefore been doubly necessary.

The facts which have so far been advanced, with the minimum of argumentation accompanying them or entailed by their selection, are intended to enable the reader to form a well-founded judgement of the nature of the Arab-Israeli conflict. The author begs leave to give his own opinion on this matter and on the future possibilities as he sees them. The reader may accept or reject them. At least he will know on what these conclusions are based.

The immediate causes of every event described in the pages of this book, especially the causes of the war of June 1967, could be discussed *ad infinitum*. The study made above, based on documentation available to the author, is of necessity provisional in character. Many facts are still unknown and will come to light only gradually, some no doubt only after a long period has elapsed. The details of crises of this sort, with their inextricable web of political, diplomatic and military manoeuvrings, is always very difficult to unravel. Who was it who initiated such and such a move? Why? What results did he expect to achieve? The disputes continue – for example, on the immediate causes of the war of 1914–18. The discussion of the origins of this conflict is likely to go on for as long and prove as complex. I readily accept that my opinion of the matter may need to be revised in the light of new evidence.

Let me say only this, that all new evidence produced since the first edition of this book – especially the statements of Israeli generals and statesmen – confirmed my views as against the views held at the time by most of the Western authors of books and papers. On the other hand it is comparatively easy to form a judgement as to the more fundamental causes of the conflict of which this war was only the most recent and the most spectacular manifestation. The pertinent facts are well known and abundantly documented. The origin of the conflict lies in the settlement of a new population on a territory already occupied by a people unwilling to accept that settlement. This is as undeniable as it is obvious. The settlement may be justified, in whole or in part; but it cannot be denied. Likewise the refusal of the indigenous population to accept it may be thought justifiable, or it may not.

It was indeed a new population, radically different from the indigenous one. It is true, as everyone knows, that the newcomers claimed that they had inhabited the territory of Palestine in ancient times and had formed a state there, and that they had merely been dispossessed and driven out by force. That is true: in the main at any rate. We may accept – though not without some reservations – that this was the same people, the former occupiers of this land. Indeed, it is generally agreed that a people continues to exist as a collectivity no matter what internal renewal takes place in its constituent elements, in the mass of individuals that constitute this people. In the case of the Jews this process of renewal has certainly gone very far since ancient times; but that is, consequently, not a pertinent factor. On the other hand, the Jewish people did see the states which they had built destroyed by force or constraint – the last of them, though, that of the Hasmoneans and those (vassals of Rome) ruled by the kings of Herod's family, with the acquiescence of a large part of the population. The national revolts launched with a view to establishing an independent state were then crushed by the Romans. But, despite the legend, the Jewish population of Palestine was, in fact, reduced to minority status much less as a result of deportations, which were limited in scope, than through assimilation, conversion and emigration.

More important is the question of what sort of people the Jews became after the end of the epoch when most of them lived in Palestine. Everything depends on how one defines the terms 'people' and 'ethnic group'. As was said at the beginning of this book, since the time of the Emancipation, the Jews, in every case, though at different dates from one country to another, were no longer a coherent whole possessing some unity despite their extreme dispersion. They were persons who were identified by themselves and by others as having originated from the ancient people of Israel, even if this was only partly true. Many of them were still bound by loyalty to the old ethnic religion, or at least to some of its rites. In certain countries the Jewish groups possessed a common culture, but this was localized so that there were several distinct 'Jewish peoples'.

In addition there were many individuals of the same origin who no longer regarded themselves as Jews in any sense at all, but whom others could identify as Jews. The feeling of solidarity and common identity, when this went beyond the sphere of religion, resulted above all from that attitude on the part of others.

To simplify the argument, however, we can accept that that section of the Jews who wished to form once more a Jewish people, a community of the national type, continued the entity that had been constituted by the Jewish religious communities of the Middle Ages (which possessed only a few ethnic features) and, beyond them, the Jewish people of Antiquity.

This in no way detracts from the heterogeneity of the Jews. The alleged ancestors of today's Jews did indeed possess Palestine for centuries as their national territory – after, according to their own tradition, conquering it from another people, the Canaanites. They then formed the majority, though not the whole, of its population. After the passage of fifteen or twenty centuries, however, the population of Palestine was different, or at least had a different identification, a different culture, different religions, a different language. Nowhere have such remote descendants of former occupiers of a country been welcomed as native sons of the soil. Nowhere can people who have been attached to a land or a city for generations welcome as 'brothers' immigrants coming from afar, speaking another language, possessing a different culture, aliens in every respect, on the basis merely of these immigrants' claim that they are descendants of former inhabitants, whether this claim be true or false – something which, moreover, the 'natives' have no means of checking.

This does not diminish the differences. Certainly the Zionist Jews who were 'returning' to Palestine were in some measure related in any case, according to the criteria of physical anthropology, to the Palestinian Arabs. Despite innumerable mixtures of blood they must, in very different degrees, have included among their ancestors Jews from ancient Palestine, and have retained something of those ancestors in their genetic heritage. Moreover in spite of an equally large number of admixtures, the basis of the Palestinian Arab population, as explained earlier, must likewise have been descendants of these same Jews or Hebrews of Antiquity. But this implies no homogeneity between the two peoples in the sociological sense. What does count, if at all, in the conflicts and compacts between peoples is the identification as a people, or as an ethnic group. The English, the French, the Spaniards, the Germans also have a great number of ancestors in common and are the bearers, in different proportions, of the same genetic heritage. This fact has not in the very least prevented wars between them, nor the desperate assertion of independence of one from the other, nor a hatred which has often reached a pitch which it would be difficult to exceed.

The same is true of the linguistic relationship, often misleadingly defined by the assertion that both peoples are 'Semites'. This means one thing only, that the Hebrew and Arabic languages are linguistically related, they derive from the same root tongue, they both belong to the linguistic group conventionally termed 'Semitic'. The Hebrew language was the ancient tongue of the Jews, and had become a dead language some centuries before the Christian era. It had been preserved as an erudite, 'holy' tongue, to some extent as a literary language among the Jewish communities, and was resuscitated in the twentieth century by Eliazar Ben Yehuda to serve as a living tongue, common to Jews of different origins called to colonize Palestine. It should be noted in passing that the great majority of Zionists did not know this Semitic tongue, neo-Hebrew, when they first set foot on Palestine soil, although they were shortly to learn it. However, none of this is of the slightest importance. Kinship between languages (often implying some anthropological kinship, in very different degrees, between some at least of those who speak those languages) has never prevented antagonism between peoples. The Spanish and the Portuguese have often been in violent opposition to one another, although Portuguese is only another Iberian dialect. The French of the '*Langue d'oïl*' in the north conquered by force the France of the '*Langue d'oc*' in the south, despite the fact that the southern dialects are fairly closely related to those of the north. The Pakistanis and the Indians speak Indo-Aryan languages, sometimes the same ones. Is it necessary to recall the bloody struggles between the Greek city-states? To repeat: what counts is the identification as special social unit or as an ethnic group.

Palestine therefore was being populated anew. Not only did the newcomers have no community of identification, in the sociological sense, with the native inhabitants, their difference was also accentuated by a gross cultural disparity. The great majority of the first wave of immigrants spoke a different language from the local population in more senses than one: they had different values, different customs, different modes of behaviour, different attitudes to life. They were altogether of a different world – the European world. Not only were they foreigners, they were also Europeans, that is to say they came from that world which was everywhere known as the world of the colonizers, of peoples who dominated their neighbours by their technical and military power and by their wealth. That they may have been the poorest and most underprivileged of this other world mattered not – they were of it.

The only ones in whom the difference was not so marked were the Oriental or Orientalized Jews, such as already lived in Palestine. But the moving spirits of the Jewish colony and then of the state of Israel regarded them as backward elements, which somehow had to be assimilated. They had to be impregnated with the values of the Western Jews, their social customs and their attitudes would have to be made to conform. The numbers of these Oriental Jews became very great in the years which followed 1948, mainly through the emigration to Israel of Jews from the Arab countries. These were undoubtedly much closer to the Arab population of Palestine. Indeed many of them might, if the problem had followed a different line of development, have become or remained Jewish Arabs; they even spoke various dialects of the same language. However, they were sharply divided from the Muslim and Christian Arabs by communal hostility and a long-standing grudge; as well as this, the Western Jews conducted a vigorous campaign to assimilate them, fearing 'levantinization' of the state more than anything else. Hence these Middle Eastern Jews tried to model themselves on their Western cousins, whose culture they envied. I should like to quote an example insignificant in itself, but symbolic of what was happening. The Yemeni Jews, who pronounced Hebrew with its ancient Semitic consonants, which appear in the written language and are preserved in their Arabic vernacular, are making strenuous efforts, in Israel, to lose these 'bad habits'. They are learning to repronounce Hebrew in the manner of the European Jews, i.e. leaving out consonants which the latter have forgotten how to pronounce for twenty centuries, confusing others, etc. In other words, they are moving as far as possible away from the standard of the Hebrew once spoken in Palestine in ancient times, and away from the Semitic model which they had partially preserved.

A foreign people had come and imposed itself on a native population. The Arab population of Palestine were native in all the usual senses of that word. Ignorance, sometimes backed up by hypocritical propaganda, has spread a number of misconceptions on this subject, unfortunately very widely held. It has been said that since the Arabs took the country by military conquest in the seventh century, they are occupiers like any other, like the Romans, the Crusaders and the Turks. Why therefore should they be regarded as any more native than the others, and in particular than the Jews, who were native to that country in ancient times, or at least occupiers of longer standing? To the historian the answer is obvious. A small contingent of Arabs from Arabia did indeed conquer the country in the seventh century. But as a result of factors which were briefly outlined in the first chapter of this book, the Palestinian population soon became Arabized under Arab domination, just as earlier it had been Hebraicized, Aramaicized, to some degree even Hellenized. It became Arab in a way that it was never to become Latinized or Ottomanized. The invaded melted with the invaders. It is ridiculous to call the English of today invaders and occupiers, on the grounds that England was conquered from Celtic peoples by the Angles, Saxons and Jutes in the fifth and sixth centuries. The population was 'Anglicized' and nobody suggests that the peoples which have more or less preserved the Celtic tongues – the Irish, the Welsh or the Bretons – should be regarded as the true natives of Kent or Suffolk, with greater titles to these territories than the English who live in those counties.

The native population did not accept the settlement of what must be regarded as foreigners, who, moreover, presented themselves as colonists, as is demonstrated by the titles which they gave to their own institutions. Again, the Arabs have been condemned for this. Without for the moment attempting to assign moral values to the various attitudes which might be taken, it must be made clear that their reaction was entirely understandable. It is certainly true that at other periods alien peoples have succeeded in imposing themselves on a given territory, and that sooner or later custom and law ratified the deed. Usually this was initially effected by force. The best example for present purposes is furnished by the Arabs themselves. The Arabs imposed themselves by force and the native population gave little resistance, then allowed itself to be assimilated by its conquerors. But this native population was already subject to foreign rule, and merely changed masters. Similarly, when Jewish colonization first started, the Palestinians were subjects of the Ottoman Empire, which was dominated by the Turks. Why not accept the new domination which might, as in earlier times, have been followed by assimilation?

This might indeed have happened were it to have taken place some centuries or even some decades earlier. But the Zionists were unlucky. The conscience of the world had developed, and no longer accepted right of conquest, or accepted it more reluctantly. Cultural assimiliation between peoples is possible; but each people now tends to cling fiercely to its own identity. This is a fact that nobody can do anything about. Zionism began as a living force in the era of nationalism, of which it was itself a manifestation, and it pursued its career during the era of decolonization. Peoples are no longer willing to accept conquest and will fight to preserve their identity and to keep or win back their independence. Once delivered from Turkish tutelage, the Palestinian Arabs desired domination neither by the British nor by the Zionists. They wished to become neither Englishmen nor Israelis, although they accepted gratefully many elements of that European culture which both brought with them and which the Arabs had slowly been absorbing in small doses for a long time. They wanted to keep their Arab identity, and therefore they wanted to live under the rule of an Arab state. In view of the division of Arab south-west Asia in 1920, they tended to form a Palestinian national community within the framework of the various different Arab national communities, which were pledged to some degree of unity in accordance with certain widely held conceptions. They consequently hoped to see an Arab state in Palestine. Moreover the conscience of the world now supports peoples fighting to defend their identity. It seemed to the Palestinians a flagrant injustice that an exception should be made of them on the sole grounds that the colonists were Jews. The whole world was proclaiming 'Down with colonialism!' They had recently seen many Frenchmen renounce the proviso '– except for French colonialism' and many Englishmen their proviso '– except for British colonialism'. All they wanted was to do away with the reservation '– except for Jewish colonialism'.

The natives had not accepted the foreigners. One point remains to be clarified. The Arab world has frequently accepted foreign settlement on its territory – witness the example of the Armenians, fleeing from Turkish persecution in 1920, who came and settled in the Arab countries. Many had come even earlier than this. As a general rule, they had been accepted. Yet the majority of the refugees, especially those in the latest migration, wanted to preserve their identity as a people, their language, their culture, their own special traditions. It is possible that if this partial refusal to assimilate persists it will one day be the source of conflict. Nonetheless up to the present time, there has been no hostility towards them comparable with that felt towards Zionist immigration. To all appearances this is due to the fact that the Armenians had no intention of constructing an Armenian state in territory populated by Arabs. If they do still harbour any claims of the 'Zionist' type, these relate to territory which is currently Turkish. Similarly no opposition to Jewish settlement existed until Jewish immigration took on its Zionist aspect. Arab opposition manifested itself the moment that the Zionist intention to establish a Jewish state by detaching Palestine territory from the Arab world became clear. This opposition mounted as the true nature of the Zionist project became obvious, and grew more irreconcilable as the Zionists came nearer to success. Therefore the Arabs were not rejecting the foreigners as such; they were rejecting foreign occupation of their territory – whether we choose to classify this phenomenon as colonialism or not.

The conflict therefore appears essentially as the struggle of an indigenous population against the occupation of part of its national territory by foreigners. Of course there are many other sides to the conflict which could be brought out. None of these, however, seems relevant to its basic definition.

It seems to me that what we have here is an objective conclusion, that is, one which ought to convince any person who is acquainted with the pertinent facts and who has decided to submit to the conditions of rational analysis, leaving aside prejudices and passions. Yet this conclusion is rejected by many, who prefer other explanations of the conflict. Some of these explanations relate to facts which, though real, are of secondary importance. Others are basically imaginary. Most are inspired, whether consciously or not, by some specific feeling, others by false notions of social and historical causality – especially those which conceive of earthly conflicts as merely pale incarnations of conflicts between metaphysical or mythical entities.

Generally speaking, the feeling that gives rise to these false explanations is a sympathy or an antipathy for a particular people or human group. In this case it is either the Arabs (with whom all Muslims are often identified) or the Zionists (with whom some are ready to identify all Jews). Thus, this type of explanation can be put into one of two categories: explanations derived from antipathy towards the Arabs and sympathy with the Jews, and explanations derived from hostility to the Jews, whether or not this be linked with some pro-Arab feeling.

In the first of these categories we have, first and foremost, the explanation of the conflict as being due to the alleged hatred felt by the Muslims (and by the Christian Arabs) for the Jews. This is said to be the primary phenomenon from which everything else follows. It is the thesis adopted, emotionally, by most Jews and by many non-Jews. Among the Jews of Europe, it is rooted in their tragic experience of modern anti-Semitism, which continues the Christian Judeophobia of earlier times. The Jews, a tiny minority, despised and restricted to contemptible occupations, were for centuries throughout the Christian world the object of a holy horror, a religious hatred, as the murderers of the Christ-God. When the effect of these denunciations weakened, with the withering-away of religious ideologies generally, this hatred was re-motivated by a pseudo-scientific racial theory which denounced the Jews as sub-men from the biological standpoint, maleficent creatures on the social plane, and aliens from the national angle. It is not surprising that the Jews in general came to see the whole world as leagued against them in universal hatred, whatever the concrete and theoretical pretexts of this hatred might be. Hostility to the Israeli settlement on Arab territory could not but appear to them as just a fresh manifestation of this general phenomenon. Rare are those who try to understand why others are hostile to them! The Jews were followed by the many non-Jews who had been conditioned by European history. Men and women of the Left had become accustomed to seeing in the Jews only victims of calumny, persecution and massacre. Profoundly ignorant of Near-Eastern conditions and of the history of the Zionist movement, of which they knew only the ideological Zionist version, they, too, were naturally inclined to see in hostility to Zionism only a fresh manifestation of anti-Semitic persecution. Oddly enough, a considerable section of the Right, formerly anti-Semitic, adopted the same thesis, now that the Jews were identified, essentially, with the Israelis, with whom they felt a sympathy the reasons for which have been analysed earlier.

The Jews of the Muslim world accepted this version more or less generally. That world had been governed for more than a thousand years by the regime of separate religious communities, each largely autonomous, dominated by a state which officially subscribed to Islam and accorded preponderance to the Muslim community over the rest. The Jews, a minority and subject community, had always been subordinated and often humiliated – differently from one country, epoch or situation to another. Familiar with the covert competition between these communities, in a setting that was usually one of tolerance but with flare-ups of violence from which they had suffered, and in certain regions deliberately humiliated, they were bound to see in the struggle going on in the Near East mainly a new phase in these relations of competition or conflict between communities.

This explanation of the Israeli-Arab conflict is nevertheless fundamentally false. Relations between communities in the Muslim world were indeed as has been described. They were not at all as idyllic as is alleged by Arab and Muslim apologetics, though neither were they marked by constant and brutal persecution of minorities, as Zionist apologetics claims. Just as in relations between nations, there was an infinitely varying mixture of hostility and peaceful coexistence.

The Muslim religious ideology is, of course, hostile to Judaism, but less so than Christianity. It allows to Judaism, as to Christianity, a certain share of essential validity, as being a monotheistic religion. In principle, it does not compel the adherents of these religions to convert to Islam and, in practice, it has tried to do this only very rarely. The Muslim conception of three legitimate faiths coexisting under Muslim domination and preponderance was much more favourable to the underdogs than was the Christian theory. This was usually true of Muslim practice as well, the best proof being the many occasions on which numbers of Jews persecuted in Christian states (as also Hungarian Protestants threatened by Catholic reaction) sought refuge in the Muslim world.

In any case, these features of the classical Muslim world were in process of changing in the course of the nineteenth century, especially in the region where Palestine is situated, the Arab Middle East. Evolution was proceeding in the direction of a secular society on the European pattern, starting with a tendency towards equality of status for the three communities. At the beginning of the twentieth century the Jews were, in *these* countries – let us be clear on the geographical point – in a peaceful, prosperous and often envied situation.

This evolution was partly checked, first by the reaction to the Zionist implantation in Palestine and then by the creation of the state of Israel. True, hostility to Zionism, like every similar movement, made use of every means available. It exploited what was left of the religious hostility to Judaism and the feelings of contempt towards the Jews which had been inherited from the medieval situation. It quoted those verses from the Koran which date from the period when the Prophet was combating the Jews of Medina. But there can be no doubt that the hostility felt towards any implanting of an alien state on Arab soil would have been the same whether those involved had been Chinese or Greeks, Christians or Buddhists. It would simply have found other texts, sacred or otherwise, to exploit.

Arab propaganda against Zionism also frequently utilizes arguments and images borrowed from European anti-Semitism. That is deeply disagreeable, but it does not justify one in identifying the two phenomena. European anti-Semitism, in the sense of hatred of the Jews in their very essence, considering them as possessed of a fundamentally maleficent nature, was not born of any actions or initiatives on the part of Jews. Whatever its real motives, the reproaches it levelled against the Jews were purely mythical or, if they referred to anything concrete, it was to phenomena and activities connected with the humiliating situation imposed on the Jews for more than a thousand years by European society. The prime responsibility lay with the latter. Arab anti-Zionism, on the contrary, even if it sometimes led to a comprehensive hatred of the Jews, originated in a concrete initiative taken by some Jews, to the detriment of the Arabs, namely, the plan to transform an Arab land into a Jewish state.

In the inevitable conflict that followed, between the Arabs and this Zionist enterprise, the Arabs had recourse to all the resources of the ideological war which normally accompanies every concrete conflict, and which inevitably piles argument upon argument without worrying about their value. In the past, likewise, every war throughout history, though perhaps fought for thoroughly insignificant reasons, has led to improper generalizations directed against the nature, the very essence, of the opponent. This is what I prefer to term 'war racialism'. Plentiful examples can be found in the 1914–18 war, among others. Among the Allies, it was common to think of the Germans as an accursed race. It was dangerous to point out that certain pure-bred Germans had been moderately competent musicians, for instance, or that others had made some small contribution to Western philosophy. This is a deplorable phenomenon, but apparently inherent in the human species as we know it. Looking for arguments and images, the Arabs drew, *inter alia*, upon the plentiful material supplied by European anti-Semitism. This would tend to show, incidentally, that their own arsenal was pretty poor where that item was concerned.

To conclude on this point, everything seems to indicate that, in the absence of the Zionist scheme and its realization, relations between Muslims, Christians and Jews in the Arab world would have developed in the direction of a general abatement of old conflicts and an equalization of status. Even if the drive towards Muslim 'integrism' which we observe at the present time had occurred anyway (and the Zionists' 'successes' are among the factors which have favoured it), with tendencies to lower the status of Jews and Christians in certain countries and during certain phases, it would not have resulted in so strong a hostility towards the Jews as has become apparent, here and there, since the establishment of the state of Israel.

In the same circles the conflict is often explained as being due to a vicious Arab expansionism, and we hear denunciations of Pan-Arabism, a tendency so named in order to call to mind phenomena from which Europe has suffered, such as Pan-Germanism and Pan-Slavism. However, without expressing any view as to the legitimacy or the realism of tendencies towards uniting all the Arab countries in a single state, these tendencies cannot (so far) be identified with a plan for expansion. The projects referred to have aimed at bringing together the Arab countries in the same way as the Italian nationalists strove to unite in one state all the regions where Italian was spoken. These projects were linked with an ideology which sometimes, in certain countries, aimed at denying the specific character of ethnic (but not religious) minorities and Arabizing them completely wherever they were Arabized only in part (the Berber speakers of the Maghreb), or else scarcely or not at all (the Blacks in the Sudan, the Kurds in Iraq). But these tendencies toward Arabization of minorities have been opposed within the Arab world itself, sometimes by great men of Arab nationalism like Nasser, and they have never met with such widespread approval as has opposition to the state of Israel. The reason for this is obvious. There was no ethnic minority of any significance in Palestine before the Zionist plan began to be realized. Palestine was Arab (with more than one religion) in the same sense that Venezia was Italian.

Among the fantastic explanations of the conflict which have been developed in the West in complete ignorance of Middle-Eastern conditions, one has often come upon the idea that hostility to Israel has resulted from a profound reaction to the progress which the Jewish settlement in Palestine is said to have brought with it. Some who think like this have in mind economic progress towards industrialization, others progress in democratic procedures, and yet others towards the abolition of classes, towards a socialist society. It is indubitable that Israel has brought to the Middle East the example of a more highly developed society, industrialized or on the way to becoming so, technically advanced, with a large and valuable technocracy. Her superiority in this respect over the surrounding countries is undeniable, and her victories are merely the manifestation of this fact on the military plane. But the case is exactly the same as that of the European colonies which did not eliminate the populations at whose expense they installed themselves. The technical lessons to be learned from the invader were in every case accepted, in principle at least. Nevertheless the local population revolted against the domination or annexation imposed from outside. The value of Israel's example is diminished to the extent that the Arabs can take their lessons from many other sources, from Europe direct or from America, for instance. They do not need to pay for them by the cession of territory. Moreover the enemy may be admired, even imitated, as witness France's attitude towards her conqueror Germany between 1871 and 1914. This in no way diminishes the hostility and desire for revenge which the conquered feel towards the victorious conqueror.

Again, the struggle is not a struggle for democracy. It is true enough that Israel has parliamentary institutions which may be regarded as models of their kind. This does not mean, any more than it does elsewhere, that the will of the majority of the population and its interests are bound to prevail over the wishes and interests of small but economically or politically powerful pressure-groups. In any case, Israel's political institutions are intimately bound up with her high level of economic development. Once again, there are other examples which the Arabs could turn to, and the value which they might attach to such institutions in no way reduces their hostility. It should be added that given the social, economic and cultural conditions of the Arab nations, the most perfect parliamentary system would only ensure that the most reactionary social groups would be guaranteed power. Parliamentary institutions are not the panacea that the Americans take them to be. This is well illustrated by the case of Egypt between 1923 and 1952. The illiteracy of the masses and the great social power wielded by the large landed proprietors meant that universal suffrage merely underwrote the political power of the latter class. Moreover when the state has to make choices which entail drastic limitations on popular aspirations in order to make the investment necessary to development, it may be said that parliamentary institutions are the enemy of economic development.

Neither does the conflict reside in the struggle between Israeli socialism and the reactionary or Fascist Arab societies, as one version fairly widely accepted in some Left-wing circles would have it. The Zionists settled in Palestine as pioneers of a Jewish state, not as apostles of socialism. I have already given my opinion on the interpretation to be placed on the socialist ideological currents in Israel and on the socialist sector of the Israeli economy. At the very least, it may be said without reservation that Israeli society is not as a whole a socialist society, and that the state of Israel's foreign policy is not directed towards the extension of the socialist system. The Arabs are opposing not the propagation of socialism, but an expansionist encroachment on their national territory. If the Arabs wanted a model, they could find it elsewhere; even if they were to imitate some of Israel's achievements in some respects, this would not weaken their hostility.

Thus, the Arab reaction against Israel is not derived from hatred of industrial society, parliamentary democracy or socialism. It has involved states or political forces among the Arabs which were keen supporters of these three tendencies or structures. True, in recent years, it has become the fashion, in the Arab countries as elsewhere, to denounce them, at any rate in the form which they have assumed in the West and, consequently, in the West's prolongation in Israel. Israel has come to represent one of the most highly developed crystallizations of the vices which are ascribed to the world of Europe and America. But the reaction against Israel began well before that way of thinking became predominant, and it continues to involve firm supporters of industrialization, parliamentarianism and socialism. Once again, the essential cause of hostility towards Israel lies elsewhere.

Finally, wide sections of Western opinion have tended, or still tend, to see the conflict as an effect of manipulations by international great powers, political or financial. Israelis, Palestinians and Arabs are seen as mere pawns, conscious or unconscious, in a game which is bigger than themselves. This interpretation enjoys the advantage of satisfying a deep-seated human taste for explaining things in terms of mysterious machinations. For the Left, besides, there was the temptation to re-discover here once more the usual mythology according to which all peoples are, by nature, guiltless of any warlike tendency, and are drawn into wars against their will, by the diabolical manoeuvres of profiteers. For a long time this was one of the ideological means whereby the Western Left avoided facing up to the idea, repugnant to the Left's hasty manicheism, that Jews – victims by their very essence – might be engaged in an activity of the colonial type. There was therefore often talk on the Left about the perfidious intrigues of the British imperialists and, much more vaguely, without going into the details of the mech-anism, about a struggle waged by the oil companies. At all events, it was believed, if the Jews and Arabs of Palestine had been left face to face without any outside interference, they would certainly have come to an agreement. This mythological picture drawn by the Left stood in contrast to no less fallacious pictures drawn by the Right. Clearly, it was easy to put the blame on Jewish finance. But not all on the Right remained faithful on all points to their basic anti-Semitism of pre-Second-World-War days. Many of them, as has been said, had become or remained Arab-haters first and foremost, while the Soviet Union was still their devilish enemy in perpetuity, engaged in inspiring the most diverse manoeuvres directed against the interests of the West. Everything, therefore, had to be explained by these manoeuvres.

There is no reason to doubt that in certain phases of the conflict, in one way or another, the great powers, especially Britain and the U.S.S.R., did not, to say the least, exercise an influence for peace. They may sometimes have thrown oil on the flames. This may have been true, too, on some occasions, of the policy followed by the big oil companies. At other moments, however, all these forces were, on the contrary, embarrassed by this incessant conflict, and took steps directed towards peacemaking. An attempt has been made earlier to show what their respective positions were, and what their influence was, at various times.

However, it is possible to manipulate over a long period only those who let themselves be manipulated. The hostility of the Palestine Arabs to the installation on their territory of a movement aiming at the crea-tion of a Jewish state is a reaction which we have tried to show to be quite normal, in accordance with the criteria of normality in reactions between peoples at the end of the nineteenth century and in the twentieth. This reaction began under the Ottoman Empire. While it may have been encouraged or reinforced by this or that factor and by these or those agents, they did not create it.

To the series of explanations resulting from sympathy, whether interested or not, with the Jews, or from a readiness to take sides, directly or indirectly, against the Arabs, must be added another series inspired by the opposite sentiments and interests.

Naturally, the supporters of classical anti-Semitism were able to find in this conflict an illustration of their familiar thesis of an international Jewish plot to secure world domination. This thesis might have a religious basis (the Jews' alleged hatred of everything Christian or Muslim) or it might be based on a secular argument. In this connection, that classic forgery, the 'Protocols of the Elders of Zion', might be brought into play.

This thesis cannot stand up to rational examination of the most elementary sort, on this point any better than on others. For a long time the Zionist scheme had no opponents more resolute than those to be found in Jewish circles, whether they were clergy or were laymen determined on more or less thorough-going assimilation. Those Jewish communities that were relatively satisfied with their lot showed lukewarmness, at the very least, towards the Zionist organizations, which often deplored the lack of support they encountered in such quarters.

It is true that, after the creation of the state of Israel, and especially after the war of June 1967 and even more after the Palestinian threat had become more credible, Jewish solidarity with the Jewish state became widespread and immensely stronger. But this was a phenomenon which manifested itself on such a scale only *after* the process of conflict had already developed very far – a phenomenon, again, which was predictable and normal in the circumstances in question, given what we know the usual reactions of human communities to be, even if we deplore their blindness. It was not at all a matter of a plan concerted by some mysterious centre controlling the reactions, throughout the world, of all the Jews, whatever meaning we give to that term and whatever the relations of the individuals concerned with the Jewish religious community or the many organizations (as varied and contrasting as possible) which attempt to mobilize them.

Furthermore, in so far as a relative degree of solidarity was secured, this was directed not towards world domination but towards the Jewish political community which had been forged in Palestine. Although the majority of the Jews had been reticent towards the establishment of this community, the Zionist organizations gradually succeeded in convincing many of them that if it were to disappear, even without any accompanying human catastrophe, that would constitute a threat to their own security. The threats uttered, or the political formulations propounded, by the Arabs convinced the majority, moreover, that it was indeed a question of a human catastrophe of which the Jews of Palestine would be physically the victims. That could not fail to provoke general repulsion among persons whose near and dear ones, relatives and friends, had recently been victims of a massacre on a huge scale. There is nothing in all this development that presupposes anything but phenomena well known in other contexts, nothing that gives support to the idea that the conflict is to be explained by a special maleficence on the part of the Jews, mobilized in obedience to a concerted plan. It is enough to consider the very real Zionist plan, the sole aim of which was to establish a Jewish state in an Arab country.

An explanation which sometimes takes forms similar to the foregoing is very widespread at present in the ranks of the international Left. This is the explanation based on the 'myth' of Imperialism. It is sometimes accepted in the West out of unconscious antipathy to the Jews, and often through instinctive sympathy with the Arabs. This is the favourite explanation among Arab and Muslim nationalists. Generally, though, what we have here is a consequence of support for a great cause which transcends by far those two groups, Arabs and Jews: an attractive and worthy cause which seems to me truly deserving of profound commitment. In the usual way, however, it has undergone an ideological shaping which, starting out from very real facts, ends in a veritable mythology. This mythology has been widely accepted by many enthusiasts without any critical spirit; it has been legitimized in learned economic works, many of which, though valid, contain extrapolations that are open to criticism; and it has been applied in a mechanical way to the elements of the problem which concerns us.

I am not saying that this is a myth in the colloquial sense of the word, that is, a mere fable. I am using the concept 'myth' in Sorel's sense, to mean a mobilizing ideological theme which may correspond to many real facts and may even inspire valid strategies. But the ideological shaping has entailed extrapolations and distortions, the mechanism of which I have just briefly indicated.

In its application to the conflict in the Middle East the myth in question presents the Jewish colony established in Palestine, and which has taken the form of the state of Israel, as a tentacle or bastion of 'Imperialism'. This world force is supposed to have assigned to Israel the task of combating, in this particular spot, the liberation of the Arab peoples, Arab unity and Arab socialism. It is regarded as just one specific example of the constant struggle being waged by Imperialism against the efforts of the peoples of the Third World to emancipate themselves. In view of the tremendous vogue it enjoys, this thesis calls for fairly close rational analysis.

Imperialisms are very real tendencies on the part of certain powerful states, under certain conditions, to expand at the expense of other states and other peoples. In ancient times there were the imperialisms of Egypt, Assyria, Persia, Macedonia and Rome, among others. In the nineteenth century the European countries with a capitalist structure manifested this tendency, and they even legitimized it and furnished it with a theory. They annexed most of the countries of what is now called the Third World, turning them into colonies, and brought the rest into strict dependence. It seems probable that their capitalist structure gave rise to economic mechanisms which contributed to urging them in this direction.

In any case, before, during and after the period of direct colonization, it is certain that the crushing superiority acquired by the industrial capitalist states in the economic sphere enabled them, even without using military force, to dominate almost absolutely the world's economic mechanisms. In this way they were able, at the very least, to exert very strong influence on the policies, political and other, of all other states. Marxist economists have tried to prove that this world economic 'centre' has been able not merely to exercise dominating pressure on the underdeveloped 'periphery' but also to 'plunder' the latter, to exploit it in the Marxist sense of the word. This means that the centre lives on the fruits of the labour of the masses of the Third World, that it grows rich at their expense, that its own citizens profit from this process. Moreover, this mechanism is said to bring about a 'development of underdevelopment', preventing the underdeveloped countries from engaging in the process of economic development which has enriched the centre, keeping them in a dependent situation and increasing their misery to an ever greater extent.

This is what is supposed to make it possible to designate this world centre as Imperialism *par excellence*. This Marxist denunciation has had a huge and understandable success in the Third World, even among social groups having no sympathy with the revolutionary tendencies suggested by Marxist analysis on the *internal* plane. It is, indeed, the only explanation offered to them which does not bring into question factors such as the cultural distinctions to which they are attached, theses of a racialist sort, and so on. It offers them, too, an immense hope, since the overthrow of this Western supremacy is something which is conceivable, and which would open up possibilities for an evolution of these countries towards independence and increased well-being. It suggests and justifies a militant mobilization which provides a reason for living to many individuals in the Third World and on the Left. It offers to the ideological intellectuals the opportunity for almost infinite discourse, together with pride of place in this mobilization.

To the writer of these lines it seems that this analysis contains at least a good deal of truth, but those who have adopted it have drawn from it a picture of the facts which is to a large extent mythological. In conformity with the universal tendencies of ideological thought, this pressure from the industrial capitalist centre is depicted as possessing a unity of leadership and planning which is both improbable and contradicted by the facts. The imperialist and capitalist enemy of the peoples' aspirations to liberty and equality is depicted as a sort of monster with one head and brain but equipped with numerous tentacles. The latter are said to obey without hesitation the orders that emanate from this brain (which is situated somewhere between the Pentagon and Wall Street), without any will-power of their own. Israel is supposed to be one of those tentacles, charged with special responsibility for putting down the anti-imperialist revolution in the Arab countries. This crude schema, mythological and pseudo-Marxist, is obviously false.

The industrial capitalist states are many and their interests diverge on numerous points, even if what they have in common often impels them to act in concerted fashion and, in some cases, to form political and military alliances among themselves. The economic mechanism of capitalist production can give rise to different political options. Tendencies to take advantage of a position of strength (economic, political or military) in order to dominate other peoples existed before and exist outside the capitalist system of production. The countries now called 'socialist' clearly exhibit such tendencies. Their economic system may be called 'state capitalism', as is done by Left-wing economists who are not Communists, thus putting the blame on the capitalist system as a whole. But we know of no concretely realized economic system today apart from these two types and combinations thereof. One may, of course, imagine that another system, one 'truly' socialist, is possible: for the future no possibility can be excluded. But no convincing argument has been put forward to show that a country living in accordance with such a system, if it possessed some superior power, would not be moved to operate mechanisms of domination externally. The experience of human history tends to persuade us to the contrary: of the universality of the tendency to yield to 'selfish interest – attempts to saddle others', as Lenin wrote in 1916, foreseeing the reality of this tendency in the case of the victorious proletariat in a socialist revolution. 'Just because the proletariat has carried out a social revolution,' he said, 'it will not become holy and immune from errors and weaknesses.' * Denouncing 'Imperialism' as such, leaving out such adjectives as 'capitalist', 'American' and so on – in practice, most often referring to American actions, but also amalgamating with these, in a vague, woolly and incoherent way, actions taken by European capitalist states – means implying an automatism of the economic structure that animates all these actions, and seeing in them the result of an evil master-plan conceived heaven knows where or by whom. This is a set of irrational ideological discourses which, though certainly useful for mobilizing the masses, must, in this form, be rejected by the rational analyst. He can only try to sort out the valid elements in it and draw conclusions therefrom.

As regards the application of this schema to Israel, one must at least modify the analysis, without, as has been said, rejecting those valid elements which it includes, under the influence of a Western ideological conformism which is no less given to myth-making and to a mechanical and crude conception of Soviet imperialism, seen as the main enemy to be fought. The Zionist plan and the creation of the state of Israel are processes which cannot be understood except in the context of Western capitalist imperialism. I believe that I have proved this in another place.† However, the Zionists had their own specific aim, the creation of a Jewish state. They conceived this plan as one to be realized *in Palestine*, and that choice of location possessed some realism only in the setting of European colonialist conceptions of the nineteenth and twentieth centuries. The realization and consolidation of the plan could take place only if it was fitted into the imperialist activity of Britain's rulers, and subsequently, by securing support from American forces moving in the same direction, along with transient backing from the U.S.S.R., which was also motivated by desire to extend its influence beyond its own borders. However, one must repeat, the Zionists'

* Lenin, 'The Discussion on Self-Determination Summed Up', *Collected Works* (4th ed.), vol. 22, London, 1964, p. 353.

† M. Rodinson, op. cit., pp. 17–88.

objective was always the Jewish state, and nothing else. The Zionist and Israeli leaders made use of the imperialist forces, just as the latter made use of them, with each side endeavouring, in the course of cease-less haggling, to avoid compromising its own aims by associating them with those of its allies.

This means, in particular, that Israel, even with all the hindrances resulting from its dependent situation, has its own will and its own aims. It does not automatically obey all orders received from the U.S.A., any more than from the monster called 'Imperialism'. It is interested above all in its own survival. Its expansion does not result from any irresistible tendency, any essence or nature connected with its alleged imperialist character. It results from an inner aspiration to achieve maximum realization of the objectives set out from the start by the Zionist nationalist ideology. The decisions taken to expand, on each historical occasion, have had to overcome much resistance from relatively moder-ate Zionist leaders, and circumstances have favoured this expansion.

Israel has no interest in Arab liberation, Arab unity, or the revolu-tionary and socialist movements among the Arabs, except in so far as they affect its own survival and consolidation. It assumes the role of 'gendarme of reaction' only in certain circumstances and when its own interest, direct or indirect, requires this.

All these explanatory theses are thus seen to be fallacious, whether their source lies in a false notion of historical and social causality in general; in preconceived general ideas applied mechanically to events in the Near East, without knowledge of their actual conditions; in sympathy or antipathy for one side or the other; or in several of these factors at once. It seems to me that they do not shake the fundamental explanation which I have put forward: the reaction of a people to the occupation of its territory by foreigners.

The parties to the conflict themselves often make use of some of these explanations, which are always touched with an apologetic colouring that favours one side or the other. The Arabs naturally sup-port the explanation which I believe correct, while imagining that they strengthen it by also using more debatable arguments. The Israelis generally repudiate it, but many of them accept it with various modifi-cations and some even accept it completely. They merely justify their occupation of Palestine with certain arguments of their own. In any case, both here and there, we find an efflorescence of apologetical themes developing around fundamental theses, as happens in every struggle. These borrow a great deal from the fallacious explanations set out above. Going beyond an estimation of the facts, they aim to endow the struggle with the character of a sacred duty which must entail a total mobilization. There is a move from the category of causal explanation, more or less correct or incorrect, to the category of morals, to which belong the concepts of right and duty. These apologetical arguments are often accepted by outsiders – especially, though not solely, by unconditional supporters of one or other of the two parties to the conflict.

On the Israeli and Zionist side, we therefore see a development of the theme of an eternal and unconditional right to Palestine on the part of the Jews. When this thesis is defended with the religious argument of a divine promise, as happens not only with religious Jews but also with Christians (especially Protestants) who ascribe a value of supernatural truth to the texts of the Old Testament, there is nothing to be said in reply. One cannot argue about faith. Let us note, however, that there are still some religious Jews – all that are left of a majority of only a few decades ago – who interpret these texts as *ruling out* any anticipation, by human political initiatives, of the 'return' to Palestine, prophesied for the end of time, through God's direct action. Many Christians, when they show some interest in their religious texts, share this negative interpretation.

When the Jews' right to Palestine is defended by secular arguments it is, on the contrary, easy to show the weakness of the thesis. It is difficult, moreover, to appeal to general rules of what is right where this matter is concerned. If we set aside a clear supernatural decree, no authority is left, in heaven or on earth, that can define what are the rights and duties of nations. International public law is a man-made affair, constantly being revised, and greatly influenced by concrete situations which it often legitimizes after the event. It includes matters still in dispute, with opposite standpoints taken up by jurists.

Never, in any case, has either theory or practice assumed the eternal right of a given people to a territory which it once occupied, even for a long period, after an interruption of two thousand years which have seen the prolonged existence of another people on this territory (using here the word 'people' in the sense discussed above, page 316). We do not find Arabs claiming sovereignty over Spain, which was, to a large extent at least, Arabized and the seat of Arab states during more than seven centuries. Celtic Ireland does not claim the whole of England, which was Celtic before the fifth and sixth centuries. Nobody denies the right of the Spaniards and the English – who are what they are by virtue of their cultural, linguistic and historical identification, regardless of the share in their genetic inheritance contributed by earlier genes, Hispanic, Gothic and Arab in Spain, Celtic, pre-Celtic or Anglo-Saxon in England – to preserve the whole of their territory, with their language and traditions. Nobody thinks of declaring it their duty to hand over a piece of Spanish or English territory so that an Arab or Celtic state can be established there. If international public law does not deal with this problem, it is because it assumes, as a postulate which it does not even expect to be questioned, that a people has an absolute right to the land on which it has been settled for many generations.

Let us note that, fortunately, Zionist activity is not in practice entirely faithful to its own theory. If the right to Palestine is based on the presence there of the Jewish people in ancient times, the territory claimed should also embrace the present Kingdom of Jordan, which was occupied for centuries by Jewish tribes and formed part of the Israelitish kingdoms. The Revisionist party of Jabotinsky (which is continued by Menachem Begin's Heruth) was being logical, in the days of the British Mandate, when, together with the religious fundamentalists, it laid claim to *both* banks of the Jordan. The majority of the Jewish colony, however, followed those who confined their demands, between 1948 and 1967, to the territory which had by that time been acquired by military means, and then, after 1967, to the whole of the west bank of the Jordan. Very few, nowadays, speak of occupying King Hussein's kingdom. This means that they implicitly accept that 'historic rights' are not enough to provide a basis for a claim in the present.

Zionist and pro-Zionist apologetics embroider a great deal on the theme of the aspiration of the Jews for nearly two thousand years to return to the land of their ancestors, and on the presence of a small number of Jews in Palestine all through the ages since Antiquity. A strong faith is needed to see in this even the shadow of an argument. No juridical doctrine bases a right on a mere aspiration: no judge, anywhere, would assign the smallest bit of land to a family because they can prove that they had always wanted to occupy it. And although there have always been Italians in France, ever since the fall of the Roman Empire, no Italian political entity has ever used that fact as an argument for asserting rights over France!

The same type of apologetics lists a number of complaints against the Arabs, designed to show that they did not deserve to keep Palestine. Here a procedure is fallen into which cannot be described otherwise than as racist. The Arabs are said to have many faults: carelessness, laziness, fanaticism, aggressiveness, a propensity to quarrel, a tendency to favour out-of-date attitudes; and so on. Some concede that this is due not so much to their genetic inheritance as to the traditional structures of their society, or to the influence of Islam, seen as detrimental. In any case, the Arabs, it is said, allowed a Palestine that was rich and prosperous when inhabited by Jews to sink into decline. In their hands, it is said, Palestine became a desert. Quotations from disgusted travellers in the nineteenth century and at the beginning of the twentieth are adduced in support of this indictment.

All that is merely so much empty ideological discourse. No one has the power to sit in sovereign judgement on the qualities and faults of peoples, so as to reward or punish them, even if the validity of this ethnic characterization were better founded than, in fact, it is. What we have here is merely what is said by conquerors in order to legitimize their conquests – nothing more. During the Second World War the Germans propounded a similar judgement of the faults of the French, who, they said, had made very poor use of the possibilities of their territory, owing to their inadequate sense of organization and discipline. No one has been able seriously to uphold the notion of a tribunal empowered to deprive a people of its territory because of its moral defects.

The idea that the Jews alone are capable of bringing prosperity to the land of Palestine is obviously fantastic. The Jews' own sacred books are there to disprove it. The ancient people of Israel wanted to conquer Canaan because the Canaanites had made of it, before they arrived, a land 'flowing with milk and honey'. In the epoch of Christian, and later of Muslim, predominance in Palestine, many documents point to activity in agriculture and the crafts at a reasonable and sometimes a remarkable level. If this tendency was on the downgrade from the nineteenth century onwards, this was due to the Ottoman administration, which became extremely bad in that period. But Palestine was certainly not a desert when the Jewish colonization began, as Zionist propaganda alleges. It was, of course, an underdeveloped country, and from that standpoint could fill Europeans and Americans with disdain and disgust. But its production was not by any means negligible. Let us merely mention here that the German scholar Gustaf Dalman, who lived in Palestine from 1902 to 1914, was able to publish an unfinished eight-volume work of more than 3,000 pages (*Arbeit und Sitte in Palästina*, Gütersloh, 1928–42) on the farming and handicraft techniques practised in this so-called desert. Full details are given regarding agriculture, milling, wine-growing and olive-growing, the raising of chickens and pigeons, weaving and other manufacturing activities, and so on.

Zionist propaganda has succeeded so well in propagating throughout the world this picture of a desert Palestine transformed at last by Jewish hands into a rich and prosperous country, that it has become a cliché accepted as evidence without any need for proof. It would surprise many people, and evoke a sceptical response, if one were to tell them, for instance, that the famous Jaffa oranges are not the creation of Jewish technique. It is an indisputable fact of history, however, that the growing of these oranges was begun and long continued by Arabs. In 1880, when the orange groves were entirely in Arab hands, they included 765,000 trees, and thirty million oranges were harvested there and, in part, exported to Europe.*

The argument derived from Jewish sufferings is based, alas, on less mythical foundations. The anti-Semitic persecutions of the late nineteenth century and the early twentieth century, and the great massacre of millions of Jews in the countries under Hitlerite domination, are sad and massive realities. It is indeed true that Judeophobic sentiments still exist in many countries, that they have been exploited quite recently, here and there, for political ends, and that we cannot rule out the possibility of renewed developments in the direction of Nazism. But one cannot jump quickly and rashly from recognizing such facts to legitimizing the construction of a Jewish state in general, and still less to the establishment of this Jewish state in Palestine.

In the nineteenth century the solution of the Jewish question seemed certainly to be, in Western Europe, the assimilation of the Jews into the societies in which they lived. This did not necessarily mean breaking with the faith and practices of the Jewish religion, or renouncing Jewish historical traditions and the forms of conduct these had shaped, even if many persons classified as Jews were able freely to break with some or all of these. This Western model seemed certain to spread gradually all over the world.

As we have said, however, evolution in this direction was checked.

* The orange groves of Jaffa go back to the beginning of the eighteenth century – see S. Tolkowsky, *The Gateway of Palestine: A History of Jaffa*, London, 1924, pp. 140 ff., 178–81 and 184–5 – or perhaps even to the seventeenth century – see S. Tolkowsky, *Hesperides: A History of the Culture and Use of Citrus Fruits*, London, 1938, p. 236 and Elisée Reclus, *Nouvelle Géographie Universelle*, vol. IX, *L'Asie antérieure*, Paris, 1884, p. 817 (*The Earth and Its Inhabitants: The Universal Geography*, vol. IX, *South-West Asia*, London, n.d., p. 425). There were no Jews in Jaffa – an ancient anathema kept them from there – before the 1830s, and a Jewish community did not develop there until the 1880s (see Tolkowsky, 1924, op. cit., pp. 155 ff., 159 ff., 163 and 174).

Perhaps it will one day be resumed. For a long time, though, we must expect that a Jewish identity will persist in many countries. Whether or not they adhere to religious Judaism, and whether or not they have retained, or even developed, cultural traces and forms of conduct inherited from their religious Jewish ancestors, many will continue to be seen as members of a specific Jewish community and, consequently, will see themselves as such. The ideology at present in vogue which accepts the right to difference, to the coexistence of many communities with more or less differing cultures, as in the U.S.A. (a model which is being widely imitated), may result in this situation not creating too many problems; but one cannot rule out the possibility of hostile reactions.

Can a Jewish state, though, offer a guarantee against this possibility? We may doubt it. Who can seriously suppose that Hitler would have shrunk from his massacre of the Jews because a Jewish state had already been formed in Palestine? It will be answered that this would at least have provided a place of refuge. In that way we should have been spared the painful and often atrocious scenes of Jewish refugees fleeing towards inaccessible places of safety during the last world war and the succeeding years, and being repulsed wherever they went.

It has to be said that the Zionist organizations bear a big share of responsibility for those tragedies. They urged the refugees to insist on Palestine as their only acceptable destination, and contributed to dissuading certain governments from offering other openings. Even, however, without discussing the Zionist theses on this point, it is not certain that a Jewish state, by itself, can constitute a permanently accessible place of refuge for Jews who are persecuted or dissatisfied with their lot in other countries. The existence of the Vietnamese, Cambodian and Chinese states has not saved millions of members of these ethnic groups either from fleeing from them in dramatic circumstances or from being subjected to persecution and massacre when outside, without being able to obtain protection. During the two thousand years when there was no Jewish state, Jews persecuted in one country or expelled therefrom have always been able to find refuge in others.

An Arab-American ideologist once maintained that he would be opposed to a Jewish state even if it were situated on the moon, because he is against any state based on religion (Pakistan, too). One may disagree with this view, and accept that there is nothing scandalous about the existence of a Jewish state as such, even if, as a Jew aiming at assimilation, for example, one may be aware of the ill consequences for one's own choice that result from this state's existence. Any dissatisfied group of human beings who wish to acquire an independent political existence ought to be able to do this by leaving the political entity in which they live. But common ethics demands that they refrain from doing this at the expense of other peoples. States cannot be founded on the moon. The earth is completely divided up. Any new state can be founded only on a territory either conceded by its present possessor or else wrested from that possessor.

Well, the Zionists – despite Herzl himself and some others – insisted on having Palestine. Regardless of the many warnings voiced even in Jewish circles and among the trends of non-political Zionism, the fact that Palestine was occupied by another people was ignored, and the state was established in Palestine, thanks to outside powers which protected the formation in that country of a large-scale Jewish base.

The result is now clear, and could not have been other than it is. In 1926 the old theoretician of German Social Democracy, Karl Kautsky, wrote: 'Jewish colonization in Palestine must collapse as soon as the Anglo-French hegemony over Asia Minor (including Egypt) [i.e. the Near East] collapses, and this is merely a question of time, perhaps of the very near future.' * Whatever the future may hold, it is at least doubtful that the life of a Jew in Israel will be more secure or, in general, better than in a lot of other countries. Many Israelis have now replied to this question 'with their feet'. Emigration to other countries by Israeli Jews has always been substantial. At the beginning of 1980 the immigration commission of the Knesset estimated it at a total of 400,000 since the creation of the state, or about 13 per cent of the country's Jewish population. Because the situation in Israel is now better known in the U.S.S.R., the passionate idealization of the country that was current at first has given way to more reasonable views. Thus, during the first quarter of that same year, 70 per cent of the Jews who left the U.S.S.R. headed for the U.S.A. In the last week of March an all-time record was achieved, when out of 102 Jewish emigrants who arrived at Vienna, only four chose to go on to Israel. A large group in the Israeli Parliament, together with various associations, indignantly urged the government of Israel to intervene to prevent philanthropic societies from helping these refugees, and to obtain the insertion of some restrictions in the new American law welcoming refugees, which

* Karl Kautsky, *Are the Jews a Race?*, London, 1926, p. 211 ff. This passage appears in the additions and changes made by Kautsky to his 1914 article, 'Rasse und Judentum', *Ergänzungshefte zur Neuen Zeit*, no. 20, pp. 1–94, one of the most remarkable restatements of this question.

facilitated this turning-away from Israel.* Rarely has one seen a more literal application of the Gospel formula which in former times was applied in the repression of heretics: *Compelle intrare!* – 'Compel them to come in!' What power can an ideal retain when it has to be imposed by coercion?

When one sets against the 'right' of the Jewish people to their own state the right of the Palestinian Arabs to remain in their ancestral land, Zionist apologetics often replies by referring to the huge amount of space at the disposal of the Arab people and, nowadays, the wealth of this space in terms of oil resources. Could not the Arabs give up a little bit of this territory to unfortunate victims? This argument has slightly more validity than the others, and some Arab leaders are themselves sensible of that fact. It is indeed possible to dream of a world in which resources, including land, would be shared out more equitably. But what happens in practice is very different, and one cannot contemplate persuading a people to make such a sacrifice willingly if nobody sets it an example. This is particularly so when the people of whom such a sacrifice is required have not been consulted but have had it imposed upon them by force in the recent past; when, too, those who require a fresh sacrifice to be made by the same people present their demand in a most coercive way, allying themselves with that people's enemies and trying to profit from the strength of the latter; and especially when those demanding the sacrifice seem to the people concerned to be enjoying, if not at the outset a state of their own, at least advantages (increased by propaganda and imagination) which appear enviable, namely, participation in the freedom and prosperity of the industrial capitalist world.

Golda Meir and many others used to claim, when one wished to speak more particularly of the rights of the Palestinian people to Palestine, that no such people existed. Nobody had spoken of them when, as a young Zionist militant, she landed in Palestine in 1921. To be sure, few spoke of the Palestinians in her circles. To be sure, Palestine was then only a small region of Arab Asia, a southern district of Syria. Other ways of dividing up that area which had been detached from the Ottoman Empire were possible at that time, but the fact is that the way it was divided up, thanks to the action of the European powers, was the way with which we are familiar. Frontiers were established which created, in the usual manner, networks of interests and aspirations. Within these frontiers each section of the Arab people in Asia has experienced its own destiny during the last sixty years. While Palestine

* *Le Monde*, 4 April 1980, p. 3.

always had certain specific features marking it off from the rest of Syria and the Fertile Crescent (the Jews are not well placed to deny that), the Arab people of this province experienced a reinforcement of that relative specificity. They had, in fact, to confront two major problems unknown to the other Arabs of Asia – the Syrians, Lebanese and Iraqis: namely, direct British administration and Zionist immigration.

There remains an argument of greater weight. This is the authority of the United Nations Organization, which created the state of Israel by its decision of 29 November 1947. International law must be respected: a recognized nation must not be attacked. We may pass over the fact that this legalistic argument is often put forward by revolutionaries who everywhere denounce the status quo, the solutions established and consecrated by law. We may accept the argument, even while smiling, for example, at the passionate expression, used by a Zionist philosopher of strongly revolutionary outlook, for whom violation of this legality by the Arabs would signify a return to the law of the jungle, to the so-called primitive epoch described by Hobbes, wherein man was a wolf to man. Philosophers are given to making such leaps out of the realm of reason. We may consider that the Arabs were wrong to challenge the decision of the United Nations. However, to excuse them, it ought to be noted all the same, that the U.N.O. of 1947 was a machine dominated by the great powers, and the Third World of colonies and dependent countries was hardly represented in it, so that this decision was, in practice, a *Diktat* by the dominant members. It should be pointed out also that Israel has been no less contemptuous of the U.N.O.'s recommendations. In 1948 it went beyond the limits laid down in the partition plan propounded by the international Areopagus, and in 1967, as we have seen, it went still further beyond them. It has treated with the greatest contempt the U.N.O.'s decisions on Jerusalem, which, under that same plan, was to constitute a separate entity. Israel even displays great indignation because foreign countries are reluctant to establish their legations in Jerusalem rather than in Tel Aviv, so as not to seem to endorse this violation of U.N.O. decisions. How dare these countries flout the will of the Israeli people on account of some miserable decisions taken by an assembly of foreigners? It must be admitted that such reactions can discourage some people from supporting Israel when it invokes international law, but, at bottom, this alters nothing. Either one accepts the validity of the decision of November 1947, and then Israel should withdraw to the lines laid down by that decision, when most states will support it in defending its existence within those new, reduced limits (perhaps subject to modification by mutual consent); or one does not accept that decision, in which case there is no rule to which reference can be made, and there is no reason to be excessively indignant about the Arabs' reactions.

Confronting the Zionist-Israeli apologetics we have, of course, the Arab apologetics. The Arabs have less need than the Zionists to resort to secondary explanations, dubious rationalizations and apologetical developments. Generally recognized international morality accepts (on the plane of principle, at any rate) a people's right to keep its territory and defend it against invaders. It should therefore be sufficient for the Arabs to bring forward precise historical facts in order to justify their attitudes, at least as regards principles, if not as regards all the initiatives, strategies, tactics and programmes that these attitudes have inspired. But every political movement always tends to develop an apologia for *all* its actions and *all* the ideas it has expressed. Its ideologists (who have an interest in the matter) also tend to add arguments one to another, beyond what is necessary, to extrapolate and to exaggerate their side's merits and the misdeeds of the adversary, provoking a scepticism which may extend to the sound points in their arguments.

The Arabs have not proved an exception to these general laws of ideological struggle. Moreover, a starting point was ready to hand in the previous ideology of Arab nationalism. Like every other nationalism (and Jewish nationalism in particular), one of its favourite tendencies is to indulge in an 'auto-apologia' of the people concerned, overflowing with narcissism. The Arabs of the past, the present and the future are decked out with all the virtues and all the qualities. They have never wanted to do anything but good, are disinterested, have produced the most admirable ideas, the finest culture, and so on. All their misfortunes and all their apparent defects result from external influences. On the other hand, the enemy who attacks such a people cannot but be hateful in the extreme and characterized by the vilest faults. Its role in history can only be negative.

This manichean description of oneself and of one's opponent is to be found among all peoples, especially in phases of nascent nationalism and fierce struggle. As regards the conflict with which we are concerned, it will be enough to mention that the Arabs often endow it, in their propaganda, with an almost cosmic dimension. The vestiges of old religious antagonisms can help them here, and likewise the new theories about imperialism. The Zionist scheme is no longer seen as something that can be criticized, a mistake, an unjustified act of aggression. It is an unimaginable monstrosity, an unprecedented atrocity, the suffering of the Palestinian people is without parallel in the world, and so forth. The details of military operations and Israeli actions are said to reveal unheard-of atrocities. All the faults, defects, inadequacies, contradictions and misfortunes of the Arab countries are often attributed to the Zionist encroachment, so that getting rid of *that* has become problem number one – which provides a facile and precious excuse. Extrapolations of this sort are, of course, exaggerated. There can be no doubt that, if Israel were to disappear, the tensions and contradictions between Arab countries, their internal social and political difficulties, and those concerned with relations with other countries would still remain. Every war and every occupation are, always and everywhere, accompanied by more or less atrocious acts. The Zionist scheme has as its principal fault that it has ignored the rights of the Arabs to Palestine. Ignoring or despising other people's rights and exaggerating one's own are, unfortunately, very frequent phenomena. The Arabs, too, have behaved in that way, and some of them can be reproached, even today, with actions of the same sort – towards the Kurds, for instance. No people is everywhere and always innocent. Having taken some trouble (and suffered many attacks in consequence) to express publicly the view that the Jews are not to be considered a sacred people, I find it all the easier to dissociate myself from equally excessive apologetics on behalf of the Arabs. They do not constitute, any more than the Jews, a quasi-divine group miraculously free from the vices, individual and collective, of our common humanity.

However, while all this Arab apologetics may arouse scepticism and annoyance, even irritation and disgust, especially when it emanates from ideologist intellectuals who expound it in order to derive personal profit and prestige therefrom, we must not forget that the initial reaction against the Zionist encroachment was due to perfectly legitimate motives, which it is for the most sober analysis to bring out.

From the description of the conflict given above follows the whole dynamic of the reactions and policies applied by the two sides. It is of no use to be surprised at them or to become indignant about them, in detail. They are the logical consequence of the fundamental theme of the conflict.

The Arabs have always recoiled as far as possible from accepting the *fait accompli* carried out at their expense and without their agreement by Israeli power, backed up by the support of the European and American world. At every Israeli victory, the most conciliatory of them have resigned themselves to accepting the previous victory but have attempted to reject all the consequences of the latest one. They have always been one war behind, because their protests against the encroachments on what they believe to be their rights have been continuous.

Until 1948 they refused to countenance the seizure of Palestine territory to form a Jewish state. They therefore fought against the Balfour Declaration, which was apparently intended to bring this about (a unilateral act on the part of Great Britain, be it once more noted). At least, this was the interpretation of the Balfour Declaration to which they objected. They directed their efforts towards limiting Jewish immigration, either by appealing to the British, or, as some of them did, by negotiating directly with the Zionists. The object was to prevent immigration from resulting in the formation of a Jewish majority in Palestine, or even a population numerous enough to provide a basis for the creation of a Jewish state. Their failure to achieve this end was sealed by the U.N. partition plan of November 1947. The international community, dominated by the American and Soviet super-powers, wanted to impose on them a dismemberment of Arab territory. They refused to accept this *Diktat*, and embarked on the guerrilla war of 1947–8, and the war of 1948. They were defeated in the field, and obliged to sign armistice agreements (all except Iraq). From that time on, the Arab states bordering on Palestine recognized Israel's existence, in practice. They still rejected the new boundaries, and refused to accept the Israeli conquests which went beyond the territory granted to Israel by the U.N. They were also outraged at the expulsion of the Palestinians from Israeli territory. They were supported by the U.N. on these two points, but Israel ignored the U.N. decisions and refused to implement them. The general Arab claim was still maintained, and found expression in the competitive militancy of the various states and national movements. This prevented the Arab governments, who were on the whole disposed to do so, from bluntly expressing *de facto* recognition of Israel within the frontiers laid down by the U.N. plan, let alone establishing diplomatic relations with Israel. The Israelis, for their part, provided them with excellent grounds for non-recognition, by refusing to accept the *principle* of a return to the U.N. plan or to implement the Organization's decisions on the refugees and on Jerusalem.

The same process has repeated itself after the conquests of June 1967. Some of the Arab states were now ready to accord *de facto* recognition to the Jewish state within its frontiers of 1948–67, but refused to endorse its latest conquests. The general Arab claim prevented them from going any further than this.

It was only in November 1977 that Anwar El-Sadat thought he could take the decisive step of recognizing the legitimacy of the Israeli state while continuing to dispute the legitimacy of its authority over its conquests of 1967. By so doing he was able, in 1980, to establish diplomatic relations with Israel. This was possible only through a convergence of exceptional factors: Egypt's limited success in the war of October 1973 and the prestige this gave to Sadat; the strength of a specific Egyptian patriotism weary of suffering to the utmost from the consequences of a conflict of only partial concern to Egypt, engaged in out of love for the other Arabs; and the existence of a region of Egypt, the Sinai Peninsula, which had been conquered by Israel but did not form part of the territory claimed by mainstream Zionist ideology, and which it was therefore relatively easy for the Israelis to give back, thus endowing Sadat with a gain of which he could boast. We must not, of course, forget Sadat's personality, his inclinations, his psychology and the whole conjuncture which had given him power. The hesitations of the other Arab leaders, including those of the P.L.O., when Sadat made his amazing trip to Jerusalem, show that a road was then opened, perhaps, towards a wider acceptance of part of the accomplished fact. But Israel's refusal, in practice, to make any concessions of substance to the demands of the Palestinians meant that this opening was closed. The general condemnation of the Egyptian leader as a traitor, a deserter from the common struggle, ensued. If that tendency is to be overcome, spectacular gestures (whether spontaneous or induced by coercion) will be needed from Israel, such as would justify Sadat *a posteriori* – if, that is, Sadat stays in power and if he continues to follow his present line. In mid 1980 it is hard to see such a development taking place.

In any case, intransigence is a theme too easy to use in inter-Arab political struggles for anyone to believe that there can be universal acquiescence in a compromise solution. The only question is: will the number and importance of the unshakable opponents of such a solution be such as to weigh heavily on the political decisions taken and so, in one way or another, prolong the conflict? It is clear that, broadly speaking, the strength of the opposition will be the less in proportion to the magnitude of the concessions made by Israel to the most essential Arab demands (first and foremost on the Palestinian problem).

On the other side, Israel's consistent policy has been to make the Arabs recognize her existence, first of all – itself established by conquest – and secondly the conquests of 1948. These seem to the more moderate

Israelis to provide the minimum guarantee for the survival of their state. At the same time, the departure of the refugees, for whatever reasons, seems to them essential if the Jewish character of the state is to be preserved, this being the prime aim and postulate of Zionist ideology. Only a very limited return would be acceptable. The Arab refusal results in a feeling of insecurity which makes any concession extremely difficult. The refusal means that the war is still on, and in no war will either side let go of any part of the advantage it has won.

The activist policy of Ben Gurion and his school was designed to obtain Arab recognition by terror, by the deployment of force. Whatever the judgement to be passed on its results, the fact is that nobody was able to devise any coherent alternative policy in Israel. Neither Sharett nor Eshkol and Eban have been able to make any substantial concession on the frontiers or the refugees, given the state of Israeli public opinion. Sharett, who in 1950 went furthest in this direction, met with violent internal opposition. The Israeli Left was just as intransigent on this point as the Right. At most, some were prepared to envisage a conditional return of some of the refugees, which was very far from satisfying the Arabs. Moreover no Israeli was able to point to any clearly stated Arab concession on the formal recognition of the state, or on the renunciation of part, at least, of the Arab claim. They were reduced to making oblique manoeuvres which may, at most and only after a long interval, create a climate more favourable to mutual concessions. But they have not got the time.

The causes of the 1967 crisis seem to lie on the one hand in the weakness of the moderate sector of Israeli public opinion and its representatives in the government, and on the other hand in the internal contradictions which prevented the Arabs from presenting a united front, able to choose a coherent policy and stick to it, and, above all, to offer to Israelis of good will any other programme than their destruction. The pacific intentions of some Arab leaders have in practice been nullified in any effect that they might have had on the Israelis by the fact that these leaders did not dare to give clear and public expression to them. This has enabled the Israeli activists to persuade the masses that no faith could be placed in them. Moreover, the divisions within the Arab world have meant that some rulers have been in a position to commit acts of war against Israel while others had to take the consequences. Combinations of circumstances like this occurred on several occasions. It was a rather special chain of events which, on this occasion, led to war, and to its manifold and grave consequences.

*

After 1967 there was more doubt in Israel regarding the necessity of clinging to the new conquests. The territory won was inhabited over-whelmingly by Arabs. Their integration in Israel presented problems, if it was desired to preserve the Jewish character of the state: de-mographic evolution, taken together with the drying-up of Jewish immigration, must eventually confront Israel with the choice between a policy of apartheid and an Arab majority. While many Israelis were ready to take the most extreme measures to avoid giving back these territories, others (whose numbers fluctuated according to circum-stances) agreed to accept that they might have to be given back, but only on condition that, in return, this or that was obtained. Many were disposed to demand a great deal. For all, however, the minimum was, of course, recognition of the state of Israel. In any case, the triumph that reigned in Israel after the glaring defeat suffered by the Arabs in June 1967 seemed, falsely, to make it possible to put off till later, much later, the solution of the problem, anticipating an eventual complete submission of the Arabs to all the accomplished facts.

The conquests of 1967 had at least provided the Israelis with means of barter (Sinai, the West Bank, Gaza and Golan) which a larger number of Israelis were prepared to give up, or which they could be led to give up if the Arabs agreed to recognize the *fait accompli* on the territory Israel had acquired prior to that date. This exchange of con-cessions proved feasible – with Egypt alone and affecting Sinai alone – when Sadat's semi-success in 1973 and his spectacular appearance in the Knesset in November 1977 had convinced the Israelis that some-thing had to be conceded. But this does not solve the problem as long as the other Arab states persist in refusing to recognize Israel, and as long as Israel persists in maintaining a *de facto* sovereignty over the West Bank, Gaza and Golan, the legitimacy of which is denied by everyone, including Egypt.

While the profound cause of the conflict, the encroachment of a new population on an Arab territory, explains by itself the attitudes of the two parties, we also find in this the underlying explanation of the particular alliances sought and obtained by them.

If the Jewish state had been created on a desert island, or in a territory almost empty of previous inhabitants, it would have been able to choose its alliances more or less freely, except for what economic constraints might have dictated. But the Jewish colony, which later became a state, was established on the soil of Arab Palestine, which it fully intended to transform into Jewish territory. It is not certain that any policy whatsoever could have succeeded in disarming the natural hostility of the indigenous population towards this takeover, virtual at first and then actual. Efforts at conciliation were not lacking but, as we have seen, fears on the part of the Arabs that the plan clearly set forth by Herzl would be realized, and profound impulses on the part of the Jews towards realizing it indeed, meant that these attempts came to nothing; and the state of Israel was, in fact, created, consecrating the alienation of an Arab territory and the expulsion of nine tenths of its inhabitants, with subordination of the fraction that remained.

Thereafter, Arab opposition could no longer be disarmed. For a short time still, rulers could keep that tendency at a secondary level. Perhaps a more flexible and conciliatory policy by Israel, such as Sharett proposed, might have resulted in a viable compromise, but no opposition force in any Arab country could fail to utilize against established authority the advantages for its propaganda of an irredentist programme, and these opposition forces were quite soon to triumph almost everywhere.

The mobilizing ideology employed by their leaders could not fail to denounce, behind the élites in power whom they wished to bring down, the support that they relied on in the world system dominated by European and American capitalism. Their own allies could not but be the opposition movements of the same order which were active in the Third World. Consequently, Israel was bound to find support only among the enemies of its enemies, that is, in the group of dominant countries denounced in all those circles as forming the bloc of 'Imperialism'. The fact of this support, this alliance, enabled the Arabs to denounce Israel as a member of that bloc. We have seen how they succeeded in convincing many of those movements and states in the Third World which were hesitant at first. In doing this they were greatly helped by such actions as the Suez expedition, which gave concrete, factual expression to an alliance between Israel, France and Britain.

Arab hostility to the Zionist encroachment on Palestine, an hostility to which some Arab rulers might, if pushed, show themselves disloyal in practice but which they could not repudiate, conditioned Israel's alliance with the capitalist powers and principally with the most important of them, the U.S.A., on which the substantial Jewish-American community gave Israel powerful means of pressure. This alliance, in turn, provoked or reinforced the hostility of the Soviet Union, America's great rival in international politics. This hostility found expression only gradually, despite the impulsion given it by the Communists' anti-Zionist doctrine, owing to the caution of Soviet policy and to a series of counter-factors. Nevertheless, it grew and grew. For the same reasons the Arab rulers were pressed to seek at least some degree of support from the Soviets, in so far as their masses, always in a state of virtual revolt, would hardly forgive them an orientation towards America.

Alliance with Israel thus became a symbol of alignment with the American bloc, and the enemies of one's enemies being necessarily one's friends, the Israelis were led to ally themselves with all the forces denounced by the Third World – for example, with another symbol of the resistance of the European 'island', namely South Africa. In the Muslim countries, where religious ideologists could make use of the anti-Jewish verses of the Koran, the alliance, or connivance, of Turkey and Iran with Israel, increasingly denounced, was bound to become impossible to maintain, as movements grew in strength in which hostility to the European and American system was coloured with Islamic fundamentalism.

At the time of writing (May 1980), what can be predicted? In the view of a very large section of opinion and of the political forces in Israel, Sadat has opened a breach in the Arab rejection of Israel, and, sooner or later, the other Arab leaders will take the same path. It will be enough, they think, to wait, while strengthening Israel's military power and demonstrating it when necessary, and while discouraging foreign pressure for concessions by means of the pro-Israeli lobbies in the various states, especially in the U.S.A. Some Israelis, however, are ready to make concessions in order to obtain Arab recognition. Many criticize the provocative policy of the religious Right, protected by Begin, which obviously aims at gradual Judaization of the occupied territories. But the majority of Israel's political forces want to retain at least a certain degree of control over the occupied territories, lest a base for attacking Israel be established there. To justify this point of view, they can invoke yet again the absence of any clear and public undertaking by the Arabs (other than Sadat) to respect the Jewish state that would remain in being after all possible concessions had been made. For this Jewish state the great majority of Israelis are prepared, rightly or wrongly, to give their lives. Why concede something to an opponent who hints that he will use that something the better to attack you?

The result is a vicious circle: the refusal by the Arabs to give the undertaking required strengthens the Israelis' refusal to make con-

cessions and *vice versa*. Most of the Arab states that wish to rid themselves of this problem maintain their refusal of recognition only because
this is the attitude of the Palestinians. The Arab leaders fear the wrath
that would be aroused if they were to dissociate themselves from the
Palestinian demands. Political oppositions would unfailingly seize upon
this and take strength from it. They do not hold such strong cards as
Sadat holds, and the firmness of his position is open to question. The
mighty wave raised throughout the Muslim world by the Iranian Revolution encourages no one to compromise himself too openly with
elements linked with the West, and especially with the United States.

With a view to escaping from this vicious circle, a mutual and sim-
ultaneous recognition by Israel and the P.L.O. has been proposed. The
word 'recognition' may create misunderstandings. Let us say that what
is meant is that the P.L.O. should proclaim clearly that, once a Palestinian state has been established on the West Bank (after conditions
for this have been negotiated), it will not challenge the legitimacy of a
predominantly Jewish state in the rest of Palestine; and that, in return,
Israel should recognize the P.L.O. as the sole representative of the
Palestinian people, to which would be retroceded the territory destined
to form the Palestinian state.

The simultaneity of these recognitions is aimed at taking the sting
out of the objection (in our view, rather an artificial one) that could be
raised on both sides – 'It's for the other side to make the first move!'
This would be an ideal process, indeed, for those who prefer peaceful
solutions. For the moment, however, we are far from a conclusion such
as this.

If, though, this road is not taken, the war can only continue and
continue, with phases of semi-peaceful hostility and phases of real
military operations, with their usual horrors and with their disastrous
economic and political consequences. With or without simultaneity,
the procedure of the two 'recognitions' is the only procedure that can
avoid perpetuating the war. This is a simple fact.

Otherwise, we are no longer engaged in a peace process, which
assumes arrival at a compromise, but in a process leading to the absolute
victory of one or other of the two camps. But in that process there is no
symmetry. Will Israel's temporary position of strength cause the majority of the Arab leaders involved to follow in Sadat's wake and sign
treaties of peace recognizing the full and entire legitimacy of the Jewish
state as its exists? It is hard to suppose that this will happen without
major concessions by Israel, including the creation of a Palestinian
state. Sadat himself has been able to move in this direction only by

allowing to be foreseen a process which is to culminate in that result. For the moment at least, though, there is no political force in Israel possessing real weight that is willing to make such a concession, and the U.S.A., which alone might be able to compel Israel to make it, does not wish to do so and would find it difficult to exercise such pressure.

So, then: would another victorious war compel Israel's Arab adversaries to accept peace treaties giving form to this absolute victory for the Jewish state? The experience of Israel's past victories hardly obliges one to think so. Whatever the attitude of the rulers, the most likely effect would be to stimulate oppositional forces, intransigent counter-states which, one day, would take power. There can be no question of Israel being able to occupy such vast territories with its military forces. Already occupation of the little West Bank has created inextricable problems for Israel.

On the other hand, a total victory for the Arabs some day is not out of the question. Israel's military superiority will not last for ever, or, at least, will not be absolute for ever. But we can be sure that the Israelis, with or without allies (and this means raising the question of a world-wide conflagration), will fight to the last man against this destruction of their state. Those, throughout the world, who, whether Jews or not, among the non-Arabs, have fought against the Zionist line of a Jewish state, those who have not attached capital importance to the existence of such a state, and those who have gradually become frightened at the price which has had to be paid for this state, would be able to imagine without horror a world without Israel – but not the human catastrophes that this military process would entail, the numberless tragedies that would descend upon families which have already suffered terribly. They will strive, to the poor extent of their resources, to promote a peaceful outcome, even if this does not give full satisfaction to the demands of either side.

A book such as this cannot be confined to a mere description of the conflict and the factors in it, a general characterization and analysis of future possibilities. It would be thought wrong if we avoided altogether considerations of a moral order. In cases of this kind opinion wishes strongly to distinguish between the innocent and the guilty, between the one who is in the wrong and the one who is in the right.

Like all fighters and those closely linked with them, the first to react in this way are, of course, on one side, the Arabs, and, on the other, the Israelis – and, with the latter, today, most Jews. For them the choice presents no difficulty, and the adjectives they use are unmitigated. For most of the Arabs 'the Zionist aggression' is a crime, and those who participate in it or who support it are criminals. For the Zionist Jews and their innumerable sympathizers, it was, on the contrary, criminal on the Arabs' part not to agree to the establishment of a persecuted people in their region – this being, moreover, the solution willed by God and by the U.N.O. To these fundamental 'crimes' are added, of course, the countless particular crimes (much less debatable) which are committed every day by the participants in a war or a conflict of this kind. The infamous and atrocious character of these crimes (often, unfortunately, quite true) is ceaselessly denounced – that is, of course, when they are the work of the other side.

In contradiction with themselves, those committed to support of one side or the other, who deny the very notion of objectivity, clamour for a universally valid moral judgement which shall condemn their adversary. By desiring that this judgement be universally valid, they implicitly accept that it can be impartial and objective. So, then, being both importuned *and* repudiated in advance if our conclusions are displeasing, let us undertake as best we can this perilous exercise. He who has done undeserved harm to another is, it would appear, an object of universal condemnation. However, mitigating circumstances may be found for him, such as need, ignorance or social conditioning, if he has blindly followed the custom of his milieu. The Zionists have quite clearly done harm to the Arabs and, more particularly, to the Arabs of Palestine. This needs to be reiterated all the time, because the tendency to deny it is so widespread. Those who deny this obvious fact, or pass over it in silence, put themselves by so doing in the category of biased judges, and are consequently to be repudiated. One may reprove the Arabs, calling upon them not to carry their resentment to extremes. But one's right to do that is lost if one begins by denying the wrong that has been done to them, or by justifying it. Imagine that you have injured someone through clumsiness. You may ask him to excuse you, to understand your own situation, to accept some compensation; but what will his reaction be if you begin by telling everyone that you have done him no harm, or that he deserved to be harmed in this way?

The Zionists have inflicted undeserved harm upon the Arabs, harm that was programmed in advance when, before the Arabs even had the slightest knowledge of what was being planned (and consequently had not the slightest reaction to it), they decided to make of Arab Palestine a Jewish state. On their behalf it may be pleaded that there were mitigating circumstances. Those concerned were driven by persecutions to seek a way out; but let us not forget that persecutions were much less severe in the period in which the plan in question was conceived than they became later on, and also that, in the same period, there were other ways out available. Those concerned were utterly ignorant of conditions in Palestine. They were strengthened in that ignorance and encouraged to preserve it by the ideas prevalent in their period. One may blame them for not having been able to transcend this ignorance of theirs and the ideas of their time, and for not having sought more difficult ways out of the situation that was constraining them. But who can cast the first stone? It is clear that few communities and few individuals – among the Arabs as among the rest of us – could or can boast of showing such virtue.

The Arabs experienced an infliction of harm that they had not deserved. One can, at most, reproach them with the way they reacted. But, again, who can pride himself on reacting any better in comparable circumstances? Nor can it be forgotten that they were the ones attacked. Only those communities and those individuals who strictly apply the prescriptions of Jesus of Nazareth about forgiveness of trespasses are in a position to blame the Arabs on that score. Where are such people to be found?

In any case, the harm was done. The conflict, with all its vicissitudes, is going on before our eyes. How can it now be ended? It is for the man of peace and goodwill to advocate compromise. An honourable compromise is now possible for both sides, and the broad lines of such a compromise have been indicated by the international organizations. This would leave to Israel all the territory that it held between 1948 and 1967, a period when Israel proclaimed that it had no further territorial demands. It would call upon the Palestinians to resign themselves to the loss of part of their national territory, but would give them an independent state of their own.

The future alone will tell us if this compromise is going to be accepted. Much will depend on the international situation at the most general level, the relation of strength between the superpowers, the bargaining they will undertake on behalf or to the detriment of their respective *protégés*. We do not know how these circumstances will evolve – and they greatly transcend the regional setting to which we have confined ourselves. One thing, however, is certain: namely, that the situation cannot be perpetuated in its present form. The West has created the term 'destabilization' as a bogey, but hundreds of millions of individuals throughout the world look towards this destabilization hopefully, because the existing situation signifies for them oppression, exploitation and, often, death. It is futile to hope to maintain against wind and weather all established situations. Compromises are still possible. Those who reject them – especially when they are the ones who originated the injustices being challenged – will bear the responsibility for terrible disasters.

Index

More about Penguins and Pelicans

ISLAM AND CAPITALISM
Maxime Rodinson

What influences do ideology and cultural tradition have over economic and political activity? In *Islam and Capitalism* Maxime Rodinson asks this question of the Muslim world. He examines the social and economic development of the countries of Islam to discover how the precepts of the Muslim religion – mutual aid, respect for property, equality before God, the prohibitions on profit – could affect those practices which make up the capitalist mode of production. In particular, have the exhortations to justice, charity and cooperation anything to do with the inclination of the Muslim world towards socialism?

'Maxime Rodinson, the French sociologist and orientalist ... happily combines immense erudition with great clarity of expression ...

'The translator and publisher are to be congratulated on the production of this important book, which should be of absorbing interest to anyone concerned with the sociology of the third world' – Peter Mansfield in *New Society*

THREAT FROM THE EAST
Fred Halliday

From Afghanistan through Iran and the Arab Middle East to the Horn of Africa – this is the area known as the 'Arc of Crisis'. The countries included in it vary from time to time but it is the focus for contemporary international conflict. For the West, the underlying cause of turmoil has been the policy of the Soviet Union – and the thesis of the 'Soviet threat' is often offered as an explanation. This book, however, takes a closer look at the facts. In an area where Afghanistan is in the grip of war, where the monarchies of the Arabian peninsular remain fragile, where there is no peace in the Horn of Africa and where – most important of all – Iran is in chaos, pressures from the West play a vital part.

Author of *Iran: Dictatorship or Development*, Fred Halliday has written a clear and accurate analysis of this potentially explosive and worrying state of affairs.

THE ARABS
Peter Mansfield

The Arabs, which draws upon Peter Mansfield's many years experience as historian and journalist in the Middle East, is a concise and authoritative general introduction – social, political and historical – to the modern Arab world.

The history is brilliantly summarized – from the pre-Islamic nomads of Arabia, the life of Muhammad and the astonishing rise of Arab power which followed, through the great Arab empires and the centuries of Ottoman rule, to the Western colonial period, the tragedy of Palestine and the modern Arab renaissance, reinforced by the new power of oil. It shows how the consequences of the centuries of struggle for dominance between Christendom and the Islamic world survive to this day in various forms.

An important section of the book surveys the Arab countries in gazetteer fashion. The final section, from a personal point of view, considers the Arabs, their characteristics, aspirations and future.

'Should be studied by anyone who wants to know about the Arab world and how the Arabs have become what they are today' – Steven Runciman in the *Sunday Times* (London)

TO JERUSALEM AND BACK
Saul Bellow

'Here you sit at dinner with charming people in a dining room like any other. Yet you know that your hostess has lost a son; that her sister lost children in the 1973 war ... In the domestic ceremony of passed dishes and filled glasses the thoughts of a destructive enemy are hard to grasp. What you do know is that there is one fact of Jewish life left unchanged by the creation of a Jewish state: you cannot take your right to live for granted ...'

'Mr Bellow's conversation with friends old and new, as well as his solitary musings, are predictably intelligent and amusing ... *To Jerusalem and Back* is, in fact, essentially a plea for a greater understanding of the state of Israel by one of its most articulate admirers' – E. C. Hodgkin in *The Times*